GREGG
SHORTHAND
DICTIONARY

A Compilation of Shorthand Outlines for 34,055 Words;
1,314 Names and Geographical Expressions;
1,368 Frequently Used Phrases;
and 120 Abbreviations

GREGG
SHORTHAND
DICTIONARY

Diamond Jubilee Series
Second Edition

John Robert Gregg

Louis A. Leslie

Charles E. Zoubek

Shorthand Written by Charles Rader

Gregg Division|McGraw-Hill Book Company
New York   St. Louis   Dallas   San Francisco
Düsseldorf   Johannesburg   Kuala Lumpur   London
Mexico   Montreal   New Delhi   Panama
Rio de Janeiro   Singapore   Sydney   Toronto

Cover and Title Design / Gail Young

Library of Congress Cataloging in Publication Data

Gregg, John Robert, 1867-1948.
Gregg shorthand dictionary.

(Diamond jubilee series)
1. Shorthand—Gregg—Dictionaries.   I. Leslie,
Louis A., date.   joint author.   II. Zoubek,
Charles E., date.   joint author.   III. Title.
Z55.5.G7   1974   653'.427'03   73-12581
ISBN 0-07-024632-7
ISBN 0-07-024633-5 (mini. ed.)

Gregg Shorthand Dictionary, Diamond Jubilee Series
Second Edition

7890DODO098

ISBN 07-024632-7

FOREWORD

Gregg Shorthand Dictionary, Diamond Jubilee Series, Second Edition, is divided into four parts:

Part One contains, in alphabetic order, the shorthand outlines for 34,055 words. However, these 34,055 words represent a considerably larger vocabulary, as many simple derivatives of these words have been omitted—those ending in *-ing* and *-s,* for example.

Part Two contains, in alphabetic order, the shorthand outlines for 1,314 entries for personal and geographical names.

Part Three contains, in alphabetic order, the shorthand outlines for 1,368 phrases frequently used in business dictation.

Part Four contains shorthand outlines for 120 abbreviations.

It is easily possible to construct briefer outlines for many of the scientific and literary words for which full outlines are given in this dictionary. It is not advisable to do so, however, unless the writer is certain that he will use those briefer outlines with sufficient frequency to justify the effort of learning them. Otherwise, the brief, but half-remembered, outlines will cause mental hesitation that will result in slower, rather than faster, writing.

Research techniques using high-speed motion pictures have proved that most shorthand writers actually write each outline at about the same speed, regardless of the speed of the dictation. That is why the writer who can take dictation at only 100 words a minute writes each outline as rapidly as it is written by another writer taking the same material at 200 words a minute. What, then, is the difference between the two writers?

The difference is that the writer who can write 100 words a minute is consuming time thinking, pausing, hesitating. The writer who can write 200 words a minute does not need to stop to think. He writes the outlines little, if any, faster than the 100-word writer, but the 200-word writer writes *continuously.*

The problem of increasing shorthand speed, therefore, is actually a problem of decreasing hesitations in writing. What causes hesitations in writing? They are caused by the struggle of the mind to remember and use the abbreviating material provided in the shorthand system.

The fewer shortcuts and exceptions the mind must remember and use, the easier it is for the writer to decrease or eliminate the hesitations that reduce speed. Therefore, any attempt by the writer to manufacture additional shortcuts is more likely to reduce his speed than to increase it, unless the new shortcuts are used in his daily work with such frequency that they readily become automatized.

The experience of expert shorthand writers of every system is conclusive in establishing the inadvisability of attempting to gain speed by devising and learning lists of brief outlines. Longer outlines that are quickly constructed by the mind under pressure of dictation give the writer more speed; the attempt to remember and use large numbers of abbreviated outlines tends to reduce the writer's speed.

There is often room for some difference of opinion as to the most appropriate outline for a word. This dictionary offers outlines that have been discussed and considered by experts. Sometimes an apparently obvious improvement in an outline will actually create the danger of a conflict in reading. More often an outline different from that provided in this dictionary would be individually satisfactory but would not be consistent with the outlines for other members of the same word family.

Of one thing the reader may be sure—every outline in this dictionary is the result of serious thought and consideration. Where possible alternate outlines exist, each alternate has been discussed and considered. This dictionary as a whole represents the accumulated experience of all those who have worked with Gregg Shorthand since its first publication in 1888.

The compilers of this dictionary are confident that this volume will render a valuable service to the shorthand writer by placing at his disposal a facile and fluent outline for any word or phrase in which he may be interested.

The Publishers

PART ONE

Part One of the Second Edition of *Gregg Shorthand Dictionary, Diamond Jubilee Series,* contains shorthand outlines for 34,055 words, arranged in alphabetical order.

Of these 34,055 words, more than 100 did not appear in the First Edition. Some are words that have been added to the language in the last decade—*skyjacker, disadvantaged, miniskirt, Amtrak.* Some are words that have been added to the language as a result of advances in technology—*astroturf, circuitry, recycling, blast-off, splashdown.* Some are words that were rarely used in the past but because of changes in the times, are today frequently used—*racist, multiethnic, ecology.*

Experience has proved that those using a shorthand dictionary often consult it for the simple words formerly omitted from shorthand dictionaries or for rare and unusual words likewise formerly omitted.

The present list, therefore, includes many of the apparently simple words formerly omitted. Most readily apparent will be the addition of the many rare and unusual words that experience has proved are wanted by users of a list such as this.

Many words are included because the shorthand learner, while still in school, has occasion to use them in his schoolwork. For this reason many mathematical, mineralogical, chemical, botanical, and physiological terms are included. For the same reason many literary words are included, words that are usually of no business value but that the high school or college learner uses in his schoolwork. The bulk of the vocabulary, however, consists of words generally used in business-office dictation.

It must be remembered, too, that in many types of office work the stenographer may have occasion to use these scientific or literary words. The editor's stenographer will need the literary words. The professor's secretary will need many of the mathematical or chemical or physiological words—according to the professor's field of interest.

Consistency, rather than brevity of outline, has been the guiding principle in the construction of the shorthand outlines in this dictionary. The fastest shorthand outline (within reasonable limits) is the outline that requires the least mental effort, the outline that is written consistently and analogically. The speed of a shorthand outline is not to be judged by its brevity to the eye, nor even by its facility for the hand; it is to be judged by the speed with which it may be constructed by the mind and supplied by the mind to the hand.

Many shorthand writers experience difficulty in understanding the principle that guides the shorthand author in devising shortcuts. If the preceding paragraph is true, why are there *any* shortcuts? Why not write out everything in full? The secret of the good shortcut is the frequency of use of the word or phrase. If a dictator says *bacteriological* day after day, the shorthand writer should, of course, use a very brief shortcut for that word. Because of this extreme frequency of use, the shortcut will come as quickly to the mind as though the word has been written in full.

There is no value, however, in having every shorthand writer learn a shortcut for a word like *bacteriological,* for some dictators may never use the word, and if it should occur infrequently in the dictation, the mental effort needed to recall the word would require far more time than would have been necessary to write it in full.

It is strongly urged, therefore, that the outline in this dictionary be accepted as the normal outline for any expression unless that expression occurs so frequently in the writer's dictation that learning a shortcut for it is thoroughly justified. A long list of seldom-used shortcuts can be a very heavy burden on the mind and will almost invariably result in decreasing the writer's shorthand speed rather than increasing it. As a famous shorthand reporter of an earlier generation once said, "The longer I write shorthand, the *longer* I write shorthand."

A

ab′a·cus

a·baft′

ab′a·lo′ne

a·ban′don

a·ban′doned

a·ban′don·ment

a·base′

a·based′

a·base′ment

a·bash′

a·bat′a·ble

a·bate′

a·bat′ed

a·bate′ment

ab′bess

ab′bey

ab′bot

ab·bre′vi·ate

ab·bre′vi·at′ed

ab·bre′vi·a′tion

ab′di·cate

ab′di·cat′ed

ab′di·ca′tion

ab·do′men

ab·dom′i·nal

ab·duct′

ab·duc′tion

a·bed′

ab′er·ra′tion

ab′er·ra′tion·al

a·bet′

a·bet′ted

a·bet′tor

a·bey′ance

ab·hor′

ab·horred′

ab·hor′rence

ab·hor′rent

a·bide′

a·bil′i·ty

ab′ject

ab′ju·ra′tion

ab·jure′

ab·jured′

ab·jure′ment

ab′la·tive

ab′laut

a·blaze′

a′ble

a′ble-bod′ied

ab·lu′tion

a′bly

ab′ne·ga′tion

ab·nor′mal

ab′nor·mal′i·ty

ab·nor′mi·ty

a·board′

a·bode′

a·bol′ish

a·bol′ished

ab′o·li′tion

ab′o·li′tion·ism

ab′o·li′tion·ist

a·bom′i·na·ble

a·bom′i·na·bly

a·bom′i·nate

1

a·bom′i·na′tion
ab′o·rig′i·nal
ab′o·rig′i·ne
a·bor′tive
a·bound′
a·bound′ing·ly
a·bout′
a·bove′
ab·rade′
ab·rad′ed
ab·ra′sion
ab·ra′sive
ab′re·ac′tion
a·breast′
a·bridge′
a·bridged′
a·bridg′ment
a·broad′
ab′ro·gate
ab′ro·gat′ed
ab′ro·ga′tion
ab′ro·ga′tive
ab·rupt′
ab·rupt′ly
ab·rupt′ness
ab′scess
ab′scessed
ab·scis′sa
ab·scis′sion
ab·scond′
ab·scond′ed
ab·scond′er

ab′sence
ab′sent
ab′sen·tee′
ab′sen·tee′ism
ab′sent·ly
ab′sinthe
ab′so·lute
ab′so·lute·ly
ab′so·lute·ness
ab′so·lu′tion
ab′so·lut·ism
ab′so·lut·ist
ab·solve′
ab·solved′
ab·sorb′
ab·sorbed′
ab·sorb′en·cy
ab·sorb′ent
ab·sorb′ing·ly
ab·sorp′tion
ab·sorp′tive
ab·stain′
ab·stained′
ab·stain′er
ab·ste′mi·ous
ab·ste′mi·ous·ly
ab·ste′mi·ous·ness
ab·sten′tion
ab′sti·nence
ab′sti·nent
ab′sti·nent·ly
ab′stract

ab·stract′ed
ab·stract′ed·ly
ab·strac′tion
ab·strac′tion·ist
ab′stract·ly
ab·struse′
ab·struse′ness
ab·surd′
ab·surd′i·ty
ab·surd′ly
a·bun′dance
a·bun′dant
a·bun′dant·ly
a·buse′
a·bused′
a·bu′sive
a·bu′sive·ly
a·bu′sive·ness
a·but′
a·but′ment
a·but′tal
a·but′ted
a·but′ter
a·bysm′
a·bys′mal
a·byss′
a·ca′cia
ac′a·dem′ic
a·cad′e·mi′cian
a·cad′e·mies
a·cad′e·my
A·ca′di·an

a·can'thus

ac·cede'

ac·ced'ed

ac·cel'er·an'do

ac·cel'er·ant

ac·cel'er·ate

ac·cel'er·at·ed

ac·cel'er·a'tion

ac·cel'er·a'tive

ac·cel'er·a'tor

ac·cel'er·a·to'ry

ac'cent

ac·cent'ed

ac·cen'tu·ate

ac·cen'tu·at'ed

ac·cen'tu·a'tion

ac·cept'

ac·cept'a·bil'i·ty

ac·cept'a·ble

ac·cept'ance

ac'cep·ta'tion

ac·cept'ed

ac'cess

ac·ces'si·bil'i·ty

ac·ces'si·ble

ac·ces'sion

ac·ces'so·ry

ac'ci·dence

ac'ci·dent

ac'ci·den'tal

ac'ci·den'tal·ly

ac·cip'i·trine

ac·claim'

ac·claimed'

ac'cla·ma'tion

ac·clam'a·to'ry

ac·cli'mate

ac·cli'mat·ed

ac'cli·ma'tion

ac·cli'ma·ti·za'tion

ac·cli'ma·tize

ac·cli'ma·tized

ac·cliv'i·ty

ac'co·lade'

ac·com'mo·date

ac·com'mo·dat'ed

ac·com'mo·dat'ing·ly

ac·com'mo·da'tion

ac·com'mo·da'tive

ac·com'pa·nied

ac·com'pa·ni·ment

ac·com'pa·nist

ac·com'pa·ny

ac·com'plice

ac·com'plish

ac·com'plished

ac·com'plish·ment

ac·cord'

ac·cord'ance

ac·cord'ed

ac·cord'ing·ly

ac·cor'di·on

ac·cost'

ac·cost'ed

ac·count'

ac·count'a·bil'i·ty

ac·count'a·ble

ac·count'an·cy

ac·count'ant

ac·count'ed

ac·cou'tered

ac·cou'ter·ment

ac·cred'it

ac·cred'it·ed

ac·cre'tion

ac·cru'al

ac·crue'

ac·crued'

ac·cu'mu·late

ac·cu'mu·lat'ed

ac·cu'mu·lates

ac·cu'mu·la'tion

ac·cu'mu·la'tive

ac·cu'mu·la'tor

ac'cu·ra·cy

ac'cu·rate

ac'cu·rate·ly

ac'cu·sa'tion

ac·cu'sa·tive

ac·cu'sa·to'ry

ac·cuse'

ac·cused'

ac·cus'er

ac·cus'ing·ly

ac·cus'tom

ac·cus'tomed

ace	ac'o·lyte	ac'ri·mo'ni·ous·ness
a·cerb'	ac'o·nite	ac'ri·mo'ny
a·cer'bic	a'corn	ac'ro·bat
a·cer'bi·ty	a·cous'tic	ac'ro·bat'ic
ac'e·tate	a·cous'ti·cal	ac'ro·bat'i·cal·ly
a·ce'tic	a·cous'ti·cal·ly	ac'ro·bat'ics
ac'e·tone	a·cous'tics	a·crop'o·lis
a·cet'y·lene	ac·quaint'	a·cross'
ache	ac·quaint'ance	a·cryl'ic
ached	ac·quaint'ance·ship	act
a·chiev'a·ble	ac·quaint'ed	act'ed
a·chieve'	ac'qui·esce'	ac·tin'ic
a·chieved'	ac'qui·esced'	ac·tin'i·um
a·chieve'ment	ac'qui·es'cence	ac'tion
ach'ro·mat'ic	ac'qui·es'cent	ac'tion·a·ble
ach'ro·mat'i·cal·ly	ac·quire'	ac'ti·vate
a·chro'ma·to'sis	ac·quired'	ac'ti·vat'ed
ac'id	ac·quire'ment	ac'ti·va'tion
a·cid'i·fi·ca'tion	ac·quires'	ac'ti·va'tor
a·cid'i·fi'er	ac'qui·si'tion	ac'tive
a·cid'i·fy	ac·quis'i·tive	ac'tive·ly
a·cid'i·ty	ac·quis'i·tive·ness	ac'tiv·ist
ac'i·do'sis	ac·quit'	ac·tiv'i·ty
ac'id·proof'	ac·quit'tal	ac'tiv·ize
a·cid'u·late	ac·quit'ted	ac'tor
a·cid'u·lat'ed	a'cre	ac'tress
a·cid'u·lous	a'cre·age	ac'tu·al
ac·knowl'edge	ac'rid	ac'tu·al'i·ties
ac·knowl'edged	a·crid'i·ty	ac'tu·al'i·ty
ac·knowl'edg·ment	ac'rid·ly	ac'tu·al·ly
ac'me	ac'ri·mo'ni·ous	ac'tu·ar'i·al
ac'ne	ac'ri·mo'ni·ous·ly	ac'tu·ar'y

ac'tu·ate

ac'tu·at'ed

a·cu'i·ty

a·cu'men

ac'u·punc'ture

a·cute'

a·cute'ness

ad'age

a·da'gio

ad'a·mant

ad'a·man'tine

a·dapt'

a·dapt'a·bil'i·ty

a·dapt'a·ble

ad'ap·ta'tion

a·dapt'ed

a·dapt'er

a·dap'tive

add

add'ed

ad·den'da

ad·den'dum

ad'der

ad'dict

ad·dict'ed

ad·dic'tion

ad·di'tion

ad·di'tion·al

ad·di'tion·al·ly

ad'di·tive

ad'dle

ad'dled

ad·dress

ad·dressed'

ad'dress·ee'

Ad·dres'so·graph

ad·duce'

ad·duced'

ad·duct'

ad·duc'tion

ad·duc'tive

ad·duc'tor

ad'e·noid

ad'e·nol'o·gy

ad'e·no'ma

a·dept'

ad'e·qua·cy

ad'e·quate

ad'e·quate·ly

ad'e·quate·ness

ad·here'

ad·hered'

ad·her'ence

ad·her'ent

ad·he'sion

ad·he'sive

ad·he'sive·ness

a·dieu'

ad'i·pose

ad'i·pos'i·ty

ad·ja'cen·cy

ad·ja'cent

ad'jec·ti'val

ad'jec·tive

ad·join'

ad·joined'

ad·journ'

ad·journed'

ad·journ'ment

ad·judge'

ad·judged'

ad·ju'di·cate

ad·ju'di·cat'ed

ad·ju'di·ca'tion

ad·ju'di·ca'tive

ad·ju'di·ca'tor

ad'junct

ad'ju·ra'tion

ad·jur'a·to'ry

ad·jure'

ad·jured'

ad·just'

ad·just'a·ble

ad·just'ed

ad·just'er

ad·just'ment

ad'ju·tan·cy

ad'ju·tant

ad·min'is·ter

ad·min'is·tered

ad·min'is·tra·tion

ad·min'is·tra·tive

ad·min'is·tra·tive·ly

ad·min'is·tra·tor

ad·min'is·tra·trix

ad'mi·ra·ble

ad'mi·ra·bly
ad'mi·ral
ad'mi·ral·ty
ad'mi·ra'tion
ad·mire'
ad·mired'
ad·mis'si·bil'i·ty
ad·mis'si·ble
ad·mis'sion
ad·mit'
ad·mit'tance
ad·mit'ted
ad·mit'ted·ly
ad·mix'ture
ad·mon'ish
ad'mo·ni'tion
ad·mon'i·to'ry
a·do'be
ad'o·les'cence
ad'o·les'cent
a·dopt'
a·dopt'ed
a·dop'tion
a·dop'tive
a·dor'a·ble
ad'o·ra'tion
a·dore'
a·dored'
a·dor'ing·ly
a·dorn'
a·dorned'
a·dorn'ment

ad·re'nal
ad·ren'al·ine
a·drift'
a·droit'
a·droit'ly
a·droit'ness
ad·sorb'
ad·sorp'tion
ad'u·la'tion
ad'u·la·to'ry
a·dult'
a·dul'ter·ant
a·dul'ter·ate
a·dul'ter·at'ed
a·dul'ter·a'tion
a·dul'ter·er
a·dul'ter·ous
a·dul'ter·y
a·dult'hood
ad·um'brate
ad·um'brat·ed
ad'um·bra'tion
ad·vance'
ad·vanced'
ad·vance'ment
ad·van'tage
ad'van·ta'geous
ad'vent
Ad'vent·ist
ad'ven·ti'tious
ad·ven'ture
ad·ven'tur·er

ad·ven'ture·some
ad·ven'tur·ess
ad·ven'tur·ous
ad'verb
ad·ver'bi·al
ad·ver'bi·al·ly
ad'ver·sar'y
ad·ver'sa·tive
ad·verse'
ad·verse'ly
ad·ver'si·ty
ad·vert'
ad'ver·tise
ad·ver'tise·ment
ad'ver·tis'er
ad·vice'
ad·vis'a·bil'i·ty
ad·vis'a·ble
ad·vise'
ad·vised'
ad·vis'ed·ly
ad'vi·see'
ad·vise'ment
ad·vi'so·ry
ad'vo·ca·cy
ad'vo·cate
ad'vo·cat'ed
ad·vow'son
adz
ae'gis
ae·o'li·an
ae'on

a′er·ate

a′er·at′ed

a′er·a′tion

a′er·a′tor

a·e′ri·al

a′er·o·nau′ti·cal

a′er·o·sol

a′er·o·space

aes·thet′ic

af′fa·bil′i·ty

af′fa·ble

af′fa·bly

af·fect′

af·fec·ta′tion

af·fect′ed

af·fect′ed·ly

af·fect′ing·ly

af·fec′tion

af·fec′tion·ate

af·fec′tion·ate·ly

af′fec·tiv′i·ty

af·fi′ance

af·fi′anced

af·fi′ant

af′fi·da′vit

af·fil′i·ate

af·fil′i·at′ed

af·fil′i·a′tion

af·fin′i·ty

af·firm′

af·firm′a·ble

af′fir·ma′tion

af·firm′a·tive

af·firm′a·to′ry

af·firmed′

af·fix′

af·fixed′

af·fla′tus

af·flict′

af·flict′ed

af·flic′tion

af·flic′tive

af′flu·ence

af′flu·ent

af·ford′

af·ford′ed

af·for′est

af·for′est·a′tion

af·fray′

af·fright′

af·fright′ed

af·front′

af·front′ed

af′ghan

a·field′

a·fire′

a·flame′

a·float′

a·foot′

a·fore′said′

a·fore′thought′

a·fore′time′

a·foul′

a·fraid′

Af′ro-A·mer′i·can

aft′er

aft′er·beat′

aft′er·care′

aft′er·clap′

aft′er·deck′

aft′er·din′ner

aft′er·ef·fect′

aft′er·glow′

aft′er·growth′

aft′er·guard′

aft′er·hatch′

aft′er·hold′

aft′er·im′age

aft′er·life′

aft′er·math

aft′er·most

aft′er·noon′

aft′er·part′

aft′er·taste′

aft′er·thought′

aft′er·time′

aft′er·ward

a·gain′

a·gainst′

a·gape′

ag′ate

ag′ate·ware′

a·ga′ve

age

aged

age′less

a'gen·cy	ag'i·ta'tor	ai'ler·on
a·gen'da	a·gleam'	ail'ment
a·gen'dum	ag'nate	aim
a'gent	ag·nos'tic	aim'less
a·ger'a·tum	ag·nos'ti·cism	air
ag·glom'er·ate	a·gog'	air'brush'
ag·glom'er·at'ed	ag'o·nize	air'-dry'
ag·glom'er·a'tion	ag'o·nized	aired
ag·glom'er·a'tive	ag'o·niz'ing·ly	air'field'
ag·glu'ti·nate	ag'o·ny	air'freight
ag·glu'ti·na'tion	a·grar'i·an	air'i·ly
ag·glu'ti·na'tive	a·gree'	air'lin'er
ag'gran·dize	a·gree'a·bil'i·ty	air'mail'
ag·gran'dize·ment	a·gree'a·ble	air'man
ag'gra·vate	a·gree'a·ble·ness	air'plane'
ag'gra·vat'ed	a·greed'	air'port'
ag'gra·vat'ing·ly	a·gree'ment	air'ship'
ag'gra·va'tion	ag'ri·cul'tur·al	air'sick'
ag'gre·gate	ag'ri·cul'ture	air'space'
ag'gre·ga'tion	a·gron'o·my	air'tight'
ag·gres'sion	a·ground'	air'way'
ag·gres'sive	a'gue	air'wor'thy
ag·gres'sor	a·head'	air'y
ag·grieve'	a·hoy'	aisle
ag·grieved'	a·hun'gered	a·jar'
a·ghast'	aid	a·kim'bo
ag'ile	aid'ed	a·kin'
a·gil'i·ty	ai·grette'	al'a·bas'ter
ag'i·o	ai'guil·lette'	a·lac'ri·ty
ag'i·tate	ail	al'a·mo
ag'i·tat'ed	ai·lan'thus	a·larm'
ag'i·ta'tion	ailed	a·larmed'

a·larm′ing·ly

a·larm′ist

a·las′

al′ba·core

al′ba·tross

al·bi′no

al′bum

al·bu′min

al·bu′mi·nous

al′che·mist

al′che·my

al′co·hol

al′co·hol′ic

al′co·hol·ism

al′co·hol·ize

al′cove

al′der

al′der·man

al′der·man′ic

Al′der·ney

a′le·a·to′ry

a·lem′bic

a·lem′bi·cate

Al′e·mite

a·lert′

a·lert′ly

a·lert′ness

ale′wife′

al′ex·an′drite

al·fal′fa

al′ge·bra

al′ge·bra′ic

Al·ge′ri·an

a′li·as

al′i·bi

al′i·dade

al′ien

al′ien·a·bil′i·ty

al′ien·a·ble

al′ien·ate

al′ien·at′ed

al′ien·a′tion

al′ien·ist

a·light′

a·lign′

a·lign′ment

a·like′

al′i·men′ta·ry

al′i·men·ta′tion

al′i·mo′ny

al′i·quant

al′i·quot

a·live′

a·live′ness

a·liz′a·rin

al′ka·li

al′ka·lin′i·ty

all

al·lay′

al·layed′

al′le·ga′tion

al·lege′

al·leged′

al·leg′ed·ly

al·le′giance

al′le·gor′i·cal

al′le·go·rize

al′le·go′ry

al′le·gret′to

al·le′gro

al′ler·gen

al·ler′gic

al′ler·gy

al·le′vi·ate

al·le′vi·at′ed

al·le′vi·a′tion

al′ley

al′ley·way′

al·li′ance

al·lied′

al′li·ga′tor

al·lit′er·ate

al·lit′er·a′tion

al·lit′er·a′tive

al·lit′er·a′tive·ly

al′lo·ca·ble

al′lo·cate

al′lo·cat′ed

al′lo·ca′tion

al′lo·cu′tion

al′lo·path

al′lo·path′ic

al·lop′a·thy

al·lot′

al·lot′ment

al·lot′ted

al·low'

al·low'a·ble

al·low'ance

al·lowed'

al·low'ed·ly

al·loy'

al·loy'age

al·loyed'

all'spice'

al·lude'

al·lud'ed

al·lure'

al·lured'

al·lure'ment

al·lur'ing·ly

al·lu'sion

al·lu'sive

al·lu'sive·ly

al·lu'sive·ness

al·lu'vi·al

al·lu'vi·um

al·ly'

al'ma·nac

al·might'y

al'mond

al'mon·er

al'most

alms

alms'house'

a·lo'di·um

al'oe

a·loft'

a·lo'ha

a·lone'

a·long'

a·long'side'

a·loof'

a·loof'ly

a·lo'pe'ci·a

a·loud'

al·pac'a

al'pha·bet

al'pha·bet'ic

al'pha·bet'i·cal

al'pha·bet·ize

al·read'y

al'so

al'tar

al'tar·piece'

al'ter

al'ter·a·ble

al'ter·a'tion

al'ter·a'tive

al'ter·cate

al'ter·ca'tion

al'tered

al'ter·nate

al'ter·nat'ed

al'ter·na'tion

al·ter'na·tive

al'ter·na'tor

al·though'

al'ti·graph

al·tim'e·ter

al'ti·pla'no

al·tis'si·mo

al'ti·tude

al'to

al'to·geth'er

al'tru·ism

al'tru·ist

al'tru·is'tic

al'tru·is'ti·cal·ly

al'um

a·lu'mi·na

a·lu'mi·nate

a·lu'mi·nif'er·ous

a·lu'mi·no'sis

a·lu'mi·num

a·lum'na

a·lum'nae

a·lum'ni

a·lum'nus

al·ve'o·lar

al·ve'o·lus

al'ways

a·lys'sum

a·mal'gam

a·mal'gam·ate

a·mal'gam·at'ed

a·mal'gam·a'tion

a·man'u·en'sis

am'a·ranth

am'a·ran'thine

a·mass'

a·massed'

am'a·teur'

am'a·teur'ish

am'a·teur'ism

am'a·tive

am'a·tive·ness

am'a·to'ry

a·maze'

a·mazed'

a·maze'ment

a·maz'ing·ly

Am'a·zon

Am'a·zo'ni·an

am·bas'sa·dor

am·bas'sa·do'ri·al

am·bas'sa·do'ri·al·ly

am·bas'sa·dress

am'ber

am'ber·gris

am'bi·dex·ter'i·ty

am'bi·dex'trous

am'bi·dex'trous·ly

am'bi·dex'trous·ness

am'bi·ent

am·bi·gu'i·ty

am·big'u·ous

am·big'u·ous·ly

am·big'u·ous·ness

am·bi'tion

am·bi'tious

am·bi'tious·ly

am·biv'a·lence

am·biv'a·lent

am'ble

am·bro'si·a

am·bro'si·al

am·bro'si·al·ly

am'bro·type

am'bu·lance

am'bu·lant

am'bu·la·to'ry

am'bus·cade'

am'bush

a·mel'io·rate

a·mel'io·rat'ed

a·mel'io·ra'tion

a·mel'io·ra'tive

a'men'

a·me'na·bil'i·ty

a·me'na·ble

a·mend'

a·mend'ed

a·mend'ment

a·men'i·ty

A·mer'i·can

A·mer'i·can·i·za'tion

A·mer'i·can·ize

am'e·thyst

a'mi·a·bil'i·ty

a'mi·a·ble

am'i·ca·bil'i·ty

am'i·ca·ble

a·mid'ships

a·midst'

a·miss'

am'i·ty

am'me'ter

am·mo'ni·a

am·mo'ni·um

am'mu·ni'tion

am·ne'si·a

am'nes·ty

a·moe'ba

a·mong'

a·mongst'

a·mor'al

am'o·rous

am'o·rous·ly

am'o·rous·ness

a·mor'phous

a·mor'ti·za'tion

a·mor'tize

a·mor'tized

a·mount'

a·mount'ed

a·mour'

am·per'age

am'pere

am·phet'a·mine

am·phib'i·an

am·phib'i·ous

am·phib'i·ous·ly

am'phi·the'a·ter

am'pho·ra

am'ple

am'pli·fi·ca'tion

am'pli·fied

am'pli·fi'er

am'pli·fy

am'pli·tude

am'ply

am·pul'la

am'pu·tate

am'pu·tat'ed

am'pu·ta'tion

am'pu·ta'tive

am'pu·tee'

Am'trak

am'u·let

a·muse'

a·mused'

a·muse'ment

a·mus'ing·ly

a·nab'o·lism

a·nach'ro·nism

a·nach'ro·nis'tic

a·nach'ro·nous

an'a·con'da

an'a·gram

an'a·lects

an'al·ge'si·a

an'al·ge'sic

an'a·log'i·cal

a·nal'o·gies

a·nal'o·gous

a·nal'o·gous·ly

an'a·logue

a·nal'o·gy

a·nal'y·ses

a·nal'y·sis

an'a·lyst

an'a·lyt'ic

an'a·lyt'i·cal

an'a·lyt'i·cal·ly

an'a·lyze

an'a·lyzed

an'a·lyz'er

an'am·ne'sis

an·ar'chic

an·ar'chi·cal

an'arch·ism

an'arch·ist

an'arch·y

an·as'tig·mat'ic

a·nath'e·ma·tize

an'a·tom'ic

an'a·tom'i·cal

a·nat'o·mist

a·nat'o·mize

a·nat'o·mized

a·nat'o·my

an'ces'tor

an'ces'tors

an·ces'tral

an·ces'try

an'chor

an'chor·age

an'chored

an'cho·rite

an·cho'vy

an'cient

an'cil·lar'y

and

an·dan'te

and'i'ron

an'ec·dot'age

an'ec·dote

a·ne'mi·a

an'e·mom'e·ter

an'e·mom'e·try

a·nem'o·ne

a·nent'

an'er·oid

an'es·the'si·a

an'es·the'si·ol'o·gy

an'es·the'sis

an'es·thet'ic

an'es·thet'i·za'tion

an·es'the·tize

an·es'the·tized

an'eu·rysm

a·new'

an'gel

an·gel'ic

An'ge·lus

an'ger

an'gered

an'gle

an'gled

an'gler

An'gli·can

An'glo-Sax'on

An·go'ra

an'gri·er

an'gri·est

an'gri·ly

an'gry

an'guish

an'guished

an'gu·lar

an'gu·lar'i·ty

an'gu·la'tion

an·hy'drous

an'i·line

an'i·mad·ver'sion

an'i·mal

an'i·mate

an'i·mat'ed

an'i·mat'ed·ly

an'i·ma'tion

an'i·ma'tor

an'i·mism

an'i·mist

an'i·mis'tic

an'i·mos'i·ty

an'i·mus

an'ise

an'ise·root'

an'kle

an'kle·bone'

an'klet

an'ky·lo'sis

an'nal·ist

an'nals

an·neal'

an·nealed'

an·nex'

an'nex·a'tion

an'nex·a'tion·ist

an·nexed'

an·ni'hi·late

an·ni'hi·lat'ed

an·ni'hi·la'tion

an'ni·ver'sa·ry

an'no·tate

an'no·tat'ed

an'no·ta'tion

an·nounce'

an·nounced'

an·nounce'ment

an·nounc'er

an·noy'

an·noy'ance

an·noyed'

an·noy'ing·ly

an'nu·al

an'nu·al·ly

an·nu'i·tant

an·nu'i·ty

an·nul'

an'nu·lar

an·nulled'

an·nul'ment

an·nun'ci·a'tion

an·nun'ci·a'tor

an'ode

an'o·dyne

a·noint'

a·noint'ed

a·nom'a·lies

a·nom'a·lous

a·nom'a·lous·ly

a·nom'a·ly

a·non'

an'o·nym'i·ty

a·non'y·mous

a·non'y·mous·ly

a·noph'e·les

an·oth'er

an'swer

an'swer·a·ble

an'swered

ant

ant·ac'id

an·tag'o·nism

an·tag'o·nist

an·tag'o·nis'tic

an·tag'o·nis'ti·cal·ly

an·tag'o·nize

an·tag'o·nized

ant·arc'tic

an'te

ant'eat'er

an'te·ced'ent

an'te·cham'ber

an'te·date'

an'te·dat'ed

an'te·lope

an'te·na'tal

an·ten'na

an·te'ri·or

an'te·room'

an'them

an·thol'o·gies

an·thol'o·gist

an·thol'o·gize

an·thol'o·gy

an'thra·cite

an'thrax

an'thro·poid

an'thro·po·log'i·cal

an'thro·pol'o·gy

an'ti·bod'y

an'tic

an'ti·christ'

an·tic'i·pate

an·tic'i·pat'ed

an·tic'i·pa'tion

an·tic'i·pa·to'ry

an'ti·cli'max

an'ti·cline

an'ti·dote

an'ti·gen

an'ti·knock'

an'ti·mo'ny

an·tin'o·my

an·tip'a·thies

an·tip'a·thy

an·tiph'o·nal

an·tip'o·des

an'ti·quar'i·an

an'ti·quar'y

an'ti·quat'ed

an·tique'

an·tiqued'

an·tiq'ui·ty

an'ti·sep'sis

an'ti·sep'tic

an'ti·sep'ti·cal·ly

an'ti·so'cial

an'ti·tank'

an·tith'e·ses

an·tith'e·sis

an'ti·thet'i·cal

an'ti·tox'in

an'ti·trust'

ant'ler

ant'lered

an'to·nym

an'trum

an'vil

anx·i'e·ty

anx'ious

anx'ious·ly

an'y

an'y·bod'y

an'y·one

an'y·thing

an'y·way

an'y·where

a·or'ta

a·or'tic

a·pace'

a·part'

a·part'ment

ap'a·thet'ic

ap'a·thet'i·cal·ly

ap'a·thy

a·pe'ri·ent

a·per'i·tive

ap'er·ture

a'pex

a'pex·es

a·pha'si·a

a'phid

aph'o·rism

aph'o·ris'tic

a'pi·a·rist

a'pi·ar'y

ap'i·cal

ap'i·ces

a·piece'

a·poc'a·lypse

ap'o·gee

A·pol'lo

a·pol'o·get'ic

a·pol'o·get'i·cal

a·pol'o·gies

a·pol'o·gist

a·pol'o·gize

a·pol'o·gized

a·pol'o·gy

ap'o·plec'tic

ap'o·plex'y

a·pos'ta·sy

a·pos′tate

a·pos′tle

ap′os·tol′ic

ap′os·tol′i·cal

a·pos′tro·phe

a·pos′tro·phize

a·poth′e·car′y

ap′o·thegm

a·poth′e·o′sis

ap·pall′

ap·palled′

ap·pall′ing·ly

ap′pa·nage

ap′pa·ra′tus

ap′pa·ra′tus·es

ap·par′el

ap·par′eled

ap·par′ent

ap′pa·ri′tion

ap·peal′

ap·pealed′

ap·peal′ing·ly

ap·pear′

ap·pear′ance

ap·peared′

ap·peas′a·ble

ap·pease′

ap·peased′

ap·pease′ment

ap·peas′ing·ly

ap·pel′lant

ap·pel′late

ap′pel·la′tion

ap′pel·lee′

ap·pend′

ap·pend′age

ap′pen·dec′to·my

ap·pend′ed

ap·pen′di·ci′tis

ap·pen′dix

ap·pen′dix·es

ap′per·ceive′

ap′per·ceived′

ap′per·cep′tion

ap′per·cep′tive

ap′per·tain′

ap′per·tained′

ap′pe·tite

ap′pe·tiz′er

ap′pe·tiz′ing·ly

ap·plaud′

ap·plaud′ed

ap·plause′

ap′ple

ap′ple·jack′

ap′ple·nut′

ap′ple·sauce′

ap·pli′ance

ap′pli·ca·bil′i·ty

ap′pli·ca·ble

ap′pli·cant

ap′pli·ca′tion

ap′pli·ca′tor

ap·plied′

ap′pli·qué′

ap·ply′

ap·point′

ap·point′ed

ap·point′ee′

ap·poin′tive

ap·point′ment

ap·por′tion

ap·por′tioned

ap·por′tion·ment

ap′po·site

ap′po·si′tion

ap·prais′al

ap·praise′

ap·praised′

ap·prais′er

ap·prais′ing·ly

ap·pre′ci·a·ble

ap·pre′ci·a·bly

ap·pre′ci·ate

ap·pre′ci·at′ed

ap·pre′ci·a′tion

ap·pre′ci·a′tive

ap·pre′ci·a′tive·ly

ap′pre·hend′

ap′pre·hend′ed

ap′pre·hend′ing·ly

ap′pre·hen′sion

ap′pre·hen′sive

ap′pre·hen′sive·ly

ap′pre·hen′sive·ness

ap·pren′tice

ap·pren'ticed

ap·pren'tice·ship

ap·prise'

ap·prised'

ap·proach'

ap·proach'a·ble

ap·proached'

ap·pro·ba'tion

ap·pro·ba'tive

ap·pro·ba'tive·ness

ap·pro'pri·ate

ap·pro'pri·at'ed

ap·pro'pri·ate·ly

ap·pro'pri·ate·ness

ap·pro'pri·a'tion

ap·prov'al

ap·prove'

ap·proved'

ap·prov'ing·ly

ap·prox'i·mate

ap·prox'i·mat'ed

ap·prox'i·mate·ly

ap·prox'i·ma'tion

ap·pur'te·nance

ap·pur'te·nant

a'pri·cot

A'pril

a'pron

ap'ro·pos'

apse

ap'sis

apt

ap'ti·tude

apt'ly

apt'ness

aq'ua·ma·rine'

aq'ua·relle'

a·quar'i·um

aq'ua·scu'tum

a·quat'ic

aq'ua·tint'

aq'ue·duct

a'que·ous

Ar'ab

ar'a·besque'

A·ra'bi·an

Ar'a·bic

ar'a·bil'i·ty

Ar'ab·ist

ar'a·ble

a·rach'nid

a·rach'noid

a·rag'o·nite

Ar'a·ma'ic

ar'ba·lest

ar'bi·ter

ar'bi·tra·ble

ar'bi·trage

ar·bit'ra·ment

ar'bi·trar'i·ly

ar'bi·trar'i·ness

ar'bi·trar'y

ar'bi·trate

ar'bi·trat'ed

ar'bi·tra'tion

ar'bi·tra'tive

ar'bi·tra'tor

ar'bor

ar·bo're·al

ar·bo're·ous

ar·bo·re'tum

ar·bu'tus

arc

ar·cade'

ar·cad'ed

Ar·ca'di·a

ar·ca'num

arch

ar'chae·ol'o·gist

ar'chae·ol'o·gy

ar·cha'ic

arch'an'gel

arch'an·gel'ic

arch'bish'op

arch'dea'con

arch'di'o·cese

arch'du'cal

arch'duch'ess

arch'duch'y

arch'duke'

arch'er

arch'er·fish'

arch'er·y

ar'che·typ'al

ar'che·type

arch'fiend'	ar'gu·men'ta·tive	arm'scye'
ar'chi·pel'a·go	Ar'gy·rol	ar'my
ar'chi·tect	a'ri·a	ar'ni·ca
ar'chi·tec·ton'ic	ar'id	a·ro'ma
ar'chi·tec'tur·al	a·rid'i·ty	ar'o·mat'ic
ar'chi·tec'tur·al·ly	a·right'	a·round'
ar'chi·tec'ture	a·rise'	a·rouse'
ar'chi·trave	a·ris'en	ar·peg'gio
ar'chives	ar'is·toc'ra·cy	ar·raign'
ar'chi·vist	a·ris'to·crat	ar·raigned'
arch'ly	a·ris'to·crat'ic	ar·raign'ment
arch'ness	a·rith'me·tic	ar·range'
arch'way	ar'ith·met'i·cal	ar·ranged'
arc'tic	ark	ar·range'ment
ar'dent	arm	ar·rang'er
ar'dent·ly	ar·ma'da	ar'ras
ar'dor	ar'ma·dil'lo	ar·ray'
ar'du·ous	ar'ma·ment	ar·rayed'
ar'du·ous·ly	ar'ma·ture	ar·rear'age
are	arm'chair	ar·rears'
a're·a	armed	ar·rest'
a·re'na	Ar·me'ni·an	ar·rest'er
ar'gent	arm'ful	ar·rhyth'mic
ar'gen·tif'er·ous	arm'hole'	ar·riv'al
ar'gon	ar'mi·stice	ar·rive'
Ar'go·naut	arm'let	ar·rived'
ar'got	ar'mor	ar'ro·gance
ar'gu·a·ble	ar'mored	ar'ro·gant
ar'gue	ar·mo'ri·al	ar'ro·gant·ly
ar'gued	ar'mor·y	ar'ro·gate
ar'gu·ment	arm'pit'	ar'ro·gat'ed
ar'gu·men·ta'tion	arm'rest'	ar'ro·ga'tion

ar'row	ar·tif'i·cer	a·sep'tic
ar'row·head'	ar'ti·fi'cial	ash
ar'row·head'ed	ar'ti·fi·ci·al'i·ty	a·shamed'
ar'row·wood'	ar'ti·fi'cial·ly	ash'en
ar'row·y	ar·til'ler·ist	ash'es
ar·roy'o	ar·til'ler·y	ash'lar
ar'se·nal	ar'ti·san	a·shore'
ar'se·nate	art'ist	ash'pit'
ar·sen'ic	ar·tis'tic	ash'wort'
ar·sen'i·cal	art'ist·ry	ash'y
ar'se·nide	art'less	A'sian
ar'se·nite	Ar'y·an	A'si·at'ic
ar'son	as	a·side'
ar'son·ist	as'a·fet'i·da	as'i·nine
art	as·bes'tos	as'i·nin'i·ty
ar·te'ri·al	as·cend'	ask
ar'ter·y	as·cend'an·cy	a·skance'
art'ful	as·cend'ant	a·skew'
art'ful·ly	as·cend'er	a·slant'
ar·thrit'ic	as·cen'sion	a·sleep'
ar·thrit'i·cal	as·cent'	asp
ar·thri'tis	as'cer·tain'	as·par'a·gus
ar'thro·plas'ty	as'cer·tain'ment	as'pect
ar'ti·choke	as·cet'ic	as'pen
ar'ti·cle	as·cet'i·cism	as·per'i·ty
ar'ti·cled	as·ci'tes	as·perse'
ar·tic'u·late	a·scor'bic	as·persed'
ar·tic'u·lat'ed	as'cot	as·per'sion
ar·tic'u·la'tion	as·cribe'	as'phalt
ar·tic'u·la'tive	as·cribed'	as·phal'tic
ar'ti·fact	as·crip'tion	as'pho·del
ar'ti·fice	a·sep'sis	as·phyx'i·a

as·phyx′i·ate

as·phyx′i·a′tion

as′pic

as·pir′ant

as′pi·rate

as′pi·rat′ed

as′pi·ra′tion

as′pi·ra′tor

as·pire′

as·pired′

as′pi·rin

as′sa·gai

as·sail′

as·sail′ant

as·sailed′

as·sas′sin

as·sas′si·nate

as·sas′si·nat′ed

as·sas′si·na′tion

as·sault′

as·sault′ed

as·say′

as·sayed′

as·say′er

as·sem′blage

as·sem′ble

as·sem′bled

as·sem′bler

as·sem′bly

as·sent′

as·sent′ed

as·sent′ing·ly

as·sert′

as·sert′ed

as·ser′tion

as·ser′tive

as·ser′tive·ly

as·sess′

as·sess′a·ble

as·sessed′

as·sess′ment

as·ses′sor

as·ses′sor·ship

as′set

as·sev′er·ate

as·sev′er·a′tion

as′si·du′i·ty

as·sid′u·ous

as·sid′u·ous·ly

as·sign′

as·sign′a·ble

as′sig·na′tion

as·signed′

as′sign·ee′

as·sign′ment

as′sign·or′

as·sim′i·la·ble

as·sim′i·late

as·sim′i·lat′ed

as·sim′i·la′tion

as·sim′i·la′tive

as·sim′i·la·to′ry

as·sist′

as·sist′ance

as·sist′ant

as·sist′ed

as·sists′

as·size′

as·so′ci·ate

as·so′ci·at′ed

as·so′ci·a′tion

as·so′ci·a′tive

as′so·nance

as′so·nant

as·sort′

as·sort′ed

as·sort′ment

as·suage′

as·suaged′

as·sum′a·ble

as·sum′a·bly

as·sume′

as·sumed′

as·sum′ed·ly

as·sump′sit

as·sump′tion

as·sur′ance

as·sure′

as·sured′

as·sur′ed·ly

as·sur′ed·ness

as·sur′er

As·syr′i·an

as′ter

as′ter·isk

a·stern′

as'ter·oid	as·tute'ly	a·tone'
as·the'ni·a	as·tute'ness	a·toned'
as·then'ic	a·sun'der	a·tone'ment
asth'ma	a·sy'lum	a'tri·um
asth·mat'ic	a'sym·met'ric	a·tro'cious
as'tig·mat'ic	a'sym·met'ri·cal	a·tro'cious·ly
a·stig'ma·tism	a·sym'me·try	a·troc'i·ty
as·ton'ish	at	at'ro·phied
as·ton'ish·ing·ly	at'a·rax'i·a	at'ro·phy
as·ton'ish·ment	at'a·vism	at'ro·pine
as·tound'	at'a·vis'tic	at·tach'
as·tound'ed	a'the·ism	at·tached'
as·tound'ing·ly	a'the·ist	at·tach'ment
a·strad'dle	a'the·is'tic	at·tack'
as·trag'a·lus	ath'e·nae'um	at·tack'er
as'tra·khan	A·the'ni·an	at·tain'
as'tral	ath'lete	at·tain'a·ble
a·stray'	ath·let'ic	at·tain'der
a·stride'	ath·let'ics	at·tained'
as·trin'gen·cy	a·thwart'	at·tain'ment
as·trin'gent	at'mos·phere	at'tar
as'tro·dome	at'mos·pher'ic	at·tempt'
as·trol'o·ger	at'oll	at·tempt'ed
as·trol'o·gy	at'om	at·tend'
as'tro·nau'tics	at'om·at'ic	at·tend'ance
as·tron'o·mer	a·tom'ic	at·tend'ant
as'tro·nom'i·cal	at'om·is'tic	at·ten'tion
as·tron'o·my	at'om·ize	at·ten'tive
as'tro·phys'i·cal	at'om·ized	at·ten'tive·ly
as'tro·phys'i·cist	at'om·iz'er	at·ten'tive·ness
as'tro·phys'ics	a·ton'al	at·ten'u·ate
as'tro·turf	a'to·nal'i·ty	at·ten'u·at'ed

at·ten'u·a'tion	au'di·bil'i·ty	aus'cul·tate
at·test'	au'di·ble	aus'cul·ta'tion
at'tes·ta'tion	au'di·bly	aus'pice
at·tests'	au'di·ence	aus'pic·es
at'tic	au'di·o	aus·pi'cious
at·tire'	au'di·om'e·ter	aus·tere'
at·tired'	au'dio·vis'u·al	aus·tere'ly
at'ti·tude	au'dit·ed	aus·ter'i·ty
at'ti·tu'di·nize	au·di'tion	Aus·tral'ian
at·tor'ney	au'di·tor	Aus'tri·an
at·tor'neys	au'di·to'ri·um	au·then'tic
at·tract'	au'di·to'ry	au·then'ti·cate
at·tract'ed	au'ger	au·then'ti·cat'ed
at·trac'tion	aught	au·then'ti·ca'tion
at·trac'tive	aug·ment'	au'then·tic'i·ty
at·trac'tive·ly	aug'men·ta'tion	au'thor
at·trib'ute	aug·ment'a·tive	au·thor'i·tar'i·an
at·trib'ut·ed	aug·ment'ed	au·thor'i·ta'tive
at'tri·bu'tion	au'gur	au·thor'i·ta'tive·ly
at·trib'u·tive	au'gured	au·thor'i·ty
at·tri'tion	au'gu·ry	au·thor'i·za'tion
at·tune'	au·gust'	au'thor·ize
at·tuned'	Au'gust	au'thor·ized
a·twit'ter	aunt	au'thor·ship
a·typ'i·cal	au'ra	au'to·bi'o·graph'i·cal
au'burn	au'ral	au'to·bi·og'ra·phy
auc'tion	au're·ole	au·toch'tho·nous
auc'tioned	au'ri·cle	au'to·clave
auc'tion·eer'	au·ric'u·lar	au·toc'ra·cy
au·da'cious	au·rif'er·ous	au'to·crat
au·da'cious·ly	au·ro'ra	au'to·crat'ic
au·dac'i·ty	au·ro'ral	au'to·crat'i·cal·ly

au'to·graph

au'to·in·tox'i·ca'tion

au'to·mat'ic

au'to·ma'tion

au·tom'a·tize

au·tom'a·ton

au'to·mo·bile'

au·ton'o·mize

au·ton'o·mous

au·ton'o·my

au'top·sies

au'top·sy

au'to·sug·ges'tion

au'tumn

au·tum'nal

aux·il'ia·ry

a·vail'

a·vail'a·bil'i·ty

a·vail'a·ble

a·vailed'

av'a·lanche

av'a·rice

av'a·ri'cious

av'a·ri'cious·ly

av'a·tar'

a·venge'

a·venged'

av'e·nue

a·ver'

av'er·age

av'er·aged

a·ver'ment

a·verred'

a·verse'

a·ver'sion

a·vert'

a·vert'ed

a'vi·ar'y

a'vi·a'tion

a'vi·a'tor

av'id

a·vid'i·ty

av'id·ly

av'i·ga'tion

av'o·ca'do

av'o·ca'tion

a·void'

a·void'a·ble

a·void'ed

a·vow'al

a·vow'ed·ly

a·vun'cu·lar

a·wait'

a·wait'ed

a·wake'

a·wak'en

a·wak'ened

a·ward'

a·ward'ed

a·ware'

a·ware'ness

a·wash'

a·way'

awe

awe'some

aw'ful

aw'ful·ly

awk'ward

awk'ward·ly

awk'ward·ness

awl

awn'ing

a·woke'

a·wry'

ax

ax'i·om

ax'i·o·mat'ic

ax'is

ax'le

a·za'le·a

az'i·muth

Az'tec

az'ure

az'u·rite

B

bab'bitt

bab'ble

ba·boon'

ba'by

Bab'y·lo'ni·an

bac'ca·lau're·ate

bac'cha·nal

bac'cha·na'li·an

bach'e·lor

bach'e·lor·hood'

ba·cil'lus

back

back'ache'

back'board'

back'bone'

back'break'er

back'drop'

back'er

back'fire'

back'gam'mon

back'ground'

back'hand'

back'hand'ed

back'lash'

back'log'

back'saw'

back'slide'

back'slid'er

back'spin'

back'stage'

back'stamp'

back'stitch'

back'stop'

back'stroke'

back'track'

back'ward

back'ward·ness

back'wash'

back'wa'ter

back'woods'

ba'con

bac·te'ri·a

bac·te'ri·al

bac·te'ri·cid'al

bac·te'ri·cide

bac·te'ri·o·log'i·cal

bac·te'ri·ol'o·gy

bac·te'ri·um

bad

badge

badg'er

bad'i·nage'

bad'lands'

bad'ly

bad'min·ton

bad'ness

baf'fle

baf'fled

bag

ba·gasse'

bag'a·telle'

bag'gage

bagged

bag'pipe'

bail

bailed

bail'ee'	bal·loon'	bang
bail'iff	bal·loon'ist	bang'board'
bail'i·wick	bal'lot	banged
bail'ment	ball'play'er	bang'le
bait	ball'room'	ban'ish
baize	balm	ban'ish·ment
bake	bal'sa	ban'is·ter
Ba'ke·lite	bal'sam	ban'jo
bak'er	bal'sam·if'er·ous	bank
bak'er·y	bal'us·ter	bank'book'
bal'ance	bal'us·trade'	banked
bal'anced	bam·boo'	bank'er
bal·bo'a	bam·boo'zle	bank'rupt
bal·brig'gan	bam·boo'zled	bank'rupt·cy
bal'co·ny	ban	banned
bald	ba'nal	ban'ner
bal'da·chin	ba·nal'i·ty	banns
bal'der·dash	ba·nan'a	ban'quet
bald'ness	band	ban'quet·ed
bal'dric	band'age	ban'shee
bale	ban·dan'na	ban'tam
baled	band'box'	ban'ter
bale'ful	ban·deau'	ban'tered
balk	band'ed	ban'ter·ing·ly
ball	ban'de·role	ban'yan
bal'lad	ban'di·coot	ban'zai'
bal'last	ban'dit	bap'tism
balled	band'mas'ter	bap·tis'mal
bal'le·ri'na	ban'do·leer'	Bap'tist
bal'let	band'stand'	bap·tize'
bal·let'o·mane	ban'dy	bap·tized'
bal·lis'tics	bane'ful	bap·tize'ment

bar	bar'na·cle	base'board'
barb	barn'yard'	based
bar·bar'i·an	bar'o·gram	base'less
bar·bar'ic	bar'o·graph	base'ly
bar'ba·rism	ba·rom'e·ter	base'ment
bar·bar'i·ty	bar'o·met'ric	base'ness
bar'ba·rous	bar'on	bas'er
bar'be·cue	bar'on·age	bas'est
barbed	bar'on·ess	bash'ful
bar'ber	bar'on·et	bas'ic
bar'ber'ry	bar'on·et·cy	bas'i·cal·ly
bar·bette'	ba·ro'ni·al	ba·sil'i·ca
bar'bi·tu'rate	bar'o·ny	bas'i·lisk
bard	ba·roque'	ba'sin
bare	bar'rack	ba'sis
bare'back'	bar'ra·cu'da	bask
bared	bar·rage'	bas'ket
bare'faced'	bar'ra·try	bas'ket·ball'
bare'foot'	bar'rel	bas'ket·work'
bare'head'ed	bar'ren	bas'-re·lief'
bare'ly	bar'ren·ness	bass
bare'ness	bar'ri·cade'	bas'si·net'
bar'gain	bar'ri·cad'ed	bas'so
bar'gained	bar'ri·er	bas·soon'
barge	bar'ris·ter	bass'wood'
barge'man	bar'row	bast'ed
bar'i·tone	bar'ter	bas'ti·na'do
bar'i·um	bar'tered	bas'tion
bark	bas'al	bat
bar'ley	ba·salt'	batch
bar'maid'	bas'cule	bath
barn	base	bathe

bathed

bath'er

bath'house'

ba'thos

bath'robe'

bath'room'

ba·tiste'

ba'ton'

bat·tal'ion

bat'ten

bat'tened

bat'ter

bat'tered

bat'ter·y

bat'tle

bat'tled

bat'tle·ment

bat'tle·ship'

bawl

bawled

bay'ber'ry

bay'o·net

bay'o·net'ed

bay'ou

ba·zaar'

be

beach

beached

beach'comb'er

bea'con

bead

bead'ed

bea'dle

bead'work'

bea'gle

beak

beak'er

beam

beamed

bean

bear

bear'a·ble

beard

beard'ed

bear'er

bear'ish

bear'skin'

beast

beast'li·ness

beast'ly

beat

beat'en

beat'er

be·a·tif'ic

be·at'i·fi·ca'tion

be·at'i·fy

beat'ings

beat'nik

beau'te·ous

beau'ti·ful

beau'ti·ful·ly

beau'ti·fy

beau'ty

bea'ver

be·calm'

be·calmed'

be·came'

be·cause'

beck'on

beck'oned

be·cloud'

be·come'

be·com'ing·ly

be·com'ing·ness

bed

be·daub'

bed'bug'

bed'cham'ber

bed'clothes'

bed'ded

be·deck'

be·dev'il

be·dev'iled

bed'fel'low

be·diz'en

bed'lam

bed'post'

bed'rid'den

bed'rock'

bed'roll'

bed'room'

bed'side'

bed'spread'

bed'spring'

bed'stead

bed'time'

bee	be·hav'ior	bell'bird'
beech	be·hav'ior·al	bell'boy'
beef	be·hav'ior·ism	bel'li·cose
beef'steak'	be·head'	bel'li·cos'i·ty
bee'line'	be·head'ings	bel·lig'er·ence
beer	be·held'	bel·lig'er·en·cy
bees'wax'	be·he'moth	bel·lig'er·ent
bee'tle	be·hest'	bel·lig'er·ent·ly
be·fall'	be·hind'	bel'lowed
be·fell'	be·hold'	bel'lows
be·fit'	be·hold'en	be·long'
be·fog'	be·hold'er	be·longed'
be·fore'	be·hoove'	be·long'ings
be·fore'hand'	beige	be·lov'ed
be·friend'	be·jew'el	be·low'
be·fud'dle	be·jew'eled	belt
be·fud'dled	be·la'bor	belt'ed
beg	be·lat'ed	bel've·dere'
be·get'	be·lat'ed·ly	be·moan'
beg'gar	belch	be·moaned'
begged	be·lea'guer	be·mused'
be·gin'	be·lea'guered	bench
be·gone'	bel'fry	bend
be·go'ni·a	Bel'gi·an	bend'ed
be·got'	be·lie'	be·neath'
be·grime'	be·lief'	ben'e·dic'tion
be·guile'	be·liev'a·ble	ben'e·fac'tion
be·guiled'	be·lieve'	ben'e·fac'tor
be'gum	be·lit'tle	ben'e·fac'tress
be·gun'	be·lit'tled	be·nef'i·cent
be·half'	bell	ben'e·fi'cial
be·have'	bel'la·don'na	ben'e·fi'ci·ar'y

ben′e·fit

ben′e·fit′ed

be·nev′o·lence

be·nev′o·lent

be·night′ed

be·nign′

be·nig′nan·cy

be·nig′nant

be·nig′ni·ty

bent

ben′zene

be·queath′

be·quest′

be·rate′

be·rat′ed

be·reave′

be·reaved′

be·reave′ment

ber′ry

berth

ber′yl

be·seech′

be·seeched′

be·seech′ing·ly

be·set′

be·side′

be·sides′

be·siege′

be·sieged′

be·smirch′

be·sot′ted

be·span′gle

be·speak′

Bes′se·mer

best

bes′tial

bes′ti·al′i·ty

be·stow′

be·stowed′

be·stride′

bet

be·take′

be·tide′

be·times′

be·to′ken

be·tray′

be·tray′al

be·tray′er

be·troth′

be·troth′al

bet′ter

bet′tered

bet′ter·ment

be·tween′

be·twixt′

bev′el

bev′eled

bev′er·age

bev′y

be·wail′

be·wailed′

be·ware′

be·wil′der

be·wil′dered

be·wil′der·ing·ly

be·wil′der·ment

be·witch′

be·witch′ing·ly

be·yond′

bez′el

bi·an′nu·al

bi·an′nu·al·ly

bi′as

bi′ased

bi′be·lot′

Bi′ble

Bib′li·cal

bib′li·o·graph′i·cal

bib′li·og′ra·phy

bib′u·lous

bi·cam′er·al

bi·car′bon·ate

bi·cen′te·nar′y

bi′ceps

bi·chlo′ride

bi·chro′mate

bi·cus′pid

bi′cy·cle

bid

bid′der

bide

bi·en′ni·al

bi·en′ni·um

bier

bi·fo′cal

big

big'a·mist

big'a·mous

big'a·my

big'ger

big'gest

big'horn'

bight

big'ot

big'ot·ed

big'ot·ry

bi'jou

bi·lat'er·al

bile

bilge

bil'i·ar'y

bi·lin'gual

bil'ious

bilk

bill

bill'board'

billed

bil'let

bil'let·ed

bill'fish'

bill'fold'

bill'head'

bil'liards

bil'lings

bil'lion

bil'lion·aire'

bil'low

bill'post'er

bill'stick'er

bi'me·tal'lic

bi·met'al·lism

bi·met'al·list

bi·month'ly

bin

bi'na·ry

bin·au'ral

bind

bind'er

bind'er·y

bind'ing·ly

bind'ings

bind'weed'

bin'go

bin'na·cle

bin·oc'u·lar

bi·no'mi·al

bi·og'ra·pher

bi'o·graph'ic

bi'o·graph'i·cal

bi'o·graph'i·cal·ly

bi·og'ra·phy

bi'o·log'i·cal

bi'o·log'i·cal·ly

bi·ol'o·gist

bi·ol'o·gy

bi'op·sy

bi·par'tite

bi'ped

bi'plane'

bi·po'lar

birch

bird

bird'lime'

bird'man'

birth

birth'day'

birth'mark'

birth'place'

birth'right'

bis'cuit

bi'sect

bish'op

bish'op·ric

bis'muth

bi'son

bisque

bit

bite

bit'er

bit'ing·ly

bit'ten

bit'ter

bit'ter·est

bit'ter·ly

bit'tern

bit'ter·ness

bit'ters

bit'ter·weed'

bi·tu'men

bi·tu'mi·nous

biv'ouac

bi·zarre'

black

black'ball'

black'ber'ry

black'bird'

black'board'

black'en

black'er

black'est

black'fish'

black'guard

black'head'

black'ish

black'jack'

black'leg'

black'mail'

black'mail'er

black'ness

black'smith'

black'strap'

black'thorn'

blad'der

blade

blame

blamed

blame'less

blame'less·ly

blame'less·ness

blame'wor'thy

blanch

blanc·mange'

bland

blan'dish

blan'dish·ing·ly

blan'dish·ment

bland'ly

bland·ness

blank

blanked

blank'er

blank'est

blan'ket

blank'ly

blare

blared

blar'ney

blas·pheme'

blas·phemed'

blas·phem'er

blas'phe·mous

blas'phe·my

blast

blast'ed

blast-off

blaze

blazed

blaz'er

bla'zon

bla'zoned

bleach

bleached

bleach'er

bleak

bleat

bleed

bleed'er

blem'ish

blench

blend

blend'ed

blend'ings

bless

bless'ed·ness

bless'ings

blew

blight

blight'ed

blimp

blind

blind'ed

blind'er

blind'fold'

blind'ly

blind'ness

blink

blinked

blink'er

bliss

bliss'ful

bliss'ful·ly

blis'ter

blis'tered

blis'ter·ing·ly

blis'ter·y

blithe

blithe'ly

blithe'some

bliz'zard	blow	blunt'ness
bloat	blow'er	blur
bloat'ed	blow'fish'	blurb
block	blow'fly'	blurred
block·ade'	blow'gun'	blurt
block·ad'ed	blow'hard'	blush
block·ad'er	blow'hole'	blushed
block'head'	blown	blush'ing·ly
block'house'	blow'off'	blus'ter
blond	blow'out'	blus'tered
blood	blow'pipe'	blus'ter·ing·ly
blood'ed	blow'torch'	blus'ter·y
blood'hound'	blow'y	bo'a
blood'i·est	blub'ber	board
blood'less	bludg'eon	board'ed
blood'let'ting	bludg'eoned	board'er
blood'line'	blue	boast
blood'root'	blue'fish'	boast'ed
blood'shed'	blue'grass'	boast'er
blood'shot'	blue'nose'	boast'ful
blood'stain'	blue'stock'ing	boast'ful·ly
blood'wood'	bluff	boat
blood'y	bluffed	boat'load'
bloom	bluff'er	boat'man'
bloomed	blun'der	boat'swain'
bloom'er	blun'dered	bob'bin
blos'som	blun'der·buss	bob'cat'
blos'somed	blun'der·er	bob'o·link
blot	blun'der·ing·ly	bob'tail'
blotch	blunt	bode
blot'ter	blunt'ed	bod'ice
blouse	blunt'ly	bod'i·ly

bod'kin

bod'y

bod'y·guard'

bod'y·mak'er

bog

bo'gey

bog'gle

bog'gled

bo'gus

bog'wood'

Bo·he'mi·an

boil

boiled

boil'er

bois'ter·ous

bois'ter·ous·ly

bo'la

bold

bold'er

bold'est

bold'face'

bold'ly

bold'ness

bo·le'ro

bole'weed'

bo·liv'i·a

bo·li'via'no

boll

bo'lo

bo·lom'e·ter

bol'she·vik

bol'ster

bol'stered

bolt

bolt'ed

bolt'head'

bo'lus

bomb

bom·bard'

bom·bard'ed

bom'bard·ier'

bom·bard'ment

bom'bast

bom·bas'tic

bombed

bomb'er

bomb'proof'

bomb'shell'

bo·nan'za

bon'bon'

bond

bond'age

bond'ed

bond'hold'er

bond'man

bond'slave'

bonds'man

bone

boned

bone'fish'

bone'less

bone'set'

bon'fire'

bon'go

bo·ni'to

bon'net

bon'net·ed

bo'nus

bon'y

boo'by

boo'dle

book

book'bind'er

booked

book'ings

book'ish

book'keep'er

book'keep'ing

book'let

book'lets

book'mak'er

book'man

book'mark'

book'plate'

book'rack'

book'rest'

book'sell'er

book'shelf

book'stall'

book'stand'

book'worm'

boom

boomed

boom'er·ang

boon

boor

boor'ish	bo'rine	bot'tle·bird'
boost	bor'ings	bot'tled
boost'ed	born	bot'tle·head'
boost'er	bo'ron	bot'tle·hold'er
boot	bor'ough	bot'tle·neck'
boot'black'	bor'row	bot'tle·nose'
boot'ed	bor'rowed	bot'tom
boot'ee'	bor'row·er	bot'tom·less
boot'er·y	bor'row·ings	bot'tom·ry
booth	borsch	bot'u·lism
boot'jack'	bosk'y	bou'doir
boot'leg'	Bos'ni·an	bough
boot'leg'ger	bos'om	boughed
boot'less	boss	bought
boot'strap'	bossed	bouil'la·baisse'
boo'ty	boss'ism	bouil'lon'
booze	boss'y	boul'der
bo·rac'ic	bo·tan'ic	bou'le·vard
bo'rate	bo·tan'i·cal	bounce
bo'rax	bot'a·nist	bounced
Bor'deaux'	bot'a·nize	bounc'er
bor'der	bot'a·nized	bound
bor'de·reau'	bot'a·ny	bound'a·ry
bor'dered	botch	bound'ed
bore	botched	bound'en
bored	bot'fly'	bound'er
bo're·al	both	bound'less
bo're·a'lis	both'er	boun'te·ous
bore'dom	both'ered	boun'te·ous·ly
bor'er	both'er·some	boun'ti·ful
bore'some	Both'ni·an	boun'ty
bo'ric	bot'tle	bou·quet'

bour·geois'

bour'geoi'sie'

bourse

bout

bo'va·rysm

bo'vine

bow

bow

bowd'ler·ize

bowed

bowed

bow'el

bow'er

bow'er·bird'

bow'fin'

bow'ie

bow'knot'

bowl

bowled

bow'leg'ged

bowl'er

bow'man

bow'shot'

bow'sprit

bow'string'

box

box'board'

box'car'

boxed

box'er

box'wood'

boy

boy'cott

boy'hood

boy'ish

boy'ish·ness

brace

braced

brace'let

brack'en

brack'et

brack'et·ed

brack'ish

brad'awl'

brag

bragged

brag'ga·do'ci·o

brag'gart

Brah'man

braid

braid'ed

Braille

brain

brained

brain'fag'

brain'less

brain'sick'

brain'work'

brain'y

braise

braised

brake

brake'age

braked

brake'man

bram'ble

bran

branch

branched

branch'ling

brand

brand'ed

bran'died

bran'dish

bran'dished

brand'-new'

bran'dy

brash

brass

bras'sard

brass'bound'

brass'ie

brass'i·ness

brass'y

brat

brat'ling

bra·va'do

brave

brave'ly

brav'er

brav'er·y

brav'est

bra'vo

bra·vu'ra

brawl

brawled

brawl'er

brawn

brawn'y

bray

brayed

braze

brazed

bra'zen

bra'zened

bra'zier

bra·zil'ite

bra·zil'wood'

breach

breached

bread

bread'bas'ket

bread'board'

bread'ed

bread'fruit'

bread'root'

bread'stuff'

breadth

bread'win·ner'

break

break'a·ble

break'age

break'down'

break'er

break'fast

break'neck'

break'off'

break'out'

break'o·ver'

break'-through'

break'up'

break'wa'ter

breast

breast'band'

breast'bone'

breast'ed

breast'-fed'

breast'mark'

breast'pin'

breast'plate'

breast'weed'

breast'work'

breath

breathed

breath'less

bred

breech

breed

breed'er

breeze

breezed

breez'y

breth'ren

breve

bre·vet'

bre'vi·ar'y

bre·vier'

brev'i·ty

brew

brewed

brew'er

brew'er·y

brew'house'

bribe

bribed

brib'er·y

bric'-a-brac'

brick

brick'bat'

bricked

brick'lay'er

brick'ma'son

brick'yard'

brid'al

bride

bride'groom'

brides'maid'

bridge

bridged

bridge'head'

bridge'work'

bri'dle

bri'dled

brief

brief'er

brief'est

brief'ly

brief'ness

bri'er

brig

bri·gade'

brig'a·dier'

brig'and

brig'and·age

brig'an·tine

bright

bright'en

bright'er

bright'est

bright'ly

bright'ness

bright'work'

bril'liance

bril'lian·cy

bril'liant

bril'lian·tine'

bril'liant·ly

bril'liant·ness

brim

brim'ful'

brimmed

brim'stone'

brin'dled

brine

bring

brink

brin'y

bri·oche'

bri·quette'

brisk

brisk'en

bris'ket

brisk'ly

brisk'ness

bris'tle

bris'tled

bris'tli·er

bris'tli·est

bris'tly

Bri·tan'ni·a

Bri·tan'nic

Brit'i·cism

Brit'ish

Brit'ish·er

Brit'on

brit'tle

brit'tle·ness

broach

broached

broad

broad'ax'

broad'bill'

broad'brim'

broad'cast'

broad'cast'er

broad'en

broad'er

broad'est

broad'leaf'

broad'loom'

broad'ly

broad'side'

broad'way'

broad'wise'

bro·cade'

bro·cad'ed

broc'a·tel'

broc'co·li

bro·chette'

bro·chure'

bro'gan

brogue

broil

broiled

broil'er

broke

bro'ken

brok'en·ly

bro'ker

bro'ker·age

bro'mate

bro'mide

bro·mid'ic

bro'mine

bron'chi·al

bron·chi'tis

bron'cho·scope

bron'chus

bron'co

bronze

bronzed

brooch

brood

brood'ed

brood'er

brood'ling

brook

brook'let

broom	brush'work'	bu·col'ic
broom'weed'	brusque	bud
broom'wood'	bru'tal	bud'ded
broth	bru·tal'i·ty	bud'dy
broth'er	bru'tal·i·za'tion	budge
broth'er·hood	bru'tal·ize	budged
broth'er-in-law'	bru'tal·ized	budg'et
broth'er·li·ness	bru'tal·ly	budg'et·ar'y
broth'er·ly	brute	budg'et·ed
brougham	brut'ish	bud'wood'
brought	brut'ish·ly	bud'worm'
brow	brut'ish·ness	buff
brown	bub'ble	buf'fa·lo
brown'er	bub'bled	buff'er
brown'est	bub'bly	buff'ered
brown'out	bu·bon'ic	buf'fet
browse	buc'cal	buf·fet'
browsed	buc'ca·neer'	buf'fet·ed
bru'in	buck	buf·foon'
bruise	buck'board'	buf·foon'er·y
bruised	bucked	bug
bruit	buck'et	bug'bear'
brum'ma·gem	buck'et·ed	bug'ging
brunch	buck'et·ful	bug'gy
bru·net'	buck'le	bu'gle
bru·nette'	buck'led	bu'gler
brunt	buck'ler	bu'gle·weed'
brush	buck'ram	bug'proof'
brushed	buck'saw'	bug'weed'
brush'ful	buck'shot'	build
brush'less	buck'skin'	build'ed
brush'wood'	buck'wheat'	build'er

build'ing

build'ings

built

bulb

bulb'ous

bulge

bulged

bulk

bulk'head'

bulk'i·er

bulk'i·est

bulk'y

bull

bull'doze'

bull'dozed'

bull'doz'er

bul'let

bul'le·tin

bull'fight'

bull'finch'

bull'frog'

bull'head'

bul'lion

bull'ish

bull'ock

bull'weed

bul'ly

bul'ly·rag'

bul'rush'

bul'wark

bum

bum'boat'

bump

bump'er

bump'i·er

bump'i·est

bump'kin

bump'y

bu'na

bunch

bunched

bun'dle

bun'dled

bung

bun'ga·low

bun'gle

bun'gled

bun'gler

bun'ion

bunk'er

bunk'house'

bunt

buoy

buoy'ant

buoy'ant·ly

bur'den

bur'dened

bur'den·some

bu'reau

bu·reauc'ra·cy

bu'reau·crat

bu·rette'

bur'gee

bur'geon

bur'geoned

bur'gess

bur'glar

bur'i·al

bu'rin

bur'lap

bur·lesque'

bur·lesqued'

bur'ly

burn

burned

burn'er

bur'nish

bur'nish·er

burn'out'

burnt

burr

bur'ro

bur'row

bur'rowed

bur'sar

bur·si'tis

burst

bur'y

bus

bus'es

bush

bushed

bush'el

bush'el·er

bush'ings

bus'i·ly

busi'ness	but'ter·ball'	bux'om
busi'ness·es	but'ter·cup'	buy
busi'ness·like'	but'tered	buy'er
bus'kin	but'ter·fat'	buzz
bust	but'ter·fish'	buz'zard
bus'tard	but'ter·fly'	buzzed
bus'tle	but'ter·nut'	buzz'er
bus'tled	but'ter·scotch'	by
bus'y	but'ter·y	by'gone'
bus'y·bod'y	but'ton	by'pass'
but	but'toned	by'path'
butch'er	but'ton·hole'	by'play'
butch'ered	but'ton·holed'	by'-prod'uct
butch'er·y	but'ton·weed'	By·ron'ic
but'ler	but'ton·wood'	by'stand'er
butt	but'tress	by'way'
but'ter	but'tressed	by'word'

C

cab	cac′tus·es	cai′tiff
ca·bal′	ca·dav′er	ca·jole′
cab′bage	ca·dav′er·ous	ca·joled′
cab′in	cad′die	ca·jol′er·y
cab′i·net	ca′dence	cake
ca′ble	ca·den′za	cake′walk′
ca′bled	ca·det′	cal′a·bash
ca′ble·gram	cad′mi·um	cal′a·mine
ca·boose′	Cad′mus	ca·lam′i·tous
cab′ri·o·let′	ca′dre	ca·lam′i·tous·ly
ca·ca′o	ca·du′ce·us	ca·lam′i·ty
cach′a·lot	cad′weed	cal·car′e·ous
cache	Cae·sar′e·an	cal′ci·fi·ca′tion
ca·chet′	cae·su′ra	cal′ci·fy
cach′in·na′tion	ca·fé′	cal′ci·mine
cack′le	caf′e·te′ri·a	cal′cine
cack′led	caf′fe·ine	cal·cined′
ca·coph′o·nous	cage	cal′ci·um
ca·coph′o·ny	caged	cal′cu·late
cac′ti	cairn	cal′cu·lat′ed
cac′toid	cais′son	cal′cu·la′tion
cac′tus	cais′soned	cal′cu·la′tor

40

cal'dron

cal'en·dar

cal'en·der

cal'en·dered

calf

calf'skin'

cal'i·ber

cal'i·brate

cal'i·brat'ed

cal'i·bra'tion

cal'i·co

cal'i·per

ca'liph

cal'is·then'ics

calk

calked

calk'er

call

cal'la

call'a·ble

called

cal'ler

cal·lig'ra·phy

cal·li'o·pe

cal·los'i·ty

cal'lous

cal'loused

cal'lous·ly

cal'low

cal'low·ly

cal'lus

calm

calmed

calm'er

calm'est

calm'ly

calm'ness

cal'o·mel

ca·lor'ic

cal'o·rie

cal'u·met

ca·lum'ni·ate

ca·lum'ni·at'ed

ca·lum'ni·a'tion

ca·lum'ni·a'tor

cal'um·ny

Cal'va·ry

calved

ca·lyp'so

ca'lyx

ca'ma·ra'de·rie

cam'ber

cam'bi·um

cam'bric

came

cam'el

cam'el·eer'

Cam'e·lot

Cam'em·bert'

cam'e·o

cam'er·a

cam'er·a·man'

cam'i·sole

cam'o·mile

cam'ou·flage

camp

cam·paign'

cam'pa·ni'le

camp'er

camp'fire'

cam'phor

cam'phor·ate

cam'phor·at'ed

cam'pus

can

ca·nal'

ca·nal'i·za'tion

ca·nar'y

can'can

can'cel

can'celed

can'cel·la'tion

can'cer

can'cer·ous

can'cer·weed'

can'de·la'brum

can'did

can'di·da·cy

can'di·date

can'did·ly

can'died

can'dle

can'dled

can'dle·fish'

can'dle·light'

can'dle·nut'

can'dle·stick'
can'dor
can'dy
can'dy·mak'er
cane
cane'brake'
ca'nine
can'is·ter
can'ker
can'kered
can'ker·ous
can'ker·weed'
can'ker·worm'
canned
can'ner
can'ner·y
can'ni·bal
can'ni·bal·ism
can'ni·ly
can'non
can'non·ade'
can'non·eer'
can'ny
ca·noe'
can'on
ca·non'i·cal
ca·non'i·cals
can'on·i·za'tion
can'on·ize
can'o·py
cant
can't

can'ta·loupe
can·tan'ker·ous
can·ta'ta
can·teen'
cant'er
can'tered
can'ti·cle
can'ti·cles
can'ti·le'ver
can'tle
can'to
can'ton
can·ton'ment
can'tor
can'vas
can'vased
can'vass
can'vassed
can'vass·er
can'yon
caou'tchouc
ca'pa·bil'i·ties
ca'pa·bil'i·ty
ca'pa·ble
ca'pa·bly
ca·pa'cious
ca·pac'i·tance
ca·pac'i·tate
ca·pac'i·tat'ed
ca·pac'i·tor
ca·pac'i·ty
cape

ca'per
ca'pered
ca'per·ings
cap'il·lar'i·ty
cap'il·lar'y
cap'i·tal
cap'i·tal·ism
cap'i·tal·ist
cap'i·tal·is'tic
cap'i·tal·ists
cap'i·tal·i·za'tion
cap'i·tal·ize
cap'i·tal·ized
cap'i·tol
ca·pit'u·late
ca·pit'u·lat'ed
ca·pit'u·lates
ca·pit'u·la'tion
ca'pon
capped
ca·price'
ca·pri'cious
cap·size'
cap·sized'
cap'stan
cap'sule
cap'tain
cap'tain·cy
cap'tion
cap'tious
cap'tious·ly
cap'tious·ness

cap'ti·vate	car'bo·run'dum	car'go
cap'ti·vat'ed	car'boy	car'i·bou
cap'ti·va'tion	car'bun·cle	car'i·ca·ture
cap'tive	car'bu·ret'or	car'i·es
cap·tiv'i·ty	car'cass	car'il·lon
cap'ture	car'ci·no'ma	car'load·ings'
cap'tured	card	car·min'a·tive
car	card'board'	car'mine
ca'ra·ba'o	card'ed	car'nage
car'a·bi·neer'	car'di·ac	car'nal
car'a·cal	car'di·gan	car'nal·ly
car'a·cole	car'di·nal	car·na'tion
ca·rafe'	car'di·nal·ate	car·nel'ian
car'a·mel	car'di·o·gram'	car'ni·val
car'a·mel·ize	car'di·o·graph'	car·niv'o·rous
car'a·pace	car'di·ol'o·gy	car'ol
car'at	care	car'oled
car'a·van	cared	car'om
car'a·van'sa·ry	ca·reen'	car'omed
car'a·vel	ca·reened'	ca·rot'id
car'a·way	ca·reer'	ca·rous'al
car'bide	care'free'	ca·rouse'
car'bine	care'ful	ca·roused'
car'bo·hy'drate	care'ful·ly	carp
car·bol'ic	care'less	car'pal
car'bon	care'less·ly	car'pen·ter
car'bon·ate	care'less·ness	car'pet
car·bon·at'ed	ca·ress'	car'pet·ed
car·bon'ic	ca·ressed'	car'riage
car'bon·if'er·ous	ca·ress'ing·ly	car'ried
car'bon·ize	car'et	car'ri·er
car'bon·ized	car'fare'	car'ri·on

car'rot	cash·ier'	cat'a·lep'sy
car'rou·sel'	cash·iered'	cat'a·lep'tic
car'ry	cash'mere	cat'a·log
cart	ca·si'no	cat'a·loged
cart'age	cask	ca·tal'pa
cart'ed	cas'ket	ca·tal'y·sis
car'tel	cas·sa'tion	cat'a·lyst
car'ti·lage	cas·sa'va	cat'a·lyt'ic
car'ti·lag'i·nous	cas'se·role	cat'a·lyze
car·tog'ra·phy	cas·sette'	cat'a·mount
car'ton	cas·si'no	cat'a·pult
car·toon'	cas'sock	cat'a·ract
car·touche'	cast	ca·tarrh'
car'tridge	cas'ta·net'	ca·tarrh'al
carve	caste	ca·tas'tro·phe
carved	cast'er	cat'a·stroph'ic
carv'er	cas'ti·gate	cat'a·stroph'i·cal·ly
carv'ings	cas'ti·gat'ed	cat'a·ton'ic
car'y·at'id	cas'ti·ga'tion	Ca·taw'ba
ca·sa'ba	cas'tle	cat'bird'
cas·cade'	cast'off'	cat'boat'
cas·cad'ed	cas'tor	cat'call'
cas·car'a	cas'tra·me·ta'tion	catch
case	cas'u·al	catch'er
ca'se·in	cas'u·al·ly	catch'weed'
case'ment	cas'u·al·ty	catch'word'
case'work'	cas'u·ist	catch'y
cash	cas'u·ist·ry	cat'e·che'sis
cash'book'	ca·tab'o·lism	cat'e·chet'i·cal
cash'box'	cat'a·clysm	cat'e·chism
cashed	cat'a·comb	cat'e·chize
ca·shew'	cat'a·falque	cat'e·gor'i·cal

cat'e·go·rize	cau·sal'i·ty	cease'less
cat'e·go'ry	cau·sa'tion	cease'less·ly
cat'e·nar'y	caus'a·tive	ce'cum
ca'ter	cause	ce'dar
ca'tered	caused	ce'dar·bird'
ca'ter·er	cause'less	cede
cat'er·pil'lar	cau'se·rie'	ced'ed
cat'fish'	cause'way'	ce·dil'la
cat'gut'	caus'tic	ced'ing
ca·thar'sis	cau'ter·i·za'tion	ceil'ings
ca·thar'tic	cau'ter·ize	cel'e·brant
cat'head'	cau'ter·ized	cel'e·brate
ca·the'dral	cau'ter·y	cel'e·brat'ed
cath'e·ter	cau'tion	cel'e·bra'tion
cath'e·ter·ize	cau'tion·ar'y	ce·leb'ri·ty
cath'ode	cau'tioned	ce·ler'i·ty
cath'o·lic	cau'tious	cel'er·y
ca·thol'i·cism	cav'al·cade'	ce·les'ta
cath'o·lic'i·ty	cav'a·lier'	ce·les'tial
ca·thol'i·cize	cav'al·ry	ce·les'tial·ly
cat'kin	ca·va·ti'na	cel'i·ba·cy
cat'like'	cave	cel'i·bate
cat'nip	ca've·at	cell
cat'tail'	cav'ern	cel'lar
cat'tle	cav'ern·ous	cel'lar·er
cat'walk'	cav'i·ar	cel'lar·et'
cau'cus	cav'il	cel'list
cau'cused	cav'i·ty	cel'lo
cau'dal	ca·vort'	cel'lo·phane
caught	cay·enne'	cel'lu·lar
cau'li·flow'er	cease	cel'lu·li'tis
caus'al	ceased	cel'lu·loid

cel'lu·lose
Celt'ic
ce·ment'
ce'men·ta'tion
cem'e·ter'y
cen'a·cle
cen'o·bite
cen'o·taph
cen'ser
cen'sor
cen'sored
cen·so'ri·al
cen·so'ri·ous
cen'sor·ship
cen'sur·a·ble
cen'sure
cen'sured
cen'sus
cent
cen'taur
cen'te·nar'i·an
cen'te·nar'y
cen·ten'ni·al
cen'ter
cen'ter·board'
cen'tered
cen'ter·piece'
cen'ti·grade
cen'ti·me'ter
cen'ti·pede
cen'tral
cen'tral·i·za'tion

cen'tral·ize
cen'tral·ized
cen·trif'u·gal
cen'tri·fuge
cen·trip'e·tal
cen'trist
cen·tu'ri·on
cen'tu·ry
ce·phal'ic
ce·ram'ic
ce're·al
cer'e·bel'lum
cer'e·bral
cer'e·bra'tion
cer'e·brum
cere'ment
cer'e·mo'ni·al
cer'e·mo'ni·al·ly
cer'e·mo'ni·ous
cer'e·mo'ni·ous·ly
cer'e·mo'ni·ous·ness
cer'e·mo'ny
ce·rise'
ce'ri·um
cer'tain
cer'tain·ly
cer'tain·ty
cer·tif'i·cate
cer·tif'i·cat'ed
cer·ti·fi·ca'tion
cer'ti·fied
cer'ti·fy

cer'ti·o·ra'ri
cer'ti·tude
cer'vi·cal
cer'vix
ce'si·um
ces·sa'tion
ces'sion
cess'pool'
ces'tus
ce·ta'cean
chafe
chaf'fer
chaf'fered
chaf'finch
chaff'weed'
cha·grin'
cha·grined'
chain
chained
chain'work'
chair
chair'man
chaise
chal·ced'o·ny
cha·let'
chal'ice
chalk
chalk'i·ness
chal'lenge
chal'lenged
cham'ber
cham'bered

cham'ber·lain

cham'ber·maid'

cha·me'le·on

cham'ois

cham·pagne'

cham'per·ty

cham'pi·on

cham'pi·on·ship'

chance

chanced

chan'cel

chan'cel·ler·y

chan'cel·lor

chan'cer·y

chan'de·lier'

chan'dler

chan'dler·y

change

change'a·ble

changed

change'less

change'ling

chan'nel

chan'neled

chant

chant'ed

cha'os

cha·ot'ic

cha·ot'i·cal·ly

chap'ar·ral'

chap'el

chap'er·on

chap'lain

chap'let

chap'ter

char

char'ac·ter

char'ac·ter·is'tic

char'ac·ter·is'ti·cal·ly

char'ac·ter·i·za'tion

char'ac·ter·ize

char'ac·ter·ized

cha·rade'

char'coal'

cha·ris'ma

charge

charge'a·ble

charged

charg'er

char'i·ly

char'i·ness

char'i·ot

char'i·ot·eer'

char'i·ta·ble

char'i·ta·bly

char'i·ty

char'la·tan

charm

charmed

charm'ing·ly

char'nel

charred

chart

chart'ed

char'ter

char'tered

char·treuse'

char'y

chase

chased

chasm

chas'sis

chaste

chas'ten

chas'tened

chas'ten·ing·ly

chas·tise'

chas·tised'

chas'tise·ment

chas'ti·ty

chas'u·ble

châ·teau'

chat'e·laine

chat'tel

chat'ter

chat'tered

chat'ter·er

chat'ty

chauf·feur'

chau'vin·ism

cheap

cheap'en

cheap'ened

cheap'er

cheap'est

cheap'ly

cheap′ness

cheat

cheat′ed

cheat′er

check

check′book′

checked

check′er

check′er·board′

check′ered

check′mate′

check′mat′ed

check′off′

check′rein′

cheek′y

cheer

cheered

cheer′ful

cheer′ful·ly

cheer′ful·ness

cheer′i·ly

cheer′less

cheer′less·ly

cheer′y

cheese

cheese′cake′

cheese′cloth′

chef

chem′i·cal

chem′i·cal·ly

che·mise′

chem′ist

chem′is·try

che·nille′

cher′ish

che·root′

cher′ry

cher′ub

che·ru′bic

cher′u·bim

cher′vil

chess

chess′board′

chess′man

chest

ches′ter·field′

chest′nut

chev′ron

chew

chic

chi·can′er·y

chick′a·dee

chick′en

chick′weed′

chic′le

chic′o·ry

chide

chief

chief′ly

chief′tain

chif′fon

chif′fo·nier′

chig′ger

chil′blain′

child

child′hood

child′ish

child′ish·ly

child′ish·ness

child′less

child′like′

chil′dren

chil′i

chill

chilled

chill′i·er

chill′i·est

chill′ing·ly

chill′y

chime

chimed

chi·me′ra

chi·mer′i·cal

chim′ney

chim′pan·zee′

chin

chi′na

chinch

chin·chil′la

chine

Chi′nese′

chink

chintz

chip

chip′munk

chipped

chip′per

chi·rog′ra·phy

chi·rop′o·dist

chi′ro·prac′tor

chirp

chis′el

chis′eled

chit′chat′

chit′ter·ling

chiv′al·ric

chiv′al·rous

chiv′al·ry

chive

chlo′ral

chlo′rate

chlo′ride

chlo′rin·ate

chlo′rine

chlo′rite

chlo′ro·form

chlo′ro·phyll

chlo·ro′sis

choc′o·late

choice

choir

choir′boy′

choke

chok′er

chol′er

chol′er·a

chol′er·ic

choose

chop

chop′house′

chopped

chop′per

cho·ral′

chord

cho·re′a

cho′re·og′ra·phy

chor′is·ter

chor′tle

cho′rus

chose

cho′sen

chow

chow′der

chrism

chris′ten

Chris′ten·dom

chris′tened

chris′ten·ings

Chris′tian

Chris′ti·an′i·ty

Christ′mas

chro′mate

chro·mat′ics

chrome

chro′mic

chro′mite

chro′mi·um

chro′mo·some

chron′ic

chron′i·cal·ly

chron′i·cle

chron′i·cled

chron′i·cler

chron′i·cles

chron′o·graph

chron′o·log′i·cal

chron′o·log′i·cal·ly

chro·nol′o·gy

chro·nom′e·ter

chron′o·met′ric

chrys′a·lis

chrys·an′the·mum

chrys′o·lite

chub′bi·ness

chub′by

chuck

chuck′le

chuck′led

chuck′le·head′

chuck′ling·ly

chum

chum′my

chump

chunk

chunk′i·ness

chunk′y

church

church′man

churl

churl′ish

churl′ish·ly

churl′ish·ness

churn	cir′cu·lat′ed	cite
churned	cir′cu·la′tion	cit′ed
chute	cir′cu·la·to′ry	cit′i·zen
chut′ney	cir′cum·am′bi·ent	cit′i·zen·ry
chyle	cir·cum′fer·ence	cit′i·zen·ship′
ci·ca′da	cir·cum′fer·en′tial	cit′rate
cic′a·trix	cir′cum·flex	cit′ric
ci′der	cir′cum·lo·cu′tion	cit′ron
ci·gar′	cir′cum·loc′u·to′ry	cit′y
cig′a·rette′	cir′cum·nav′i·gate	civ′ic
cinch	cir′cum·scribe′	civ′il
cinc′ture	cir′cum·scribed′	ci·vil′ian
cinc′tured	cir′cum·spect	ci·vil′i·ty
cin′der	cir′cum·spec′tion	civ′i·li·za′tion
cin′e·ma	cir′cum·spect′ly	civ′i·lize
cin′e·mat′o·graph	cir′cum·spect′ness	civ′i·lized
cin′na·bar	cir′cum·stance	civ′il·ly
cin′na·mon	cir′cum·stanc·es	clack
cinque′foil′	cir′cum·stan′tial	claim
ci′on	cir′cum·stan′ti·al′i·ty	claim′ant
ci′pher	cir′cum·stan′ti·ate	claimed
ci′phered	cir′cum·stan′ti·at′ed	clair·voy′ance
cir′cle	cir′cum·vent′	clair·voy′ant
cir′cled	cir′cum·vent′ed	cla′mant
cir′cuit	cir′cum·ven′tion	clam′bake′
cir·cu′i·tous	cir′cus	clam′ber
cir·cu′i·tous·ly	cir·rho′sis	clam′bered
cir′cuit·ry	cir·rhot′ic	clam′my
cir′cu·lar	cir′rus	clam′or
cir′cu·lar·i·za′tion	cis′tern	clam′ored
cir′cu·lar·ize	cit′a·del	clam′or·ous
cir′cu·late	ci·ta′tion	clamp

clam'shell'

clan

clan·des'tine

clang

clanged

clang'or

clank

clanked

clan'nish

clan'ship

clans'man

clap

clapped

clap'per

clap'trap'

claque

clar'et

clar'i·fi·ca'tion

clar'i·fied

clar'i·fy

clar'i·net'

clar'i·on

clar'i·ty

clash

clasp

class

clas'sic

clas'si·cal

clas'si·cal·ism

clas'si·cal·ist

clas'si·cal·ly

clas'si·cist

clas'si·fi·ca'tion

clas'si·fied

clas'si·fi'er

clas'si·fy

class'mate'

class'room'

class'work'

clat'ter

clat'tered

clause

claus'tro·pho'bi·a

clav'i·chord

clav'i·cle

claw

clay

clean

cleaned

clean'er

clean'est

clean'li·ness

clean'ly

clean'ness

cleanse

cleans'er

clean'up'

clear

clear'ance

cleared

clear'er

clear'est

clear'head'ed

clear'ing·house'

clear'ly

clear'ness

cleat

cleat'ed

cleav'age

cleave

cleav'er

clef

cleft

clem'a·tis

clem'en·cy

clem'ent

clench

clere'sto'ry

cler'gy

cler'gy·man

cler'i·cal

cler'i·cal·ism

clerk

clev'er

clev'er·er

clev'er·est

clev'er·ness

clew

cli·ché'

click

cli'ent

cli'en·tele'

cliff

cli·mac'ter·ic

cli·mac'tic

cli'mate

cli·mat'ic	close'ness	club'man
cli'max	clos'er	cluck
climb	clos'est	clump
climbed	clos'et	clum'si·er
climb'er	clos'et·ed	clum'si·est
clinch	clo'sure	clum'si·ly
clinch'er	clot	clum'si·ness
cling	cloth	clum'sy
cling'ing·ly	clothed	clus'ter
clin'ic	clothes	clus'tered
clin'i·cal	clothes'pin'	clutch
cli·ni'cian	cloth'ier	clut'ter
clink	clot'ted	clut'tered
clinked	cloud	coach
clink'er	cloud'i·er	coach'man
clip	cloud'i·est	co·ad'ju·tor
clip'per	cloud'i·ness	co·ag'u·late
clip'pings	cloud'less	co·ag'u·lat'ed
clique	cloud'y	co·ag'u·lates
cloak	clout	co·ag'u·la'tion
clock	clout'ed	co·ag'u·la'tive
clock'wise'	clove	coal
clock'work'	clo'ven	co·a·lesce'
clod	clo'ver	co·a·lesced'
clog	clown	co·a·les'cence
cloi'son'né'	clowned	co·a·les'cent
clois'ter	clown'ish	co·a·li'tion
clois'tered	cloy	coal'sack'
clon'ic	cloyed	coarse
close	club	coars'en
closed	clubbed	coars'ened
close'ly	club'house'	coars'er

coars'est	co'co·nut'	cog'nate
coast	co·coon'	cog·ni'tion
coast'al	co'da	cog'ni·zance
coast'er	code	cog'ni·zant
coast'wise'	cod'ed	cog·no'men
coat	co'de·fend'ant	co·hab'it
coat'ed	co'de·ine	co·here'
coat'ings	co'dex	co·hered'
co·au'thor	cod'fish'	co·her'ence
coax	cod'i·cil	co·her'ent
coaxed	cod'i·fi·ca'tion	co·her'ent·ly
co·ax'i·al	cod'i·fy	co·her'er
coax'ing·ly	co'ed'	co·he'sion
co'balt	co'ed'u·ca'tion	co·he'sive
cob'ble	co'ef·fi'cient	co'hort
cob'bled	co·erce'	coif
Co'bol	co·erced'	coif·fure'
cob'web'	co·er'cion	coign
co·caine'	co·er'cive	coil
coc'cyx	co·e'val	coiled
coch'i·neal'	co'ex·ec'u·tor	coin
cock·ade'	cof'fee	coin'age
cock'a·too'	cof'fer	co'in·cide'
cock'le	cof'fin	co'in·cid'ed
cock'le·shell'	cog	co·in'ci·dence
cock'ney	co'gen·cy	co·in'ci·den'tal
cock'pit'	co'gent	coined
cock'roach'	cog'i·tate	coin'er
cock'sure'	cog'i·tat'ed	co'in·sur'ance
cock'sure'ness	cog'i·ta'tion	co'in·sure'
cock'tail'	cog'i·ta'tive	co'in·sur'er
co'coa	co'gnac	coke

col·an·der	col·lec'tor·ship	col'or·less
cold	col'lege	co·los'sal
cold'er	col·le'gi·ate	Col'os·se'um
cold'est	col·lide'	co·los'sus
cold'ly	col·lid'ed	col'por'teur
cole'slaw'	col'lie	colt
col'ic	col'lier	col'um·bine
col'i·se'um	col·li'sion	col'umn
co·li'tis	col'lo·ca'tion	co·lum'nar
col·lab'o·rate	col·lo'di·on	co'ma
col·lab'o·rat'ed	col'loid	com'a·tose
col·lab'o·ra'tion	col·loi'dal	comb
col·lapse'	col·lo'qui·al	com'bat
col·lapsed'	col'lo·quy	com'bat·ant
col·laps'i·ble	col'lo·type	com'ba·tive
col'lar	col·lu'sion	com·bat'ive·ness
col'lar·band'	col·lu'sive	combed
col'lar·bone'	co·logne'	com'bi·na'tion
col·late'	co'lon	com·bine
col·lat'ed	colo'nel	com·bined'
col·lat'er·al	co·lo'ni·al	comb'ings
col·la'tion	col'o·nist	com·bust'
col·la'tor	col'o·ni·za'tion	com·bus'ti·ble
col·league'	col'o·nize	com·bus'tion
col'lect	col'o·nized	come
col·lect'ed	col'on·nade'	co·me'di·an
col·lect'i·ble	col'o·ny	com'e·dy
col·lec'tion	col'o·phon	come'li·ness
col·lec'tive	col'or	come'ly
col·lec'tiv·ism	col'or·a'tion	co·mes'ti·ble
col·lec'tiv·ist	col'o·ra·tu'ra	com'et
col·lec'tor	col'ored	com'fit

com'fort

com'fort·a·ble

com'fort·a·bly

com'fort·ed

com'fort·er

com'fort·less

com'ic

com'i·cal

com'ings

com'ma

com·mand'

com'man·dant'

com·mand'ed

com'man·deer'

com·mand'er

com·mand'er·y

com·mand'ing·ly

com·mand'ment

com·man'do

com·mem'o·rate

com·mem'o·rat'ed

com·mem'o·ra'tion

com·mem'o·ra'tive

com·mence'

com·menced'

com·mence'ment

com·mend'

com·mend'a·ble

com'men·da'tion

com·mend'a·to'ry

com·mend'ed

com·men'su·ra·ble

com·men'su·rate

com'ment

com'men·tar'y

com'men·ta'tor

com'ment·ed

com'merce

com·mer'cial

com·mer'cial·ism

com·mer'cial·i·za'tion

com·mer'cial·ize

com·min'a·to'ry

com·min'gle

com·min'gled

com'mi·nute

com'mi·nut'ed

com'mi·nu'tion

com·mis'er·ate

com·mis'er·a'tion

com'mis·sar'

com'mis·sar'i·at

com'mis·sar'y

com·mis'sion

com·mis'sioned

com·mis'sion·er

com·mit'

com·mit'ment

com·mit'ted

com·mit'tee

com·mo'di·ous

com·mod'i·ty

com'mo·dore'

com'mon

com'mon·al·ty

com'mon·er

com'mon·est

com'mon·ly

com'mon·place'

com'mon·wealth'

com·mo'tion

com'mu·nal

com·mune'

com·mu'ni·ca·ble

com·mu'ni·cant

com·mu'ni·cate

com·mu'ni·cat'ed

com·mu'ni·ca'tion

com·mu'ni·ca'tive

com·mun'ion

com·mu'ni·qué'

com'mu·nism

com'mu·nist

com·mu·nis'tic

com·mu'ni·ty

com'mu·ni·za'tion

com'mu·nize

com'mu·ta'tion

com'mu·ta'tor

com·mute'

com·mut'ed

com·mut'er

com·pact'

com·pan'ion

com·pan'ion·a·ble

com·pan'ion·ship

com·pan'ion·way'
com'pa·ny
com'pa·ra·bil'i·ty
com'pa·ra·ble
com·par'a·tive
com·pare'
com·pared'
com·par'i·son
com·part'ment
com'pass
com·pas'sion
com·pas'sion·ate
com·pas'sion·ate·ly
com·pat'i·bil'i·ty
com·pat'i·ble
com·pa'tri·ot
com·peer'
com·pel'
com·pelled'
com·pel'ling·ly
com'pend
com·pen'di·ous
com·pen'di·um
com'pen·sate
com'pen·sat'ed
com'pen·sa'tion
com'pen·sa'tor
com·pen'sa·to'ry
com·pete'
com·pet'ed
com'pe·tence
com'pe·ten·cy

com'pe·tent·ly
com·pe·ti'tion
com·pet'i·tive
com·pet'i·tor
com'pi·la'tion
com·pile'
com·piled'
com·pil'er
com·pla'cence
com·pla'cen·cy
com·pla'cent
com·plain'
com·plain'ant
com·plained'
com·plain'ing·ly
com·plaint'
com·plai'sance
com·plai'sant
com'ple·ment
com'ple·men'tal
com'ple·men'ta·ry
com'ple·ment·ed
com·plete'
com·plet'ed
com·ple'tion
com·plex'
com·plex'ion
com·plex'i·ty
com·pli'ance
com·pli'ant
com'pli·cate
com'pli·cat'ed

com'pli·ca'tion
com·plic'i·ty
com·plied'
com'pli·ment
com'pli·men'ta·ry
com'plin
com·ply'
com·po'nent
com·port'
com·pose'
com·posed'
com·pos'er
com·pos'ite
com·po·si'tion
com·pos'i·tor
com'post
com·po'sure
com'pote
com'pound
com'pre·hend'
com'pre·hend'ed
com'pre·hen'si·bil'i·ty
com'pre·hen'si·ble
com'pre·hen'sion
com'pre·hen'sive
com·press'
com·press'i·bil'i·ty
com·press'ible
com·pres'sion
com·pres'sor
com·prise'
com'pro·mise

com'pro·mis'ing·ly

Comp·tom'e·ter

comp·trol'ler

com·pul'sion

com·pul'sive

com·pul'so·ry

com·punc'tion

com'pu·ta'tion

com·pute'

com·put'er

com·put'er·ized

com'rade

con'cave

con·cav'i·ty

con·ceal'

con·cealed'

con·ceal'ment

con·cede'

con·ced'ed

con·ceit'

con·ceit'ed

con·ceit'ed·ly

con·ceiv'a·ble

con·ceiv'a·bly

con·ceive'

con·ceived'

con'cen·trate

con'cen·trat'ed

con'cen·tra'tion

con·cen'tric

con'cept

con·cep'tion

con·cep'tu·al

con·cern'

con·cerned'

con'cert

con·cert'ed

con'cer·ti'na

con·ces'sion

con·ces'sion·aire'

conch

con·cil'i·ate

con·cil'i·at'ed

con·cil'i·a'tion

con·cil'i·a·to'ry

con·cise'

con·cise'ness

con'clave

con·clude'

con·clud'ed

con·clu'sion

con·clu'sive

con·clu'sive·ly

con·coct'

con·coct'ed

con·coc'tion

con·com'i·tant

con'cord

con·cord'ance

con'course

con·crete'

con·cur'

con·curred'

con·cur'rence

con·cur'rent

con·cus'sion

con·demn'

con·dem·na'tion

con·dem'na·to'ry

con·demned'

con'den·sa'tion

con·dense'

con·densed'

con·dens'er

con'de·scend'

con'de·scend'ing·ly

con'de·scen'sion

con·dign'

con'di·ment

con·di'tion

con·di'tion·al

con·di'tion·al·ly

con·di'tioned

con·dole'

con·do'lence

con'do·min'i·um

con'do·na'tion

con·done'

con·doned'

con'dor

con·du'cive

con·duct'

con·duct'ed

con·duc'tion

con'duc·tiv'i·ty

con·duc'tor

con'duit

con'dyle

cone

con·fec'tion

con·fec'tion·er

con·fec'tion·er'y

con·fed'er·a·cy

con·fed'er·ate

con·fed'er·a'tion

con·fer'

con'fer·ee'

con'fer·ence

con·ferred'

con·fess'

con·fess'ed·ly

con·fes'sion

con·fes'sion·al

con·fes'sor

con·fide'

con·fid'ed

con'fi·dence

con'fi·dent

con'fi·den'tial

con'fi·den'tial·ly

con'fi·dent·ly

con·fid'ing·ly

con·fig'u·ra'tion

con·fine'

con·fined'

con·fine'ment

con·firm'

con'fir·ma'tion

con·firmed'

con'fis·cate

con'fis·cat'ed

con'fis·ca'tion

con·fis'ca·to'ry

con'fla·gra'tion

con·flict'

con·flict'ed

con·flic'tion

con'flu·ence

con'flu·ent

con·form'

con·form'a·ble

con'for·ma'tion

con·formed'

con·form'er

con·form'i·ty

con·found'

con·found'ed

con'frere

con·front'

con'fron·ta'tion

con·front'ed

con·fuse'

con·fused'

con·fus'ed·ly

con·fus'ing·ly

con·fu'sion

con'fu·ta'tion

con·fute'

con·fut'ed

con·geal'

con·gealed'

con'ge·la'tion

con'ge·ner

con·gen'ial

con·ge'ni·al'i·ty

con·gen'i·tal

con·gest'

con·gest'ed

con·ges'tion

con·glom'er·ate

con·glom'er·a'tion

con·grat'u·late

con·grat'u·lat'ed

con·grat'u·lates

con·grat'u·la'tion

con·grat'u·la·to'ry

con'gre·gate

con'gre·gat'ed

con'gre·ga'tion

con'gre·ga'tion·al

con'gress

con·gres'sion·al

con'gru·ence

con'gru·ent

con·gru'i·ty

con'gru·ous

con'ic

con'i·cal

co'ni·fer

co·nif'er·ous

con·jec'tur·al

con·jec'ture

con·jec'tured
con'ju·gal
con'ju·gate
con'ju·gat'ed
con'ju·ga'tion
con·junc'tion
con·junc'tive
con·junc'ti·vi'tis
con'ju·ra'tion
con·jure'
con·jured'
con'jur·er
con·nect'
con·nect'ed·ly
con·nec'tion
con·nec'tive
con·nec'tor
con·niv'ance
con·nive'
con·nived'
con'nois·seur'
con'no·ta'tion
con·note'
con·not'ed
con·nu'bi·al
con'quer
con'quered
con'quer·or
con'quest
con'san·guin'i·ty
con'science
con'sci·en'tious

con'sci·en'tious·ly
con'scious
con'scious·ly
con'scious·ness
con'script
con·scrip'tion
con'se·crate
con'se·crat'ed
con'se·cra'tion
con'se·cra'tive
con·sec'u·tive
con·sen'sus
con·sent'
con·sent'ed
con'se·quence
con'se·quent
con'se·quen'tial
con'se·quent·ly
con'ser·va'tion
con·serv'a·tism
con·serv'a·tive
con·serv'a·to'ry
con·serve'
con·served'
con·sid'er
con·sid'er·a·ble
con·sid'er·ate
con·sid'er·a'tion
con·sid'ered
con·sign'
con·signed'
con'sign·ee'

con·sign'ment
con·sign'or
con·sist'
con·sist'en·cy
con·sist'ent
con·sis'to·ry
con·so·la'tion
con·sole'
con·soled'
con·sol'i·date
con·sol'i·dat'ed
con·sol'i·da'tion
con·sol'ing·ly
con'sols
con'som·mé'
con'so·nance
con'so·nant
con'so·nan'tal
con·sort'
con·sort'ed
con·spic'u·ous
con·spic'u·ous·ly
con·spir'a·cy
con·spir'a·tor
con·spir'a·to'ri·al
con·spire'
con·spired'
con'sta·ble
con·stab'u·lar'y
con'stan·cy
con'stant
con'stant·ly

con·stel·la'tion

con'ster·na'tion

con'sti·pa'tion

con·stit'u·en·cy

con·stit'u·ent

con'sti·tute

con'sti·tut'ed

con'sti·tu'tion

con'sti·tu'tion·al

con'sti·tu'tion·al'i·ty

con'sti·tu'tion·al·ly

con·strain'

con·strained'

con·straint'

con·strict'

con·strict'ed

con·stric'tion

con·struct'

con·struct'ed

con·struc'tive

con·strue'

con·strued'

con'sul

con'su·lar

con'su·late

con'su·lates

con·sult'

con·sult'ant

con'sul·ta'tion

con·sult'a·tive

con·sult'ed

con·sum'a·ble

con·sume'

con·sumed'

con·sum'er·ism

con'sum·mate

con'sum·ma'tion

con·sump'tion

con·sump'tive

con'tact

con·ta'gion

con·ta'gious

con·tain'

con·tained'

con·tain'er·ize

con·tam'i·nate

con·tam'i·nat'ed

con·tam'i·na'tion

con'tem·plate

con'tem·plat'ed

con'tem·pla'tion

con·tem'pla·tive

con·tem'po·ra'ne·ous

con·tem'po·rar'y

con·tempt'

con·tempt'i·ble

con·temp'tu·ous

con·tend'

con·tend'ed

con·tend'er

con·tent'

con·tent'ed

con·ten'tion

con·ten'tious

con·tent'ment

con'test

con'test·ant

con'tes·ta'tion

con'text

con·tex'tu·al

con'ti·gu'i·ty

con·tig'u·ous

con'ti·nence

con'ti·nent

con'ti·nen'tal

con·tin'gen·cy

con·tin'gent

con·tin'u·al

con·tin'u·al·ly

con·tin'u·ance

con·tin'u·ant

con·tin'u·a'tion

con·tin'ue

con·tin'ued

con·ti·nu'i·ty

con·tin'u·ous

con·tin'u·ous·ly

con·tin'u·um

con·tort'

con·tort'ed

con·tor'tion

con·tor'tion·ist

con'tour

con'tra·band

con'tra·bass'

con'tract

con·tract'ed

con·trac'tile

con·trac'tion

con·trac'tor

con·trac'tu·al

con'tra·dict'

con'tra·dic'tion

con'tra·dic'to·ry

con'tra·dis·tinc'tion

con'tra·in'di·cate

con'tra·in'di·ca'tion

con·tral'to

con·trap'tion

con'tra·ri·ly

con'tra·ri·ness

con'tra·ri·wise'

con'tra·ry

con'trast

con'tra·vene'

con'tra·ven'tion

con·trib'ute

con'tri·bu'tion

con·trib'u·tive

con·trib'u·tor

con·trib'u·to'ry

con'trite

con'trite·ly

con·tri'tion

con·triv'ance

con·trive'

con·trol'

con·trol'la·ble

con·trolled'

con·trol'ler

con'tro·ver'sial

con'tro·ver'sy

con'tro·vert

con'tu·ma'cious

con'tu·ma·cy

con'tu·me'li·ous

con'tu·me'ly

con·tuse'

con·tused'

con·tu'sion

co·nun'drum

con'va·lesce'

con'va·les'cence

con'va·les'cent

con·vec'tion

con·vene'

con·vened'

con·ven'ience

con·ven'ienc·es

con·ven'ient

con·ven'ient·ly

con·vent'

con·ven'tion

con·ven'tion·al

con·ven'tion·al'i·ty

con·ven'tion·al·ize

con·ven'tion·al·ly

con·ven'tu·al

con·ven'tu·al·ly

con·verge'

con·verged'

con·ver'gence

con·ver'gent

con'ver·sant

con'ver·sa'tion

con'ver·sa'tion·al

con'ver·sa'tion·al·ist

con·verse'

con·ver'sion

con·vert'

con·vert'ed

con·vert'i·bil'i·ty

con·vert'i·ble

con·vex

con·vex'i·ty

con·vey'

con·vey'ance

con·veyed'

con·vey'er

con·vict'

con·vict'ed

con·vic'tion

con·vince'

con·vinc'ing·ly

con·viv'i·al

con·viv'i·al'i·ty

con·viv'i·al·ly

con'vo·ca'tion

con·voke'

con·voked'

con'vo·lute

con'vo·lut'ed

con'vo·lu'tion

con·voy'

con·voyed'

con·vulse'

con·vul'sion

con·vul'sive

cook'book'

cook'er

cook'er·y

cook'house'

cool

cooled

cool'er

cool'est

cool'head'ed

cool'house'

coo'lie

cool'ly

cool'ness

coop

co-op

coop'er·age

co-op'er·ate

co-op'er·at'ed

co-op'er·a'tion

co-op'er·a'tive

co-opt'

co-opt'ed

co-or'di·nate

co-or'di·nat'ed

co-or'di·na'tion

co-or'di·na'tor

coot

co'pal

co·part'ner

co·part'ner·ship

cope

coped

Co·per'ni·can

cop'ied

cop'i·er

cop'ing

co'pi·ous

co'pi·ous·ly

co'pi·ous·ness

cop'per

cop'per·head'

cop'per·plate'

cop'per·smith'

cop'pice

cop'ra

cop'y

cop'y·hold'er

cop'y·ist

cop'y·read'er

cop'y·right'

co'quet·ry

co·quette'

co·quet'tish

cor'a·cle

cor'a·coid

cor'al

cor'al·line

cord

cord'age

cord'ed

cor'dial

cor·dial'i·ty

cor'dial·ly

cord'ite

cor'don

Cor'do·van

cor'du·roy

cord'wood'

core

cored

co're·spond'ent

co·ri·an'der

Co·rin'thi·an

cork

cork'age

cork'screw'

cork'wood'

cor'mo·rant

corn

cor'ne·a

cor'ner

cor'nered

cor'ner·stone'

cor'net

corn'field'

corn'flow'er

cor'nice

corn'stalk'

cor'nu·co'pi·a

cor'ol·lar'y

co·ro'na

cor'o·nar'y

cor'o·na'tion

cor'o·ner

cor'o·net

cor'po·ral

cor'po·rate

cor'po·rate·ly

cor'po·ra'tion

cor'po·ra'tive

cor·po're·al

corps

corpse

cor'pu·lence

cor'pu·lent

cor'pus

cor'pus·cle

cor·pus'cu·lar

cor·ral'

cor·rect'

cor·rect'ed

cor·rec'tion

cor·rec'tion·al

cor·rec'tive

cor·rect'ly

cor·rect'ness

cor·rec'tor

cor're·late

cor're·lat'ed

cor're·la'tion

cor·rel'a·tive

cor're·spond'

cor're·spond'ed

cor're·spond'ence

cor're·spond'ent

cor·re·spond'ing·ly

cor're·sponds'

cor'ri·dor

cor·rob'o·rate

cor·rob'o·ra'tion

cor·rob'o·ra'tive

cor·rob'o·ra·to'ry

cor·rode'

cor·rod'ed

cor·ro'si·ble

cor·ro'sion

cor·ro'sive

cor'ru·gate

cor'ru·gat'ed

cor'ru·ga'tion

cor·rupt'

cor·rupt'ed

cor·rupt'i·bil'i·ty

cor·rupt'i·ble

cor·rup'tion

cor·rupt'ly

cor·sage'

cor'sair

corse'let

cor'set

cor·tege'

cor'tex

cor'ti·cal

co·run'dum

cor'us·cate

cor'us·cat'ed

cor'us·ca'tion

cor·vette'

co·ry'za

co·sig'na·to'ry

co·sign'er

cos'i·ly

co'sine

cos·met'ic

cos'me·ti'cian

cos'mic

cos·mog'o·ny

cos·mol'o·gy

cos'mo·naut

cos'mo·pol'i·tan

cos·mop'o·lite

cos'mos

Cos'sack

cost

cos'tal

cos'tive

cost'li·ness

cost'ly

cos'tume

cos·tum'er

co'sy

cot

co'te·rie

co·ter'mi·nous

co·til'lion

cot'tage

cot'ter	coun'ter·of·fen'sive	cour'te·sy
cot'ton	coun'ter·pane'	court'house'
cot'ton·tail'	coun'ter·part'	cour'ti·er
cot'ton·wood'	coun'ter·plot'	court'li·ness
couch	coun'ter·point'	court'ly
cou'gar	coun'ter·shaft'	court'-mar'tial
cough	coun'ter·sign'	court'ship
could	coun'ter·sink'	court'yard'
coun'cil	coun'ter·vail'	cous'in
coun'ci·lor	coun'ter·weight'	cove
coun'sel	count'ess	cov'e·nant
coun'seled	count'less	cov'er
count	coun'try	cov'er·age
count'down	coun'try·man	cov'ered
coun'te·nance	coun'try·side'	cov'er·let
count'er	coun'ty	cov'ert
coun'ter·act'	coup	cov'et
coun'ter·at·tack'	cou'pé'	cov'et·ed
coun'ter·bal'ance	cou'ple	cov'et·ous
coun'ter·blast'	cou'pler	cov'ey
coun'ter·change'	cou'plet	cow'ard
coun'ter·check'	cou'pling	cow'ard·ice
coun'ter·claim'	cou'pon	cow'ard·ly
coun'ter·clock'wise'	cour'age	cow'bell'
count'ered	cou·ra'geous	cow'boy'
coun'ter·feit	cour'i·er	cow'catch'er
coun'ter·feit'er	course	cow'er
coun'ter·foil'	coursed	cowl
coun'ter·ir'ri·tant	cours'er	cow'lick'
coun'ter·mand'	court	co-work'er
coun'ter·march'	court'ed	cow'slip
coun'ter·mine'	cour'te·ous	cox'comb'

cox'swain	crane	craze
coy	craned	cra'zi·er
coy'ly	cra'ni·al	cra'zi·est
coy'ness	cra·ni·om'e·try	cra'zi·ly
coy'ote	cra'ni·ot'o·my	cra'zi·ness
coz'en	cra'ni·um	cra'zy
co'zi·er	crank	creak
co'zi·est	crank'case'	creak'ing·ly
co'zi·ly	cranked	cream
co'zi·ness	crank'i·ly	creamed
co'zy	crank'i·ness	cream'er·y
crab	crank'y	cream'i·er
crack	cran'ny	cream'i·est
cracked	crape	cream'y
crack'er	crash	crease
crack'le	crass	cre·ate'
crack'led	crass'ly	cre·at'ed
cra'dle	crass'ness	cre·a'tion
cra'dled	crate	cre·a'tive
craft	crat'ed	cre·a'tive·ly
craft'i·er	cra'ter	cre·a'tive·ness
craft'i·est	cra·vat'	cre'a·tiv'i·ty
craft'i·ly	crave	cre·a'tor
craft'i·ness	craved	crea'ture
crafts'man	cra'ven	crèche
craft'y	cra'ven·ette'	cre'dence
crag	crav'ings	cre·den'tial
cram	craw'fish'	cre·den'za
crammed	crawl	cred'i·bil'i·ty
cramp	crawled	cred'i·ble
cram'pon	cray'fish'	cred'it
cran'ber'ry	cray'on	cred'it·a·bil'i·ty

cred'it·a·ble	cre'tin·ous	criss'cross'
cred'it·ed	cre·tonne'	cri·te'ri·a
cred'i·tor	cre·vasse'	cri·te'ri·on
cre'do	crev'ice	crit'ic
cre·du'li·ty	crew	crit'i·cal
cred'u·lous	crew'el	crit'i·cal·ly
cred'u·lous·ness	crib	crit'i·cism
creed	crib'bage	crit'i·cize
creek	crib'work'	crit'i·cized
creel	crick'et	cri·tique'
creep	crime	croak
creep'er	crim'i·nal	croaked
creep'i·ness	crim'i·nal'i·ty	croak'er
cre'mate	crim'i·nal·ly	croak'ing·ly
cre'mat·ed	crim'i·nol'o·gist	croch'et
cre·ma'tion	crim'i·nol'o·gy	crock
cre'ma·to'ry	crimp	crock'er·y
Cre·mo'na	crim'son	croc'o·dile
cre'ole	cringe	cro'cus
cre'o·sote	cringed	crook
crepe	crin'kle	crook'ed
crep'i·tant	crin'kled	crook'ed·ness
crep'i·tate	crin'o·line	croon
crep'i·ta'tion	crip'ple	crooned
cre·scen'do	crip'pled	croon'er
cres'cent	cri'ses	crop
crest	cri'sis	cro·quet'
crest'ed	crisp	cro·quette'
crest'fall'en	crisp'er	cro'sier
cre'tin	crisp'est	cross
cre'tin·ism	crisp'ly	cross'bar'
cre'tin·oid	crisp'ness	cross'bow'

cross'bow'man	crud'est	cry
cross'bred'	cru'di·ty	cry'o·lite
cross'cut'	cru'el	crypt
cross'hatch'	cru'el·ly	cryp'tic
cross'ings	cru'el·ty	cryp'ti·cal
cross'o'ver	cru'et	cryp'ti·cal·ly
cross'road'	cruise	cryp'to·gram
cross'walk'	cruis'er	cryp'to·graph
cross'wise'	crul'ler	cryp·tog'ra·phy
cross'word'	crumb	crys'tal
crotch'et	crum'ble	crys'tal·line
crouch	crum'bled	crys'tal·li·za'tion
crouched	crump	crys'tal·lize
croup	crum'pet	crys'tal·lized
crou'pi·er	crum'ple	crys'tal·loid
crow	crum'pled	cub
crow'bar'	crunch	cub'by·hole'
crowd	crup'per	cube
crowd'ed	cru·sade'	cu'beb
crown	cru·sad'er	cu'bic
crowned	cruse	cu'bi·cle
crown'work'	crush	cub'ism
cru'cial	crushed	cu'bit
cru'cial·ly	crush'er	cuck'oo
cru'ci·ble	crush'ing·ly	cu'cum·ber
cru'ci·fied	crust	cud'dle
cru'ci·fix	crust'ed	cud'dled
cru'ci·fix'ion	crust'i·er	cudg'el
cru'ci·form	crust'i·est	cudg'eled
cru'ci·fy	crust'y	cue
crude	crutch	cuff
crud'er	crux	cuffed

cui·rass'

cui·sine'

cu'li·nar'y

cull

culled

cul'mi·nate

cul'mi·nat'ed

cul'mi·na'tion

cul'pa·bil'i·ty

cul'pa·ble

cul'prit

cult

cul'ti·vate

cul'ti·vat'ed

cul'ti·va'tion

cul'ti·va'tor

cul'tur·al

cul'tur·al·ly

cul'ture

cul'tured

cul'vert

cum'ber

cum'bered

cum'ber·some

cum'brous

cum'mer·bund'

cu'mu·la'tive

cu'mu·lus

cu·ne'i·form

cun'ning

cun'ning·ly

cup

cup'board

cup'cake'

cu'pel

cu'pel·la'tion

cup'ful

Cu'pid

cu·pid'i·ty

cu'po·la

cupped

cu'pric

cu'prous

cur

cur'a·ble

cu'ra·çao'

cu'ra·cy

cu·ra're

cu'rate

cur'a·tive

cu·ra'tor

curb

curbed

curd

cure

cured

cu·ret'tage

cu·rette'

cur'few

cu'rie

cu'ri·o

cu'ri·os'i·ties

cu'ri·os'i·ty

cu'ri·ous

cu'ri·ous·ly

curl

curled

curl'er

cur'lew

curl'i·cue

curl'y

cur·mudg'eon

cur'rant

cur'ren·cy

cur'rent

cur'rent·ly

cur·ric'u·la

cur·ric'u·lar

cur·ric'u·lum

cur'ry

curse

curs'ed

cur'sive

cur'so·ry

curt

cur·tail'

cur·tailed'

cur'tain

cur'te·sy

curt'ly

cur'va·ture

curve

curved

cur'vi·lin'e·ar

cush'ion

cush'ioned

cusp	cut'out'	cy'clo·pe'dic
cus'pi·dor	cut'purse'	Cy'clops
cuss'ed·ness	cut'ter	cy'clo·ra'ma
cus'tard	cut'tings	cyg'net
cus·to'di·al	cut'tle·fish'	cyl'in·der
cus·to'di·an	cut'weed'	cy·lin'dric
cus'to·dy	cut'worm	cy·lin'dri·cal
cus'tom	cy'a·nate	cym'bal
cus'tom·ar'i·ly	cy·an'ic	cyn'ic
cus'tom·ar'y	cy'a·nide	cyn'i·cal
cus'tom·er	cy'a·nite	cyn'i·cal·ly
cut	cy·an'o·gen	cyn'i·cism
cu·ta'ne·ous	cy'a·no'sis	cy'no·sure
cut'a·way'	cy'ber·net'ics	cy'press
cut'back'	cy'cla·mate	Cy·ril'lic
cute	cy'cle	cyst
cu'ti·cle	cy'clic	cys·ti'tis
cut'lass	cy'cloid	cyst'oid
cut'ler·y	cy·clom'e·ter	cys'to·lith
cut'let	cy'clone	czar
cut'off'	cy·clon'ic	Czech

D

dab'ble	dal'ly	dan'dle
dachs'hund'	dal·ma'tian	dan'dled
da·coit'	dam	dan'druff
dae'dal	dam'age	dan'dy
dae'mon	dam'aged'	dan'ger
daf'fo·dil	dam'a·scene'	dan'ger·ous
daft	dam'a·scened'	dan'ger·ous·ly
dag'ger	da·mas'cus	dan'gle
da·guerre'o·type	dam'ask	dan'gled
dahl'ia	dammed	Dan'ish
dai'ly	dam'na·ble	dank
dain'ti·er	dam·na'tion	dap'per
dain'ti·est	damp	dap'ple
dain'ti·ly	damp'en	dap'pled
dain'ti·ness	damp'ened	dare
dain'ty	damp'er	dared
dair'y	damp'est	dar'ing·ly
dair'y·maid'	damp'ness	dark
dair'y·man	dam'sel	dark'en
da'is	dance	dark'er
dai'sy	danc'er	dark'est
dal'li·ance	dan'de·li'on	dark'ly

dark'ness

dar'ling

darned

dart

dart'ed

dash

dash'board'

dashed

dash'ing·ly

das'tard·ly

da'ta

date

dat'ed

da'tive

da'tum

daub

daubed

daugh'ter

daugh'ter-in-law'

daunt

daunt'ed

daunt'less

dau'phin

dav'en·port

dav'it

daw'dle

daw'dled

dawn

dawned

day

day'book'

day'break'

day'dream'

day'light'

day'time'

daz'zle

daz'zled

dea'con

dead

dead'en

dead'ened

dead'fall'

dead'head'

dead'light'

dead'li·ness

dead'lock

dead'ly

deaf

deaf'en

deaf'ened

deaf'en·ing·ly

deaf'er

deaf'est

deal

deal'er

deal'ings

dean

dean'er·y

dear

dear'er

dear'est

dear'ly

dear'ness

dearth

death

death'bed'

death'blow'

death'less

death'like'

death'ly

de·ba'cle

de·bar'

de·bark'

de·barred'

de·base'

de·based'

de·base'ment

de·bat'a·ble

de·bate'

de·bat'ed

de·bat'er

de·bauch'

de·bauched'

de·bauch'er·y

de·ben'ture

de·bil'i·tate

de·bil'i·tat'ed

de·bil'i·ty

deb'it

deb'it·ed

de·bris'

debt

debt'or

de·bug'ging

de'but

deb'u·tante'

dec'ade

de·ca'dence

de·ca'dent

de·cal'co·ma'ni·a

de·camp'

de·cant'

de·cant'er

de·cap'i·tate

de·cap'i·ta'tion

de·car'bon·ize

de·cath'lon

de·cay'

de·cayed'

de·cease'

de·ceased'

de·ce'dent

de·ceit'

de·ceit'ful

de·ceit'ful·ness

de·ceive'

de·ceived'

de·cel'er·a'tion

De·cem'ber

de'cen·cy

de·cen'ni·al

de'cent

de'cent·ly

de·cen'tral·i·za'tion

de·cen'tral·ize

de·cep'tion

de·cep'tive

de·cep'tive·ly

de·cep'tive·ness

de·cide'

de·cid'ed·ly

de·cid'u·ous

dec'i·mal

dec'i·mate

dec'i·mat'ed

dec'i·ma'tion

de·ci'pher

de·ci'pher·a·ble

de-ci'phered

de·ci'sion

de·ci'sive

de·ci'sive·ly

de·ci'sive·ness

deck

decked

deck'house'

deck'le

de·claim'

de·claimed'

dec'la·ma'tion

de·clam'a·to'ry

dec'la·ra'tion

de·clar'a·tive

de·clar'a·to'ry

de·clare'

de·clared'

de·clen'sion

dec'li·na'tion

de·cline'

de·clined'

de·cliv'i·ty

de·coc'tion

dé·col'le·tage

dé·col'le·té

de·com'pen·sate

de·com'pen·sa'tion

de'com·pose'

de'com·posed'

de'com·po·si'tion

dec'o·rate

dec'o·rat'ed

dec'o·ra'tion

dec'o·ra'tive

dec'o·ra'tor

dec'o·rous

dec'o·rous·ly

dec'o·rous·ness

de·co'rum

de·coy'

de·crease'

de·creased'

de·creas'ing·ly

de·cree'

de·creed'

de·crep'it

de·crep'i·tude

de·cre'tal

de·cried'

de·cry'

ded'i·cate

ded'i·cat'ed

ded'i·ca'tion

ded'·i·ca·to'ry

de·duce'

de·duced'

de·duc'i·ble

de·duct'

de·duct'ed

de·duct'i·ble

de·duc'tion

de·duc'tive·ly

deed

deed'ed

deem

deemed

deep

deep'en

deep'ened

deep'er

deep'est

deep'ly

deep'ness

deer

deer'hound'

deer'skin'

deer'stalk'er

deer'weed'

de·face'

de·faced'

de·fal'cate

de·fal'cat·ed

de·fal·ca'tion

def'a·ma'tion

de·fam'a·to'ry

de·fame'

de·famed'

de·fault'

de·fault'ed

de·fault'er

de·fea'si·ble

de·feat'

de·feat'ed

de·feat'ism

de·fect'

de·fec'tion

de·fec'tive

de·fec'tor

de·fend'

de·fend'ant

de·fend'ed

de·fend'er

de·fense'

de·fen'si·ble

de·fen'sive

de·fen'sive·ly

de·fen'sive·ness

de·fer'

def'er·ence

def'er·en'tial

def'er·en'tial·ly

de·fer'ment

de·fer'ral

de·ferred'

de·fi'ance

de·fi'ant

de·fi'ant·ly

de·fi'cien·cy

de·fi'cient

def'i·cit

def'i·lade'

def'i·lad'ed

de·file'

de·filed'

de·file'ment

de·fin'a·ble

de·fine'

de·fined'

def'i·nite

def'i·nite·ly

def'i·nite·ness

def'i·ni'tion

de·fin'i·tive

de·fin'i·tive·ly

de·fin'i·tive·ness

de·fin'i·tize

de·flate'

de·flat'ed

de·fla'tion

de·fla'tion·ar'y

de·flect'

de·flect'ed

de·flec'tion

de·for'est·a'tion

de·form'

de·for·ma'tion

de·formed'

de·form'i·ty

de·fraud'

de·fraud'ed

de·fray'

de·frayed'

deft

deft'ly

deft'ness

de·funct'

de·fied'

de·fy'

de·gen'er·a·cy

de·gen'er·ate

de·gen'er·at'ed

de'gen·er·a'tion

deg'ra·da'tion

de·grade'

de·grad'ed

de·grad'ing·ly

de·gree'

de·hy'drate

de·hy'drat·ed

de'i·fi·ca'tion

de'i·fied

de'i·fy

deign

deigned

de'ism

de'ist

de'i·ty

de·ject'ed

de·ject'ed·ly

de·jec'tion

de·lay'

de·layed'

de·lec'ta·bil'i·ty

de·lec'ta·ble

de·lec·ta'tion

del'e·gate

del'e·gat'ed

del'e·ga'tion

de·lete'

de·let'ed

del'e·te'ri·ous

del'e·te'ri·ous·ly

de·le'tion

delft'ware'

de·lib'er·ate

de·lib'er·at'ed

de·lib'er·a'tion

de·lib'er·a'tive

del'i·ca·cy

del'i·cate

del'i·cate·ly

del'i·ca·tes'sen

de·li'cious

de·li'cious·ly

de·light'

de·light'ed

de·light'ful

de·light'ful·ly

de·lim'it

de·lim'i·ta'tion

de·lin'e·ate

de·lin'e·at'ed

de·lin'e·a'tion

de·lin'e·a'tive

de·lin'e·a'tor

de·lin'quen·cy

de·lin'quent

del'i·quesce'

del'i·ques'cence

del'i·ques'cent

de·lir'i·ous

de·lir'i·um

de·liv'er

de·liv'er·ance

de·liv'ered

de·liv'er·er

de·liv'er·y

del·phin'i·um

del'ta

del'toid

de·lude'

de·lud'ed

del'uge

del'uged

de·lu'sion

de·lu'sive

de luxe'

delve

de·mag'net·ize

dem'a·gog'ic

dem'a·gogue

de·mand'

de·mand'ed

de·mand'ing·ly

de'mar·ca'tion

de·mean'

de·meaned'

de·mean'or

de·ment'ed

de·men'ti·a

de·mer'it

dem'i·god'

de·mil'i·ta·rize

de·mise'

de·mo'bi·li·za'tion

de·mo'bi·lize

de·mo'bi·lized

de·moc'ra·cy

dem'o·crat

dem'o·crat'ic

dem'o·crat'i·cal·ly

de·moc'ra·ti·za'tion

de·moc'ra·tize

de·mol'ish

de·mol'ished

dem'o·li'tion

de'mon

de·mon'e·ti·za'tion

de·mon'e·tize

de'mo·ni'a·cal

de·mon'stra·ble

dem'on·strate

dem'on·strat'ed

dem'on·stra'tion

dem'on·stra·tive

dem'on·stra'tor

de·mor'al·i·za'tion

de·mor'al·ize

de·mor'al·ized

de·mot'ic

de·mount'able

de·mur'

de·mure'

de·mure'ly

de·mur'rage

de·murred'

de·mur'rer

den

de·na'ture

de·na'tured

den·drol'o·gy

de·ni'al

de·nied'

den'i·grate

den'i·zen

de·nom'i·nate

de·nom'i·nat'ed

de·nom'i·na'tion

de·nom'i·na'tion·al

de·nom'i·na'tor

de'no·ta'tion

de·note'

de·not'ed

de·noue'ment

de·nounce'

de·nounced'

dense

dens'er

dens'est

den'si·ty

dent

den'tal

den·tal'gi·a

dent'ed

den'ti·frice

den'tine

den'tist

den'tist·ry

den·ti'tion

den'u·da'tion

de·nude'

de·nun'ci·a'tion

de·nun'ci·a·to'ry

de·ny'

de·o'dor·ant

de·o'dor·ize

de·o'dor·ized

de·part'

de·part'ed

de·part'ment

de'part·men'tal

de'part·men'tal·ize

de·par'ture

de·pend'

de·pend'ed

de·pend'en·cy

de·pend'ent

de·per'son·al·ize

de·pict'

de·pict'ed

de·pic'tion

de·pil'a·to'ry

de·plete'

de·plet'ed

de·ple'tion

de·plor'a·ble

de·plore'

de·plored'

de·ploy'

de·ployed'

de·ploy'ment

de·po'lar·i·za'tion

de·po'lar·ize

de·po'nent

de·pop'u·late

de·pop'u·lat'ed

de·port'

de'por·ta'tion

de·port'ed

de·port'ment

de·pose'

de·posed'

de·pos'it

de·pos'i·tar'y

de·pos'it·ed

dep'o·si'tion

de·pos'i·tor

de·pos'i·to'ry

de'pot

dep'ra·va'tion

de·prave'

de·praved'

de·prav'i·ty

dep're·cate

dep're·cat'ed

dep're·ca'tion

dep're·ca·to'ry

de·pre'ci·ate

de·pre'ci·at'ed

de·pre'ci·a'tion

dep're·da'tion

de·press'

de·pres'sant

de·pressed'

de·press'ing·ly

de·pres'sion

de·pres'sive

dep'ri·va'tion

de·prive'

de·prived'

depth

dep'u·ta'tion

de·pute'

de·put'ed

dep'u·tize

dep'u·tized

dep'u·ty

de·rail'

de·railed'

de·rail'ment

de·range'

de·ranged'

de·range'ment

der'by

der'e·lict

der'e·lic'tion

de·ride'

de·rid'ed

de·ri'sion

de·ri'sive

de·riv'a·ble

der'i·va'tion

de·riv'a·tive

de·rive'

de·rived'

der'mal

der'ma·ti'tis

der'ma·tol'o·gy

der'ma·to'sis

der'o·gate

der'o·gat'ed

der'o·ga'tion

de·rog'a·to'ry

der'rick

der'vish

des'cant

de·scend'

de·scend'ant

de·scent'

de·scribe'

de·scribed'

de·scrip'tion

de·scrip'tive

de·scry'

des'e·crate

des'e·crat'ed

des'e·cra'tion

de·sen'si·tize

de·sen'si·tiz'er

de·sert'

de·sert'ed

de·sert'er

de·ser'tion

de·serve'

de·served'

des'ic·cant

des'ic·cate

des'ic·cat'ed

des'ic·ca'tion

des'ic·ca'tive

de·sid'er·a'ta

de·sid'er·a'tum

de·sign'

des'ig·nate

des'ig·nat'ed

des'ig·na'tion

de·signed'

de·sign'ed·ly

de·sign'er

de·sir'a·bil'i·ty

de·sir'a·ble

de·sire'

de·sired'

de·sires'

de·sir'ous

de·sist'

de·sists'

desk

des'o·late

des'o·lat'ed

des'o·late·ly

des'o·la'tion

de·spair'

de·spaired'

de·spair'ing·ly

des'per·a'do

des'per·ate

des'per·ate·ly

des'per·a'tion

des'pi·ca·ble

de·spise'

de·spised'

de·spite'

de·spoil'

de·spoiled'

de·spond'en·cy

de·spond'ent

de·spond'ing·ly

des'pot

des·pot'ic

des'pot·ism

des'qua·ma'tion

des·sert'

des'ti·na'tion

des'tine

des'tined

des'ti·ny

des'ti·tute

des'ti·tu'tion

de·stroy'

de·stroyed'

de·stroy'er

de·struct'i·ble

de·struc'tion

de·struc'tive

des'ue·tude

des'ul·to'ri·ly

des'ul·to'ry

de·tach'

de·tach'a·ble

de·tached'

de·tach'ment

de·tail'

de·tailed'

de·tain'

de·tained'

de·tect'

de·tect'ed

de·tec'tion

de·tec'tive

de·tec'tor

de·ten'tion

de·ter'

de·ter'gent

de·te'ri·o·rate

de·te'ri·o·rat'ed

de·te'ri·o·ra'tion

de·ter'mi·na·ble

de·ter'mi·nant

de·ter'mi·na'tion

de·ter'mi·na'tive

de·ter'mine

de·ter'mined

de·ter′min·ism

de·terred′

de·ter′rent

de·test′

de·test′a·ble

de′tes·ta′tion

de·test′ed

de·throne′

de·throned′

det′o·nate

det′o·nat′ed

det′o·na′tion

det′o·na′tor

de·tour′

de·toured′

de·tract′

de·tract′ed

de·trac′tion

de·trac′tor

det′ri·ment

det′ri·men′tal

de·tri′tus

de·val′u·ate

de·val′u·at′ed

de·val′u·a′tion

dev′as·tate

dev′as·tat′ed

dev′as·tat′ing·ly

dev′as·ta′tion

de·vel′op

de·vel′oped

de·vel′op·ment

de·vel′op·men′tal

de′vi·ate

de′vi·at′ed

de′vi·a′tion

de·vice′

dev′il

dev′il·try

de′vi·ous

de′vi·ous·ness

de·vise′

de·vised′

de·vi′tal·ize

de·void′

de·volve′

de·volved′

de·vote′

de·vot′ed

de·vot′ed·ly

dev′o·tee′

de·vo′tion

de·vo′tion·al

de·vour′

de·voured′

de·vout′ly

dew

dew′y

dex′ter

dex·ter′i·ty

dex′ter·ous

dex′ter·ous·ly

dex′trose

di′a·be′tes

di′a·bet′ic

di′a·bol′ic

di′a·bol′i·cal

di·ac′o·nal

di′a·crit′i·cal

di′a·dem

di·aer′e·sis

di′ag·nose′

di′ag·nosed′

di′ag·no′ses

di′ag·no′sis

di′ag·nos′tic

di′ag·nos·ti′cian

di·ag′o·nal

di·ag′o·nal·ly

di′a·gram

di′al

di′a·lect

di′a·lec′tic

di′aled

di′a·logue

di·al′y·sis

di·am′e·ter

di′a·met′ric

di′a·met′ri·cal·ly

di′a·mond

di′a·pa′son

di′a·per

di·aph′a·nous

di′a·phragm

di′a·rist

di′a·ry

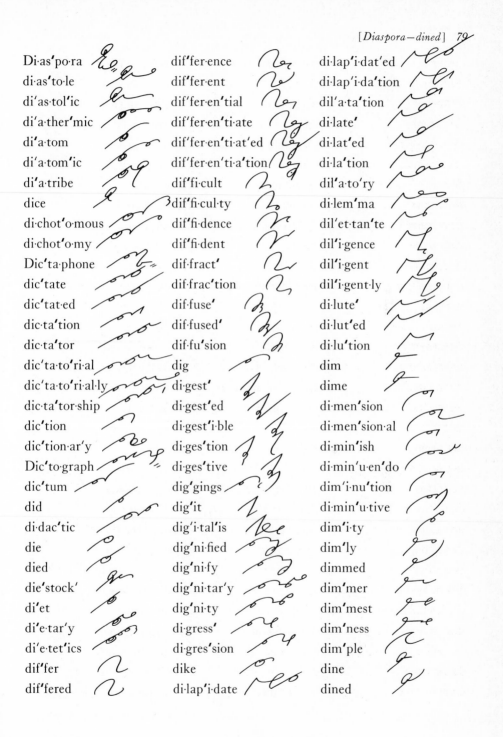

Di·as'po·ra
di·as'to·le
di·as·tol'ic
di·a·ther'mic
di'a·tom
di·a·tom'ic
di'a·tribe
dice
di·chot'o·mous
di·chot'o·my
Dic'ta·phone
dic'tate
dic'tat·ed
dic·ta'tion
dic·ta'tor
dic'ta·to'ri·al
dic'ta·to'ri·al·ly
dic·ta'tor·ship
dic'tion
dic'tion·ar'y
Dic'to·graph
dic'tum
did
di·dac'tic
die
died
die'stock'
di'et
di'e·tar'y
di'e·tet'ics
dif'fer
dif'fered

dif'fer·ence
dif'fer·ent
dif'fer·en'tial
dif'fer·en'ti·ate
dif'fer·en'ti·at'ed
dif'fer·en'ti·a'tion
dif'fi·cult
dif'fi·cul·ty
dif'fi·dence
dif'fi·dent
dif·fract'
dif·frac'tion
dif·fuse'
dif·fused'
dif·fu'sion
dig
di·gest'
di·gest'ed
di·gest'i·ble
di·ges'tion
di·ges'tive
dig'gings
dig'it
dig'i·tal'is
dig'ni·fied
dig'ni·fy
dig'ni·tar'y
dig'ni·ty
di·gress'
di·gres'sion
dike
di·lap'i·date

di·lap'i·dat'ed
di·lap'i·da'tion
dil'a·ta'tion
di·late'
di·lat'ed
di·la'tion
dil'a·to'ry
di·lem'ma
dil'et·tan'te
dil'i·gence
dil'i·gent
dil'i·gent·ly
di·lute'
di·lut'ed
di·lu'tion
dim
dime
di·men'sion
di·men'sion·al
di·min'ish
di·min'u·en'do
dim'i·nu'tion
di·min'u·tive
dim'i·ty
dim'ly
dimmed
dim'mer
dim'mest
dim'ness
dim'ple
dine
dined

din'er

din'gy

din'ner

di'no·saur

dint

di·oc'e·san

di'o·cese

di'o·ra'ma

diph·the'ri·a

diph'thong

di·plo'ma

di·plo'ma·cy

dip'lo·mat

dip'lo·mat'ic

dip'lo·mat'i·cal·ly

di·plo'ma·tist

di·plo'pi·a

dip'per

dip'so·ma'ni·a

dip'so·ma'ni·ac

di·rect'

di·rect'ed

di·rec'tion

di·rec'tion·al

di·rec'tive

di·rect'ly

di·rect'ness

di·rec'tor

di·rec'to·ry

dire'ful

dir'est

dirge

dir'i·gi·ble

dirt

dirt'i·ly

dirt'y

dis'a·bil'i·ty

dis·a'ble

dis·a'bled

dis·a'buse'

dis'ad·van'tage

dis'ad·van'taged

dis·ad'van·ta'geous

dis'af·fec'tion

dis'af·firm'

dis'af·firmed'

dis'a·gree'

dis'a·gree'a·ble

dis'a·gree'ment

dis'al·low'

dis'al·lowed'

dis'ap·pear'

dis'ap·pear'ance

dis'ap·peared'

dis'ap·point'

dis'ap·point'ment

dis'ap·pro·ba'tion

dis'ap·prov'al

dis'ap·prove'

dis·arm'

dis·ar'ma·ment

dis·armed'

dis·arm'ing·ly

dis'ar·range'

dis'ar·ranged'

dis'ar·ray'

dis'ar·tic'u·late

dis·as·so'ci·a'tion

dis·as'ter

dis·as'trous

dis·a·vow'

dis·a·vow'al

dis·band'

dis·band'ed

dis·bar'

dis·bar'ment

dis·barred'

dis·be·lieve'

dis·be·lieved'

dis·be·liev'er

dis·be·liev'ing·ly

dis·burse'

dis·burse'ment

disc

dis'card

dis·card'ed

dis·cern'

dis·cerned'

dis·cern'i·ble

dis·cern'ing·ly

dis·cern'ment

dis·charge'

dis·charged'

dis·ci'ple

dis·ci'ple·ship

dis·ci·pli·nar'y

dis'ci·pline	dis·cour'age·ment	dis'em·bar'rass
dis'ci·plined	dis·cour'ag·ing·ly	dis'em·bod'y
dis·claim'	dis·course'	dis'en·chant'
dis·claimed'	dis·cour'te·ous	dis'en·gage'
dis·close'	dis·cour'te·sy	dis'es·tab'lish
dis·clo'sure	dis·cov'er	dis'es·teem'
dis·col'or	dis·cov'ered	dis·fa'vor
dis·col'or·a'tion	dis·cov'er·er	dis·fea'ture
dis·col'ored	dis·cov'er·y	dis·fig'ure
dis·com'fit	dis·cred'it	dis·fig'ured
dis·com'fi·ture	dis·cred'it·a·ble	dis·fig'ure·ment
dis·com'fort	dis·cred'it·ed	dis·fran'chise
dis'com·pose'	dis·creet'	dis·gorge'
dis'com·posed'	dis·crep'an·cy	dis·grace'
dis'com·po'sure	dis·crete'	dis·grace'ful
dis'con·cert'	dis·cre'tion	dis·grun'tle
dis'con·nect'	dis·cre'tion·ar'y	dis·guise'
dis'con·nect'ed	dis·crim'i·nate	dis·gust'
dis·con'so·late	dis·crim'i·nat'ed	dis·gust'ed
dis'con·tent'	dis·crim'i·na'tion	dis·gust'ed·ly
dis'con·tent'ed	dis·crim'i·na'tive	dis·gust'ing·ly
dis'con·tin'u·ance	dis·crim'i·na·to'ry	dish
dis'con·tin'ue	dis·cur'sive	dis'ha·bille'
dis'con·tin'ued	dis'cus	dis·har'mo·ny
dis'cord	dis·cuss'	dis·heart'en
dis·cord'ance	dis·cuss'es	di·shev'el
dis·cord'ant	dis·dain'	di·shev'eled
dis'count	dis·dained'	dis·hon'est
dis'count·ed	dis·dain'ful	dis·hon'est·ly
dis·coun'te·nance	dis·ease'	dis·hon'or
dis·cour'age	dis·eased'	dis·hon'or·a·ble
dis·cour'aged	dis·em'bar·ka'tion	dis·hon'ored

dis·il·lu'sion

dis·in·cli·na'tion

dis·in·cline'

dis·in·clined'

dis·in·fect'

dis·in·fect'ant

dis·in·gen'u·ous

dis·in·her'it

dis·in'te·grate

dis·in'te·gra'tion

dis·in'ter·est·ed

dis·join'

dis·joined'

dis·join'ings

dis·joint'ed

dis·junc'tion

dis·junc'tive

disk

dis·like'

dis'lo·cate

dis'lo·cat'ed

dis'lo·ca'tion

dis·lodge'

dis·loy'al

dis·loy'al·ty

dis'mal

dis'mal·ly

dis·man'tle

dis·man'tled

dis·mast'

dis·mast'ed

dis·may'

dis·mayed'

dis·mem'ber

dis·mem'bered

dis·mem'ber·ment

dis·miss'

dis·miss'al

dis·mount'

dis·mount'ed

dis'o·be'di·ence

dis'o·be'di·ent

dis'o·bey'

dis'o·beyed'

dis'o·blige'

dis'o·blig'ing·ly

dis·or'der

dis·or'dered

dis·or'der·ly

dis·or'gan·ize

dis·or'gan·ized

dis·own'

dis·par'age

dis·par'age·ment

dis·par'ag·ing·ly

dis'pa·rate

dis·par'i·ty

dis·pas'sion·ate

dis·patch'

dis·patched'

dis·patch'er

dis·pel'

dis·pelled'

dis·pen'sa·ble

dis·pen'sa·ry

dis'pen·sa'tion

dis·pense'

dis·pensed'

dis·per'sal

dis·perse'

dis·persed'

dis·per'sion

dis·pir'it·ed

dis·place'

dis·place'ment

dis·play'

dis·please'

dis·pleas'ure

dis·port'

dis·pos'al

dis·pose'

dis·posed'

dis'po·si'tion

dis'pos·sess'

dis'pos·sessed'

dis·po'sure

dis·praise'

dis·proof'

dis'pro·por'tion

dis'pro·por'tion·ate

dis'pu·ta·ble

dis'pu·tant

dis'pu·ta'tion

dis'pu·ta'tious

dis·pute'

dis·put'ed

dis·qual'i·fi·ca'tion

dis·qual'i·fy

dis·qui'et·ed

dis·qui'e·tude

dis'qui·si'tion

dis're·gard'

dis·re·pair'

dis·rep'u·ta·ble

dis're·pute'

dis're·spect'

dis're·spect'ful

dis·robe'

dis·root'

dis·rupt'

dis·rup'tion

dis·rup'tive

dis'sat·is·fac'tion

dis·sat'is·fied

dis·sect'

dis·sect'ed

dis·sem'ble

dis·sem'i·nate

dis·sem'i·nat'ed

dis·sem'i·na'tion

dis·sen'sion

dis·sent'

dis·sent'er

dis·sen'tient

dis'ser·ta'tion

dis·serv'ice

dis'si·dence

dis'si·dent

dis·sim'i·lar

dis·sim'i·lar'i·ty

dis·sim'u·late

dis·sim'u·lat'ed

dis·sim'u·la'tion

dis'si·pate

dis'si·pat'ed

dis'si·pa'tion

dis·so'ci·ate

dis·so'ci·at'ed

dis·so'ci·a'tion

dis'so·lute

dis'so·lu'tion

dis·solv'a·ble·ness

dis·solve'

dis·solved'

dis'so·nance

dis'so·nant

dis·suade'

dis·sua'sion

dis'taff

dis'tal

dis'tance

dis'tant

dis·taste'

dis·taste'ful

dis·tem'per

dis·tend'

dis·ten'si·ble

dis·till'

dis'til·late

dis'til·la'tion

dis·tilled'

dis·till'er

dis·till'er·y

dis·tinct'

dis·tinc'tion

dis·tinc'tive

dis·tinct'ly

dis·tinct'ness

dis·tin'guish

dis·tin'guished

dis·tort'

dis·tort'ed

dis·tor'tion

dis·tract'

dis·tract'ing·ly

dis·trac'tion

dis·train'

dis·trained'

dis·traught'

dis·tress'

dis·trib'ute

dis'tri·bu'tion

dis·trib'u·tive

dis·trib'u·tor

dis'trict

dis·trust'

dis·trust'ful

dis·turb'

dis·turb'ance

dis·turbed'

dis·turb'er

dis·un'ion

dis'u·nite'

dis·use'

ditch

ditched

dith'y·ram'bic

dit'to

dit'ty

di·ur'nal

di'va·gate

di'van

dive

dived

div'er

di·verge'

di·verged'

di·ver'gence

di·ver'gent

di·verg'ing·ly

di·verse'

di·ver'si·fi·ca'tion

di·ver'si·fy

di·ver'sion

di·ver'sion·ar·y

di·ver'si·ty

di·vert'

di·vest'

di·vide'

di·vid'ed

div'i·dend

di·vid'er

di·vine'

di·vined'

di·vine'ly

di·vin'i·ty

di·vis'i·bil'i·ty

di·vis'i·ble

di·vi'sion

di·vi'sor

di·vorce'

di·vor·cee'

di·vorce'ment

di·vulge'

di·vulged'

diz'zi·er

diz'zi·est

diz'zi·ly

diz'zi·ness

diz'zy

do

doc'ile

do·cil'i·ty

dock

dock'et

dock'yard'

doc'tor

doc'tor·ate

doc'tri·naire'

doc'tri·nal

doc'trine

doc'u·ment

doc'u·men'ta·ry

doc'u·men·ta'tion

doc'u·ment'ed

dod'der

dodge

dodged

do'do

doe

doe'skin'

doff

dog

dog'cart'

doge

dog'ged

dog'ger·el

dog'ma

dog·mat'ic

dog'ma·tism

dog'ma·tize

dog'trot'

dog'wood'

doi'ly

do'ings

dol'drums

dole

doled

dole'ful

doll

dol'lar

dol'man

dol'phin

dolt

do·main'

dome

domed

do·mes'tic

do·mes'ti·cal·ly	door'stop'	dough'y
do·mes'ti·cate	door'way'	dour
do·mes'ti·cat'ed	door'yard'	dove
do'mes·tic'i·ty	dope	dove
dom'i·cile	dor'mant	dove'cot'
dom'i·cil'i·ar'y	dor'mer	dove'tail'
dom'i·nance	dor'mi·to'ry	dow'a·ger
dom'i·nant	dor'mouse'	dow'di·er
dom'i·nate	dor'sal	dow'di·est
dom'i·nat'ed	do'ry	dow'di·ly
dom'i·na'tion	dos'age	dow'dy
dom'i·neer'	dose	dow'el
dom'i·neered'	dos'si·er	dow'eled
dom'i·neer'ing·ly	dot	dow'er
dom'i·nie	dot'age	down
do·min'ion	do'tard	down'cast'
dom'i·no	dote	down'fall'
do'nate	dot'ing·ly	down'heart'ed
do'nat·ed	dot'ted	down'hill'
do·na'tion	dou'ble	down'pour'
don'a·tive	dou'bled	down'right'
done	dou'ble·knit	down'stairs'
don'key	doubt	down'town'
do'nor	doubt'ed	down'ward
doom	doubt'ful	down'y
doomed	doubt'ful·ly	dow'ry
door	doubt'ing·ly	dows'er
door'bell'	doubt'less	dox·ol'o·gy
door'frame'	dough	doze
door'knob'	dough'boy'	doz'en
door'nail'	dough'nut'	drab
door'sill'	dough'ty	drach'ma

draft	dra'per·y	drear'i·er
draft'ed	dras'tic	drear'i·est
draft'ee'	draught	drear'i·ly
draft'i·er	draw	drear'i·ness
draft'i·est	draw'back'	drear'y
draft'i·ly	draw'bar'	dredge
draft'y	draw'bridge'	dredged
drag	draw'ee'	dreg
drag'gle	draw'er	drench
drag'gled	draw'ings	drenched
drag'net'	drawl	dress
drag'on	drawled	dressed
drag'on·fly'	drawn	dress'er
dra·goon'	draw'plate'	dress'ings
dra·gooned'	draw'string'	dress'mak'er
drain	dray	dress'y
drain'age	dray'age	drew
drained	dray'man	drib'ble
drain'er	dread	drib'bled
drake	dread'ed	dried
dra'ma	dread'ful	dri'er
dra·mat'ic	dream	dri'est
dra·mat'i·cal·ly	dreamed	drift
dra·mat'ics	dream'er	drift'wood'
dram'a·tist	dream'i·er	drill
dram'a·ti·za'tion	dream'i·est	drilled
dram'a·tize	dream'i·ly	drill'er
dram'a·tized	dream'i·ness	drink
dram'a·tur'gy	dream'land	drink'a·ble
drank	dream'less	drink'er
drape	dream'like	drip
drap'er	dream'y	drip'pings

drive	drudg'er·y	duc'tile
driv'el	drug	duc·til'i·ty
driv'en	drug'gist	dudg'eon
driv'er	drug'store'	due
drive'way'	dru'id	du'el
driz'zle	dru·id'i·cal	du'el·ist
driz'zled	drum	du·en'na
droll	drum'head'	du·et'
droll'er·y	drummed	duf'fel
drom'e·dar'y	drum'mer	duff'er
drone	drum'stick'	dug
dron'ing·ly	drunk	du'gong
drool	drunk'ard	dug'out'
drool'ings	drunk'en	duke
droop	dry	duke'dom
drop	dry'ly	dul'cet
drop'out'	dry'ness	dul'ci·mer
drop'per	du'al	dull
drop'pings	du'al·ism	dull'ard
drop'si·cal	du'al·is'tic	dull'er
drop'sy	du·al'i·ty	dull'est
dross	du·bi'e·ty	dull'ness
drought	du'bi·ous	du'ly
drove	du'cal	dumb
drown	duc'at	dumb'bell'
drowned	duch'ess	dum'my
drown'ings	duch'y	dump
drowse	duck	dump'ing
drow'si·ly	duck'ling	dump'ling
drow'si·ness	duck'pin'	dun
drow'sy	duck'weed'	dunce
drudge	duct	dune

dun'ga·ree'

dun'geon

dun'nage

dunned

dupe

du'plex

du'pli·cate

du'pli·cat'ed

du'pli·ca'tion

du'pli·ca'tor

du·plic'i·ty

du'ra·bil'i·ty

du'ra·ble

du·ral'u·min

dur'ance

du·ra'tion

du'ress

dur'ing

dusk'y

dust

dust'ed

dust'er

dust'i·er

dust'i·est

dust'y

du'te·ous

du'ties

du'ti·ful

du'ty

dwarf

dwarf'ish

dwell

dwel'lings

dwelt

dwin'dle

dwin'dled

dy·nam'ic

dy'na·mism

dy'na·mite

dy'na·mit'ed

dy'na·mo

dy'nas·ty

dys'en·ter'y

dys·func'tion

dys·pep'si·a

dys·pep'tic

dys'tro·phy

E

each	ear'shot'	East'er
ea'ger	earth	east'er·ly
ea'ger·ly	earth'en	east'ern
ea'ger·ness	earth'en·ware'	east'ern·er
ea'gle	earth'li·ness	east'ward
ea'glet	earth'ly	east'ward·ly
ear	earth'men	eas'y
earl	earth'quake'	eas'y·go'ing
earl'dom	earth'ward	eat
ear'li·er	earth'work'	eat'a·ble
ear'li·est	earth'worm'	eat'en
ear'ly	ear'wax'	eat'er
ear'mark'	ear'wig'	eaves'drop'
earn	ease	ebb
earned	eased	ebbed
earn'er	ea'sel	eb'on·ize
ear'nest	ease'ment	eb'on·ized
ear'nest·ly	eas'i·er	eb'on·y
ear'nest·ness	eas'i·est	e·bul'li·ence
earn'ings	eas'i·ly	e·bul'li·ent
ear'ring'	eas'i·ness	eb'ul·li'tion
ear'rings'	east	ec·cen'tric

ec'cen·tric'i·ty

ec'chy·mo'sis

ec·cle'si·as'tic

ec·cle'si·as'ti·cal

ech'e·lon

ech'o

ech'oed

é·clair'

é·clat'

ec·lec'tic

ec·lec'ti·cism

e·clipse'

e·col'o·gy

e'co·nom'ic

e'co·nom'i·cal

e'co·nom'i·cal·ly

e·con'o·mist

e·con'o·mize

econ'omized

econ'omy

ec'ru

ec'sta·sy

ec·stat'ic

ec·stat'i·cal·ly

ec'ze·ma

ed'dy

e'del·weiss

e·de'ma

edge

edged

edg'er

edge'ways'

edge'wise'

ed'i·bil'i·ty

ed'i·ble

e'dict

ed'i·fi·ca'tion

ed'i·fice

ed'i·fied

ed'i·fy

ed'it

ed'it·ed

e·di'tion

ed'i·tor

ed'i·to'ri·al

ed'i·to'ri·al·ize

ed'i·to'ri·al·ly

ed'u·ca·ble

ed'u·cate

ed'u·cat'ed

ed'u·ca'tion

ed'u·ca'tion·al

ed'u·ca'tion·al·ly

ed'u·ca'tor

e·duce'

eel

eel'pot'

eel'worm'

ee'rie

ef·face'

ef·face'ment

ef·fect'

ef·fect'ed

ef·fec'tive

ef·fec'tu·al

ef·fec'tu·al·ly

ef·fec'tu·ate

ef·fem'i·na·cy

ef·fem'i·nate

ef'fer·ent

ef'fer·vesce'

ef'fer·ves'cence

ef'fer·ves'cent

ef·fete'

ef'fi·ca'cious

ef'fi·ca·cy

ef·fi'cien·cy

ef·fi'cient

ef'fi·gies

ef'fi·gy

ef'flo·resce'

ef'flo·res'cence

ef'flo·res'cent

ef·flu'vi·a

ef·flu'vi·um

ef'flux

ef'fort

ef'fort·less

ef·fron'ter·y

ef·ful'gence

ef·ful'gent

ef·fu'sion

ef·fu'sive

ef·fu'sive·ly

ef·fu'sive·ness

e·gal'i·tar'i·an

egg'nog'	e·la'tion	e·lec'trom'e·ter
egg'plant'	el'bow	e·lec'tro·mo'tive
egg'shell'	el'bowed	e·lec'tron
eg'lan·tine	el'bow·room'	e·lec'tron'ic
e'go	eld'er	e·lec'tro·plate'
e'go·cen'tric	el'der·ber'ry	e·lec'tro·pos'i·tive
e'go·cen·tric'i·ty	eld'er·ly	e·lec'tro·scope
e'go·ism	eld'est	e·lec'tro·type
e'go·is'tic	e·lect'	e·lec'tro·typ'er
e'go·tism	e·lect'ed	el'ee·mos'y·nar'y
e'go·tis'tic	e·lec'tion	el'e·gance
e'go·tis'ti·cal	e·lec'tion·eer'	el'e·gant
e·gre'gious	e·lec'tive	el'e·gy
e'gress	e·lec'tor	el'e·ment
e'gret	e·lec'tor·al	el'e·men'tal
E·gyp'tian	e·lec'tor·ate	el'e·men'tal·ly
ei'der	e·lec'tric	el'e·men'ta·ry
ei'ther	e·lec'tri·cal	el'e·phant
e·jac'u·late	e·lec'tri·cal·ly	el'e·phan·ti'a·sis
e·jac'u·la'tion	e·lec'tri'cian	el'e·phan'tine
e·ject'	e·lec'tric'i·ty	el'e·vate
e·jec'tion	e·lec'tri·fi·ca'tion	el'e·vat'ed
e·ject'ment	e·lec'tri·fy	el'e·va'tion
e·jec'tor	e·lec'tro·cute	el'e·va'tor
e·lab'o·rate	e·lec'tro·cu'tion	elf'in
e·lab'o·rate·ly	e·lec'trode	e·lic'it
e·lab'o·ra'tion	e·lec'tro·lier'	e·lic'it·ed
e·lapse'	e·lec'trol'y·sis	e·lide'
e·lapsed'	e·lec'tro·lyt'ic	el'i·gi·bil'i·ty
e·las'tic	e·lec'tro·lyt'i·cal	el'i·gi·ble
e·las'tic'i·ty	e·lec'tro·lyze	e·lim'i·nate
e·lat'ed	e·lec'tro·mag'net	e·lim'i·nat'ed

e·lim'i·na'tion

e·lim'i·na'tive

e·li'sion

e·lite'

e·lix'ir

E·liz'a·be'than

elk

el·lip'sis

el·lips'oid

el·lip'tic

el·lip'ti·cal

elm

el'o·cu'tion

el'o·cu'tion·ist

e·lon'gate

e·lon'gat·ed

e·lon'ga'tion

e·lope'

e·lope'ment

el'o·quence

el'o·quent

el'o·quent·ly

else

else'where

else'wise

e·lu'ci·date

e·lu'ci·dat'ed

e·lu'ci·da'tion

e·lude'

e·lud'ed

e·lu'sive

e·lu'sive·ness

e·lu'so·ry

e·ma'ci·ate

e·ma'ci·at'ed

e·ma'ci·a'tion

em'a·nate

em'a·nat'ed

e·man'ci·pate

e·man'ci·pat'ed

e·man'ci·pa'tion

e·man'ci·pa'tor

e·mas'cu·late

e·mas'cu·la'tion

em·balm'

em·balmed'

em·balm'er

em·bank'ment

em·bar'go

em·bar'goed

em·bark'

em'bar·ka'tion

em·bar'rass

em·bar'rassed

em·bar'rass·ment

em'bas·sy

em·bat'tle

em·bat'tled

em·bel'lish

em·bel'lished

em·bel'lish·ment

em'ber

em·bez'zle

em·bez'zled

em·bez'zle·ment

em·bez'zler

em·bit'ter

em·bit'tered

em·bla'zon

em'blem

em'blem·at'ic

em'blem·at'i·cal

em·bod'ied

em·bod'i·ment

em·bod'y

em·bold'en

em·bold'ened

em'bo·lism

em'bo·lus

em·boss'

em·bossed'

em·brace'

em·braced'

em·bra'sure

em'bro·cate

em'bro·ca'tion

em·broi'der

em·broi'dered

em·broi'der·y

em·broil'

em·broiled'

em'bry·o

em'bry·ol'o·gy

em'bry·on'ic

e·mend'

e'men·da'tion

e·mend'ed

em'er·ald

e·merge'

e·merged'

e·mer'gence

e·mer'gen·cy

e·mer'gent

e·mer'i·tus

em'er·y

e·met'ic

em'i·grant

em'i·grate

em'i·grat'ed

em'i·gra'tion

em'i·nence

em'i·nent

em'is·sar'y

e·mis'sion

e·mit'

e·mit'ted

e·mol'li·ent

e·mol'u·ment

e·mo'tion

e·mo'tion·al

e·mo'tion·al·ly

em·pan'el

em'per·or

em'pha·ses

em'pha·sis

em'pha·size

em'pha·sized

em·phat'ic

em·phat'i·cal·ly

em'pire

em·pir'ic

em·pir'i·cal

em·pir'i·cism

em·place'ment

em·ploy'

em·ployed'

em·ploy'ee

em·ploy'er

em·ploy'ment

em·po'ri·um

em·pow'er

em·pow'ered

em'press

emp'tied

emp'ti·ly

emp'ti·ness

emp'ty

em'py·re'an

e'mu

em'u·late

em'u·lat'ed

em'u·lates

em'u·la'tion

em'u·la'tive

em'u·la·to'ry

em'u·lous

e·mul'si·fi·ca'tion

e·mul'si·fi'er

e·mul'si·fy

e·mul'sion

en·a'ble

en·a'bled

en·act'

en·act'ed

en·act'ment

en·am'el

en·am'eled

en·am'ored

en·camp'

en·camp'ment

en·cap'su·late

en·caus'tic

en'ce·phal'ic

en·ceph'a·li'tis

en·chant'

en·chant'ed

en·chant'ing·ly

en·chant'ment

en·cir'cle

en·cir'cled

en·cir'cle·ment

en'clave

en·close'

en·closed'

en·clo'sure

en·co'mi·a

en·co'mi·as'tic

en·co'mi·um

en·com'pass

en·core'

en·coun'ter

en·coun'tered

en·cour′age	en·dog′e·nous	en·gage′
en·cour′aged	en·dorse′	en·gaged′
en·cour′age·ment	en·dorse′ment	en·gage′ment
en·cour′ag·ing·ly	en·dow′	en·gag′ing·ly
en·croach′	en·dowed′	en·gen′der
en·croached′	en·dow′ment	en·gen′dered
en·croach′ment	en·due′	en′gine
en·cum′ber	en·dued′	en′gi·neer′
en·cum′bered	en·dur′a·ble	Eng′lish
en·cum′brance	en·dur′ance	Eng′lish·man
en·cy′cli·cal	en·dure′	en·gorge′
en·cy′clo·pe′di·a	en·dured′	en·gorge′ment
en·cy′clo·pe′dic	en·dur′ing·ly	en·grain′
en·cyst′	end′ways	en·grained′
en·cyst′ed	end′wise	en·grave′
end	en′e·my	en·graved′
en·dan′ger	en′er·get′ic	en·grav′er
en·dan′gered	en′er·gize	en·gross′
en·dear′	en′er·gized	en·grossed′
en·deared′	en′er·vate	en·gross′er
en·deav′or	en′er·va′tion	en·gulf′
en·deav′ored	en·fee′ble	en·hance′
end′ed	en·fee′bled	en·hanced′
en·dem′ic	en′fi·lade′	en·hance′ment
end′ings	en·fold′	en·har·mon′ic
en′dive	en·force′	e·nig′ma
end′less	en·force′a·ble	e′nig·mat′ic
end′less·ly	en·forced′	e′nig·mat′i·cal
end′long′	en·force′ment	en·join′
en′do·crine	en·forc′er	en·joined′
en′do·cri·nol′o·gy	en·fran′chise	en·joy′
en′do·derm	en·fran′chised	en·joy′a·ble

en·joyed'

en·joy'ment

en·large'

en·larged'

en·large'ment

en·larg'er

en·light'en

en·light'ened

en·light'en·ing·ly

en·light'en·ment

en·list'

en·list'ed

en·list'ment

en·liv'en

en·liv'ened

en·mesh'

en'mi·ty

en·no'ble

en·no'bled

e·nor'mi·ty

e·nor'mous

e·nough'

en·rage'

en·raged'

en·rap'ture

en·rap'tured

en·rich'

en·riched'

en·rich'ment

en·roll'

en·rolled'

en·roll'ment

en·shrine'

en·shrined'

en'sign

en'si·lage

en·slave'

en·slave'ment

en·sue'

en·sued'

en·sure'

en·sured'

en·tab'la·ture

en·tail'

en·tailed'

en·tan'gle

en·tan'gled

en·tan'gle·ment

en'ter

en'tered

en'ter·i'tis

en'ter·prise

en'ter·tain'

en'ter·tained'

en'ter·tain'er

en'ter·tain'ing·ly

en'ter·tain'ment

en·thrall'

en·thralled'

en·throne'

en·throned'

en·thu'si·asm

en·thu'si·ast

en·thu'si·as'tic

en·thu'si·as'ti·cal·ly

en·tice'

en·ticed'

en·tice'ment

en·tic'ing·ly

en·tire'

en·tire'ly

en·tire'ty

en·ti'tle

en·ti'tled

en'ti·ty

en·tomb'

en·tombed'

en·tomb'ment

en'to·mol'o·gist

en'to·mol'o·gy

en'trails

en'trance

en·tranc'ing·ly

en'trant

en·trap'

en·treat'

en·treat'ed

en·treat'y

en·trench'

en·trust'

en'try

en'try·way'

en·twine'

e·nu'cle·ate

e·nu'cle·a'tion

e·nu'mer·ate

e·nu'mer·at'ed	ep'i·gas'tric	eq'ua·bly
e·nu'mer·a'tion	ep'i·glot'tis	e'qual
e·nu'mer·a'tor	ep'i·gram	e'qualed
e·nun'ci·ate	ep'i·gram·mat'ic	e·qual'i·tar'i·an
e·nun'ci·at'ed	ep'i·graph	e·qual'i·ty
e·nun'ci·a'tion	ep'i·lep'sy	e'qual·i·za'tion
e·nun'ci·a'tor	ep'i·lep'tic	e'qual·ize
en·vel'op	ep'i·lep'toid	e'qual·ized
en've·lope	ep'i·logue	e'qual·iz'er
en·ven'om	e·piph'y·sis	e'qual·ly
en'vi·a·ble	e·pis'co·pa·cy	e'qua·nim'i·ty
en'vi·ous	e·pis'co·pal	e·quate'
en·vi'ron·ment	e·pis'co·pa'li·an	e·quat'ed
en·vi'ron·men'tal	e·pis'co·pate	e·qua'tion
en·vi'ron·men'tal·ly	ep'i·sode	e·qua'tor
en·vi'rons	ep'i·sod'ic	e'qua·to'ri·al
en·vis'age	e·pis'te·mol'o·gy	eq'uer·ry
en·vis'aged	e·pis'tle	e·ques'tri·an
en'voy	e·pis'to·lar'y	e·ques'tri·enne'
en'voys	e·pis'to·la·to'ry	e'qui·an'gu·lar
en'vy	ep'i·taph	e'qui·dis'tance
en'zyme	ep'i·tha·la'mi·um	e'qui·dis'tant
e'on	ep'i·the'li·um	e'qui·lat'er·al
e·phem'er·al	ep'i·thet	e'qui·lib'ri·um
ep'ic	e·pit'o·me	e'quine
ep'i·cure	e·pit'o·mize	e'qui·noc'tial
ep'i·cu·re'an	ep'i·zo·ot'ic	e'qui·nox
ep'i·dem'ic	ep'och	e·quip'
ep'i·der'mal	ep'och·al	eq'ui·page
ep'i·der'mic	ep'o·nym	e·quip'ment
ep'i·der'mis	ep·ox'y	e'qui·poise
ep'i·der'moid	eq'ua·ble	eq'ui·ta·ble

eq'ui·ta'tion	er·rat'ic	es·pe'cial·ly
eq'ui·ty	er·rat'i·cal·ly	Es'pe·ran'to
e·quiv'a·lence	er·ra'tum	es'pi·o·nage
e·quiv'a·len·cy	erred	es'pla·nade'
e·quiv'a·lent	er·ro'ne·ous	es·pous'al
e·quiv'o·cal	er'ror	es·pouse'
e·quiv'o·cal·ly	erst'while'	es'prit'
e·quiv'o·cate	er'u·dite	es·py'
e·quiv'o·ca'tion	er'u·di'tion	es·quire'
e'ra	e·rupt'	es·say'
e·rad'i·cate	e·rup'tion	es·sayed'
e·rad'i·cat'ed	e·rup'tive	es'say·ist
e·rad'i·ca'tion	er'y·sip'e·las	es'sence
e·rase'	es'ca·lade'	es·sen'tial
e·rased'	es'ca·la'tor	es·sen'tial·ly
e·ras'er	es'ca·pade'	es·tab'lish
e·ra'sure	es·cape'	es·tab'lished
e·rect'	es·cape'ment	es·tab'lish·ment
e·rect'ed	es·cap'ist	es·tate'
e·rec'tile	es·carp'ment	es·teem'
e·rec'tion	es·cheat'	es·teemed'
e·rect'ness	es·chew'	es'ter
erg	es'cort	es·thet'ic
er'go	es·cort'ed	es'ti·ma·ble
er'got	es'cri·toire'	es'ti·mate
er'mine	es'crow'	es'ti·mat'ed
e·rode'	es·cutch'eon	es'ti·ma'tion
e·ro'sion	Es'ki·mo	es'ti·ma'tor
e·rot'ic	e·soph'a·gus	es'ti·vate
err	es'o·ter'ic	es·top'pel
er'rand	es·par'to	es·trange'
er·ra'ta	es·pe'cial	es·tranged'

es·trange′ment

es′tu·ar·y

e·su′ri·ent

etch

etch′er

etch′ings

e·ter′nal

e·ter′nal·ly

e·ter′ni·ty

eth′ane

e′ther

e·the′re·al

e·the′re·al·ly

eth′i·cal

eth′ics

eth′nic

eth·nol′o·gy

eth′yl

e′ti·ol′o·gy

et′i·quette

e′tude

et′y·mo·log′i·cal

et′y·mol′o·gy

eu′ca·lyp′tus

Eu′cha·rist

eu′chre

Eu·clid′e·an

eu·gen′ics

eu·lo·gis′tic

eu′lo·gize

eu′lo·gy

eu′phe·mism

eu′phe·mis′tic

eu·pho′ni·ous

eu·pho·ny

Eur·a′sian

eu·re′ka

Eu′ro·pe′an

Eu·sta′chi·an

eu·tec′tic

eu′tha·na′si·a

e·vac′u·ate

e·vac′u·at′ed

e·vac′u·a′tion

e·vade′

e·vad′ed

e·val′u·ate

e·val′u·a′tion

ev′a·nesce′

ev′a·nes′cence

ev′a·nes′cent

e·van·gel′i·cal

e·van′ge·list

e·vap′o·rate

e·vap′o·rat′ed

e·vap′o·ra′tion

e·vap′o·ra′tor

e·va′sion

e·va′sive

e·va′sive·ly

e·va′sive·ness

e′ven

eve′ning

eve′nings

e′ven·ly

e′ven·ness

e·vent′

e·vent′ful

e·vent′ful·ly

e·ven′tu·al

e·ven′tu·al′i·ty

e·ven′tu·al·ly

e·ven′tu·ate

ev′er

ev′er·glade

ev′er·green′

ev′er·last′ing

ev′er·last′ing·ly

ev′er·y

ev′er·y·bod′y

ev′er·y·day′

ev′er·y·one′

ev′er·y·thing′

ev′er·y·where′

e·vict′

e·vict′ed

e·vic′tion

ev′i·dence

ev′i·dent

ev′i·den′tial

ev′i·den′tial·ly

e′vil

e′vil·ly

e·vince′

e·vinced′

e·vis′cer·ate

ev·o·ca'tion

e·voc'a·tive

e·voke'

e·voked'

ev'o·lu'tion

ev'o·lu'tion·ar'y

ev'o·lu'tion·ist

e·volve'

ewe

ew'er

ex·ac'er·bate

ex·ac'er·ba'tion

ex·act'

ex·act'ed

ex·ac'tion

ex·act'i·tude

ex·act'ly

ex·act'ness

ex·ag'ger·ate

ex·ag'ger·at'ed

ex·ag'ger·a'tion

ex·alt'

ex'al·ta'tion

ex·alt'ed

ex·a'men

ex·am'i·na'tion

ex·am'ine

ex·am'ined

ex·am'in·er

ex·am'ple

ex·as'per·ate

ex·as'per·at'ed

ex·as'per·a'tion

ex'ca·vate

ex'ca·vat'ed

ex'ca·va'tion

ex'ca·va'tor

ex·ceed'

ex·ceed'ed

ex·ceed'ing·ly

ex·cel'

ex·celled'

ex'cel·lence

ex'cel·len·cy

ex'cel·lent

ex·cel'si·or

ex·cept'

ex·cept'ed

ex·cep'tion

ex·cep'tion·al

ex·cep'tion·al·ly

ex·cerpt'

ex·cess'

ex·cess'es

ex·ces'sive

ex·ces'sive·ly

ex·change'

ex·change'a·ble

ex·cheq'uer

ex·cip'i·ent

ex'cise

ex·ci'sion

ex·cit'a·bil'i·ty

ex·cit'a·ble

ex·cit'ant

ex·ci·ta'tion

ex·cite'

ex·cit'ed·ly

ex·cite'ment

ex·claim'

ex·claimed'

ex·cla·ma'tion

ex·clam'a·to·ry

ex·clude'

ex·clud'ed

ex·clu'sion

ex·clu'sive

ex'com·mu'ni·cate

ex'com·mu·ni·ca'tion

ex·co'ri·ate

ex·co'ri·at'ed

ex·co'ri·a'tion

ex·cres'cence

ex·cres'cent

ex·crete'

ex·cret'ed

ex·cre'tion

ex'cre·to·ry

ex·cru'ci·ate

ex·cru'ci·at'ing·ly

ex·cru'ci·a'tion

ex'cul·pate

ex'cul·pat'ed

ex'cul·pa'tion

ex·cur'sion

ex·cus'a·ble

ex·cuse′

ex·cused′

ex·cus′es

ex′e·cra·ble

ex′e·crate

ex′e·crat′ed

ex′e·cra′tion

ex·ec′u·tant

ex′e·cute

ex′e·cut′ed

ex′e·cu′tion

ex′e·cu′tion·er

ex·ec′u·tive

ex·ec′u·tor

ex·ec′u·trix

ex′e·ge′sis

ex·em′plar

ex·em′pla·ry

ex·em′pli·fi·ca′tion

ex·em′pli·fy

ex·empt′

ex·empt′ed

ex·emp′tion

ex′e·qua′tur

ex′er·cise

ex′er·cised

ex′er·cis′er

ex·ert′

ex·ert′ed

ex·er′tion

ex′ha·la′tion

ex·hale′

ex·haled′

ex·haust′

ex·haus′tion

ex·haus′tive

ex·haust′less

ex·hib′it

ex·hib′it·ed

ex′hi·bi′tion

ex·hib′i·tor

ex·hil′a·rate

ex·hil′a·rat′ed

ex·hil′a·ra′tion

ex·hort′

ex′hor·ta′tion

ex·hort′ed

ex·hu·ma′tion

ex·hume′

ex·humed′

ex′i·gen·cy

ex′i·gent

ex·ig′u·ous

ex′ile

ex′iled

ex·ist′

ex·ist′ed

ex·ist′ence

ex·ist′ent

ex′it

ex′o·dus

ex·on′er·ate

ex·on′er·at′ed

ex·on′er·a′tion

ex·or′bi·tant

ex·or′bi·tant·ly

ex′or·cise

ex′or·cised

ex′or·cism

ex·or′di·um

ex′o·ter′ic

ex·ot′ic

ex·ot′i·cism

ex·pand′

ex·pand′ed

ex·panse′

ex·pan′sion

ex·pan′sive

ex·pa′ti·ate

ex·pa′ti·at′ed

ex·pa′tri·ate

ex·pa′tri·a′tion

ex·pect′

ex·pect′an·cy

ex·pect′ant

ex′pec·ta′tion

ex·pect′ed

ex·pec′to·rant

ex·pec′to·rate

ex·pec′to·ra′tion

ex·pe′di·en·cy

ex·pe′di·ent

ex′pe·dite

ex′pe·dit′ed

ex′pe·di′tion

ex′pe·di′tion·ar′y

ex'pe·di'tious

ex'pe·di'tious·ly

ex·pel'

ex·pelled'

ex·pend'

ex·pend'ed

ex·pend'i·ture

ex·pense'

ex·pen'sive·ly

ex·pe'ri·ence

ex·pe'ri·enced

ex·pe'ri·enc·es

ex·per'i·ment

ex·per'i·men'tal

ex·per'i·men'tal·ly

ex·per'i·men·ta'tion

ex·per'i·ment·er

ex·pert'

ex'per'tise'

ex·pert'ly

ex·pert'ness

ex'pi·ate

ex'pi·a'tion

ex'pi·ra'tion

ex·pire'

ex·pired'

ex·plain'

ex·plained'

ex'pla·na'tion

ex·plan'a·to'ry

ex'ple·tive

ex'pli·ca·ble

ex'pli·cate

ex·plic'it

ex·plic'it·ly

ex·plode'

ex·plod'ed

ex'ploit

ex'ploi·ta'tion

ex·ploit'ed

ex'plo·ra'tion

ex·plor'a·to'ry

ex·plore'

ex·plored'

ex·plor'er

ex·plor'ing·ly

ex·plo'sion

ex·plo'sive

ex·po'nent

ex'po·nen'tial

ex·port'

ex'por·ta'tion

ex·pose'

ex·posed'

ex'po·si'tion

ex·pos'i·to'ry

ex·pos'tu·late

ex·pos'tu·lat'ed

ex·pos'tu·la'tion

ex·po'sure

ex·pound'

ex·press'

ex·pres'sion

ex·pres'sive

ex·pres'sive·ly

ex·press'ly

ex·press'man

ex·pro'pri·ate

ex·pro'pri·a'tion

ex·pul'sion

ex·punge'

ex·punged'

ex'pur·gate

ex'pur·gat'ed

ex'pur·ga'tion

ex'qui·site

ex'tant

ex·tem'po·ra'ne·ous

ex·tem'po·rar'y

ex·tem'po·re

ex·tem'po·ri·za'tion

ex·tem'po·rize

ex·tend'

ex·tend'ed

ex·ten'si·ble

ex·ten'sion

ex·ten'sive

ex·tent'

ex·ten'u·ate

ex·ten'u·at'ed

ex·ten'u·a'tion

ex·te'ri·or

ex·ter'mi·nate

ex·ter'mi·nat'ed

ex·ter'mi·na'tion

ex·ter'mi·na'tor

ex·ter′nal	ex′tra·di′tion	ex′u·date
ex·ter′nal·i·za′tion	ex·tra′ne·ous	ex′u·da′tion
ex·ter′nal·ly	ex·traor′di·nar′i·ly	ex·ude′
ex·tinct′	ex·traor′di·nar′y	ex·ud′ed
ex·tinc′tion	ex·trap′o·late	ex·ult′
ex·tin′guish	ex′tra·ter′ri·to′ri·al′i·ty	ex·ult′ant
ex·tin′guished	ex·trav′a·gance	ex′ul·ta′tion
ex·tin′guish·er	ex·trav′a·gant	ex·ult′ed
ex′tir·pate	ex·trav′a·gan′za	ex·ult′ing·ly
ex′tir·pat′ed	ex·trav′a·sate	eye
ex′tir·pa′tion	ex·trav′a·sa′tion	eye′ball′
ex·tol′	ex·treme′	eye′brow′
ex·tolled′	ex·trem′ist	eye′cup′
ex·tort′	ex·trem′i·ty	eyed
ex·tort′ed	ex′tri·cate	eye′lash′
ex·tor′tion	ex′tri·cat′ed	eye′let
ex·tor′tion·ate	ex′tri·ca′tion	eye′lid′
ex′tra	ex·trin′sic	eye′piece′
ex·tract′	ex′tro·ver′sion	eyes
ex·tract′ed	ex′tro·vert′	eye′shot′
ex·trac′tion	ex·trude′	eye′sight′
ex·trac′tive	ex·trud′ed	eye′strain′
ex′tra·cur- ric′u·lar	ex·tru′sion	eye′tooth′
ex′tra·dite	ex·u′ber·ance	eye′wash′
ex′tra·dit′ed	ex·u′ber·ant	eye′wit′ness

F

Fa′bi·an	fac′tion·al	faint′ed
fa′ble	fac′tious	faint′heart′ed
fa′bled	fac·ti′tious	faint′ly
fab′ric	fac′tor	faint′ness
fab′ri·cate	fac′to·ry	fair
fab′ri·cat′ed	fac·to′tum	fair′er
fab′ri·ca′tion	fac′tu·al	fair′est
fab′u·lous	fac′tu·al·ly	fair′ly
fa·çade′	fac′ul·ta′tive	fair′ness
face	fac′ul·ty	fair′way′
faced	fad′dist	fair′y
fac′et	fade	fair′y·land′
fa·ce′tious	fad′ed	faith
fa′cial	fad′ing·ly	faith′ful
fac′ile	Fahr′en·heit	faith′less
fa·cil′i·tate	fail	faith′less·ly
fa·cil′i·tat′ed	failed	fake
fa·cil′i·ty	fail′ing·ly	fak′er
fac′ings	fail′ings	fal′con
fac·sim′i·le	faille	fall
fact	fail′ure	fal·la′cious
fac′tion	faint	fal′la·cy

fall'en	fa·nat'i·cism	far'o
fal'li·bil'i·ty	fan'cied	far'ri·er
fal'li·ble	fan'ci·er	far'see'ing
fall'out	fan'ci·est	far'sight'ed
false	fan'ci·ful	far'ther
false'hood	fan'cy	far'thest
false'ly	fan'fare	far'thing
false'ness	fang	fas'ci·nate
fal·set'to	fanged	fas'ci·nat'ed
fal'si·fi·ca'tion	fan'light'	fas'ci·na'tion
fal'si·fi'er	fanned	fas'ci·nat'ing·ly
fal'si·fy	fan'tail'	fas'ci·na'tor
fal'si·ty	fan·ta'sia	fas'cism
fal'ter	fan·tas'tic	fas'cist
fal'tered	fan'ta·sy	fash'ion
fal'ter·ing·ly	far	fash'ion·a·ble
fame	far'ad	fash'ioned
famed	farce	fast
fa·mil'ial	far'cial	fas'ten
fa·mil'iar	far'ci·cal	fas'tened
fa·mil'i·ar'i·ty	far'cy	fas'ten·ings
fa·mil'iar·ize	fare	fast'er
fa·mil'iar·ly	fared	fast'est
fam'i·lies	fare'well'	fas·tid'i·ous
fam'i·ly	far'fetched'	fast'ness
fam'ine	fa·ri'na	fat
fam'ish	far'i·na'ceous	fa'tal
fa'mous	farm	fa'tal·ism
fa'mous·ly	farmed	fa'tal·ist
fan	farm'er	fa'tal·is'tic
fa·nat'ic	farm'house'	fa'tal'i·ty
fa·nat'i·cal	farm'yard'	fa'tal·ly

fate

fat'ed

fate'ful

fa'ther

fa'thered

fa'ther·hood

fa'ther-in-law'

fa'ther·land'

fa'ther·less

fa'ther·li·ness

fa'ther·ly

fath'om

fath'omed

fath'om·less

fa·tigue'

fat'ness

fat'ten

fat'tened

fat'ter

fat'test

fat'ty

fa·tu'i·ty

fat'u·ous

fau'cet

fault

fault'i·ly

fault'less

fault'less·ly

fault'y

fau'na

fa'vor

fa'vor·a·ble

fa'vored

fa'vor·ite

fa'vor·it·ism

fawn

fawned

fe'al·ty

fear

feared

fear'ful

fear'less

fear'less·ly

fear'some

fea'si·bil'i·ty

fea'si·ble

feast

feat

feath'er

feath'ered

feath'er·edge'

feath'er·weight'

feath'er·y

fea'ture

fea'tured

fe'brile

Feb'ru·ar'y

fe'cund

fe'cun·date

fe·cun'di·ty

fed'er·al

fed'er·al·ism

fed'er·al·ist

fed'er·al·i·za'tion

fed'er·al·ize

fed'er·al·ized

fed'er·ate

fed'er·at'ed

fed'er·a'tion

fed'er·a'tive

fe·do'ra

fee

fee'ble

fee'ble·ness

fee'blest

fee'bly

feed

feed'-back'

feed'ings

feel

feel'er

feel'ing·ly

feel'ings

feer

feered

feet

feign

feigned

feint

feld'spar'

fe·lic'i·tate

fe·lic'i·tat'ed

fe·lic'i·ta'tion

fe·lic'i·tous

fe·lic'i·tous·ly

fe·lic'i·ty

fe′line	fe·roc′i·ty	fet′id
fel′low	fer′ret	fe′tish
fel′low·ship	fer′ret·ed	fe′tish·ism
fel′on	fer′ric	fet′lock
fe·lo′ni·ous	fer′ro·chrome	fet′ter
fel′o·ny	fer′ro·type	fet′tered
felt	fer′rous	fet′tle
fe·luc′ca	fer′rule	feud
fe′male	fer′ry	feu′dal
fem′i·nine	fer′ry·boat′	feu′dal·ism
fem′i·nin′i·ty	fer′tile	feu′da·to′ry
fem′i·nism	fer·til′i·ty	fe′ver
fem′i·nist	fer′ti·li·za′tion	fe′ver·ish
fem′o·ral	fer′ti·lize	fe′ver·ish·ly
fe′mur	fer′ti·lized	few
fen	fer′ti·liz′er	few′er
fence	fer′ule	few′est
fenc′er	fer′vent	fez
fend	fer′vent·ly	fi·as′co
fend′ed	fer′vid	fi′at
fend′er	fer′vid·ly	fib
fe·nes′trat·ed	fer′vor	fi′ber
fen′es·tra′tion	fes′cue	fi′broid
Fe′ni·an	fes′tal	fib′u·la
fen′nel	fes′ter	fick′le
fe′ral	fes′tered	fic′tion
fer·ment′	fes′ti·val	fic′tion·al
fer′men·ta′tion	fes′tive	fic·ti′tious
fer·ment′ed	fes·tiv′i·ty	fid′dle
fern	fes·toon′	fid′dled
fe·ro′cious	fes·tooned′	fid′dler
fe·ro′cious·ly	fetch	fi·del′i·ty

fidg'et

fi·du'ci·ar'y

fief

field

field'ed

field'piece'

fiend

fiend'ish

fiend'ish·ly

fierce

fierce'ness

fierc'er

fierc'est

fi'er·y

fife

fig

fight

fig'ment

fig'u·ra'tion

fig'ur·a·tive

fig'ur·a·tive·ly

fig'ure

fig'ured

fig'ure·head'

fig'u·rine'

fil'a·ment

fil'a·ri'a·sis

fil'a·ture

fil'bert

filch

filched

file

filed

fil'i·al

fil'i·bus'ter

fil'i·gree

fil'ings

fill

filled

fill'er

fil'let

fill'ings

film

filmed

film'strip

fil'ter

fil'tered

filth

filth'i·er

filth'i·est

filth'i·ness

filth'y

fil'trate

fil·tra'tion

fin

fi'nal

fi'nal·ist

fi·nal'i·ty

fi'nal·ly

fi·nance'

fi·nan'cial

fi·nan'cial·ly

fin'an·cier'

finch

find

find'er

find'ings

fine

fined

fine'ly

fine'ness

fin'er

fin'er·y

fine'spun'

fi·nesse'

fin'est

fin'ger

fin'gered

fin'ger·print'

fin'i·al

fi'nis

fin'ish

fin'ished

fin'ish·er

fi'nite

fiord

fir

fire

fire'arm'

fire'boat'

fire'box'

fire'brand'

fire'break'

fire'brick'

fired

fire'fly'

fire′man

fire′place′

fire′proof′

fire′side′

fire′weed′

fire′wood′

fire′works′

fir′kin

firm

fir′ma·ment

firm′er

firm′est

firm′ly

firm′ness

first

first′ly

firth

fis′cal

fish

fish′er·man

fish′er·y

fish′hook′

fish′wife′

fish′y

fis′sile

fis′sion

fis′sure

fist

fist′ic

fist′i·cuffs

fis′tu·la

fit

fit′ful

fit′ful·ly

fit′ness

fit′ted

fit′ter

fit′ting·ly

fit′tings

fix

fix·a′tion

fix′a·tive

fixed

fix′er

fix′ings

fix′i·ty

fix′ture

fiz′zle

fiz′zled

flab′bi·er

flab′bi·est

flab′bi·ness

flab′by

flac′cid

flag

flag′el·lant

flag′el·late

flag′el·la′tion

flag′eo·let′

flag′eo·lets′

fla·gi′tious

flag′on

flag′pole′

fla′grance

fla′grant

fla′grant·ly

flag′ship′

flag′staff′

flag′stone′

flail

flailed

flair

flake

flak′i·ness

flak′y

flam′beau

flam·boy′ant

flame

flamed

fla·men′co

flame′proof′

flam′ing·ly

fla·min′go

flan

flange

flanged

flank

flanked

flan′nel

flan′nel·ette′

flap

flap′jack′

flare

flare′back′

flared

flash

flash'board'

flash'er

flash'i·ly

flash'i·ness

flash'ing·ly

flash'light'

flash'y

flask

flat

flat'-bed'

flat'boat'

flat'fish'

flat'-foot'ed

flat'head'

flat'i'ron

flat'ly

flat'ness

flat'ten

flat'tened

flat'ter

flat'tered

flat'ter·er

flat'ter·ing·ly

flat'ter·y

flat'test

flat'u·lence

flat'u·lent

flat'ware'

flat'wise'

flat'work'

flat'worm'

flaunt

flaunt'ed

flaunt'ing·ly

flau'tist

fla'vor

fla'vored

fla'vor·ings

fla'vors

flaw

flawed

flax

flax'en

flax'seed'

flay

flea

flea'bite'

fleck

fledge

fledg'ling

flee

fleece

fleeced

fleec'i·ness

fleec'y

fleet

fleet'ing·ly

Flem'ish

flesh

flesh'i·ness

flesh'ings

flesh'pot'

flesh'y

Fletch'er·ism

fleur'-de-lis'

flew

flex

flexed

flex'i·bil'i·ty

flex'i·ble

flex'ure

flick

flicked

flick'er

flick'er·ing·ly

fli'er

flight

flight'i·ness

flight'y

flim'si·er

flim'si·est

flim'si·ly

flim'si·ness

flim'sy

flinch

flinched

flinch'ing·ly

fling

flint

flint'i·ness

flint'lock'

flint'y

flip'pan·cy

flip'pant

flip'pant·ly

flip'per

flirt

flir·ta′tion

flir·ta′tious

flirt′ed

flit

flitch

fliv′ver

float

float′ed

float′er

floc′cu·lence

floc′cu·lent

flock

floe

flog

flogged

flog′gings

flood

flood′ed

flood′gate′

flood′light′

flood′wa′ter

floor

floor′walk′er

flop′pi·ness

flop′py

flo′ral

Flor′en·tine

flo′ret

flo′ri·cul′ture

flor′id

flo·rid′i·ty

flor′id·ly

flor′in

flo′rist

floss

floss′i·er

floss′i·est

floss′y

flo·ta′tion

flo·til′la

flot′sam

flounce

floun′der

floun′dered

floun′der·ing·ly

flour

flour′ish

flour′ish·ing·ly

flour′y

flout

flout′ed

flow

flowed

flow′er

flow′ered

flow′er·i·ness

flow′er·pot′

flow′er·y

flow′ing·ly

flown

fluc′tu·ate

fluc′tu·at′ed

fluc′tu·a′tion

flue

flu′en·cy

flu′ent

flu′ent·ly

fluff

fluff′i·ness

fluff′y

flu′id

flu′id·ly

flu′id·ex′tract

flu·id′i·ty

fluke

flume

flung

flunk

flunked

flunk′y

flu′o·res′cence

flu′o·res′cent

flu·or′ic

flu′o·ri·date

flu′o·ri·da′tion

flu′o·ride

flu′o·ri·nate

flu′o·rine

flu′o·ro·scope

flu′or·os′co·py

flur′ry

flush

flushed

flus′ter

flus′tered

flute	foe	fond'er
flut'ed	foe'man	fond'est
flut'ings	fog	fon'dle
flut'ist	fog'gi·er	fon'dled
flut'ter	fog'gi·est	fond'ly
flut'tered	fog'gy	fond'ness
flut'ter·ing·ly	fog'horn'	fon·due'
flut'ter·y	foi'ble	font
flux	foil	food
flux'ion	foiled	fool
fly	foist	fooled
fly'er	foist'ed	fool'har'di·ness
fly'leaf'	fold	fool'har'dy
fly'trap'	fold'ed	fool'ish
fly'wheel'	fold'er	fool'ish·ly
foal	fo'li·age	fool'ish·ness
foaled	fo'li·ate	fool'proof'
foam	fo'li·a'tion	fools'cap'
foamed	fo'li·o	foot
foam'i·er	folk	foot'age
foam'i·est	folk'way'	foot'ball'
foam'i·ness	fol'li·cle	foot'board'
foam'y	fol·lic'u·lar	foot'bridge'
fob	fol'low	foot'ed
fobbed	fol'lowed	foot'fall'
fo'cal	fol'low·er	foot'gear'
fo'cal·i·za'tion	fol'ly	foot'hill'
fo'cal·ize	fo·ment'	foot'hold'
fo'cal·ized	fo'men·ta'tion	foot'ings
fo'cus	fo·ment'ed	foot'less
fo'cused	fond	foot'lights'
fod'der	fon'dant	foot'-loose'

foot'man	for'ci·ble	fore'mast'
foot'mark'	ford	fore'most
foot'note'	ford'ed	fore'name'
foot'pace'	fore'arm'	fore'noon'
foot'pad'	fore·bear	fo·ren'sic
foot'path'	fore·bode'	fore'or·dain'
foot'print'	fore·bod'ing·ly	fore'or·dained'
foot'rest'	fore·bod'ings	fore'quar'ter
foot'sore'	fore·bore'	fore·run'ner
foot'step'	fore-cast'	fore·saw'
foot'stool'	fore'cas·tle	fore·see'
foot'wear'	fore·close'	fore·see'ing·ly
foot'work'	fore·closed'	fore·shad'ow
foot'worn'	fore·clo'sure	fore'shore'
foo'zle	fore'deck'	fore·short'en
foo'zled	fore·doom'	fore'sight'
fop'per·y	fore·doomed'	fore'sight'ed·ness
fop'pish	fore'fa'ther	for'est
for	fore'fin'ger	fore·stall'
for'age	fore'foot'	fore·stalled'
fo·ra'men	fore'front'	for'est·a'tion
for'as·much'	fore·gone'	for'est·ed
for'ay	fore'ground'	for'est·er
for·bear'	fore'hand'ed	for'est·ry
for·bear'ance	fore'head	fore·taste'
for·bid'	for'eign	fore·tell'
for·bid'den	for'eign·er	fore'thought'
for·bid'ding·ly	for'eign·ism	fore·told'
force	fore·knowl'edge	for·ev'er
force'ful	fore'leg'	fore·warn'
force'meat'	fore'lock'	fore·warned'
for'ceps	fore'man	fore'wom'an

fore'word'	for'mat	for'ti·tude·
for'feit	for·ma'tion	fort'night
for'feit·ed	form'a·tive	fort'night·ly
for'fei·ture	formed	For'tran
for·gath'er	form'er	for·tu'i·tous
for·gave'	for'mer·ly	for·tu'i·ty
forge	for'mic	for'tu·nate
forged	for'mi·da·ble	for'tune
for'ger	form'less	for'tune·tell'er
for'ger·y	for'mu·la	fo'rum
for·get'	for'mu·lar'y	for'ward
for·get'ful	for'mu·late	for'ward·ed
for·get'ful·ly	for'mu·lat'ed	for'ward·er
for·get'ful·ness	for'mu·la'tion	for'ward·ness
for·give'	for·sake'	fos'sil
for·giv'en	for·sak'en	fos'sil·if'er·ous
for·give'ness	for·sook'	fos'sil·i·za'tion
for·giv'ing·ly	for·sooth'	fos'sil·ize
for·go'	for·swear'	fos'sil·ized
for·got'	for·syth'i·a	fos'ter
for·got'ten	fort	fos'tered
fork	for'ta·lice	fought
forked	forte	foul
for·lorn'	for'te	fou·lard'
form	forth	foul'er
for'mal	forth'com'ing	foul'est
form·al'de·hyde	forth'right'	foul'ly
for'mal·ism	forth'right'ness	foul'ness
for·mal'i·ty	forth'with'	found
for'mal·i·za'tion	for'ti·fi·ca'tion	foun·da'tion
for'mal·ize	for'ti·fy	found'ed
for'mal·ly	for·tis'si·mo	found'er

found'ling

found'lings

found'ry

fount

foun'tain

foun'tain·head'

four'some

four'square'

fourth

fowl

fox

foxes

fox'glove'

fox'i·er

fox'i·est

fox'y

fra'cas

frac'tion

frac'tion·al

frac'tion·al·ly

frac'tion·ate

frac'tion·a'tion

frac'tious

frac'ture

frac'tured

frag'ile

frag'ile·ly

fra·gil'i·ty

frag'ment

frag'men·tar'i·ly

frag'men·tar'y

frag'men·ta'tion

frag'ment·ed

fra'grance

fra'grant

fra'grant·ly

frail

frail'er

frail'est

frail'ty

frame

framed

frame'work'

franc

fran'chise

Fran·cis'can

frank

frank'er

frank'est

frank'furt·er

frank'ly

frank'ness

fran'tic

frap'pé'

fra·ter'nal

fra·ter'nal·ly

fra·ter'ni·ty

frat'er·ni·za'tion

frat'er·nize

frat'er·nized

frat'ri·cid'al

frat'ri·cide

fraud

fraud'u·lent

fraught

fray

fraz'zle

fraz'zled

freak

freak'ish

freck'le

freck'led

free

free'board'

free'born'

free'dom

free'hand'

free'hold'

free'ly

free'man

free'ma'son

free'ma'son·ry

fre'er

fre'est

free'stone'

free'think'er

free'wheel'ing

freeze

freez'er

freight

freight'er

French

fren'zied

fren'zy

fre'quen·cy

fre'quent

fre'quent·ly	fright'en	frond
fres'co	fright'ened	frond'ed
fresh	fright'en·ing·ly	front
fresh'en	fright'ful	front'age
fresh'en·er	fright'ful·ly	fron'tal
fresh'er	fright'ful·ness	front'ed
fresh'est	frig'id	fron·tier'
fresh'ly	Frig'id·aire'	fron'tis·piece
fresh'man	fri·gid'i·ty	frost
fresh'ness	frig'id·ly	frost'bite'
fret	frill	frost'ed
fret'ful	frilled	frost'fish'
fret'ted	frill'i·ness	frost'i·er
fret'work'	frill'y	frost'i·est
fri'a·bil'i·ty	fringe	frost'i·ly
fri'a·ble	fringed	frost'i·ness
fri'ar	frip'per·y	frost'work'
fric'as·see'	frisk	frost'y
fric'tion	frit'ter	froth
fric'tion·al	frit'tered	frothed
Fri'day	fri·vol'i·ty	froth'y
fried	friv'o·lous	fro'ward
friend	friv'o·lous·ly	frown
friend'less	friz'zi·ness	frowned
friend'li·er	friz'zle	frown'ing·ly
friend'li·est	friz'zled	frowz'i·ly
friend'li·ness	frock	frowz'y
friend'ly	frog	froze
friend'ship	frog'fish'	fro'zen
frieze	frol'ic	fruc·tif'er·ous
frig'ate	frol'icked	fruc'ti·fy
fright	from	fru'gal

fru·gal'i·ty	full'er	fun'gus
fru'gal·ly	full'est	fu·nic'u·lar
fruit	full'ness	fun'nel
fruit'er·er	ful'ly	fun'ni·er
fruit'ful	ful'mi·nate	fun'ni·est
fruit'ful·ly	ful'mi·nat'ed	fun'ny
fruit'i·ness	ful'mi·na'tion	fur
fru·i'tion	ful'some	fur'be·low
fruit'less	fum'ble	fur'bish
fruit'less·ly	fum'bling	fu'ri·ous
fruit'less·ness	fume	fu'ri·ous·ly
fruit'worm'	fumed	furl
fruit'y	fu'mi·gate	furled
frump	fu'mi·gat'ed	fur'long
frus'trate	fu'mi·ga'tion	fur'lough
frus·tra'tion	fu'mi·ga'tor	fur'loughed
fry	fun	fur'nace
fry'er	func'tion	fur'nish
fuch'sia	func'tion·al	fur'nished
fud'dle	func'tion·al·ly	fur'nish·ings
fud'dled	func'tion·ar'y	fur'ni·ture
fudge	fund	fu'ror
fu'el	fun'da·men'tal	fur'ri·er
fu'eled	fun'da·men'tal·ly	fur'ri·est
fu·ga'cious	fund'ed	fur'row
fu'gi·tive	fu'ner·al	fur'rowed
fugue	fu·ne're·al	fur'ry
ful'crum	fu·ne're·al·ly	fur'ther
ful·fill'	fun'gi	fur'ther·ance
ful·filled'	fun'gi·ble	fur'ther·more'
ful·fill'ment	fun'gi·cide	fur'thest
full	fun'goid	fur'tive

fur'tive·ly	fu'si·bil'i·ty	fu'tile
fu'run·cle	fu'si·ble	fu'tile·ly
fu'ry	fu'sil·lade'	fu·til'i·ty
furze	fu'sion	fu'ture
fuse	fuss	fu'tur·is'tic
fused	fussed	fu·tu'ri·ty
fu'sel	fuss'i·er	fuzz
fu'se·lage	fuss'y	fuzz'i·ly
fus'es	fus'tian	fuzz'i·ness

G

gab′ar·dine′	gal′ax·y	gam′bit
ga′ble	gale	gam′ble
gad′fly′	ga·le′na	gam′bled
gad′o·lin′i·um	gall	gam′bler
ga·droon′	gal′lant	gam·boge′
gaff	gal′lant·ry	gam′bol
gag	galled	gam′brel
gage	gal′ler·y	game
gagged	gal′ley	game′ness
gag′gle	Gal′lic	gam′mon
gai′e·ty	gall′ing·ly	gam′ut
gai′ly	gal′li·um	gan′der
gain	gal′lon	gang
gained	gal′lop	ganged
gain′er	gal′lows	gan′gli·a
gain′ful	gall′stone′	gan′gli·on
gain′ful·ly	ga·lore′	gang′plank′
gain′say′	gal′va·nism	gan′grene
gait′ed	gal′va·ni·za′tion	gan′gre·nous
gai′ter	gal′va·nize	gang′ster
ga′la	gal′va·nized	gang′way′
gal′an·tine	gal′va·nom′e·ter	gan′try

118

gap	gashed	gay'ly
gaped	gas'house'	gay'ness
ga·rage'	gas'ket	gaze
garb	gas'o·line	ga·ze'bo
gar'bage	gasp	ga·zelle'
gar'ble	gas'tight'	ga·zette'
gar'den	gas·tral'gi·a	ga·zet'ted
gar'den·er	gas'tric	gaz'et·teer'
gar·de'ni·a	gas·tri'tis	gear
gar'gle	gas'tro·nom'ic	geared
gar'goyle	gas·tron'o·my	gear'shift'
gar'ish	gate	gei'sha
gar'land	gate'house'	gel'a·tin
gar'lic	gate'post'	ge·lat'i·nize
gar'ment	gate'way'	ge·lat'i·noid
gar'ner	gath'er	ge·lat'i·nous
gar'nered	gath'ered	gem
gar'net	gath'er·er	gen'der
gar'nish	gau'che·rie'	gen'e·a·log'i·cal
gar'nished	gaud'i·er	gen'e·al'o·gist
gar'nish·ee'	gaud'i·est	gen'e·al'o·gy
gar'nish·er	gaud'y	gen'er·al
gar'nish·ment	gauge	gen'er·al·is'si·mo
gar'ni·ture	gauged	gen'er·al·ist
gar'ret	gaunt'let	gen'er·al'i·ty
gar'ri·son	gauze	gen'er·al·i·za'tion
gar'ri·soned	gave	gen'er·al·ize
gar'ru·lous	gav'el	gen'er·al·ized
gar'ter	ga·votte'	gen'er·al·ly
gas	gawk'y	gen'er·al·ship'
gas'e·ous	gay	gen'er·ate
gash	gay'e·ty	gen'er·at'ed

gen'er·a'tion

gen'er·a'tive

gen'er·a'tor

ge·ner'ic

gen'er·os'i·ty

gen'er·ous

gen'er·ous·ly

gen'e·sis

ge·net'ics

ge·ni'al

ge·ni·al'i·ty

gen'ial·ly

gen'i·tive

gen'ius

gen·teel'

gen·teel'ly

gen'tian

gen'tile

gen·til'i·ty

gen'tle

gen'tle·man

gen'tle·men

gen'tle·ness

gen'tler

gen'tlest

gen'tly

gen'try

gen'u·flect

gen'u·flec'tion

gen'u·ine

gen'u·ine·ly

gen'u·ine·ness

ge'nus

ge·od'e·sy

ge'o·det'ic

ge·og'ra·pher

ge·og'ra·phy

ge'o·log'i·cal

ge·ol'o·gist

ge·ol'o·gy

ge'o·met'ric

ge'o·met'ri·cal

ge·om'e·try

ge·ra'ni·um

ge'rent

ger'i·a·tri'cian

ger'i·at'rics

germ

Ger'man

ger·mane'

ger'mi·cide

ger'mi·nal

ger'mi·nant

ger'mi·nate

ger'mi·nat'ed

ger'mi·na'tion

ger'mi·na'tive

ger'und

ge·run'di·al

ge·run'dive

ges'so

Ge·stalt'

ges·tic'u·late

ges·tic'u·la'tion

ges'ture

ges'tured

get

gew'gaw

gey'ser

ghast'li·ness

ghast'ly

gher'kin

ghet'to

ghost

ghost'li·ness

ghost'ly

ghoul

gi'ant

gi'ant·ism

gib'ber

gib'ber·ish

gib'bet

gib'bon

gibe

gib'let

gid'di·ly

gid'di·ness

gid'dy

gift

gift'ed

gig

gi·gan'tic

gi·gan'ti·cal·ly

gi·gan'tism

gig'gle

gig'gled

gild	gla'cier	gleam
gild'ed	glad	gleamed
gild'er	glad'den	glean
gill	glad'dened	glean'er
gill	glade	glean'ings
gilt	glad'i·a'tor	glee'ful
gim'bals	glad'i·a·to'ri·al	glib
gim'crack'	glad'i·o'lus	glib'ly
gim'let	glad'ly	glide
gin	glad'ness	glid'ed
gin'ger	Glad'stone	glid'er
gin'ger·ly	glam'or·ous	glim'mer
ging'ham	glam'our	glim'mered
gin'gi·vi'tis	glance	glim'mer·ings
gi·raffe'	gland	glimpse
gir'an·dole	glan'dered	glimpsed
gird	glan'ders	glint
gird'er	glan'du·lar	glint'ed
gir'dle	glare	gli·o'ma
gir'dled	glared	glis·san'do
gir'dler	glar'ing·ly	glis'ten
girl	glass	glis'tened
girl'hood	glass'ful	glis'ter
girl'ish	glass'house'	glit'ter
girt	glass'i·ly	glit'tered
girth	glass'i·ness	gloat
gist	glass'ware'	gloat'ed
give	glass'y	glob'al
giv'en	glau·co'ma	glob'al·ly
giv'er	glaze	globe
giz'zard	glazed	glob'u·lar
gla'cial	gla'zier	glob'ule

glock'en·spiel'

gloom

gloom'i·ly

gloom'i·ness

glo'ri·fi·ca'tion

glo'ri·fy

glo'ri·ous

glo'ry

gloss

glos'sal

glos'sa·ry

gloss'i·ly

gloss'i·ness

glos·si'tis

gloss'y

glot'tis

glove

glov'er

glow

glowed

glow'er

glow'ered

glow'ing·ly

glow'worm'

glu·ci'num

glu'cose

glue

glued

glue'y

glum

glut

glut'ted

glut'ton

glut'ton·ize

glut'ton·ous

glut'ton·y

glyc'er·in

gnarl

gnarled

gnash

gnashed

gnat

gnath'ic

gnaw

gnawed

gnaw'ings

gneiss

gnome

gno'mic

gno'mon

gnu

go

goad

goal

goat

goat'fish'

goat'herd'

goat'skin'

goat'weed'

gob'ble

gob'bled

gob'let

gob'lin

go'cart'

god

god'child'

god'dess

god'fa'ther

god'head

god'hood

god'less

god'like'

god'li·ness

god'ly

god'moth'er

god'par'ent

god'send'

god'son'

gog'gle

go'ings

goi'ter

gold

gold'en

gold'en·rod'

gold'finch'

gold'smith'

gold'weed'

golf

golf'er

gon'do·la

gon'do·lier'

gone

gong

goo'ber

good

good'-by'

good'ly

good'-na'tured

good'ness

goose

goose'ber'ry

goose'neck'

go'pher

Gor'di·an

gore

gored

gorge

gorged

gor'geous

gor'get

gor'gon

go·ril'la

gos'hawk'

gos'ling

gos'pel

gos'sa·mer

gos'sip

got

Goth'ic

got'ten

gouache

gouge

gouged

gou'lash

gourd

gour'mand

gour'met

gout

gov'ern

gov'ern·ance

gov'erned

gov'ern·ess

gov'ern·ment

gov'ern·men'tal

gov'er·nor

gown

grab

grabbed

grace

grace'ful

grace'less

gra'cious

gra'cious·ly

grack'le

gra·da'tion

grade

grad'ed

gra'di·ent

grad'u·al

grad'u·al·ly

grad'u·ate

grad'u·at'ed

grad'u·a'tion

graf·fi'ti

graft'ed

graft'er

grail

grain

grained

grain'field'

gram'mar

gram·mar'i·an

gram·mat'i·cal

gram·mat'i·cal·ly

gram'pus

gran'a·ry

grand

grand'child'

gran·dee'

gran'deur

grand'fa'ther

gran·dil'o·quence

gran·dil'o·quent

gran'di·ose

grand'ly

grand'moth'er

grand'ness

grand'par'ent

grand'sire'

grand'son'

grand'stand'

grange

gran'ite

gran'it·oid

gra·niv'o·rous

grant

grant'ed

gran'u·lar

gran'u·late

gran'u·lat'ed

gran'u·la'tion

gran'ule

grape	grav'en	greed
grape'shot'	grav'er	greed'i·er
graph	grav'est	greed'i·est
graph'ic	grave'stone'	greed'i·ly
graph'ics	grave'yard'	greed'i·ness
graph'ite	grav'i·tate	greed'y
grap'nel	grav'i·tat'ed	Greek
grap'ple	grav'i·ta'tion	green
grap'pled	grav'i·ta'tion·al	green'back'
grasp	grav'i·ty	green'er
grasp'ing·ly	gra·vure'	green'er·y
grass	gra'vy	green'est
grass'hop'per	gray	green'horn'
grass'plot'	gray'beard'	green'house'
grate	gray'ish	green'ish
grat'ed	gray'ness	green'ness
grate'ful	graze	green'room'
grat'er	grazed	green'stick'
grat'i·fi·ca'tion	gra'zier	green'sward'
grat'i·fy	grease	green'wood'
grat'i·fy'ing·ly	greased	greet
grat'i·nate	grease'wood'	greet'ed
grat'ings	greas'i·er	greet'ings
gra'tis	greas'i·est	gre·gar'i·ous
grat'i·tude	greas'i·ly	Gre·go'ri·an
gra·tu'i·tous	greas'i·ness	gre·nade'
gra·tu'i·ty	greas'y	gren'a·dier'
gra·va'men	great	gren'a·dine'
grave	great'er	grew
grave'dig'ger	great'est	grey'hound'
grav'el	great'ly	grid
grav'el·ly	great'ness	grid'dle

grid'i'ron	grit'ti·ness	grouch'y
grief	grit'ty	ground
griev'ance	griz'zle	ground'ed
grieve	griz'zled	ground'less
grieved	griz'zly	ground'lings
griev'ous	groan	ground'work'
griev'ous·ly	groaned	group
grif'fin	groan'ing·ly	group'ings
grill	gro'cer	grouse
grilled	gro'cer·y	grout
grim	grog	grout'ed
gri·mace'	grog'gy	grove
grime	groin	grov'el
grim'i·er	grom'met	grov'eled
grim'i·est	groom	grow
grim'i·ly	groomed	grow'er
grim'i·ness	groove	growl
grim'y	grooved	growled
grin	grope	grown
grind	grop'ing·ly	growth
grind'er	gros'beak'	grub
grind'ing·ly	gros'grain'	grubbed
grind'stone'	gross	grub'bi·ness
grinned	gross'er	grub'by
grip	gross'est	grudge
gripe	gross'ly	grudg'ing·ly
grip'per	gross'ness	gru'el
gris'ly	gro·tesque'	grue'some
grist	gro·tesque'ly	gruff
gris'tle	grot'to	gruff'er
grist'mill'	grouch	gruff'est
grit	grouch'i·ly	gruff'ly

grum'ble

grum'bled

grump'i·ly

grump'i·ness

grump'y

grunt

grunt'ed

guar'an·tee'

guar'an·tor

guar'an·ty

guard

guard'ed

guard'i·an

guard'i·an·ship'

guard'room'

guards'man

gua'va

gu·ber·na·to'ri·al

gudg'eon

guer'don

guer·ril'la

guess

guess'work'

guest

guid'ance

guide

guide'book'

guid'ed

guide'line'

gui'don

guild

guile

guile'ful

guile'less

guil'lo·tine

guilt

guilt'i·er

guilt'i·est

guilt'i·ly

guilt'i·ness

guilt'y

guin'ea

guise

guis'es

gui·tar'

gulch

gul'den

gulf

gull

gul'let

gul'li·bil'i·ty

gul'li·ble

gul'ly

gulp

gum

gum'bo

gum'boil'

gummed

gum·mo'sis

gum'my

gump'tion

gum'shoe'

gum'weed'

gum'wood'

gun

gun'boat'

gun'cot'ton

gun'fire'

gun'lock'

gun'man

gun'ner

gun'ner·y

gun'ny

gun'pa'per

gun'pow'der

gun'run'ning

gun'shot'

gun'smith'

gun'stock'

gun'wale

gur'gle

gu'ru

gush

gush'er

gush'y

gus'set

gust

gus'ta·to'ry

gust'i·ly

gus'to

gust'y

gut'ter

gut'ter·snipe'

gut'tur·al

gut'tur·al·ly

guy

guz′zle

guz′zled

guz′zler

gym·kha′na

gym·na′si·um

gym′nast

gym·nas′tic

gyn′e·col′o·gist

gyn′e·col′o·gy

gyp′sum

gyp′sy

gy′rate

gy′rat·ed

gy·ra′tion

gy′ra·to′ry

gyr′fal′con

gy′ro

gy′ro·com′pass

gy′ro·scope

gy′ro·stat

gyves

hab′er·dash′er

hab′er·dash′er·y

ha·bil′i·ment

hab′it

hab′it·a·ble

hab′i·tat

hab′i·ta′tion

hab′it·ed

ha·bit′u·al

ha·bit′u·al·ly

ha·bit′u·ate

ha·bit′u·at′ed

hab′i·tude

hack′le

hack′man

hack′ney

hack′neyed

hack saw

had

had′dock

haft

hag

hag′gard

hag′gle

hag′gled

hail

hailed

hail′stone′

hail′storm′

hair

hair′breadth′

hair′brush′

hair′cut′

hair′line′

hair′pin′

hair′split′ter

hair′spring′

hair′y

hake

ha·la′tion

hal′berd

hal′cy·on

hale

half

half′heart′ed

half′tone′

half′way′

half′-wit′ted

hal′i·but

hal′ide

hal′ite

hal′i·to′sis

hall

hall′mark′

hal′low

hal′lowed

Hal′low·een′

hal·lu′ci·na′tion

hal·lu′ci·na·to′ry

hal·lu′ci·no′sis

ha′lo

hal′o·gen

halt

halt′ed

hal′ter

halt′ing·ly

128

halves		hand'some		hard	
hal'yard		hand'spring'		hard'en	
ham		hand'work'		hard'ened	
ham'let		hand'writ'ing		hard'en·er	
ham'mer		hand'y		hard'er	
ham'mered		hang		hard'est	
ham'mer·less		hang'ar		hard'hat	
ham'mock		hanged		hard'head'ed	
ham'per		hang'er		har'di·hood	
ham'pered		hang'ings		har'di·ness	
ham'ster		hang'man		hard'ly	
ham'string'		han'ker		hard'ness	
ham'strung'		han'kered		hard'pan'	
hand		han'som		hard'ship	
hand'bag'		hap'haz'ard		hard'ware'	
hand'ball'		hap'less		har'dy	
hand'bill'		hap'loid		hare	
hand'book'		hap'pen		hare'brained'	
hand'cuff'		hap'pened		hare'lip'	
hand'ed		hap'pen·ings		ha'rem	
hand'ful		hap'pi·er		hark	
hand'i·cap		hap'pi·est		har'le·quin	
hand'i·capped		hap'pi·ly		har'le·quin·ade'	
hand'i·craft		hap'pi·ness		harm	
hand'i·er		hap'py		harmed	
hand'i·est		ha·rangue'		harm'ful	
hand'i·ly		ha·rangued'		harm'ful·ly	
hand'i·ness		har'ass		harm'ful·ness	
hand'ker·chief		har'ass·ment		harm'less	
han'dle		har'bin·ger		harm'less·ly	
han'dled		har'bor		harm'less·ness	
hand'rail		har'bored		har·mon'ic	

har·mon'i·ca

har·mo'ni·ous

har·mo'ni·ous·ly

har·mo'ni·ous·ness

har·mo'ni·um

har'mo·ni·za'tion

har'mo·nize

har'mo·nized

har'mo·ny

har'ness

har'nessed

harp

harp'er

harp'ist

har·poon'

har·pooned'

harp'si·chord

har'ri·er

har'row

harsh

harsh'er

harsh'est

harsh'ly

harsh'ness

har'te·beest'

har'vest

har'vest·ed

har'vest·er

has

hash

hashed

hash'ish

hasp

has'sock

haste

has'ten

has'tened

hast'i·er

hast'i·est

hast'i·ly

hast'i·ness

hast'y

hat

hat'band'

hatch

hatched

hatch'er·y

hatch'et

hatch'ment

hatch'way'

hate

hat'ed

hate'ful

hate'ful·ly

hate'ful·ness

hat'pin'

ha'tred

hat'ter

haugh'ti·er

haugh'ti·est

haugh'ti·ly

haugh'ty

haul

haul'age

hauled

haunch

haunt

haunt'ed

haunt'ing·ly

haut'boy

hau·teur'

have

ha'ven

hav'er·sack

hav'oc

Ha·wai'ian

hawk

hawk'er

hawk'weed'

hawse

haw'ser

haw'thorn

hay

hay'cock'

hay'fork'

hay'loft'

hay'mow'

hay'rack'

hay'seed'

hay'stack'

haz'ard

haz'ard·ed

haz'ard·ous

haz'ard·ous·ly

haze

ha'zel

ha'zel·nut'	head'stone'	heart'en
ha'zi·er	head'strong	heart'ened
ha'zi·est	head'wa'ter	heart'felt'
ha'zi·ly	head'way'	hearth
ha'zi·ness	head'work'	hearth'stone'
ha'zy	head'y	heart'i·er
he	heal	heart'i·est
head	healed	heart'i·ly
head'ache'	heal'er	heart'less
head'band'	health	heart'sick'
head'board'	health'ful	heart'sore'
head'cheese'	health'ful·ness	heart'string'
head'dress'	health'i·er	heart'wood'
head'ed	health'i·est	heart'y
head'er	health'i·ly	heat
head'first'	health'y	heat'ed
head'fore'most	heap	heat'er
head'gear'	heaped	heath
head'i·ly	hear	hea'then
head'ings	heard	hea'then·ish
head'land'	hear'er	hea'then·ish·ly
head'less	hear'ings	heath'er
head'light'	hark'en	heat'stroke'
head'line'	hark'ened	heave
head'lock'	hear'say'	heav'en
head'long	hearse	heav'en·ly
head'mas'ter	heart	heav'en·ward
head'phone'	heart'ache'	heav'i·er
head'piece'	heart'beat'	heav'i·est
head'quar'ters	heart'break'	heav'i·ly
heads'man	heart'bro'ken	heav'i·ness
head'spring'	heart'burn'	heav'y

He·bra'ic	hel'i·coid	hence
He'brew	hel'i·cop'ter	hence'forth'
hec'a·tomb	he'li·o·trope	hence'for'ward
heck'le	he'li·um	hench'man
heck'led	he'lix	hen'e·quen
heck'ler	helm	hen'na
hec'tic	hel'met	he·pat'ic
hec'to·graph	hel'met·ed	he·pat'i·ca
hedge	helms'man	hep'a·ti'tis
hedged	help	hep'ta·gon
hedge'hog'	help'er	hep·tam'e·ter
hedge'row'	help'ful	her
he'don·ism	help'ful·ly	her'ald
heed	help'ful·ness	her'ald·ed
heed'ed	help'ing	he·ral'dic
heed'ful·ly	help'less	her'ald·ry
heed'ful·ness	help'less·ly	herb
heed'less	help'less·ness	her·ba'ceous
heed'less·ness	help'mate'	herb'age
heel	hem	herb'al
heft	hem'a·tite	her·bar'i·um
he·gem'o·ny	hem'i·cy'cle	her'bi·cide
he·gi'ra	hem'i·ple'gi·a	her·biv'o·rous
heif'er	hem'i·sphere	Her·cu'le·an
height	hem'i·spher'i·cal	herd
height'en	hem'lock	herd'ed
height'ened	hemmed	here
hei'nous	hem'or·rhage	here'a·bouts'
heir	hemp	here·aft'er
heir'ess	hemp'en	here·by'
heir'loom'	hem'stitch'	he·red'i·ta·bil'i·ty
hel'i·cal	hem'stitched'	he·red'i·ta·ble

he·red′i·ta·bly	her′ring	hid
her′e·dit′a·ment	her′ring·bone′	hid′den
he·red′i·tar′y	hers	hide
he·red′i·ty	her·self′	hide′bound′
here′in·aft′er	hes′i·tance	hid′e·ous
here·in′be·fore′	hes′i·tan·cy	hid′e·ous·ly
here·on′	hes′i·tant	hid′e·ous·ness
her′e·sy	hes′i·tate	hi′er·arch′y
her′e·tic	hes′i·tat′ed	hi′er·at′ic
he·ret′i·cal	hes′i·tat′ing·ly	hi′er·o·glyph′ic
here·to′	hes′i·ta′tion	high
here′to·fore′	hes′i·ta′tive·ly	high′born′
here′un·to′	het′er·o·dox	high′boy′
here′up·on′	het′er·o·ge·ne′i·ty	high′er
here·with′	het′er·o·ge′ne·ous	high′est
her′it·a·bil′i·ty	het′er·o·nym′	high′land
her′it·a·ble	heu·ris′tic	high′land·er
her′it·a·bly	hew	high′ly
her′it·age	hewed	high′ness
her·met′ic	hew′er	high′road′
her·met′i·cal·ly	hewn	high′way′
her′mit	hex′a·gon	high′way′man
her′mit·age	hex·ag′o·nal	hi′jack′
her′ni·a	hex·am′e·ter	hi′jack′er
he′ro	hex·an′gu·lar	hik′er
he·ro′ic	hex′a·pod	hi·lar′i·ous
he·ro′i·cal	hey′day′	hi·lar′i·ty
her′o·ine	hi·a′tus	hill
her′o·ism	hi′ber·nate	hill′i·er
her′on	hi′ber·na′tion	hill′i·est
her′pes	hi·bis′cus	hill′i·ness
her′pe·tol′o·gy	hick′o·ry	hill′ock

hill'side'	hith'er	hoist'way'
hilt	hith'er·to'	ho'kum
him	hive	hold
him·self'	hoar	hold'er
hind	hoard	hold'ings
hin'der	hoard'ed	hole
hin'dered	hoard'er	hol'i·day
hin'drance	hoar'frost'	ho'li·ly
hinge	hoarse	ho'li·ness
hinged	hoars'er	Hol'land
hint	hoars'est	hol'low
hint'ed	hoax	hol'lowed
hin'ter·land'	hob'ble	hol'ly
hip'po·drome	hob'bled	hol'ly·hock
hip'po·pot'a·mus	hob'by	hol'o·caust
hire	hob'gob'lin	hol'o·graph
hired	hob'nail'	hol'o·graph'ic
hire'ling	hob'nailed'	hol'ster
hir'sute	hob'nob'	ho'ly
his	ho'bo	ho'ly·stone'
His·pan'ic	hock	hom'age
his·tol'o·gist	hock'ey	home
his·tol'o·gy	hod	home'land'
his·to'ri·an	hoe	home'like'
his·tor'ic	hog	home'li·ness
his·tor'i·cal	hog'back'	home'ly
his'to·ry	hog'fish'	ho'me·o·path'ic
his'tri·on'ic	hog'gish	ho'me·op'a·thy
hit	hogs'head	home'sick'ness
hitch	hog'weed'	home'site'
hitched	hoist	home'spun'
hitch'hike'	hoist'ed	home'stead

home'ward	hon'or·ar'y	hor'net
home'work'	hon'ored	horn'pipe'
hom'i·cid'al	hood	ho·rol'o·gy
hom'i·cide	hood'ed	hor'o·scope
hom'i·let'ics	hood'lum	hor·ren'dous
hom'i·lies	hoo'doo	hor'ri·ble
hom'i·ly	hood'wink	hor'rid
hom'i·ny	hoof	hor'ri·fi·ca'tion
ho'mo·ge·ne'i·ty	hook	hor'ri·fied
ho'mo·ge'ne·ous	hooked	hor'ri·fy
ho'mo·ge'ne·ous·ly	hook'er	hor'ror
ho·mog'e·nize	hook'worm'	horse
ho·mol'o·gous	hoop	horse'back'
hom'o·nym	Hoo'sier	horse chest'nut
ho·mun'cu·lus	hope	horse'hair'
hone	hope'ful	horse'man
honed	hope'ful·ly	horse'man·ship
hon'est	hope'ful·ness	horse'pow'er
hon'est·ly	hope'less	horse'shoe'
hon'es·ty	hope'less·ly	horse'weed'
hon'ey	hope'less·ness	horse'whip'
hon'ey·bee'	hop'lite	horse'wom'an
hon'ey·comb'	hop'per	hor'ta·tive
hon'ey·dew'	hop'scotch'	hor'ta·to'ry
hon'eyed	horde	hor'ti·cul'ture
hon'ey·moon'	hore'hound'	hose
hon'ey·suck'le	ho·ri'zon	ho'sier
honk	hor'i·zon'tal	ho'sier·y
hon'or	hor'mone	hos'pice
hon'or·a·ble	horn	hos'pi·ta·ble
hon'or·a·bly	horn'book'	hos'pi·tal
hon'o·rar'i·um	horned	hos'pi·tal'i·ty

hos'pi·tal·i·za'tion	house'moth'er	hum
hos'pi·tal·ize	house'room'	hu'man
host	house'wares'	hu·mane'
hos'tage	house'warm'ing	hu·mane'ly
hos'tel	house'wife'	hu·mane'ness
host'ess	house'work'	hu'man·ism
hos'tile	hous'ing	hu'man·ist
hos'tile·ly	hov'er	hu'man·is'tic
hos·til'i·ty	hov'ered	hu·man'i·tar'i·an
hot	hov'er·ing·ly	hu·man'i·tar'i·an·ism
hot'bed'	how	hu·man'i·ty
hot'box'	how·ev'er	hu'man·i·za'tion
ho·tel'	how'itz·er	hu'man·ize
hot'head'ed	howl	hu'man·ized
hot'house'	how'so·ev'er	hu'man·kind'
hot'ly	hoy'den	hu'man·ly
hot'ness	hub	hum'ble
hot'ter	hub'bub	hum'bled
hot'test	huck'le·ber'ry	hum'ble·ness
hound	huck'ster	hum'bler
hound'ed	hud'dle	hum'blest
hour	hud'dled	hum'bly
hour'ly	hue	hum'bug'
house	huff	hum'drum'
housed	hug	hu'mer·us
house'fly'	huge	hu'mid
house'fur'nish·ings	hug'er	hu·mid'i·fi·ca'tion
house'hold	hug'est	hu·mid'i·fied
house'hold'er	Hu'gue·not	hu·mid'i·fi'er
house'keep'er	hulk	hu·mid'i·fy
house'maid'	hull	hu·mid'i·ty
house'man	hulled	hu'mi·dor

hu·mil'i·ate	hurl	hy'drant
hu·mil'i·at'ed	hurled	hy'drate
hu·mil'i·a'tion	hur'ri·cane	hy·drau'lic
hu·mil'i·ty	hur'ry	hy'dro·car'bon
hummed	hurt	hy'dro·chlo'ric
hum'ming·bird'	hurt'ful	hy'dro·cy·an'ic
hum'mock	hurt'ful·ly	hy'dro·e·lec'tric
hu'mor	hurt'ful·ness	hy'dro·flu·or'ic
hu'mored	hur'tle	hy'dro·foil'
hu'mor·esque'	hur'tled	hy'dro·gen
hu'mor·ist	hus'band	hy·drom'e·ter
hu'mor·ous	hus'band·ry	hy'dro·pho'bi·a
hu'mor·ous·ness	hush	hy'dro·plane
hump	hushed	hy'dro·stat'ics
hu'mus	husk	hy·drox'ide
hunch	husk'i·ly	hy·e'na
hun'dred	husk'i·ness	hy'giene
hun'dred·fold'	hus'ky	hy'gi·en'ic
hun'dredth	hus'sy	hy'gi·en'i·cal·ly
Hun·gar'i·an	hus'tings	hy'gi·en·ist
hun'ger	hus'tle	hy·grom'e·ter
hun'gered	hus'tled	hy'gro·scop'ic
hun'gri·er	hus'tler	hymn
hun'gri·est	hut	hym'nal
hun'gry	hutch	hymn'book'
hunk	hy'a·cinth	hy·per'bo·la
hunt	hy'a·loid	hy·per'bo·le
hunt'ed	hy'brid	hy·per·bol'ic
hunt'er	hy'brid·ism	hy'per·crit'i·cal
hunts'man	hy'brid·i·za'tion	hy'per·e'mi·a
hur'dle	hy'brid·ize	hy'per·o'pi·a
hur'dled	hy·dran'ge·a	hy'per·sen'si·tive

hy'per·thy'roid	hyp'no·tized	hy·poth'e·ca'tion
hy·per'tro·phy	hy'po·chon'dri·a	hy·poth'e·ses
hy'phen	hy'po·chon'dri·ac	hy·poth'e·sis
hy'phen·ate	hy·poc'ri·sy	hy·poth'e·size
hy'phen·at'ed	hyp'o·crite	hy'po·thet'i·cal
hy'phen·a'tion	hyp'o·crit'i·cal	hy'po·thet'i·cal·ly
hyp·no'sis	hy'po·der'mic	hys·te'ri·a
hyp·not'ic	hy'po·der'mi·cal·ly	hys·ter'i·cal
hyp'no·tist	hy·pot'e·nuse	hys·ter'ics
hyp'no·tize	hy·poth'e·cate	hys'ter·oid

I

i·am′bic	i·de′al	id′i·ot′ic
I·be′ri·an	i·de′al·ism	id′i·ot′i·cal·ly
i′bex	i·de′al·ist	i′dle
i′bis	i·de′al·is′tic	i′dled
ice	i·de′al·i·za′tion	i′dle·ness
ice′berg′	i·de′al·ize	i′dler
ice′boat′	i·de′al·ly	i′dlest
ice′box′	i′de·a′tion	i′dly
ice′break′er	i′de·a′tion·al	i′dol
ice′house′	i·den′ti·cal	i·dol′a·ter
ice′man′	i·den′ti·fi·ca′tion	i·dol′a·trize
ich·neu′mon	i·den′ti·fy	i·dol′a·trous
i′chor	i·den′ti·ty	i·dol′a·try
ich·thy·ol′o·gy	id′e·o·log′i·cal	i′dol·ize
i′ci·cle	id′e·ol′o·gy	i′dyl
i′ci·er	id′i·o·cy	i·dyl′lic
i′ci·est	id′i·om	if
i′ci·ly	id′i·o·mat′ic	ig′loo
i′ci·ness	id′i·o·mat′i·cal·ly	ig′ne·ous
i′con	id′i·o·syn′cra·sy	ig·nite′
i′cy	id′i·o·syn·crat′ic	ig·nit′ed
i·de′a	id′i·ot	ig·ni′tion

ig·no′ble

ig′no·min′i·ous

ig′no·min·y

ig′no·ra′mus

ig′no·rance

ig′no·rant

ig′no·rant·ly

ig·nore′

ig·nored′

i·gua′na

i′lex

Il′i·ad

ilk

ill

il·le′gal

il′le·gal′i·ty

il·leg′i·ble

il·leg′i·bly

il′le·git′i·ma·cy

il′le·git′i·mate

il·lib′er·al

il·lic′it

il·lim′it·a·ble

il·lit′er·a·cy

il·lit′er·ate

ill′ness

il·log′i·cal

il·lu′mi·nant

il·lu′mi·nate

il·lu′mi·nat′ed

il·lu′mi·na′tion

il·lu′mi·na′tor

il·lu′mine

il·lu′mined

il·lu′sion

il·lu′sive

il·lu′so·ry

il′lus·trate

il′lus·trat′ed

il′lus·tra′tion

il·lus′tra·tive

il′lus·tra′tor

il·lus′tri·ous

im′age

im′age·ry

im·ag′i·na·ble

im·ag′i·nar′y

im·ag′i·na′tion

im·ag′i·na′tive

im·ag′ine

im·ag′ined

im·ag′in·ings

i·ma′go

i·mam′

im′be·cile

im′be·cil′i·ty

im·bibe′

im·bibed′

im·bro′glio

im·bue′

im·bued′

im′i·ta·ble

im′i·tate

im′i·tat′ed

im′i·ta′tion

im′i·ta′tive

im′i·ta′tor

im·mac′u·late

im·mac′u·late·ly

im·ma′nent

im·ma·te′ri·al

im·ma·ture′

im·ma·ture′ly

im·ma·tu′ri·ty

im·meas′ur·a·ble

im·me′di·a·cy

im·me′di·ate

im·me′di·ate·ly

im·me′di·ate·ness

im′me·mo′ri·al

im·mense′

im·mense′ly

im·men′si·ty

im·merse′

im·mersed′

im·mer′sion

im′mi·grant

im′mi·grate

im′mi·grat′ed

im′mi·gra′tion

im′mi·nence

im′mi·nent

im·mo′bile

im·mo′bil′i·ty

im·mo′bi·li·za′tion

im·mo′bi·lize

im·mod'er·ate

im·mod'est

im'mo·late

im'mo·la'tion

im·mor'al

im·mor'al·i·ty

im·mor'al·ly

im·mor'tal

im'mor·tal'i·ty

im·mor'tal·ize

im·mor'tal·ly

im'mor·telle'

im·mov'a·bil'i·ty

im·mov'a·ble

im·mov'a·ble·ness

im·mov'a·bly

im·mune'

im·mu'ni·ty

im'mu·ni·za'tion

im'mu·nize

im'mu·nol'o·gy

im·mure'

im'mu·ta·bil'i·ty

im·mu'ta·ble

imp

im'pact

im·pac'tion

im·pair'

im·paired'

im·pair'ment

im·pa'la

im·pale'

im·paled'

im·pale'ment

im·pal'pa·bil'i·ty

im·pal'pa·ble

im·pan'el

im·pan'eled

im·part'

im·part'ed

im·par'tial

im'par·ti·al'i·ty

im·par'tial·ly

im·pass'a·bil'i·ty

im·pass'a·ble

im·passe'

im·pas'sion

im·pas'sioned

im·pas'sive

im·pas'sive·ly

im'pas·siv'i·ty

im·pa'tience

im·pa'tient

im·peach'

im·peach'ment

im·pec'ca·bil'i·ty

im·pec'ca·ble

im'pe·cu'ni·os'i·ty

im'pe·cu'ni·ous

im·ped'ance

im·pede'

im·ped'ed

im·ped'i·ment

im·ped'i·men'ta

im·pel'

im·pelled'

im·pend'

im·pend'ed

im·pen'e·tra·bil'i·ty

im·pen'e·tra·ble

im·pen'i·tent

im·per'a·tive

im'per·cep'ti·ble

im'per·cep'tive

im·per'fect

im'per·fec'tion

im·per'fo·rate

im·pe'ri·al

im·pe'ri·al·ism

im·pe'ri·al·ist

im·pe'ri·al·is'tic

im·pe'ri·ous

im·per'ish·a·ble

im·per'ma·nent

im·per'me·a·ble

im'per·scrip'ti·ble

im·per'son·al

im·per'son·ate

im·per'son·at'ed

im·per'son·a'tion

im·per'ti·nence

im·per'ti·nent

im'per·turb'a·ble

im·per'vi·ous

im'pe·ti'go

im·pet'u·os'i·ty

im·pet′u·ous
im·pet′u·ous·ly
im·pet′u·ous·ness
im′pe·tus
im·pi′e·ty
im·pinge′
im·pinged′
im·pinge′ment
im′pi·ous
im′pi·ous·ly
imp′ish
im·pla′ca·bil′i·ty
im·pla′ca·ble
im·plant′
im·plant′ed
im·plau′si·bil′i·ty
im·plau′si·ble
im′ple·ment
im′ple·ment′ed
im′pli·cate
im′pli·cat′ed
im′pli·ca′tion
im·plic′it
im·plic′it·ly
im·plied′
im′plo·ra′tion
im·plore′
im·plored′
im·plor′ing·ly
im·plo′sion
im·ply′
im′po·lite′

im′po·lite′ly
im′po·lite′ness
im·pol′i·tic
im·pon′der·a·ble
im·port′
im·por′tance
im·por′tant
im′por·ta′tion
im′port′er
im·por′tu·nate
im′por·tune′
im′por·tu′ni·ty
im·pose′
im·posed′
im·pos′ing·ly
im′po·si′tion
im·pos′si·bil′i·ty
im·pos′si·ble
im′post
im·pos′tor
im·pos′ture
im′po·tence
im′po·tent
im·pound′
im·pov′er·ish
im·pov′er·ish·ment
im·pow′er
im·prac′ti·ca·ble
im·prac′ti·cal′i·ty
im′pre·cate
im′pre·ca′tion
im′pre·ca·to′ry

im·preg′na·bil′i·ty
im·preg′na·ble
im·preg′nate
im′preg·na′tion
im′pre·sa′ri·o
im′pre·scrip′ti·ble
im·press′
im·pressed′
im·pres′sion
im·pres′sion·a·ble
im·pres′sion·ism
im·pres′sive
im′pri·ma′tur
im·print′
im·print′ed
im·pris′on
im·pris′oned
im·pris′on·ment
im·prob·a·bil′i·ty
im·prob′a·ble
im·prob′a·bly
im·promp′tu
im·prop′er
im′pro·pri′e·ty
im·prov′a·ble
im·prove′
im·prove′ment
im′prov′i·dence
im·prov′i·dent
im′pro·vi·sa′tion
im′pro·vise
im′pro·vised

im·pru'dence

im·pru'dent

im·pru'dent·ly

im'pu·dence

im'pu·dent

im·pugn'

im·pugn'a·ble

im·pugned'

im·pugn'ment

im'pulse

im·pul'sion

im·pul'sive

im·pu'ni·ty

im·pure'

im·pure'ly

im·pu'ri·ty

im·put'a·ble

im'pu·ta'tion

im·put'a·tive

im·pute'

im·put'ed

in·a·bil'i·ty

in'ac·ces'si·bil'i·ty

in'ac·ces'si·ble

in·ac'cu·ra·cy

in·ac'cu·rate

in·ac'tion

in·ac'ti·vate

in·ac'tive

in'ac·tiv'i·ty

in·ad'e·qua·cy

in·ad'e·quate

in'ad·mis'si·bil'i·ty

in'ad·mis'si·ble

in'ad·vert'ence

in'ad·vert'ent

in'ad·vis'a·bil'i·ty

in'ad·vis'a·ble

in·al'ien·a·ble

in·am'o·ra'ta

in·ane'

in·an'i·mate

in'a·ni'tion

in·an'i·ty

in·ap'pli·ca·ble

in·ap'po·site

in'ap·pro'pri·ate

in·apt'

in·apt'i·tude

in'ar·tic'u·late

in'ar·tis'tic

in'as·much'

in'at·ten'tion

in'at·ten'tive

in·au'di·bil'i·ty

in·au'di·ble

in·au'di·bly

in·au'gu·ral

in·au'gu·rate

in·au'gu·rat'ed

in·au'gu·ra'tion

in'aus·pi'cious

in'board'

in'born'

in'bred'

in·cal'cu·la·ble

in'can·desce'

in'can·des'cence

in'can·des'cent

in'can·ta'tion

in'ca·pa·bil'i·ty

in·ca'pa·ble

in'ca·pac'i·tate

in'ca·pac'i·tat'ed

in'ca·pac'i·ta'tion

in'ca·pac'i·ty

in·car'cer·ate

in·car'cer·at'ed

in·car'cer·a'tion

in·car'nate

in'car·na'tion

in·cen'di·a·rism

in·cen'di·ar'y

in·cense'

in·censed'

in·cen'tive

in·cep'tion

in·cer'ti·tude

in·ces'sant

in·ces'sant·ly

in'cest

in·ces'tu·ous

inch

in·cho'ate

inch'worm'

in'ci·dence

in'ci·dent

in'ci·den'tal

in'ci·den'tal·ly

in·cin'er·ate

in·cin'er·at'ed

in·cin'er·a'tion

in·cin'er·a'tor

in·cip'i·ent

in·cise'

in·cised'

in·ci'sion

in·ci'sive

in·ci'sive·ly

in·ci'sive·ness

in·ci'sor

in'ci·ta'tion

in·cite'

in·cite'ment

in'ci·vil'i·ty

in·clem'en·cy

in·clem'ent

in'cli·na'tion

in·cline'

in·clined'

in·close'

in·closed'

in·clo'sure

in·clude'

in·clud'ed

in·clu'sive

in·clu'sive·ly

in·clu'sive·ness

in·cog'ni·to

in'co·her'ence

in'co·her'ent

in'com·bus'ti·bil'i·ty

in'com·bus'ti·ble

in'come

in'com·men'su·ra·ble

in'com·men'su·rate

in'com·mode'

in'com·mu'ni·ca'do

in·com'pa·ra·ble

in·com'pa·ra·bly

in'com·pat'i·bil'i·ty

in'com·pat'i·ble

in·com'pe·tence

in·com'pe·tent

in·com'pe·tent·ly

in'com·plete'

in'com·pre·hen'si·bil'i·ty

in'com·pre·hen'si·ble

in'com·press'i·bil'i·ty

in'com·press'i·ble

in'con·ceiv'a·bil'i·ty

in'con·ceiv'a·ble

in'con·clu'sive

in'con·clu'sive·ness

in'con·gru'i·ty

in·con'gru·ous

in·con'se·quen'tial

in'con·sid'er·a·ble

in'con·sid'er·ate

in'con·sid'er·ate·ly

in'con·sist'en·cy

in'con·sist'ent

in'con·sol'a·ble

in'con·spic'u·ous

in'con·spic'u·ous·ly

in·con'stan·cy

in·con'stant

in'con·test'a·ble

in·con'ti·nence

in·con'ti·nent

in'con·tro·vert'i·ble

in'con·ven'ience

in'con·ven'ienced

in'con·ven'ient

in'con·ven'ient·ly

in'con·ver'si·bil'i·ty

in'con·vert'i·bil'i·ty

in'con·vert'i·ble

in·cor'po·rate

in·cor'po·rat'ed

in·cor'po·ra'tion

in·cor'po·ra'tor

in'cor·rect'

in·cor'ri·gi·bil'i·ty

in·cor'ri·gi·ble

in'cor·rupt'i·bil'i·ty

in'cor·rupt'i·ble

in·crease'

in·creased'

in·creas'ing·ly

in·cred'i·bil'i·ty

in·cred'i·ble

in·cre·du′li·ty

in·cred′u·lous

in′cre·ment

in′cre·men′tal

in·cre′tion

in·crim′i·nate

in·crim′i·nat′ed

in·crim′i·na′tion

in·crim′i·na·to′ry

in′crus·ta′tion

in′cu·bate

in′cu·bat′ed

in′cu·ba′tion

in′cu·ba·tor

in′cu·bus

in·cul′cate

in·cul′cat·ed

in·cul·ca′tion

in·cul′pate

in·cul′pat·ed

in·cul′pa′tion

in·cul′pa·to′ry

in·cum′ben·cy

in·cum′bent

in′cu·nab′u·la

in·cur′

in·cur′a·ble

in·cur′a·bly

in·curred′

in·cur′sion

in·debt′ed

in·debt′ed·ness

in·de′cen·cy

in·de′cent

in·de′cent·ly

in′de·ci′sion

in′de·ci′sive

in′de·ci′sive·ly

in′de·ci′sive·ness

in·dec′o·rous

in′de·co′rum

in·deed′

in′de·fat′i·ga·bil′i·ty

in′de·fat′i·ga·ble

in′de·fea′si·ble

in′de·fen′si·ble

in′de·fin′a·ble

in·def′i·nite

in·def′i·nite·ly

in·def′i·nite·ness

in·del′i·bil′i·ty

in·del′i·ble

in·del′i·bly

in·del′i·ca·cy

in·del′i·cate

in·del′i·cate·ly

in·dem′ni·fi·ca′tion

in·dem′ni·fied

in·dem′ni·fy

in·dem′ni·ty

in·dent′

in′den·ta′tion

in·dent′ed

in·den′tion

in·den′ture

in·den′tured

in′de·pend′ence

in′de·pend′ent

in′de·scrib′a·ble

in′de·struct′i·ble

in′de·ter′mi·na·ble

in′de·ter′mi·nate

in′dex

in′dexed

in′dex·er

in′dex·es

In′di·an

in′di·cate

in′di·cat′ed

in′di·ca′tion

in·dic′a·tive

in′di·ca′tor

in′di·ca·to′ry

in′di·ces

in·di′ci·a

in·dict′

in·dict′a·ble

in·dict′ed

in·dict′ment

in·dif′fer·ence

in·dif′fer·ent

in·dif′fer·ent·ly

in′di·gence

in·dig′e·nous

in′di·gent

in′di·gest′i·bil′i·ty

in·di·gest'i·ble

in·di·ges'tion

in·dig'nant

in·dig'nant·ly

in·dig·na'tion

in·dig'ni·ty

in'di·go

in'di·rect'

in'di·rec'tion

in'di·rect'ly

in'di·rect'ness

in'dis·creet'

in'dis·creet'ly

in'dis·cre'tion

in'dis·crim'i·nate

in'dis·crim'i·nate·ly

in'dis·pen'sa·bil'i·ty

in'dis·pen'sa·ble

in'dis·pose'

in'dis·posed'

in'dis·po·si'tion

in·dis'pu·ta·ble

in·dis'so·lu·ble

in·dis'so·lu·bly

in'dis·tinct'

in'dis·tinct'ly

in·dis·tin'guish·a·ble

in·dite'

in·dit'ed

in'di·um

in'di·vid'u·al

in'di·vid'u·al·ism

in'di·vid'u·al·ist

in'di·vid'u·al'i·ty

in'di·vid'u·al·ize

in'di·vid'u·al·ly

in'di·vis'i·bil'i·ty

in'di·vis'i·ble

in·doc'tri·nate

in·doc'tri·nat'ed

in·doc'tri·na'tion

in'do·lence

in'do·lent

in'do·lent·ly

in·dom'i·ta·ble

in'doors'

in·dorse'

in·dorsed'

in·dorse'ment

in·dors'er

in·du'bi·ta·ble

in·duce'

in·duced'

in·duce'ment

in·duct'

in·duct'ance

in·duct'ed

in·duc'tion

in·duc'tive

in·duc'tor

in·due'

in·dued'

in·dulge'

in·dul'gence

in·dul'gent

in·dul'gent·ly

in'du·rate

in'du·rat'ed

in·dus'tri·al

in·dus'tri·al·ly

in·dus'tri·al·ism

in·dus'tri·al·ist

in·dus'tri·al·i·za'tion

in·dus'tri·al·ize

in·dus'tri·al·ized

in·dus'tri·ous

in·dus'tri·ous·ly

in·dus'tri·ous·ness

in'dus·try

in·e'bri·ate

in·e'bri·at'ed

in·e'bri·a'tion

in·e·bri'e·ty

in·ed'i·ble

in·ef'fa·ble

in·ef'fa·bly

in'ef·fec'tive

in'ef·fec'tu·al

in'ef·fec'tu·al·ly

in'ef·fi·ca'cious

in'ef·fi'cien·cy

in'ef·fi'cient

in'ef·fi'cient·ly

in'e·las'tic

in'e·las·tic'i·ty

in·el'e·gance

in·el'e·gant

in·el'e·gant·ly

in·el'i·gi·bil'i·ty

in·el'i·gi·ble

in·e·luc'ta·ble

in·ept'

in·ept'i·tude

in·e·qual'i·ty

in·eq'ui·ta·ble

in·eq'ui·ty

in·e·rad'i·ca·ble

in·e·rad'i·ca·bly

in·er'ran·cy

in·er'rant

in·ert'

in·er'tia

in·ert'ly

in·ert'ness

in·es·sen'tial

in·es'ti·ma·ble

in·es'ti·ma·bly

in·ev'i·ta·bil'i·ty

in·ev'i·ta·ble

in·ev'i·ta·bly

in·ex·act'

in·ex·act'i·tude

in·ex·cus'a·ble

in·ex·cus'a·bly

in·ex·haust'i·ble

in·ex·haust'i·bly

in·ex'o·ra·ble

in'ex·pe'di·ence

in'ex·pe'di·en·cy

in'ex·pe'di·ent

in'ex·pen'sive

in'ex·pe'ri·ence

in'ex·pert'

in·ex'pli·ca·ble

in·ex'pli·ca·bly

in·ex'tri·ca·ble

in·fal'li·bil'i·ty

in·fal'li·ble

in'fa·mous

in'fa·my

in'fan·cy

in'fant

in·fan'ti·cide

in'fan·tile

in'fan·ti·lism

in'fan·try

in'fan·try·man

in·farct'

in·farc'tion

in·fat'u·ate

in·fat'u·at·ed

in·fat'u·a'tion

in·fea'si·ble

in·fect'

in·fect'ed

in·fec'tion

in·fec'tious

in·fec'tious·ly

in·fec'tious·ness

in'fe·lic'i·tous

in'fe·lic'i·ty

in·fer'

in'fer·ence

in'fer·en'tial

in·fe'ri·or

in·fe'ri·or'i·ty

in·fer'nal

in·fer'nal·ly

in·fer'no

in·ferred'

in·fer'tile

in·fer·til'i·ty

in·fest'

in'fes·ta'tion

in'fi·del

in'fi·del'i·ty

in'field'

in'field'er

in·fil'trate

in·fil'trat·ed

in'fil·tra'tion

in'fi·nite

in·fin·i·tes'i·mal

in·fin·i·tes'i·mal·ly

in·fin'i·tive

in·fin'i·tude

in·fin'i·ty

in·firm'

in·fir'ma·ry

in·fir'mi·ty

in·flame'

in·flamed'

in·flam'ma·bil'i·ty

in·flam'ma·ble

in·flam'ma·bly

in'flam·ma'tion

in·flam'ma·to'ry

in·flate'

in·flat'ed

in·fla'tion

in·fla'tion·ar'y

in·fla'tion·ist

in·flect'

in·flect'ed

in·flec'tion

in·flex'i·bil'i·ty

in·flex'i·ble

in·flict'

in·flict'ed

in·flic'tion

in'flu·ence

in'flu·enced

in'flu·en'tial

in'flu·en'tial·ly

in'flu·en'za

in'flux

in·form'

in·for'mal

in'for·mal'i·ty

in·for'mal·ly

in·form'ant

in'for·ma'tion

in·form'a·tive

in·formed'

in·form'er

in·form'ing·ly

in·frac'tion

in·fran'gi·ble

in'fra·red'

in·fre'quent

in·fre'quent·ly

in·fringe'

in·fringed'

in·fringe'ment

in·fu'ri·ate

in·fu'ri·at'ed

in·fuse'

in·fused'

in·fus'es

in·fu'sion

in·gen'ious

in·gen'ious·ly

in'ge·nu'i·ty

in·gen'u·ous

in·gest'

in·gest'ed

in·ges'tion

in·ges'tive

in·glo'ri·ous

in'got

in·grain'

in·grained'

in'grate

in·gra'ti·ate

in·gra'ti·a'tion

in·gra'ti·a·to'ry

in·grat'i·tude

in·gre'di·ent

in'gress

in'grown'

in·hab'it

in·hab'it·a·ble

in·hab'it·ance

in·hab'it·ant

in·hab'i·ta'tion

in·hab'it·ed

in'ha·la'tion

in·hale'

in·haled'

in·hal'er

in'har·mo'ni·ous·

in·here'

in·hered'

in·her'ence

in·her'ent

in·her'ent·ly

in·her'it

in·her'it·a·ble

in·her'it·ance

in·her'it·ed

in·her'i·tor

in·hib'it

in·hib'it·ed

in'hi·bi'tion

in·hib'i·to'ry

in·hos'pi·ta·ble

in·hos'pi·ta·bly

in·hos'pi·tal'i·ty

in·hu′man	in′ju·ry	in′no·va′tive
in′hu·mane′	in·jus′tice	in′no·va′tor
in′hu·man′i·ty	in·jus′tic·es	in′nu·en′do
in′hu·ma′tion	ink	in·nu′mer·a·ble
in·hume′	inked	in′ob·serv′ant
in·humed′	ink′horn′	in·oc′u·late
in·im′i·cal	ink′ling	in·oc′u·lat′ed
in·im′i·ta·ble	ink′lings	in·oc′u·la′tion
in·im′i·ta·bly	ink′stand′	in′of·fen′sive
in·iq′ui·tous	ink′well′	in·op′er·a·ble
in·iq′ui·tous·ly	ink′y	in·op′er·a′tive
in·iq′ui·ty	in·laid′	in·op′por·tune′
in·i′tial	in′land	in·or′di·nate
in·i′tialed	in·lay′	in·or·gan′ic
in·i′tial·ly	in·let′	in′pa′tient
in·i′ti·ate	in′mate	in′put′
in·i′ti·at′ed	in′most	in′quest
in·i′ti·a′tion	inn	in·qui′e·tude
in·i′ti·a′tive	in′nate	in·quire′
in·i′ti·a′tor	in′nate·ly	in·quired′
in·i′ti·a·to′ry	in′ner	in·quir′er
in·ject′	in′ner·most	in·quires′
in·ject′ed	in′ning	in·quir′ies
in·jec′tion	in′nings	in·quir′ing·ly
in·jec′tor	inn′keep′er	in·quir′y
in′ju·di′cious	in′no·cence	in′qui·si′tion
in′ju·di′cious·ly	in′no·cent	in·quis′i·tive
in·junc′tion	in′no·cent·ly	in·quis′i·tor
in·junc′tive	in·noc′u·ous	in·quis′i·to′ri·al
in′jure	in·noc′u·ous·ly	in·road′
in′jured	in′no·vate	in·rush′
in·ju′ri·ous	in′no·va′tion	in·sane′

in·sane′ly
in·san′i·tar′y
in·san′i·ta′tion
in·san′i·ty
in·sa′ti·a·bil′i·ty
in·sa′ti·a·ble
in·scribe′
in·scribed′
in·scrib′er
in·scrip′tion
in·scru′ta·bil′i·ty
in·scru′ta·ble
in′sect
in·sec′ti·cide
in′sec·tiv′o·rous
in′se·cure′
in′se·cu′ri·ty
in·sen′sate
in·sen′si·bil′i·ty
in·sen′si·ble
in·sen′si·tive
in·sen′si·tive·ness
in·sen′ti·ence
in·sen′ti·ent
in·sep′a·ra·ble
in·sep′a·ra·bly
in·sert′
in·sert′ed
in·ser′tion
in′set′
in′shore′
in′side′

in′sid′er
in·sides′
in·sid′i·ous
in·sid′i·ous·ly
in′sight′
in·sig′ne
in·sig′ni·a
in′sig·nif′i·cance
in′sig·nif′i·cant
in′sig·nif′i·cant·ly
in′sin·cere′
in′sin·cere′ly
in′sin·cer′i·ty
in·sin′u·ate
in·sin′u·at′ed
in·sin′u·at′ing·ly
in·sin′u·a′tion
in·sin′u·a′tive
in·sip′id
in′si·pid′i·ty
in·sip′id·ly
in·sist′
in·sist′ed
in·sist′ence
in·sist′ent
in·sist′ent·ly
in′so·bri′e·ty
in′sole′
in′so·lence
in′so·lent
in′so·lent·ly
in·sol′u·bil′i·ty

in·sol′u·ble
in·solv′a·ble
in·sol′ven·cy
in·sol′vent
in·som′ni·a
in·som′ni·ac
in′so·much′
in·sou′ci·ance
in·sou′ci·ant
in·spect′
in·spect′ed
in·spec′tion
in·spec′tor
in·spec′tor·ate
in′spi·ra′tion
in′spi·ra′tion·al
in′spi·ra′tion·al·ly
in·spir′a·to′ry
in·spire′
in·spired′
in·spir′er
in·spir′ing·ly
in·spir′it·ing·ly
in′sta·bil′i·ty
in·stall′
in′stal·la′tion
in·stalled′
in·stall′ment
in′stance
in′stant
in′stan·ta′ne·ous
in·stan′ter

in'stant·ly

in·state'

in·stat'ed

in·stead'

in'step

in'sti·gate

in'sti·gat'ed

in'sti·ga'tion

in'sti·ga'tor

in·still'

in·stilled'

in·stinct'

in·stinc'tive

in·stinc'tive·ly

in·stinc'tu·al

in'sti·tute

in'sti·tut'ed

in'sti·tu'tion

in'sti·tu'tion·al

in'sti·tu'tion·al·ize

in'sti·tu'tion·al·ly

in·struct'

in·struct'ed

in·struc'tion

in·struc'tion·al

in·struc'tive

in·struc'tor

in'stru·ment

in'stru·men'tal

in'stru·men·tal·ist

in'stru·men·tal'i·ty

in'stru·men·tal·ly

in'stru·men·ta'tion

in'sub·or'di·nate

in'sub·or'di·na'tion

in·suf'fer·a·ble

in'suf·fi'cien·cy

in'suf·fi'cient

in'su·lar

in'su·lar'i·ty

in'su·late

in'su·lat'ed

in'su·la'tion

in'su·la'tor

in'su·lin

in·sult'

in·sult'ed

in·sult'ing·ly

in·su'per·a·ble

in'sup·port'a·ble

in'sup·press'i·ble

in·sur'a·bil'i·ty

in·sur'a·ble

in·sur'ance

in·sure'

in·sured'

in·sur'er

in·sur'gen·cy

in·sur'gent

in'sur·mount'a·ble

in'sur·rec'tion

in'sur·rec'tion·ar'y

in'sur·rec'tion·ist

in·tact'

in·tagl'io

in'take'

in·tan'gi·bil'i·ty

in·tan'gi·ble

in·tar'si·a

in'te·ger

in'te·gral

in'te·gral·ly

in'te·grate

in'te·grat'ed

in'te·gra'tion

in·teg'ri·ty

in·teg'u·ment

in'tel·lect

in'tel·lec'tu·al

in'tel·lec'tu·al·ism

in'tel·lec'tu·al·ize

in'tel·lec'tu·al·ly

in·tel'li·gence

in·tel'li·gent

in·tel'li·gent'si·a

in·tel'li·gi·bil'i·ty

in·tel'li·gi·ble

in·tem'per·ance

in·tem'per·ate

in·tem'per·ate·ly

in·tend'

in·tend'ant

in·tend'ed

in·tense'

in·ten'si·fi·ca'tion

in·ten'si·fi'er

in·ten'si·fy

in·ten'si·ty

in·ten'sive

in·tent'

in·ten'tion

in·ten'tion·al

in·ten'tion·al·ly

in·tent'ly

in·tent'ness

in'ter·act'

in'ter·ac'tion

in'ter·bor'ough

in'ter·breed'

in'ter·cede'

in'ter·ced'ed

in'ter·cept'

in'ter·cept'ed

in'ter·cep'tion

in'ter·cep'tor

in'ter·ces'sion

in'ter·ces'so·ry

in'ter·change'

in'ter·change'a·bil'i·ty

in'ter·change'a·ble

in'ter·col·le'gi·ate

in'ter·com·mu'ni·cate

in'ter·con·nect'

in'ter·cos'tal

in'ter·course

in'ter·de·nom'i·na'tion·al

in'ter·de·part·men'tal

in'ter·de·pend'ence

in'ter·de·pend'ent

in'ter·dict

in'ter·dic'tion

in'ter·est

in'ter·est·ed

in'ter·est·ed·ly

in'ter·est·ing·ly

in'ter·fere'

in'ter·fered'

in'ter·fer'ence

in'ter·fer'ing·ly

in'ter·im

in·te'ri·or

in'ter·ject'

in'ter·ject'ed

in'ter·jec'tion

in'ter·lace'

in'ter·laced'

in'ter·lard'

in'ter·leaf'

in'ter·leave'

in'ter·line'

in'ter·lin'e·al

in'ter·lin'e·ar

in'ter·lin'e·a'tion

in'ter·lined'

in'ter·lock'

in'ter·locked'

in'ter·loc'u·tor

in'ter·loc'u·to·ry

in'ter·lop'er

in'ter·lude

in'ter·mar'riage

in'ter·mar'ry

in'ter·me'di·ar'y

in'ter·me'di·ate

in·ter'ment

in'ter·mez'zo

in·ter'mi·na·ble

in·ter'mi·na·bly

in'ter·min'gle

in'ter·min'gled

in'ter·mis'sion

in'ter·mit'

in'ter·mit'tence

in'ter·mit'tent

in'ter·mit'tent·ly

in'ter·mix'ture

in·tern'

in·ter'nal

in·ter'nal·ly

in'ter·na'tion·al

in'ter·na'tion·al·ize

in'ter·na'tion·al·ly

in'terne

in'ter·ne'cine

in·terned'

in·tern'ment

in·ter'pel'late

in'ter·pel·la'tion

in'ter·plan'e·tar'y

in·ter'po·late

in·ter'po·lat'ed

in·ter'po·la'tion

in'ter·pose'

in'ter·posed'

in'ter·po·si'tion

in·ter'pret

in·ter'pre·ta'tion

in·ter'pre·ta'tive

in·ter'pret·ed

in·ter'pret·er

in'ter·reg'num

in'ter·re·la'tion

in·ter'ro·gate

in·ter'ro·ga'tion

in·ter'rog'a·tive

in·ter'rog'a·to'ry

in'ter·rupt'

in'ter·rupt'ed·ly

in'ter·rup'tion

in'ter·scap'u·lar

in'ter·scho·las'tic

in'ter·sect'

in'ter·sect'ed

in'ter·sperse'

in'ter·spersed'

in'ter·state'

in'ter·stel'lar

in·ter'stice

in·ter'stic·es

in'ter·sti'tial

in'ter·sti'tial·ly

in'ter·twine'

in'ter·twined'

In'ter·type

in'ter·ur'ban

in'ter·val

in'ter·vene'

in'ter·vened'

in'ter·ven'tion

in'ter·ven'tion·ist

in'ter·ver'te·bral

in'ter·view

in'ter·viewed

in'ter·view'er

in'ter·weave'

in'ter·wo'ven

in·tes'ta·cy

in·tes'tate

in·tes'ti·nal

in·tes'tine

in'ti·ma·cy

in'ti·mate

in'ti·mat'ed

in'ti·mate·ly

in'ti·ma'tion

in·tim'i·date

in·tim'i·dat'ed

in·tim'i·da'tion

in'to

in·tol'er·a·ble

in·tol'er·ance

in·tol'er·ant

in'to·na'tion

in·tone'

in·toned'

in·tox'i·cate

in·tox'i·cat'ed

in·tox'i·cat'ing·ly

in·tox'i·ca'tion

in·trac'ta·bil'i·ty

in·trac'ta·ble

in'tra·mu'ral

in·tran'si·gence

in·tran'si·gent

in·tran'si·tive

in'tra·state'

in·trench'ment

in·trep'id

in·tre·pid'i·ty

in·trep'id·ly

in'tri·ca·cies

in'tri·ca·cy

in'tri·cate

in'tri·cate·ly

in·trigue'

in·trigued'

in·trin'sic

in·trin'si·cal

in·trin'si·cal·ly

in'tro·duce'

in'tro·duced'

in'tro·duc'tion

in'tro·duc'to·ry

in·tro'it

in'tro·jec'tion

in'tro·spect'

in'tro·spec'tion

in'tro·spec'tive

in·tro·ver'sion

in'tro·vert'

in'tro·vert'ed

in·trude'

in·trud'ed

in·trud'er

in·tru'sion

in·tru'sive

in·tru'sive·ly

in·tu·i'tion

in·tu·i'tion·al

in·tu'i·tive

in·tu'i·tive·ly

in·tu·mesce'

in·tu·mes'cence

in·tu·mes'cent

in·unc'tion

in·un·date

in·un·dat'ed

in·un·da'tion

in·ure'

in·ured'

in·ur'ed·ness

in·urn'

in·vade'

in·vad'ed

in'va·lid

in·val'i·date

in·val'i·dat'ed

in·val'i·da'tion

in'va·lid'i·ty

in·val'u·a·ble

In·var'

in·var'i·a·bil'i·ty

in·var'i·a·ble

in·var'i·a·ble·ness

in·va'sion

in·va'sive

in·vec'tive

in·veigh'

in·vei'gle

in·vei'gled

in·vent'

in·vent'ed

in·ven'tion

in·ven'tive

in·ven'tive·ly

in·ven'tive·ness

in·ven'tor

in'ven·to'ry

in·verse'

in·ver'sion

in·vert'

in·vert'ed

in·vert'i·ble

in·vest'

in·vest'ed

in·ves'ti·gate

in·ves'ti·gat'ed

in·ves'ti·ga'tion

in·ves'ti·ga'tive

in·ves'ti·ga'tor

in·ves'ti·ture

in·vest'ment

in·ves'tor

in·vet'er·ate

in·vid'i·ous

in·vid'i·ous·ly

in·vig'i·late

in·vig'or·ate

in·vig'or·at'ed

in·vig'or·at'ing·ly

in·vig'or·a'tion

in·vig'or·a'tive

in·vin'ci·bil'i·ty

in·vin'ci·ble

in·vi'o·la·bil'i·ty

in·vi'o·la·ble

in·vi'o·late

in·vis'i·bil'i·ty

in·vis'i·ble

in·vis'i·bly

in'vi·ta'tion

in'vi·ta'tion·al

in·vite'

in·vit'ed

in·vit'ing·ly

in'vo·ca'tion

in'voice

in'voiced

in'voic·es

in·voke'

in·voked'

in·vol'un·tar'i·ly

in·vol'un·tar'y

in'vo·lute

in·vo·lu'tion

in·volve'

in·volve'ment

in·vul'ner·a·bil'i·ty

in·vul'ner·a·ble

in'ward

in'ward·ly

in'ward·ness

i'o·date

i·od'ic

i'o·dide

i'o·dine

i'o·dize

i·o'do·form

i'on

I·on'ic

i'on·i·za'tion

i'on·ize

i·o'ta

ip'e·cac

I·ra'ni·an

i·ras'ci·bil'i·ty

i·ras'ci·ble

i'rate

i'rate·ly

ire

ir'i·des'cence

ir'i·des'cent

i·rid'i·um

i'ris

I'rish

I'rish·man

i·ri'tis

irk

irked

irk'some

i'ron

i'ron·bound'

i'ron·clad'

i'roned

i·ron'ic

i·ron'i·cal

i·ron'i·cal·ly

i'ron·ings

i'ron·side'

i'ron·ware'

i'ron·weed'

i'ron·wood'

i'ron·work'

i'ron·work'er

i'ro·ny

Ir'o·quois

ir·ra'di·ate

ir·ra'di·at'ed

ir·ra'di·a'tion

ir·ra'tion·al

ir·ra'tion·al'i·ty

ir·ra'tion·al·ly

ir're·claim'a·ble

ir·rec'on·cil'a·ble

ir·rec'on·cil'i·a·bil'i·ty

ir·rec'on·cil'i·a·ble

ir're·cov'er·a·ble

ir're·deem'a·ble

ir're·den'ta

ir're·duc'i·ble

ir·ref'ra·ga·ble

ir're·fran'gi·ble

ir·ref'u·ta·ble

ir·reg'u·lar

ir·reg'u·lar'i·ty

ir·reg'u·lar·ly

ir·rel'e·vance

ir·rel'e·vant

ir're·li'gious

ir're·me'di·a·ble

ir're·mis'si·ble

ir're·mov'a·ble

ir·rep'a·ra·ble

ir're·place'a·ble

ir're·press'i·ble

ir're·proach'a·ble

ir're·sist'i·ble

ir·res'o·lute

ir·res'o·lu'tion

ir're·solv'a·ble

ir're·spec'tive

ir're·spon'si·bil'i·ty

ir're·spon'si·ble

ir're·spon'si·bly

ir're·trace'a·ble

ir're·triev'a·ble

ir·rev'er·ence

ir·rev'er·ent

ir're·vers'i·ble

ir·rev'o·ca·ble

ir'ri·ga·ble		i'so·late		i·tal'i·cize
ir'ri·gate		i'so·lat'ed		itch
ir'ri·gat'ed		i·so·la'tion		itched
ir'ri·ga'tion		i'so·la'tion·ism		itch'i·er
ir'ri·ta·bil'i·ty		i'so·la'tion·ist		itch'i·est
ir'ri·ta·ble		i'so·mer		itch'y
ir'ri·tant		i'so·mer'ic		i'tem
ir'ri·tate		i'so·mor'phic		i'tem·ize
ir'ri·tat'ed		i·sos'ce·les		i'tem·ized
ir'ri·ta'tion		i'so·therm		it'er·ate
ir'ri·ta'tive		i'so·tope		it'er·a'tion
ir·rup'tion		is'su·ance		it'er·a'tive
ir·rup'tive		is'sue		i·tin'er·a·cy
is'chi·um		is'sued		i·tin'er·an·cy
i'sin·glass'		is'sues		i·tin'er·ant
Is'lam		isth'mi·an		i·tin'er·ar'y
is'land		isth'mus		i·tin'er·ate
is'land·er		it		its
isle		I·tal'ian		it·self'
is'let		I·tal'ian·ate		i'vo·ry
i'so·bar		i·tal'ic		i'vy

jab'ber
jab'ber·ing·ly
ja'bot'
jack
jack'al
jack'a·napes'
jack'daw'
jack'et
jack'et·ed
jack'knife'
jack'stone'
jack'straw'
jack'weed'
Jac·o·be'an
jade
jad'ed
jade'ite
jagged
jag'uar
jail
jailed
jail'er

jal'ou·sie
jam
jam'bo·ree'
jammed
jan'gle
jan'i·tor
jan'i·tress
Jan'u·ar'y
Ja·pan'
Jap'a·nese'
ja·panned'
jar
jar'gon
jarred
jas'mine
jas'per
jaun'dice
jaunt
jaun'ti·er
jaun'ti·est
jaun'ti·ly
jaun'ti·ness

jaun'ty
jave'lin
jaw
jaw'bone'
jazz
jazz'y
jeal'ous
jeal'ous·y
jeer
jeered
jeer'ing·ly
Je·ho'vah
je·june'
je·ju'num
jel'lied
jel'ly
jel'ly·fish'
jen'net
jeop'ard·ize
jeop'ard·y
jer'e·mi'ad
jerk

157

jerked

jerk'i·ly

jer'kin

jerk'y

jer'sey

jest

jest'er

jest'ing·ly

Jes'u·it

Je'sus

jet

jet'lin·er

jet'port

jet'sam

jet'ti·son

jew'eled

jew'el·er

jew'el·ry

Jew'ish

Jew'ry

jibe

jig

jig'ger

jig'gle

jig'gled

jig'saw'

jin'gle

jin'gled

jin'go

jin'go·ism

jin·rik'i·sha

jinx

jit'ney

jit'ters

jit'ter·y

job

job'ber

jock'ey

jo·cose'

jo·cose'ly

jo·cos'i·ty

joc'u·lar

joc'u·lar'i·ty

joc'u·lar·ly

joc'und

jo·cun'di·ty

jodh'purs

jog

jogged

jog'gle

jog'gled

join

join'der

joined

join'er

join'ings

joint

joint'ed

joint'ly

join'ture

joist

joke

jok'er

jok'ing·ly

jol'li·er

jol'li·est

jol'li·fi·ca'tion

jol'li·ty

jol'ly

jolt

jolt'ed

jon'quil

jos'tle

jos'tled

jot

jot'ted

jounce

jour'nal

jour'nal·ism

jour'nal·ist

jour'nal·is'tic

jour'nal·ize

jour'nal·ized

jour'ney

jour'neyed

jour'ney·man

jo'vi·al

jo'vi·al'i·ty

jo'vi·al·ly

jowl

joy

joy'ful

joy'ful·ly

joy'ful·ness

joy'less

joy'ous

ju'bi·lance

ju'bi·lant

ju'bi·late

ju'bi·la'tion

ju'bi·lee

Ju'da·ism

judge

judged

judge'ship

judg'ment

ju'di·ca'tive

ju'di·ca·to'ry

ju'di·ca·ture

ju·di'cial

ju·di'cial·ly

ju·di'ci·ar'y

ju·di'cious

jug'gle

jug'gled

jug'gler

jug'u·lar

juice

juic'y

ju'lep

ju'li·enne'

Ju·ly'

jum'ble

jum'bled

jum'bo

jump

jumped

jump'er

junc'tion

junc'ture

June

jun'gle

jun'ior

ju'ni·per

junk

jun'ket

jun'ta

ju'rat

ju·rid'i·cal

ju'ris·con·sult'

ju'ris·dic'tion

ju'ris·pru'dence

ju'rist

ju'ror

ju'ry

ju'ry·man

just

jus'tice

jus·ti'ci·a·ble

jus'ti·fi'a·ble

jus'ti·fi·ca'tion

jus'ti·fi·ca'to·ry

jus'ti·fied

jus'ti·fy

just'ly

just'ness

jut

jute

jut'ted

ju've·nile

ju've·nil'i·ty

jux'ta·po·si'tion

kai'ser	kept	kick'off'
kale	ker'a·tin	kick'shaw'
ka·lei'do·scope	ker'chief	kid
ka·lei'do·scop'ic	ker'nel	kid'nap
kal'so·mine	ker'o·sene'	kid'naped
kan'ga·roo'	ker'sey	kid'ney
ka'o·lin	ketch	kid'skin'
ka'pok	ke·to'sis	kill
kar'ma	ket'tle	killed
kay'ak	key	kill'er
keel	key'board'	kill'ings
keen	keyed	kiln
keen'er	key'hole'	kil'o·cy'cle
keen'est	key'note'	kil'o·gram
keen'ly	key'stone'	kil'o·me'ter
keen'ness	khak'i	kilt
keep	khe·dive'	kilt'ed
keep'er	kib'itz·er	kin
keep'sake'	ki'bosh	kind
keg	kick	kind'er
kelp	kick'back'	kind'est
ken'nel	kick'er	kin'der·gar'ten

kin'dle	kite	knock'out'
kin'dled	kith	knoll
kind'li·ness	kit'ten	knot
kind'ly	klep'to·ma'ni·a	knot'hole'
kind'ness	klep'to·ma'ni·ac	knot'ted
kin'dred	knap'sack'	knot'ty
kine	knave	knot'work'
kin'es·thet'ic	knav'er·y	knout
ki·net'ic	knav'ish	know
king	knead	know'a·ble
king'bird'	knead'ed	know'ing·ly
king'bolt'	knee'cap'	know'ing·ness
king'craft	kneel	knowl'edge
king'dom	kneeled	known
king'fish'	knelt	knuck'le
king'fish'er	knew	knuck'led
king'let	knick'ers	knurl
king'li·ness	knick'knack'	knurled
king'ly	knife	knurl'y
king'pin'	knifed	ko'bold
king'ship	knight	ko'dak
kink	knight'ed	kohl'ra'bi
kinked	knight'hood	ko'peck
kink'y	knight'li·ness	Ko·ran'
kin'ship	knight'ly	Ko·re'an
kins'man	knit	ko'sher
ki·osk'	knit'ter	kraft
kip'per	knives	krem'lin
kiss	knob	kryp'ton
kissed	knock	ku·lak'
kitch'en	knock'down'	ky'mo·graph
kitch'en·ette'	knock'er	ky·pho'sis

L

la'bel

la'beled

la'bi·al

la'bor

lab'o·ra·to·ry

la'bored

la'bor·er

la·bo'ri·ous

la·bur'num

lab'y·rinth

lab'y·rin'thine

lace

laced

lac'er·ate

lac'er·at'ed

lac'er·a'tion

lac'er·a'tive

lace'wing'

lace'wood'

lace'work'

lach'es

lach'ry·mal

lach'ry·mose

lac'ings

lack

lack'a·dai'si·cal

lack'ey

lack'lus'ter

la·con'ic

lac'quer

lac'quered

la·crosse'

lac'tase

lac'tate

lac·ta'tion

lac'te·al

lac'tic

lac'tose

la·cu'na

la·cu'nae

lad'der

lad'en

la'dle

la'dled

la'dy

la'dy·like'

la'dy·ship

lag

la'ger

lag'gard

lagged

la·goon'

lair

laird

la'i·ty

lake

lamb'doid

lam'bent

lamb'kin

lamb'like'

lam'bre·quin

la'mé'

lame

lamed

lame'ly

lame'ness

la·ment′	land′slip′	large
lam′en·ta·ble	lands′man	large′ly
lam′en·ta′tion	land′ward	large′ness
la·ment′ed	lan′guage	larg′er
lam′i·na	lan′guid	lar′gess
lam′i·nae	lan′guish	larg′est
lam′i·nate	lan′guor	lar′i·at
lam′i·nat′ed	lan′guor·ous	lark
lam′i·na′tion	lank	lark′spur
lamp	lank′er	lar′va
lamp′black′	lank′est	lar′vae
lam·poon′	lank′y	lar′val
lam·pooned′	lan′o·lin	la·ryn′ge·al
lam′prey	lans′downe	lar′yn·gi′tis
lance	lan′tern	lar′ynx
lanc′er	lan′tha·num	las′car
lan′cet	lan′yard	las·civ′i·ous
lan′ci·nate	lap	lash
lan′ci·nat′ed	la·pel′	lashed
lan′ci·na′tion	lap′ful	lash′ings
land	lap′i·dar′y	lass
lan′dau	lap′i·da′tion	las′si·tude
land′ed	lapse	las′so
land′fall′	lapsed	last
land′hold′er	lap′wing′	last′ed
land′la′dy	lar′board	last′ing·ly
land′locked′	lar′ce·nous	last′ly
land′lord′	lar′ce·ny	lasts
land′mark′	larch	Lat′a·ki′a
land′own′er	lard	latch
land′scape	lard′ed	latched
land′slide′	lard′er	latch′key′

latch'string'

late

la·teen'

late'ly

la'ten·cy

late'ness

la'tent

lat'er

lat'er·al

lat'er·al·ly

lat'est

la'tex

lath

lath'er

laths

Lat'in

Lat'in·ism

La·tin'i·ty

Lat'in·i·za'tion

Lat'in·ize

lat'i·tude

lat'i·tu'di·nal

lat'i·tu'di·nar'i·an

lat'ter

lat'ter·most

lat'tice

lat'tice·work'

laud

laud'a·bil'i·ty

laud'a·ble

lau'da·num

lau·da'tion

laud'a·to'ry

laud'ed

laugh

laugh'a·ble

laugh'ing·ly

laugh'ing·stock'

laugh'ter

launch

launch'ings

laun'der

laun'dered

laun'der·ings

laun'dress

laun'dry

laun'dry·man

lau're·ate

lau'rel

la'va

lav'a·liere'

lav'a·to'ry

lav'en·der

lav'ish

lav'ished

lav'ish·ness

law

law'break'er

law'ful

law'ful·ly

law'giv'er

law'less

law'less·ness

law'mak'er

lawn

law'suit'

law'yer

lax

lax'a·tive

lax'i·ty

lax'ly

lax'ness

lay'er

lay'man

laz'a·ret'to

la'zi·er

la'zi·est

la'zi·ly

la'zi·ness

la'zy

leach

leached

lead

lead'en

lead'er

lead'er·ship

leads'man

leaf

leaf'let

league

leagued

leak

leak'age

leak'i·ness

leak'y

lean

leaned	leered	le·git'i·ma·cy
lean'ings	leer'ing·ly	le·git'i·mate
leap	lee'ward	le·git'i·mate·ly
leaped	lee'way'	le·git'i·mate·ness
learn	left	le·git'i·ma'tion
learned	left'-hand'ed	le·git'i·mist
learnt	leg	le·git'i·mize
lease	leg'a·cy	leg'ume
leased	le'gal	le·gu'mi·nous
lease'hold'	le'gal·ism	lei'sure
lease'hold'er	le'gal·is'tic	lei'sure·li·ness
leash	le·gal'i·ty	lei'sure·ly
leashed	le'gal·i·za'tion	lem'mings
least	le'gal·ize	lem'on
leath'er	le'gal·ly	lem'on·ade'
leath'ern	leg'ate	lem'on·weed'
leath'er·oid	leg'a·tee'	le'mur
leath'er·y	le·ga'tion	lend
leave	le·ga'to	length
leav'en	leg'end	length'en
leav'ened	leg'end·ar'y	length'ened
leav'ing	leg'er·de·main'	length'i·er
lec'i·thin	leg'gings	length'i·est
lec'tern	leg'i·bil'i·ty	length'i·ly
lec'ture	leg'i·ble	length'i·ness
lec'tured	le'gion	length'ways
lec'tur·er	le'gion·ar'y	length'wise
ledge	leg'is·late	length'y
ledg'er	leg'is·la'tion	le'ni·ence
leech	leg'is·la'tive	le'ni·en·cy
leek	leg'is·la'tor	le'ni·ent
leer	leg'is·la'ture	le'ni·ent·ly

Len'in·ism	let'tered	li'beled
len'i·tive	let'ter·head'	li'bel·ous
len'i·ty	let'ter·press'	lib'er·al
lens	let'ter·space'	lib'er·al·ism
lent	let'tuce	lib'er·al'i·ty
Lent'en	leu'co·cyte	lib'er·al·i·za'tion
len·tic'u·lar	leu'co·cy·to'sis	lib'er·al·ize
len'til	leu'co·der'ma	lib'er·al·ized
len'toid	leu·ke'mi·a	lib'er·al·ly
le'o·nine	lev'ant	lib'er·ate
leop'ard	lev'ee	lib'er·at'ed
le'o·tard	lev'el	lib'er·a'tion
lep'er	lev'eled	lib'er·a'tor
lep're·chaun'	lev'el·head'ed	lib'er·tar'i·an
lep'ro·sy	le'ver	lib'er·tine
lep'rous	le'ver·age	lib'er·ty
le'sion	lev'i·tate	li·bi'do
less	lev'i·tat'ed	li·brar'i·an
les·see'	lev'i·ta'tion	li'brar'y
less'en	lev'i·ty	li·bret'to
less'ened	lev'u·lose	lice
less'er	lev'y	li'cense
les'son	lex'i·cog'ra·pher	li'cen·see'
les'sor	lex'i·cog'ra·phy	li·cen'ti·ate
lest	lex'i·con	li·cen'tious
let	li'a·bil'i·ty	li·cen'tious·ness
le'thal	li'a·ble	li'chen
le·thar'gic	li'ai·son'	li'chen·oid
le·thar'gi·cal	li'ar	lic'it
leth'ar·gy	li·ba'tion	lick
let's	li'bel	lic'o·rice
let'ter	li'bel·ant	lic'tor

lie

liege

li'en

lieu

lieu·ten'an·cy

lieu·ten'ant

life

life'guard'

life'less

life'like'

life'long'

life'time'

life'work'

lift

lift'ed

lig'a·ment

li'gate

li·ga'tion

lig'a·ture

lig'a·tured

light

light'ed

light'en

light'ened

light'er

light'er·age

light'est

light'face'

light'head'ed

light'heart'ed

light'house'

light'ly

light'ness

light'ning

light'ship'

light'weight'

lig'ne·ous

lig'ni·fy

lig'nite

lik'a·ble

like

liked

like'li·er

like'li·est

like'li·hood

like'ly

lik'en

like'ness

like'wise'

lik'ings

li'lac

lil'i·a'ceous

lilt

lilt'ing·ly

lil'y

limb

lim'ber

lim'bo

lime

lime'kiln'

lime'light'

li'men

Lim'er·ick

lime'stone'

lime'wa'ter

lim'i·nal

lim'it

lim'it·a·ble

lim'i·ta'tion

lim'it·ed

lim'it·less

limn

limned

lim·nol'o·gy

lim'ou·sine'

limp

limped

limp'er

limp'est

lim'pet

lim'pid

lim·pid'i·ty

lim'pid·ly

limp'ly

limp'ness

lin'age

lin'den

line

lin'e·age

lin'e·al

lin'e·al'i·ty

lin'e·a·ment

lin'e·ar

lined

line'man

lin'en

lin'er	liq'ue·fi'a·ble	lit'er·ate
lines'man	liq'ue·fied	lit'er·a·ture
lin'ger	liq'ue·fy	lith'arge
lin'gered	li'ques'cence	lithe
lin'ge·rie'	li·queur'	lithe'some
lin'ger·ing·ly	liq'uid	lith'i·a
lin'go	liq'ui·date	lith'i·um
lin'gual	liq'ui·dat'ed	lith'o·graph
lin'guist	liq'ui·da'tion	li·thog'ra·pher
lin·guis'tic	liq'ui·da'tor	lith'o·graph'ic
lin·guis'ti·cal·ly	liq'uor	li·thog'ra·phy
lin·guis'tics	li'ra	li·tho'sis
lin'i·ment	lisp	li·thot'o·my
lin'ings	lisped	lit'i·ga·ble
link	lisp'ing·ly	lit'i·gant
link'age	lis'some	lit'i·gate
linked	list	lit'i·gat'ed
Lin·nae'an	list'ed	lit'i·ga'tion
lin'net	lis'ten	li·ti'gious
li·no'le·um	lis'tened	lit'mus
Lin'o·type	lis'ten·er	lit'ter
lin'seed'	list'ings	lit'tered
lint	list'less	lit'tle
lin'tel	lit'a·ny	lit'tlest
li'on	li'ter	lit'to·ral
li'on·ess	lit'er·a·cy	li·tur'gi·cal
li'on·ize	lit'er·al	lit'ur·gist
lip'oid	lit'er·al·ism	lit'ur·gy
li·po'ma	lit'er·al'i·ty	liv'a·ble
liq'ue·fa'cient	lit'er·al·ize	live
liq'ue·fac'tion	lit'er·al·ly	live
liq'ue·fac'tive	lit'er·ar'y	lived

live'li·er	lob'by·ist	lodg'ment
live'li·est	lob'ster	loft
live'li·hood	lo'cal	loft'i·ly
live'li·ness	lo'cal·ism	loft'i·ness
live'long'	lo·cal'i·ty	loft'y
live'ly	lo'cal·i·za'tion	log
liv'er	lo'cal·ize	lo'gan·ber'ry
liv'er·y	lo'cal·ized	log'a·rithm
liv'er·y·man	lo'cal·ly	log'book'
liv'id	lo'cate	loge
li·vid'i·ty	lo'cat·ed	log'ger·heads'
liv'ings	lo·ca'tion	log'gia
liz'ard	lo'ci	log'ic
lla'ma	lock	log'i·cal
lla'no	lock'age	log'i·cal·ly
load	lock'er	lo·gi'cian
load'ed	lock'et	lo·gis'tics
load'ings	lock'jaw'	log'or·rhe'a
loaf	lock'out'	log'o·type
loaf'er	lock'smith'	log'wood'
loam	lock'up'	loin
loan	lo'co·mo'tion	loi'ter
loaned	lo'co·mo'tive	loi'tered
loathe	lo'cus	loi'ter·er
loathed	lo'cust	loll
loath'er	lo·cu'tion	lolled
loath'ful	lode	lol'li·pop
loath'ly	lode'star'	lone
loath'some	lodge	lone'li·ness
lo'bar	lodged	lone'ly
lob'bied	lodg'er	lone'some
lob'by	lodg'ings	lone'some·ly

lone'some·ness	lop'sid'ed	lov'a·ble
long	lo·qua'cious	love
long'boat'	lo·qua'cious·ly	love'less
longed	lo·quac'i·ty	love'li·ness
lon'ger	lord	love'lorn'
long'est	lord'li·ness	love'ly
lon·gev'i·ty	lord'ly	lov'er
long'hand'	lor·do'sis	love'sick'
long'horn'	lord'ship	lov'ing·ly
long'ing·ly	lore	low
long'ings	lor'gnette'	low'born'
lon'gi·tude	lor'ry	low'boy'
lon'gi·tu'di·nal	los'a·ble	low'bred'
long'shore'man	lose	low'er
look	los'er	low'est
look'out'	los'es	low'land
loom	los'ings	low'li·er
loomed	loss	low'li·est
loon	lost	low'li·ness
loon'y	lo'tion	low'ly
loop	lot'ter·y	low'most
loop'hole'	lo'tus	loy'al
loose	loud	loy'al·ism
loose'ly	loud'er	loy'al·ist
loos'en	loud'est	loy'al·ly
loos'ened	loud'ly	loy'al·ty
loose'ness	loud'ness	loz'enge
loos'er	lounge	lu'bri·cant
loos'est	louse	lu'bri·cate
loot	lout	lu'bri·ca'tion
loot'ed	lout'ish	lu'bri·ca'tor
lop	lou'ver	lu·bric'i·ty

lu'cent

lu'cid

lu·cid'i·ty

lu'cid·ly

lu'cid·ness

luck

luck'i·ly

luck'i·ness

luck'less

luck'y

lu'cra·tive

lu'cre

lu'cu·bra'tion

lu'di·crous

lug

lug'gage

lugged

lug'ger

lu·gu'bri·ous

luke'warm'

lull

lull'a·by'

lulled

lum·ba'go

lum'ber

lum'ber·yard'

lu'mi·nar'y

lu'mi·nes'cence

lu'mi·nes'cent

lu'mi·nif'er·ous

lu'mi·nos'i·ty

lu'mi·nous

lump

lump'i·er

lump'i·est

lump'y

lu'na·cy

lu'nar

lu'na·tic

lunch

lunch'eon

lunch'eon·ette'

lunch'room'

lu·nette'

lung

lunge

lunged

lurch

lurched

lurch'ing

lure

lured

lu'rid

lurk

lurked

lus'cious

lush

lust

lus'ter

lust'ful

lust'i·ly

lust'i·ness

lus'trous

lus'trous·ly

lus'trum

lust'y

lute

Lu'ther·an

lux·u'ri·ance

lux·u'ri·ant

lux·u'ri·ate

lux·u'ri·at'ed

lux·u'ri·ous

lux'u·ry

ly·ce'um

lydd'ite

lymph

lym·phat'ic

lymph'oid

lynx

ly'on·naise'

lyre

lyre'bird'

lyr'ic

lyr'i·cal

lyr'i·cism

M

ma·ca′bre
mac·ad′am
mac·ad′am·ize
mac′a·ro′ni
mac′a·roon′
ma·caw′
mac′er·ate
mac′er·at′ed
mac′er·a′tion
Mach
ma·che′te
ma·chic′o·la′tion
mach′i·nate
mach′i·na′tion
ma·chine′
ma·chined′
ma·chin′er·y
ma·chin′ist
mack′er·el
mac′ro·cosm
mac′ro·cyte
ma′cron

mac′u·late
mad
mad′am
mad′den·ing·ly
mad′der
mad′dest
mad′house′
mad′ly
mad′man
mad′ness
ma·don′na
mad′ri·gal
mael′strom
maf′fi·a
mag′a·zine′
ma·gen′ta
mag′got
Ma′gi
mag′ic
mag′i·cal
mag′i·cal·ly
ma·gi′cian

mag′is·te′ri·al
mag′is·tra·cy
mag′is·tral
mag′is·trate
mag′is·tra·ture
mag′na·nim′i·ty
mag·nan′i·mous
mag′nate
mag·ne′sia
mag·ne′si·um
mag′net
mag·net′ic
mag·net′i·cal·ly
mag′net·ism
mag′net·i·za′tion
mag′net·ize
mag′net·ized
mag·ne′to
mag′ni·fi·ca′tion
mag·nif′i·cence
mag·nif′i·cent
mag·nif′i·co

mag'ni·fi'er	main'sheet'	mal'e·dic'to·ry
mag'ni·fy	main'spring'	mal'e·fac'tor
mag·nil'o·quent	main'stay'	ma·lef'i·cence
mag'ni·tude	main·tain'	ma·lef'i·cent
mag·no'li·a	main·tain'a·ble	ma·lev'o·lence
mag'num	main'te·nance	ma·lev'o·lent
mag'pie	ma·jes'tic	mal·fea'sance
mag'uey	maj'es·ty	mal·fea'sor
ma·ha'ra'ja	ma·jol'i·ca	mal'for·ma'tion
ma·ha'ra'ni	ma'jor	mal·formed'
ma·hat'ma	ma·jor'i·ty	mal'ice
ma·hog'a·ny	ma·jus'cule	ma·li'cious
maid	make	ma·li'cious·ly
maid'en	make'-be·lieve'	ma·li'cious·ness
maid'en·hair'	mak'er	ma·lign'
maid'en·hood	make'shift'	ma·lig'nan·cy
maid'en·ly	mak'ings	ma·lig'nant
maid'serv'ant	mal'a·chite	ma·lig'nant·ly
mail	mal'ad·just'ed	ma·ligned'
mail'a·ble	mal'ad·just'ment	ma·lig'ni·ty
mail'bag'	mal'a·droit'	ma·lign'ly
mail'box'	mal'a·dy	ma·lin'ger
mailed	mal'a·pert	ma·lin'ger·er
mail'er	mal'a·prop·ism	mall
mail'ings	mal'ap·ro·pos'	mal'lard
maim	ma·lar'i·a	mal'le·a·bil'i·ty
maimed	ma·lar'i·al	mal'le·a·ble
main	mal'as·sim'i·la'tion	mal'le·o·lar
main'land'	Ma·lay'	mal'le·o·lus
main'ly	mal'con·tent'	mal'let
main'mast'	male	mal'low
main'sail'	mal'e·dic'tion	malm'sey

mal'nu·tri'tion	man'da·to'ry	man'i·fold'er
mal·o'dor·ous	man'di·ble	man'i·kin
mal'po·si'tion	man·dib'u·lar	ma·nip'u·late
mal'prac'tice	man'do·lin	ma·nip'u·lat'ed
malt	man'drake	ma·nip'u·lates
malt'ase	man'drel	ma·nip'u·la'tion
Mal'tese'	ma·neu'ver	ma·nip'u·la'tive
malt'ose	ma·neu'vered	ma·nip'u·la'tor
mal·treat'	man'ga·nate	ma·nip'u·la·to'ry
mal·ver·sa'tion	man'ga·nese	man'kind'
mam'ba	mange	man'like'
mam'mal	man'ger	man'li·ness
mam·ma'li·an	man'gi·ly	man'ly
mam'ma·ry	man'gi·ness	man'na
mam'mon	man'gle	man'ner
mam'moth	man'gled	man'nered
man	man'go	man'ner·ism
man'a·cle	man'grove	man'ner·ly
man'a·cled	man'gy	man'nish
man'age	man'hole'	ma·nom'e·ter
man'age·a·ble	man'hood	man'o·met'ric
man'aged	ma'ni·a	man'or
man'age·ment	ma'ni·ac	ma·no'ri·al
man'ag·er	ma·ni'a·cal	man'sard
man'a·ge'ri·al	man'i·cure	man'serv'ant
man'a·ge'ri·al·ly	man'i·cur'ist	man'sion
man'ag·er·ship'	man'i·fest	man'slaugh'ter
man'a·tee'	man'i·fes·ta'tion	man'teau
man·da'mus	man'i·fest·ed	man'tel
man'da·rin	man'i·fes'to	man·til'la
man'date	man'i·fold	man'tis
man'dat·ed	man'i·fold'ed	man·tis'sa

man'tle	mar'gi·na'li·a	mar'mo·set
man'u·al	mar'gin·al·ly	mar'mot
man'u·al·ly	mar'grave	ma·roon'
man'u·fac'to·ry	mar'i·gold	ma·rooned'
man'u·fac'ture	mar'i·jua'na	mar'plot'
man'u·fac'tured	ma·rim'ba	mar·quee'
man'u·fac'tur·er	ma·ri'na	mar'qui·sette'
man'u·mis'sion	mar'i·nade'	marred
ma·nure'	mar'i·nate	mar'riage
man'u·script	mar'i·nat'ed	mar'riage·a·ble
Manx	ma·rine'	mar'ried
man'y	mar'i·ner	mar'row
Ma'o·ri	mar'i·o·nette'	mar'row·bone'
map	Mar'ist	mar'row·fat'
ma'ple	mar'i·tal	mar'row·y
mapped	mar'i·tal·ly	mar'ry
mar	mar'i·time	Mars
mar'a·bou	mar'jo·ram	mar'shal
mar'a·schi'no	mark	mar'shaled
ma·raud'	marked	marsh'i·ness
ma·raud'er	mark'ed·ly	marsh'mal'low
mar'ble	mark'er	marsh'y
mar'bled	mar'ket	mar·su'pi·al
mar'ca·site	mar'ket·a·bil'i·ty	mart
march	mar'ket·a·ble	mar'ten
march'er	mark'ings	mar'tial
mar'chion·ess	marks'man	mar'tial·ly
mar·co'ni·gram	marks'man·ship	Mar'ti·an
mare	mark'weed'	mar'ti·net'
mar'ga·rine	marl	mar'tin·gale
mar'gin	mar'lin	mar'tyr
mar'gin·al	mar'ma·lade	mar'tyr·dom

mar'tyred	mas'ter·ly	ma·te'ri·al·ized
mar'vel	mas'ter·piece'	ma·te'ri·al·ly
mar'veled	mas'ter·ship	ma·ter'nal
mar'vel·ous	mas'ter·work'	ma·ter'nal·ly
mar'zi·pan	mas'ter·y	ma·ter'ni·ty
mas·car'a	mast'head'	math'e·mat'i·cal
mas'cot	mas'tic	math'e·ma·ti'cian
mas'cu·line	mas'ti·cate	math'e·mat'ics
mas'cu·lin'i·ty	mas'ti·cat'ed	mat'in
mash	mas'ti·ca'tion	mat'i·nee'
mashed	mas'ti·ca'tor	ma'tri·arch
mash'er	mas'ti·ca·to'ry	ma'tri·arch'y
mash'ie	mas'tiff	ma'tri·ces
mask	mas'to·don	ma'tri·cide
masked	mas'toid	ma·tric'u·lant
mask'er	mas'toid·i'tis	ma·tric'u·late
ma'son	mat	ma·tric'u·lat'ed
ma·son'ic	mat'a·dor	ma·tric'u·lates
ma'son·ry	match	ma·tric'u·la'tion
mas'quer·ade'	matched	mat'ri·mo'ni·al
mas'quer·ad'ed	match'less	mat'ri·mo'ni·al·ly
mass	match'less·ly	mat'ri·mo'ny
mas'sa·cre	match'mak'er	ma'trix
mas·sage'	match'wood'	ma'tron
mas·seur'	ma'té	ma'tron·li·ness
mas'sive	ma·te'ri·al	ma'tron·ly
mast	ma·te'ri·al·ism	matte
mas'ter	ma·te'ri·al·ist	mat'ted
mas'tered	ma·te'ri·al·is'tic	mat'ter
mas'ter·ful	ma·te'ri·al'i·ty	mat'tered
mas'ter·ful·ly	ma·te'ri·al·i·za'tion	mat'tings
mas'ter·ful·ness	ma·te'ri·al·ize	mat'tock

mat'tress	maze	me·a'tus
mat'u·rate	ma·zur'ka	me·chan'ic
mat'u·rat'ed	me	me·chan'i·cal
mat'u·ra'tion	mead'ow	me·chan'i·cal·ly
ma·tur'a·tive	mead'ow·land'	mech'a·ni'cian
ma·ture'	mea'ger	me·chan'ics
ma·tured'	meal	mech'a·nism
ma·ture'ly	meal'i·er	mech'a·ni·za'tion
ma·ture'ness	meal'i·est	mech'a·nize
ma·tu'ri·ty	meal'time'	med'al
ma·tu'ti·nal	meal'y	med'al·ist
maud'lin	meal'y·mouthed'	me·dal'lion
maul	mean	med'dle
mauled	me·an'der	med'dled
maun'der	mean'ing·ful	med'dle·some
mau·so·le'um	mean'ing·less	me'di·a
mauve	mean'ing·ly	me'di·al
mav'er·ick	mean'ings	me'di·an
ma'vis	mean'ly	me'di·ate
maw	mean'ness	me'di·at'ed
mawk'ish	mean'time'	me'di·a'tion
max'il·lar'y	mean'while'	me'di·a'tive
max'im	mea'sles	me'di·a'tor
max'i·mal	meas'ur·a·ble	med'i·cal
max'i·mize	meas'ur·a·bly	med'i·cal·ly
max'i·mum	meas'ure	Med'i·care
may	meas'ured	med'i·cate
may'be	meas'ure·less	med'i·cat'ed
may'hem	meas'ure·ment	med'i·ca'tion
may'on·naise'	meas'ur·er	med'i·ca'tive
may'or	meat	me·dic'i·nal
may'or·al·ty	meat'cut'ter	me·dic'i·nal·ly

med'i·cine

me'di·e'val

me'di·e'val·ist

me'di·e'val·ly

me'di·o'cre

me'di·oc'ri·ty

med'i·tate

med'i·tat'ed

med'i·ta'tion

med'i·ta'tive

me'di·um

med'lar

me·dul'la

meek

meek'er

meek'est

meek'ly

meek'ness

meer'schaum

meet

meet'ings

meet'ing·house'

meg'a·cy'cle

meg'a·phone

mei·o'sis

mei·ot'ic

mel'an·cho'li·a

mel'an·chol'ic

mel'an·chol'y

mel'a·nism

mel'a·no'sis

meld

mel'io·rate

mel'io·rat'ed

mel'io·ra'tion

mel'io·ra'tive

me·lis'ma

mel'is·mat'ic

mel·lif'lu·ous

mel'low

mel'lowed

mel'low·er

mel'low·est

me·lo'de·on

me·lod'ic

me·lo'di·on

me·lo'di·ous

me·lo'di·ous·ly

mel'o·dra'ma

mel'o·dra·mat'ic

mel'o·dy

mel'on

me'los

melt

melt'ed

melt'ing·ly

mem'ber

mem'ber·ship

mem'brane

mem'bra·nous

me·men'to

mem'oir

mem'o·ra·bil'i·a

mem'o·ra·ble

mem'o·ran'da

mem'o·ran'dum

mem'o·ran'dums

me·mo'ri·al

me·mo'ri·al·i·za'tion

me·mo'ri·al·ize

mem'o·ri·za'tion

mem'o·rize

mem'o·rized

mem'o·ry

men'ace

men'aced

me·nage'

me·nag'er·ie

mend

men·da'cious

men·dac'i·ty

mend'ed

Men·de'li·an

men'di·can·cy

men'di·cant

men'folk'

men·ha'den

me'ni·al

me'ni·al·ly

me·nin'ges

men'in·gi'tis

me·nis'cus

Men'non·ite

men'su·ra'tion

men'su·ra'tive

men'tal

men·tal'i·ty

men'tal·ly

men'thol

men'tion

men'tioned

men'tor

men'u

me·phit'ic

mer'can·tile

mer'ce·nar'y

mer'cer·ize

mer'cer·ized

mer'chan·dise

mer'chan·dis'er

mer'chant

mer'chant·man

mer'ci·ful

mer'ci·less

mer'ci·less·ly

mer·cu'ri·al

mer'cu·ry

mer'cy

mere'ly

mer'est

mer'e·tri'cious

merge

merged

merg'er

me·rid'i·an

me·ringue'

me·ri'no

mer'it

mer'it·ed

mer'i·to'ri·ous

mer'i·to'ri·ous·ly

mer'lin

mer'maid'

mer'ri·er

mer'ri·est

mer'ri·ly

mer'ri·ment

mer'ri·ness

mer'ry

mer'ry·mak'ing

me'sa

mes·cal'

mes·cal'ine

mesh

mesh'work'

mes'mer·ism

mes'on

mess

mes'sage

mes'sen·ger

Mes·si'ah

mess'man

mess'mate'

mes·ti'zo

met'a·bol'ic

me·tab'o·lism

met'a·car'pal

met'a·car'pus

met'al

me·tal'lic

me·tal'li·cal·ly

met'al·loid

met'al·lur'gic

met'al·lur'gi·cal

met'al·lur'gy

met'al·ware'

met'al·work'

met'al·work'er

met'a·mor'phose

met'a·mor'phoses

met'a·mor'pho·sis

met'a·phor

met'a·phor'ic

met'a·phor'i·cal

met'a·phor'i·cal·ly

met'a·phys'i·cal

met'a·phys'i·cal·ly

met'a·phy·si'cian

met'a·phys'ics

me·tas'ta·sis

me·tas'ta·size

met'a·tar'sal

met'a·tar'sus

mete

met'ed

me'te·or

me'te·or'ic

me'te·or·ite

me'te·or·oid'

me'te·or·ol'o·gy

me'ter

me'tered

meth'a·done	mi·crom'e·ter	mid'year'
meth'ane	mi'cron	mien
me·thinks'	mi'cro·phone	might
meth'od	mi'cro·scope	might'i·ly
me·thod'i·cal	mi'cro·scop'ic	might'i·ness
me·thod'i·cal·ly	mi·cros'co·py	might'y
meth'od·ist	mi'cro·spore	mi'graine
meth'od·ol'o·gy	mi'cro·struc'ture	mi'grant
meth'yl	mi'cro·tome	mi'grate
me·tic'u·lous	mi·crot'o·my	mi'grat·ed
mé·tier'	Mi'das	mi·gra'tion
me·ton'y·my	mid'brain'	mi'gra·to'ry
met'ric	mid'day'	mi·ka'do
met'ri·cal	mid'dle	milch
Met'ro·lin·er	mid'dle·man'	mild
met'ro·nome	mid'dle·weight'	mild'er
me·trop'o·lis	midge	mild'est
met'ro·pol'i·tan	midg'et	mil'dew
met'tle	mid'i'ron	mild'ly
met'tled	mid'land	mild'ness
met'tle·some	mid'most	mile
Mex'i·can	mid'night'	mile'age
mez'za·nine	mid'riff	mile'post'
mi·as'ma	mid'ship'man	mil'er
mi·as'mal	mid'ships'	mile'stone'
mi'as·mat'ic	midst	mil'i·tant
mi'ca	mid'stream'	mil'i·ta·rism
mi'crobe	mid'sum'mer	mil'i·ta·rist
mi'cro·cosm	mid'way'	mil'i·ta·ris'tic
mi'cro·fiche	mid'week'	mil'i·ta·rize
mi'cro·film	mid'wife'	mil'i·tar'y
mi'cro·gram	mid'win'ter	mil'i·tate

mil′i·tat′ed	mim′ic	min′is·try
mi·li′tia	mim′ic·ry	min′i·ver
milk	mi·mo′sa	mink
milk′maid′	min′a·ret	min′now
milk′man′	min′a·to′ry	mi′nor
milk′weed′	mince	mi·nor′i·ty
milk′y	minced	min′ster
mill	mince′meat′	min′strel
mill′board′	minc′ing·ly	min′strel·sy
milled	mind	mint
mil′le·nar′y	mind′ed	mint′ed
mil·len′ni·al	mind′ful	min′u·end
mil·len′ni·um	mind′less	min′u·et′
mil′le·pede	mine	mi′nus
mill′er	min′er	mi·nus′cule
mil′let	min′er·al	min′ute
mil′line′	min′er·al′o·gy	mi·nute′
mil′li·ner	min′gle	mi·nute′ness
mil′li·ner′y	min′gled	mi·nu′ti·a
mil′lion	min′i·a·ture	mi·nu′ti·ae
mil′lion·aire′	min′i·a·tur·ist	minx
mil′lion·fold′	min′im	mir′a·cle
mil′lionth	min′i·mal	mi·rac′u·lous
mill′pond′	min′i·mi·za′tion	mi·rage′
mill′race′	min′i·mize	mire
mill′stone′	min′i·mum	mired
mill′work′	min′i·skirt	mir′ror
mill′wright′	min′is·ter	mir′rored
Mil·ton′ic	min′is·tered	mirth
mime	min′is·te′ri·al	mirth′ful
mim′e·o·graph′	min′is·te′ri·al·ly	mirth′ful·ly
mi·met′ic	min′is·tra′tion	mirth′less

mis'ad·ven'ture

mis'al·li'ance

mis'an·thrope

mis'an·throp'ic

mis'an·throp'i·cal

mis·an'thro·pism

mis·an'thro·pist

mis·an'thro·py

mis'ap·pli·ca'tion

mis'ap·ply'

mis'ap·pre·hen'sion

mis'ap·pro'pri·ate

mis'ap·pro'pri·a'tion

mis'ar·range'

mis'be·got'ten

mis'be·have'

mis'be·haved'

mis'be·hav'ior

mis'be·liev'er

mis·brand'

mis·cal'cu·late

mis·cal'cu·lat'ed

mis·call'

mis·car'riage

mis·car'ried

mis·car'ry

mis·cast'

mis'ce·ge·na'tion

mis'cel·la'ne·a

mis'cel·la'ne·ous

mis'cel·la'nist

mis'cel·la'ny

mis·chance'

mis'chief

mis'chie·vous

mis'ci·ble

mis'con·ceive'

mis'con·cep'tion

mis'con·duct'

mis'con·struc'tion

mis'con·strue'

mis·count'

mis'cre·ant

mis·cue'

mis·date'

mis·deal'

mis·deed'

mis'de·mean'or

mis'di·rect'

mis'di·rect'ed

mis'di·rec'tion

mis·doubt'

mi'ser

mis'er·a·ble

mi'ser·li·ness

mi'ser·ly

mis'er·y

mis·fea'sance

mis·fire'

mis·fired'

mis·fit'

mis·formed'

mis·for'tune

mis·giv'ings

mis·gov'ern

mis·gov'erned

mis·guide'

mis·guid'ed

mis·hap'

mish'mash'

mis'in·form'

mis'in·formed'

mis'in·ter'pret

mis'in·ter'pre·ta'tion

mis'in·ter'pret·ed

mis·judge'

mis·judged'

mis·laid'

mis·lay'

mis·lead'

mis·lead'ing·ly

mis·like'

mis·liked'

mis·made'

mis·man'age

mis·man'age·ment

mis·mate'

mis·mat'ed

mis·name'

mis·named'

mis·no'mer

mi·sog'y·nist

mis·place'

mis·placed'

mis·print'

mis·pri'sion

mis·pro·nounce'

mis·pro·nun'ci·a'tion

mis·quo·ta'tion

mis·quote'

mis·read'

mis·re·mem'ber

mis·re·mem'brance

mis·rep·re·sent'

mis·rep·re·sen·ta'tion

mis·rule'

miss

mis'sal

missed

mis·shap'en

mis'sile

mis'sion

mis'sion·ar'y

mis'sion·er

mis'sive

mis·spell'

mis·spelled'

mis·spell'ings

mis·spend'

mis·spent'

mis·state'

mis·stat'ed

mis·state'ment

mis·step'

mist

mis·take'

mis·tak'en

mis·tak'en·ly

mis·taught'

mis·teach'

mist'i·er

mist'i·est

mist'i·ly

mist'i·ness

mis'tle·toe

mis·took'

mis·treat'

mis·treat'ment

mis'tress

mis·tri'al

mis·trust'

mis·trust'ful

mist'y

mis'un·der·stand'

mis'un·der·stand'ings

mis'un·der·stood'

mis·us'age

mis·use'

mis·used'

mite

mi'ter

mi'tered

mit'i·ga·ble

mit'i·gate

mit'i·gat'ed

mit'i·ga'tion

mit'i·ga'tive

mit'i·ga·to'ry

mi·to'sis

mi·tot'ic

mi'tral

mit'ten

mit'tened

mix

mixed

mix'er

mix'ture

miz'zen·mast'

mne·mon'ic

mo'a

moan

moaned

moat

mob

mob'cap'

mo'bile

mo·bil'i·ty

mo'bi·li·za'tion

mo'bi·lize

mo'bi·lized

mob·oc'ra·cy

moc'ca·sin

Mo'cha

mock

mock'er·y

mock'ing·ly

mod'al

mo·dal'i·ty

mode

mod'el

mod'eled

mod'er·ate

mod'er·at'ed

mod'er·ate·ly

mod'er·ate·ness

mod'er·a'tion

mod'er·a'tion·ist

mod'er·a'tor

mod'ern

mod'ern·ism

mod'ern·ist

mod'ern·is'tic

mo·der'ni·ty

mod'ern·i·za'tion

mod'ern·ize

mod'ern·ized

mod'est

mod'est·ly

mod'es·ty

mod'i·cum

mod'i·fi·ca'tion

mod'i·fi·ca'tion·ist

mod'i·fied

mod'i·fi'er

mod'i·fy

mod'ish

mod'ish·ly

mod'ish·ness

mod'u·lar

mod'u·late

mod'u·lat'ed

mod'u·la'tion

mod'u·la'tive

mod'u·la'tor

mod'u·la·to'ry

mod'ule

mod'u·lus

mog'a·dore'

Mo·gul'

mo'hair'

Mo·ham'med·an

Mo'hawk

mo'ho

moi'e·ty

moil

moiled

moi·re'

moist

mois'ten

mois'tened

mois'ten·er

mois'ture

mo'lal

mo'lar

mo·lar'i·ty

mo·las'ses

mold

mold'board'

mold'ed

mold'er

mold'ings

mold'y

mole

mo·lec'u·lar

mol'e·cule

mole'hill'

mole'skin'

mo·lest'

mo·les·ta'tion

mo·lest'ed

mol'li·fi·ca'tion

mol'li·fied

mol'li·fy

mol'lusk

mol'ly·cod'dle

molt

molt'ed

mol'ten

mo'ly

mo·lyb'de·num

mo'ment

mo'men·tar'i·ly

mo'men·tar'y

mo'ment·ly

mo·men'tous

mo·men'tum

mon'ad

mo·nad'nock

mon'arch

mo·nar'chi·al

mo·nar'chi·an·ism

mo·nar'chic

mon'arch·ism

mon'arch·ist

mon'arch·is'tic

mon'arch·y

mon'as·te'ri·al

mon'as·te'ri·al·ly

mon'as·ter'y

mon'o·lith'ic

month

mo·nas'tic

mon'o·logue

month'ly

mo·nas'ti·cism

mon'o·ma'ni·a

mon'u·ment

mon'a·tom'ic

mon'o·ma'ni·ac

mon'u·men'tal

Mon'day

mon'o·ma·ni'a·cal

mon'u·men'tal·ly

mo·nel'

mon'o·mor'phic

mood

mon'e·tar'y

mon'o·plane

mood'i·ly

mon'e·ti·za'tion

mon'o·ple'gi·a

mood'i·ness

mon'e·tize

mo·nop'o·lism

mood'y

mon'ey

mo·nop'o·list

moon

mon'eyed

mo·nop'o·lis'tic

moon'beam'

mon'goose

mo·nop'o·lis'ti·cal·ly

moon'faced'

mon'grel

mo·nop'o·li·za'tion

moon'fish'

mon'ism

mo·nop'o·lize

moon'flow'er

mon'i·tor

mo·nop'o·lized

moon'light'

mon'i·tored

mo·nop'o·ly

moon'light'ed

mon'i·to'ri·al

mon'o·rail'

moon'light'er

mon'i·to'ry

mon'o·syl·lab'ic

moon'light'ing

monk

mon'o·syl'la·ble

moon'rise'

mon'key

mon'o·the·ism

moon'shine'

monk'hood

mon'o·the·is'tic

moon'stone'

monk'ish

mon'o·tone

moon'-struck

mon'o·bas'ic

mo·not'o·nous

moor

mon'o·cle

mo·not'o·ny

moor'age

mon'o·cled

mon'o·type

moored

mo·noc'u·lar

mon·ox'ide

moor'ings

mon'o·dy

mon·si'gnor

Moor'ish

mo·nog'a·mous

mon·soon'

moor'land'

mo·nog'a·my

mon'ster

moose

mon'o·gram

mon'strance

moot

mon'o·graph

mon·stros'i·ty

mop

mon'o·lith

mon'strous

mopped

mop'pet	mor'phine	most'ly
mo·raine'	mor'phin·ism	mo·tel'
mor'al	mor'phin·ize	mo·tet'
mo·rale'	mor·phol'o·gy	moth
mor'al·ist	mor'ris	moth'er
mor'al·is'tic	mor'row	moth'er·hood
mo·ral'i·ty	mor'sel	moth'er-in-law'
mor'al·i·za'tion	mor'tal	moth'er·land'
mor'al·ize	mor·tal'i·ty	moth'er·less
mor'al·ized	mor'tal·ly	moth'er·li·ness
mor'al·ly	mor'tar	moth'er·ly
mo·rass'	mor'tar·board'	moth'er-of-pearl'
mor'a·to'ri·um	mort'gage	mo·tif'
mo·ray'	mort'gaged	mo'tile
mor'bid	mort'ga·gee'	mo'tion
mor·bid'i·ty	mort'ga·gor'	mo'tioned
mor'bid·ly	mor·ti'cian	mo'tion·less
mor'dant	mor'ti·fi·ca'tion	mo'ti·vate
more	mor'ti·fied	mo'ti·vat'ed
more·o'ver	mor'ti·fy	mo'ti·va'tion
mo'res	mor'tise	mo'ti·va'tion·al
mor'ga·nat'ic	mort'main	mo'tive
morgue	mor'tu·ar'y	mot'ley
mor'i·bund	mo·sa'ic	mo'tor
Mor'mon	Mos'lem	mo'tor·boat'
morn	mosque	mo'tor·cy'cle
morn'ing	mos·qui'to	mo'tored
morn'ings	moss	mo'tor·ist
mo·roc'co	moss'back'	mo'tor·ize
mo'ron	moss'i·ness	mo'tor·man
mo·rose'	moss'y	mot'tle
mo·rose'ly	most	mot'tled

mot'to	mow	mug
mound	mow'er	mug'ging
mount	Ms.	mug'gy
moun'tain	much	mug'wump'
moun'tain·eer'	mu'ci·lage	mu·lat'to
moun'tain·ous	mu'ci·lag'i·nous	mul'ber'ry
moun'tain·ous·ly	muck	mulch
moun'te·bank	muck'er	mulched
mount'ed	muck'rak'er	mulct
mount'ings	muck'weed'	mulct'ed
mourn	muck'worm'	mule
mourned	mu'coid	mu'le·teer'
mourn'er	mu·co'sa	mu'li·eb'ri·ty
mourn'ful	mu'cous	mul'ish
mouse	mu'cus	mull
mous'er	mud	mulled
mouse'trap'	mud'di·er	mul'let
mousse	mud'di·est	mul'li·ga·taw'ny
mouth	mud'di·ly	mul'ti·eth'nic
mouthed	mud'di·ness	mul'ti·far'i·ous
mouth'ful	mud'dle	mul'ti·fold
mouth'fuls	mud'dled	mul'ti·form
mouth'piece'	mud'dle-head'ed	mul'ti·for'mi·ty
mov'a·bil'i·ty	mud'dy	Mul'ti·graph
mov'a·ble	mud'fish'	Mul'ti·lith'
mov'a·bly	mud'weed'	mul'ti·mil'lion·aire'
move	muff	mul'ti·na'tion·al
moved	muf'fin	mul'ti·ple
move'ment	muf'fle	mul'ti·plex
mov'er	muf'fled	mul'ti·pli·cand'
mov'ie	muf'fler	mul'ti·pli·cate
mov'ing·ly	muf'ti	mul'ti·pli·ca'tion

mul'ti·pli·ca'tive

mul'ti·plic'i·ty

mul'ti·plied

mul'ti·pli'er

mul'ti·ply

mul'ti·tude

mul'ti·tu'di·nous

mul'ti·va'lent

mum'ble

mum'bled

mum'mer

mum'mer·y

mum'mi·fi·ca'tion

mum'mi·fied

mum'mi·fy

mum'my

mumps

munch

munched

mun'dane

mu·nic'i·pal

mu·nic'i·pal'i·ty

mu·nic'i·pal·ly

mu·nif'i·cence

mu·nif'i·cent

mu'ni·ment

mu·ni'tion

mu'ral

mur'der

mur'dered

mur'der·er

mur'der·ous

mu'rex

mu'ri·at'ic

murk

murk'i·ly

murk'i·ness

murk'y

mur'mur

mur'mured

mur'mur·er

mur'mur·ous

mus'ca·dine

mus'cat

mus'ca·tel'

mus'cle

mus'cu·lar

mus'cu·lar'i·ty

mus'cu·lar·ly

mus'cu·la·ture

muse

mused

mu·sette'

mu·se'um

mush

mush'room

mush'roomed

mush'y

mu'sic

mu'si·cal

mu'si·cale'

mu'si·cal·ly

mu·si'cian

mu·si'cian·ly

musk

mus'keg

mus'kel·lunge

mus'ket

mus'ket·eer'

mus'ket·ry

musk'mel'on

musk'rat'

mus'lin

muss

mussed

mus'sel

muss'i·er

muss'i·est

muss'y

must

mus·tache'

mus·ta'chio

mus'tang

mus'tard

mus'ter

mus'tered

mus'ti·ness

mus'ty

mu'ta·bil'i·ty

mu'ta·ble

mu'tate

mu·ta'tion

mu'ta·tive

mute

mut'ed

mute'ness

mu′ti·late	muz′zle	mys·te′ri·ous·ly
mu′ti·lat′ed	muz′zled	mys′ter·y
mu′ti·la′tion	my	mys′tic
mu′ti·la′tor	my·col′o·gy	mys′ti·cal
mu′ti·neer′	my·co′sis	mys′ti·cal·ly
mu′ti·nied	my·dri′a·sis	mys′ti·cism
mu′ti·nous	myd′ri·at′ic	mys′ti·fi·ca′tion
mu′ti·ny	my′e·loid	mys′ti·fied
mut′ism	My′lar	mys′ti·fy
mut′ter	my·o′pi·a	myth
mut′tered	my·op′ic	myth′i·cal
mut′ter·ings	myr′i·ad	myth′o·log′i·cal
mut′ton	myrrh	my·thol′o·gist
mu′tu·al	myr′tle	my·thol′o·gy
mu′tu·al′i·ty	my·self′	
mu′tu·al·ly	mys·te′ri·ous	

N

na·celle'

na'cre

na'cre·ous

na'dir

nai'ad

nail

nailed

nail'head'

nain'sook

na·ive'

na·ive·té'

na'ked

na'ked·ly

na'ked·ness

nam'a·ble

name

named

name'less

name'less·ly

name'ly

name'sake'

nan·keen'

nap

na'per·y

naph'tha

naph'tha·lene

nap'kin

na·po'le·on

Na·po'le·on·a'na

Na·po'le·on'ic

napped

nar·cis'sism

nar·cis'sus

nar·co'sis

nar·cot'ic

nar·cot'i·cism

nar'co·tize

nar'co·tized

nar·rate'

nar·rat'ed

nar·ra'tion

nar'ra·tive

nar·ra'tor

nar'row

nar'rowed

nar'row·er

nar'row·est

nar'row·ly

nar'row·ness

nar'whal

na'sal

na·sal'i·ty

na'sal·ize

na'sal·ly

nas'cent

nas'ti·er

nas'ti·est

nas'ti·ly

nas'ti·ness

nas·tur'tium

nas'ty

na'tal

na·ta'tion

na'ta·to'ri·um

na'ta·to'ry

na'tion

na·tion·al

na·tion·al·ism

na·tion·al·is'tic

na·tion·al'i·ty

na·tion·al·i·za'tion

na·tion·al·ize

na·tion·al·ized

na·tion·al·ly

na'tive

na·tiv'i·ty

nat'u·ral

nat'u·ral·ism

nat'u·ral·ist

nat'u·ral·is'tic

nat'u·ral·i·za'tion

nat'u·ral·ize

nat'u·ral·ized

nat'u·ral·ly

nat'u·ral·ness

na'ture

na'tur·is'tic

naught

naugh'ti·ly

naugh'ti·ness

naugh'ty

nau'se·a

nau'se·ate

nau'se·at'ed

nau'seous

nau'ti·cal

nau'ti·lus

na'val

nave

na'vel

nav'i·ga·ble

nav'i·gate

nav'i·gat'ed

nav'i·ga'tion

nav'i·ga'tion·al

nav'i·ga'tor

na'vy

Naz'a·rene'

neap

Ne·a·pol'i·tan

near

near'by'

neared

near'er

near'est

near'ly

near'ness

near'sight'ed

neat

neat'er

neat'est

neat'herd'

neat'ly

neat'ness

neb'u·la

neb'u·lar

neb'u·los'i·ty

neb'u·lous

neb'u·lous·ly

nec'es·sar'i·ly

nec'es·sar'y

ne·ces'si·tar'i·an

ne·ces'si·tate

ne·ces'si·tat'ed

ne·ces'si·tous

ne·ces'si·ty

neck

neck'band'

neck'cloth'

neck'er·chief

neck'lace

neck'tie'

neck'wear'

nec'ro·log'i·cal

ne·crol'o·gy

nec'ro·man'cy

nec'ro·man'tic

nec'ro·pho'bi·a

ne·crop'o·lis

nec'rop·sy

ne·cro'sis

ne·crot'ic

nec'tar

nec'tar·ine'

need

need'ed

need'ful

need'ful·ly

need'i·er

need'i·est

need'i·ness

nee'dle

nee'dled	neigh'bor·ly	net'ted
nee'dle·ful	nei'ther	net'tings
need'less	nem'a·tode	net'tle
need'less·ly	Nem'e·sis	net'tled
need'less·ness	ne'o·for·ma'tion	net'work'
nee'dle·work'	ne'o·lith'ic	neu'ral
need'y	ne·ol'o·gism	neu·ral'gia
ne·far'i·ous	ne·ol'o·gy	neu'ras·the'ni·a
ne·gate'	ne'on	neu'ras·then'ic
ne·gat'ed	ne'o·phyte	neu·ri'tis
ne·ga'tion	ne'o·plasm	neu·ro'ses
neg'a·tive	ne·pen'the	neu·ro'sis
neg'a·tived	neph'ew	neu·rot'ic
neg'a·tiv·ism	ne·phrec'to·my	neu'ter
neg·lect'	ne·phri'tis	neu'tral
neg·lect'ed	nep'o·tism	neu'tral·ism
neg·lect'ful	nerve	neu'tral·ist
neg'li·gee'	nerve'less	neu·tral'i·ty
neg'li·gence	ner'vous	neu'tral·i·za'tion
neg'li·gent	nerv'ous·ly	neu'tral·ize
neg'li·gi·ble	nerv'ous·ness	neu'tral·ized
ne·go'ti·a·bil'i·ty	nes'ci·ence	neu'tral·iz'er
ne·go'ti·a·ble	nes'ci·ent	neu'tral·ly
ne·go'ti·ate	nest	neu'tron
ne·go'ti·at'ed	nest'ed	nev'er
ne·go'ti·a'tion	nes'tle	nev'er·more'
ne·go'ti·a'tor	nes'tled	nev'er·the·less'
Ne'gro	nest'lings	new
Ne'gro·phile	net	new'com'er
neigh'bor	neth'er	new'el
neigh'bor·hood	neth'er·most	new'er
neigh'bor·li·ness	net'su·ke	new'est

new'fan'gled

new'ly

new'ness

news'i·er

news'i·est

news'let'ter

news'pa'per

news'reel'

news'stand'

news'y

newt

next

nex'us

nib'ble

nib'bled

nib'lick

nice

nice'ly

nice'ness

nic'er

nic'est

ni'ce·ty

niche

nick

nicked

nick'el

nick'el·if'er·ous

nick'el·o'de·on

nick'name'

nick'named'

nic'o·tine

nic'o·tin'ic

niece

ni·el'lo

nig'gard

nig'gard·li·ness

nig'gard·ly

nig'gle

nig'gling·ly

nigh

night

night'cap'

night'fall'

night'fish'

night'gown'

night'hawk'

night'in·gale

night'ly

night'mare'

night'mar'ish

night'shade'

night'shirt'

night'time'

night'wear'

night'work'

night'work'er

ni'hil·ism

ni'hil·ist

ni'hil·is'tic

nim'ble

nim'bus

nin'com·poop

nine'pins'

nip'per

nip'ple

nip'py

nir·va'na

ni'ter

ni'trate

ni'tric

ni'tride

ni'tri·fi·ca'tion

ni'tri·fy

ni'tro·gen

ni·trog'e·nous

ni'tro·glyc'er·in

ni'trous

nit'wit'

no

no·bil'i·ty

no'ble

no'ble·man

no'bler

no'blest

no'bly

no'bod·y

noc·tur'nal

noc·tur'nal·ly

noc'turne

nod

nod'ded

node

nod'ule

no·el'

noise

noise'less

nois'i·er

nois'i·est

nois'i·ly

nois'i·ness

noi'some

nois'y

no'mad

no·mad'ic

no'men·cla·ture

nom'i·nal

nom'i·nal·ism

nom'i·nal·ly

nom'i·nate

nom'i·nat'ed

nom'i·na'tion

nom'i·na·tive

nom'i·nee'

non'a·ge·nar'i·an

non'a·gon

non'ap·pear'ance

non·call'a·ble

nonce

non'cha·lance

non'cha·lant

non'cha·lant·ly

non·com'bat·ant

non'com·mis'sioned

non'com·mit'tal

non'com·mu'ni·cant

non'con·duc'tor

non'con·form'ism

non'con·form'ist

non'con·form'i·ty

non'-co-op'er·a'tion

non'de·script

non·en'ti·ty

non'es·sen'tial

none'such'

non'ex·ist'ence

non·fea'sance

non·fea'sor

non·for'feit·ure

non'in·ter·ven'tion

non'met'al

non'me·tal'lic

non'pa·reil'

non'par·tic'i·pat'ing

non·par'ti·san

non·per'ma·nent

non'plus

non'plused

non·res'i·dence

non·res'i·dent

non're·sist'ance

non're·sist'ant

non'sense

non·sen'si·cal

non'skid'

non'stop'

non'sub·scrib'er

non'suit'

non'sup·port'

non·un'ion

noo'dle

nook

noon

noon'day'

noon'time'

noose

nor

norm

nor'mal

nor·mal'i·ty

nor'mal·ize

nor'mal·ized

nor'mal·ly

Nor'man

nor'ma·tive

Norse

north

north'east'

north'east'er

north'east'er·ly

north'east'ern

north'east'ward

north'east'ward·ly

north'er·ly

north'ern

north'ern·er

north'land

north'ward

north'west'

north'west'er·ly

north'west'ern

Nor·we'gian

nose

nose'band'

nose'bleed'

nose'gay'

nose'piece'

nos'ings

no·sol'o·gy

nos·tal'gi·a

nos·tal'gic

nos'tril

nos'trum

not

no'ta·bil'i·ty

no'ta·ble

no·tar'i·al

no·tar'i·al·ly

no'ta·ry

no·ta'tion

notch

notched

notch'weed'

note

note'book'

not'ed

note'wor'thi·ly

note'wor'thy

noth'ing

noth'ing·ness

no'tice

no'tice·a·ble

no'ticed

no'ti·fi·ca'tion

no'ti·fied

no'ti·fy

no'tion

no'to·ri'e·ty

no·to'ri·ous

no·to'ri·ous·ly

not'with·stand'ing

nou'gat

nou'ga·tine

nought

nou'me·non

noun

nour'ish

nour'ished

nour'ish·ing·ly

nour'ish·ment

nov'el

nov'el·ette'

nov'el·ist

nov'el·ize

no·vel'la

nov'el·ty

No·vem'ber

no·ve'na

nov'ice

no·vi'ti·ate

No'vo·cain'

now

now'a·days'

no'where

nox'ious

nox'ious·ness

noz'zle

nu·ance'

nu'cle·ar

nu'cle·ate

nu'cle·at'ed

nu'cle·a'tion

nu'cle·i

nu·cle'o·lus

nu'cle·us

nude

nudge

nudged

nud'ism

nud'ist

nu'di·ty

nu'ga·to'ry

nug'get

nui'sance

null

nul'li·fi·ca'tion

nul'li·fi·ca'tion·ist

nul'li·fied

nul'li·fy

nul'li·ty

numb

numbed

num'ber

num'bered

num'ber·less

numb'ness

nu'mer·al

nu'mer·ate

nu'mer·a'tion

nu'mer·a'tor

nu·mer'ic

nu·mer'i·cal

nu'mer·ous

nu·mis·mat'ics

nu·mis'ma·tist

num'skull'

nun

nun'ci·a·ture

nun'ci·o

nun'ner·y

nup'tial

nurse

nursed

nurse'maid'

nurs'er·y

nurs'er·y·maid'

nurs'er·y·man

nurs'lings

nur'ture

nur'tured

nut

nut'hatch'

nut'meg

nu'tri·a

nu'tri·ent

nu'tri·ment

nu·tri'tion

nu·tri'tion·al

nu·tri'tion·al·ly

nu·tri'tion·ist

nu·tri'tious

nu·tri'tious·ly

nu'tri·tive

nu'tri·tive·ly

nut'shell'

nuz'zle

nuz'zled

nyc'ta·lo'pi·a

ny'lon

nys·tag'mus

oaf	o·bit'u·ar'y	ob·lique'ness
oak	ob·ject'	ob·liq'ui·ty
oak'en	ob·ject'ed	ob·lit'er·ate
oa'kum	ob·jec'tion	ob·lit'er·at'ed
oar	ob·jec'tion·a·ble	ob·lit'er·a'tion
oar'lock'	ob·jec'tive	ob·liv'i·on
oars'man	ob·jec'tive·ly	ob·liv'i·ous
o·a'sis	ob·jec'tive·ness	ob·liv'i·ous·ly
oat'en	ob'jec·tiv'i·ty	ob·liv'i·ous·ness
oath	ob·jec'tor	ob'long
oat'meal'	ob'jur·gate	ob'lo·quy
ob'bli·ga'to	ob'late	ob·nox'ious
ob'du·ra·cy	ob·la'tion	ob·nox'ious·ly
ob'du·rate	ob'li·gate	o'boe
o·be'di·ence	ob'li·gat'ed	ob·scene'
o·be'di·ent	ob'li·ga'tion	ob·scen'i·ty
o·bei'sance	ob·lig'a·to'ry	ob·scure'
ob'e·lisk	o·blige'	ob·scure'ness
o·bese'	o·bliged'	ob·scu'ri·ty
o·bes'i·ty	o·blig'ing·ly	ob·se'qui·ous
o·bey'	ob·lique'	ob·se'qui·ous·ly
o·beyed'	ob·lique'ly	ob·se'qui·ous·ness

ob'se·quy
ob·serv'a·ble
ob·serv'ance
ob·serv'ant
ob'ser·va'tion
ob·serv'a·to'ry
ob·serve'
ob·served'
ob·serv'er
ob·serv'ing·ly
ob·sess'
ob·sessed'
ob·ses'sion
ob·ses'sion·al
ob·ses'sive
ob·sid'i·an
ob'so·les'cence
ob'so·les'cent
ob'so·lete
ob'so·lete·ly
ob'so·lete·ness
ob'sta·cle
ob·stet'ri·cal
ob·ste·tri'cian
ob·stet'rics
ob'sti·na·cy
ob'sti·nate
ob'sti·nate·ly
ob·strep'er·ous
ob·struct'
ob·struct'ed
ob·struc'tion

ob·struc'tion·ism
ob·struc'tion·ist
ob·struc'tive
ob·struc'tor
ob·tain'
ob·tain'a·ble
ob·tained'
ob·trude'
ob·trud'ed
ob·trud'er
ob·tru'sion
ob·tru'sive
ob·tuse'
ob·tuse'ly
ob·tuse'ness
ob'verse
ob'vi·ate
ob'vi·at'ed
ob'vi·a'tion
ob'vi·ous
ob'vi·ous·ly
oc'a·ri'na
oc·ca'sion
oc·ca'sion·al
oc·ca'sion·al·ly
oc·ca'sioned
oc'ci·dent
oc'ci·den'tal
oc'ci·den'tal·ly
oc·cip'i·tal
oc'ci·put
oc·clude'

oc·clud'ed
oc·clu'sion
oc·cult'
oc'cul·ta'tion
oc·cult'ism
oc·cult'ist
oc'cu·pan·cy
oc'cu·pant
oc'cu·pa'tion
oc'cu·pa'tion·al
oc'cu·pa'tion·al·ly
oc'cu·pied
oc'cu·py
oc·cur'
oc·curred'
oc·cur'rence
o'cean
o'ce·an'ic
o'ce·a·nog'ra·phy
o'ce·lot
o'cher
och·loc'ra·cy
oc'ta·gon
oc·tag'o·nal
oc·tag'o·nal·ly
oc·tam'e·ter
oc·tan'gu·lar
oc'tave
oc·ta'vo
oc·tet'
Oc·to'ber
oc'to·ge·nar'i·an

oc'to·pus

oc'u·lar

oc'u·list

odd

odd'er

odd'est

odd'i·ty

odd'ly

odd'ment

odd'ness

ode

o·de'um

o'di·ous

o'di·ous·ly

o'di·ous·ness

o'di·um

o·dom'e·ter

o'dor

o'dor·if'er·ous

o'dor·less

o'dor·ous

oe·nol'o·gy

of

off

of'fal

off'cast'

of·fend'

of·fend'ed

of·fense'

of·fen'sive

of'fer

of'fered

of'fer·ings

of'fer·to'ry

off'hand'

of'fice

of'fi·cer

of·fi'cial

of·fi'cial·ly

of·fi'ci·ate

of·fi'ci·at'ed

of·fi'ci·a'tion

of·fi'cious

of·fi'cious·ly

of·fi'cious·ness

off'ish

off'set'

off'shoot'

off'shore'

of'ten

of'ten·er

of'ten·est

of'ten·times'

o·gee'

o'give

o'gle

o'gled

o'gre

ohm

ohm'age

ohm'me'ter

oil

oiled

oil'er

oil'hole'

oil'i·er

oil'i·est

oil'i·ly

oil'i·ness

oil'man

oil'pa'per

oil'proof'

oil'seed'

oil'skin'

oil'stone'

oil'tight'

oil'y

oint'ment

o·ka'pi

o'kra

old

old'en

old'er

old'est

old'-fash'ioned

old'ish

old'ness

old'ster

o'le·ag'i·nous

o'le·an'der

o'le·ate

o·lec'ra·non

o'le·o

o'le·o·mar'ga·rine

ol·fac'to·ry

ol'i·garch'y

ol'ive	on·tol'o·gy	oph'thal·mol'o·gist
o·me'ga	o'nus	oph'thal·mol'o·gy
om'e·let	on'ward	o'pi·ate
o'men	on'yx	o·pin'ion
o·men'tum	o·öl'o·gy	o·pin'ion·at'ed
om'i·nous	oo'long	o·pin'ion·a'tive
o·mis'sion	ooze	o'pi·um
o·mit'	oozed	o·pos'sum
o·mit'ted	o·pac'i·ty	op·po'nent
om'ni·bus	o'pal	op'por·tune'
om'nip'o·tence	o'pal·esce'	op'por·tun'ism
om·nip'o·tent	o'pal·es'cence	op'por·tu'ni·ty
om'ni·pres'ent	o'pal·es'cent	op·pos'a·ble
om·nis'cience	o·paque'	op·pose'
om·nis'cient	o'pen	op·posed'
om·niv'o·rous	o'pened	op·pos'er
on	o'pen·er	op·pos'ing
on'a·ger	o'pen·ings	op'po·site
once	o'pen·ly	op'po·si'tion
one	o'pen·ness	op·press'
one'ness	o'pen·work'	op·pressed'
on'er·ous	op'er·a	op·pres'sion
one·self'	op'er·a·ble	op·pres'sive
one'time'	op'er·a·logue'	op·pres'sive·ly
on'ion	op'er·ate	op·pres'sive·ness
on'look'er	op'er·at'ed	op·pres'sor
on'ly	op'er·at'ic	op·pro'bri·ous
on'o·mat'o·poe'ia	op'er·at'i·cal·ly	op·pro'bri·ous·ly
on'set'	op'er·a'tion	op·pro'bri·ous·ness
on'slaught'	op'er·a'tive	op·pro'bri·um
on'to	op'er·a'tor	opt
on·tog'e·ny	op'er·et'ta	opt'ed

op'ta·tive

op'tic

op'ti·cal

op·ti'cian

op'tics

op'ti·mism

op'ti·mist

op'ti·mis'tic

op'ti·mis'ti·cal·ly

op'ti·mum

op'tion

op'tion·al

op'tion·al·ly

op·tom'e·trist

op·tom'e·try

op'u·lence

op'u·lent

o'pus

or

or'a·cle

o·rac'u·lar

o·rac'u·lar·ly

o'ral

o'ral·ly

or'ange

o·rang'u·tan'

o·ra'tion

or'a·tor

or'a·tor'i·cal

or'a·to'ri·o

or'a·to'ry

orb

or'bit

or'bit·al

or'bit·ed

or'chard

or'ches·tra

or·ches'tral

or'ches·trate

or'ches·trat'ed

or'ches·tra'tion

or'chid

or'chi·da'ceous

or·dain'

or·dained'

or·deal'

or'der

or'dered

or'der·li·ness

or'der·ly

or'di·nal

or'di·nance

or'di·nar'i·ly

or'di·nar'y

or'di·na'tion

ord'nance

ore

or'gan

or·gan'ic

or·gan'i·cal·ly

or'gan·ism

or'gan·ist

or'gan·i·za'tion

or'gan·i·za'tion·al

or'gan·ize

or'gan·ized

or'gy

o'ri·el

o'ri·ent

o'ri·en'tal

o'ri·en'tal·ism

o'ri·en'tal·ist

o'ri·en'tal·ly

o'ri·en·tate'

o'ri·en·ta'tion

o'ri·ent'ed

or'i·fice

or'i·gin

o·rig'i·nal

o·rig'i·nal'i·ty

o·rig'i·nal·ly

o·rig'i·nate

o·rig'i·nat'ed

o·rig'i·na'tion

o·rig'i·na'tive

o·rig'i·na'tor

o'ri·ole

O·ri'on

or'i·son

or'lop

or'mo·lu

or'na·ment

or'na·men'tal

or'na·men'tal·ly

or'na·men·ta'tion

or·nate'

or·nate'ly	os'se·ous	out'crop'
or'ni·tho·log'i·cal	os'si·fi·ca'tion	out'cry'
or'ni·thol'o·gist	os'si·fied	out·curve'
or'ni·thol'o·gy	os'si·fy	out·dis'tance
o'ro·tund	os·ten'si·ble	out·do'
o'ro·tun'di·ty	os·ten'si·bly	out'doors'
or'phan	os'ten·ta'tion	out'er
or'phan·age	os'ten·ta'tious	out'er·most
or'phaned	os'ten·ta'tious·ly	out·face'
or'phan·hood	os'te·o·path	out'field'
or'phe·um	os'te·op'a·thy	out'fit
or'rer·y	os'tra·cism	out'fit'ter
or'tho·dox	os'tra·cize	out·flank'
or'tho·ëp'y	os'tra·cized	out'flow'
or·thog'ra·phy	os'trich	out·go'
or'tho·pe'dic	o·tal'gi·a	out'growth'
or·thop'tic	oth'er	out'ings
or'to·lan	oth'er·wise'	out·land'ish
os'cil·late	o'ti·ose	out·land'ish·ness
os'cil·lat'ed	ot'ter	out·last'
os'cil·la'tion	Ot'to·man	out'law'
os'cil·la'tor	ought	out'law'ry
os'cil·la·to'ry	ounce	out'lay'
os·cil'lo·scope	our	out'let
os'cu·late	ours	out'lets
os'cu·la'tion	our·selves'	out'line'
os'cu·la·to'ry	oust	out'lined'
o'sier	oust'er	out·live'
os'mi·um	out	out·lived'
os·mo'sis	out'cast'	out·look'
os·mot'ic	out·class'	out'ly'ing
os'prey	out·come'	out'march'

out·mod′ed	ov′en·bird′	o′ver·drawn′
out·num′ber	ov′en·ware′	o′ver·dress′
out′put′	o′ver	o′ver·drew′
out′rage	o′ver·age	o′ver·drive′
out·ra′geous	o′ver·age′	o′ver·driv′en
out·ra′geous·ly	o′ver·alls′	o′ver·due′
out·ra′geous·ness	o′ver·awe′	o′ver·eat′
out·rank′	o′ver·awed′	o′ver·es′ti·mate
out·ranked′	o′ver·bal′ance	o′ver·ex·pose′
out·reach′	o′ver·bear′	o′ver·ex·po′sure
out′rid·er	o′ver·bear′ing·ly	o′ver·flow′
out′rig′ger	o′ver·bid′	o′ver·flow′ing·ly
out′right′	o′ver·board′	o′ver·grown′
out·run′	o′ver·build′	o′ver·hand′
out′set′	o′ver·built′	o′ver·hang′
out′side′	o′ver·bur′den	o′ver·haul′
out′sid′er	o′ver·cap′i·tal·ize	o′ver·head′
out′size′	o′ver·cast′	o′ver·heat′
out′skirt′	o′ver·charge′	o′ver·is′sue
out·stand′ing·ly	o′ver·charged′	o′ver·land′
out·stay′	o′ver·clothes′	o′ver·lap′
out·strip′	o′ver·coat′	o′ver·look′
out·vote′	o′ver·come′	o′ver·lord′
out′ward	o′ver·com′pen·sa′tion	o′ver·ly
out′ward·ly	o′ver·cor·rect′	o′ver·mas′ter·ing·ly
out·wear′	o′ver·count′	o′ver·mod′u·la′tion
out·wit′	o′ver·de·vel′op	o′ver·night′
out·work′	o′ver·do′	o′ver·pass′
o′val	o′ver·done′	o′ver·pay′
o′vate	o′ver·dose′	o′ver·pop′u·la′tion
o·va′tion	o′ver·draft′	o′ver·pow′er
ov′en	o′ver·draw′	o′ver·pow′ered

o'ver·pow'er·ing·ly

o'ver·pro·duc'tion

o'ver·rate'

o'ver·rat'ed

o'ver·reach'

o'ver·ride'

o'ver·ripe'

o'ver·rule'

o'ver·ruled'

o'ver·run'

o'ver·seas'

o'ver·see'

o'ver·se'er

o'ver·sell'

o'ver·shad'ow

o'ver·shad'owed

o'ver·shoe'

o'ver·side'

o'ver·sight'

o'ver·size'

o'ver·spread'

o'ver·state'

o'ver·state'ment

o'ver·stay'

o'ver·step'

o'ver·stock'

o'ver·strain'

o'ver·sub·scribe'

o'ver·sup·ply'

o'vert

o'ver·take'

o'ver·tax'

o'ver·taxed'

o'ver·threw'

o'ver·throw'

o'ver·thrown'

o'ver·time'

o'ver·tone'

o'ver·ture

o'ver·turn'

o'ver·turned'

o'ver·val'ue

o'ver·ween'ing·ly

o'ver·weight'

o'ver·whelm'

o'ver·whelmed'

o'ver·whelm'ing·ly

o'ver·wind'

o'ver·work'

o'ver·worked'

o'ver·wrought'

o'vi·duct

o·vip'a·rous

o'vi·pos'i·tor

o'vule

o'vum

owe

owed

owl

owl'et

owl'ish

own

owned

own'er

own'er·ship

ox

ox'a·late

ox·al'ic

ox'i·da'tion

ox'ide

ox'i·diz'a·ble

ox'i·dize

ox'i·dized

ox'tongue'

ox'y·gen

ox'y·gen·ate

oys'ter

oys'ter·shell'

o'zone

o'zo·nize

o'zo·nized

pab'u·lum	pack'sack'	paid
pace	pack'sad'dle	pail
pace'mak'er	pack'thread'	pain
pac'er	pact	pained
pach'y·derm	pad	pain'ful
pach'y·san'dra	pad'ded	pain'kill'er
pa·cif'ic	pad'dings	pain'less
pa·cif'i·cal·ly	pad'dle	pains'tak'ing·ly
pa·cif'i·cate	pad'dled	paint
pac'i·fi·ca'tion	pad'dle·fish'	paint'ed
pa·cif'i·ca·to'ry	pad'dock	paint'er
pac'i·fied	pad'lock'	paint'ings
pac'i·fi'er	pae'an	paint'pot'
pac'i·fism	pa'gan	pair
pac'i·fist	pa'gan·ism	paired
pac'i·fy	pa'gan·ize	pair'ings
pack	page	pa·ja'ma
pack'age	pag'eant	pal'ace
pack'aged	pag'eant·ry	pal'a·din
pack'er	paged	pal'an·quin'
pack'et	pag'i·na'tion	pal'at·a·bil'i·ty
pack'ings	pa·go'da	pal'at·a·ble

pal'a·tal

pal'a·tal·ize

pal'ate

pa·la'tial

pa·la'tial·ly

pa·lat'i·nate

pal'a·tine

pa·lav'er

pale

paled

pa'le·og'ra·phy

pal'er

pal'est

pal'ette

pal'frey

pal'imp·sest

pal'in·drome

pal'ings

pal'i·node

pal'i·sade'

pall

pal·la'di·um

pall'bear'er

palled

pal'let

pal'li·ate

pal'li·at'ed

pal'li·a'tion

pal'li·a'tive

pal'lid

pal·lid'i·ty

pal'lid·ly

pal'li·um

pal'lor

palm

pal'mate

palmed

palm'er

palm·met'to

palm'ist

palm'is·try

pal'pa·bil'i·ty

pal'pa·ble

pal'pate

pal'pat·ed

pal·pa'tion

pal'pa·to'ry

pal'pi·tant

pal'pi·tate

pal'pi·tat'ed

pal'pi·tat'ing·ly

pal'pi·ta'tion

pal'sied

pal'sy

pal'ter

pal'tered

pal'try

pam'pas

pam'per

pam'pered

pam'phlet

pam'phlet·eer'

pam'phlet·ize

pan

pan'a·ce'a

pan'a·ma'

Pan'-A·mer'i·can

Pan'-A·mer'i-
can·ism

pan'cake'

pan'chro·mat'ic

pan'cre·as

pan'cre·at'ic

pan'da

pan·dem'ic

pan'de·mo'ni·um

pan'der

pan'dered

pane

pan'e·gyr'ic

pan'e·gyr'i·cal

pan'e·gy·rize

pan'e·gy·rized

pan'el

pan'eled

pang

Pan'hel·len'ic

pan'ic

pan'icked

pan'ick·y

pan·jan'drum

panned

pan'nier

pan'ni·kin

pan'o·ply

pan'o·ra·ma

pan'o·ram'ic

pan'sy

pant

pan'ta·loon'

pant'ed

pan'the·ism

pan'the·ist

pan'the·is'tic

pan'the·on

pan'ther

pan'to·graph

pan'to·mime

pan'try

pan'try·man

pa'pa·cy

pa'pal

pa·pay'a

pa'per

pa'per·back'

pa'per·board'

pa'pered

pa'per·er

pap'e·terie

pa·poose'

pa·pri'ka

Pap'u·an

pap'ule

pa·py'rus

par

par'a·ble

pa·rab'o·la

par'a·bol'ic

par'a·bol'i·cal

pa·rab'o·loid

par'a·chute

pa·rade'

pa·rad'ed

par'a·digm

par'a·dise

par'a·dox

par'a·dox'i·cal

par'af·fin

par'a·gon

par'a·graph

par'a·graphed

par'a·keet

par'al·lax

par'al·lel

par'al·leled

par'al·lel·ism

par'al·lel'o·gram

pa·ral'y·sis

par'a·lyt'ic

par'a·lyt'i·cal·ly

par'a·lyze

par'a·lyzed

pa·ram'e·ter

par'a·mount

par'a·noi'a

par'a·noi'ac

par'a·noid

par'a·pet

par'a·pher·na'li·a

par'a·phrase

par'a·phrased

par'a·phras'tic

par'a·ple'gi·a

par'a·pleg'ic

par'a·site

par'a·sit'ic

par'a·sit'i·cal

par'a·sit'i·cide

par'a·sit·ism

par'a·sit·ize

par'a·sol

par'a·thy'roid

par'a·ty'phoid

par'a·vane

par'boil'

par'boiled'

par'cel

par'celed

parch

parched

parch'ment

par'don

par'don·a·ble

par'doned

pare

pared

par'e·gor'ic

pa·ren'chy·ma

par'ent

par'ent·age

pa·ren'tal

pa·ren'tal·ly

pa·ren'the·ses

pa·ren'the·sis

pa·ren'the·size

par'en·thet'i·cal

par'en·thet'i·cal·ly

par'ent·hood

pa·re'sis

par·fait'

pa·ri'ah

pa·ri'e·tal

par'ings

par'ish

pa·rish'ion·er

par'i·ty

park

par'ka

parked

park'way'

par'lance

par·lan'do

par'lay

par'ley

par'leyed

par'lia·ment

par'lia·men·tar'i·an

par'lia·men'ta·ri·ly

par'lia·men'ta·ry

par'lor

par'lous

Par'me·san'

Par·nas'sus

pa·ro'chi·al

pa·ro'chi·al·ism

pa·ro'chi·al·ly

par'o·dy

pa·role'

par'o·no·ma'si·a

pa·rot'id

par'ox·ysm

par'ox·ys'mal

par'ox·ys'mal·ly

par·quet'

par'ri·cid'al

par'ri·cid'al·ly

par'ri·cide

par'ried

par'rot

par'rot·ed

par'ry

parse

parsed

par'si·mo'ni·ous

par'si·mo'ny

pars'ley

pars'nip

par'son

par'son·age

part

par·take'

par·tak'er

part'ed

par·terre'

par'the·no·gen'e·sis

Par'the·non

Par'thi·an

par'tial

par'ti·al'i·ty

par'tial·ly

par·tic'i·pant

par·tic'i·pate

par·tic'i·pat'ed

par·tic'i·pa'tion

par·tic'i·pa'tive

par·tic'i·pa'tor

par'ti·cip'i·al

par'ti·cip'i·al·ly

par'ti·ci·ple

par'ti·cle

par·tic'u·lar

par·tic'u·lar'i·ty

par·tic'u·lar·ize

par·tic'u·lar·ized

par·tic'u·lar·ly

part'ings

par'ti·san

par'ti·san·ship'

par·ti'tion

par·ti'tioned

par'ti·tive

part'ner

part'ner·ship

par'tridge

par'ty

par've·nu

pas'chal

pa·sha'

pass

pass'a·ble

pas'sage

pas'sage·way'

pass'book'

passed

pas'sen·ger

pas'sion

pas'sion·ate

pas'sion·ate·ly

Pas'sion·ist

pas'sion·less

pas'sive

pas'sive·ness

pas'siv·ism

pas'siv·ist

pas·siv'i·ty

pass'key'

pass'o'ver

pass'port

pass'word'

past

paste

paste'board'

past'ed

pas·tel'

pas'tern

pas'teur·i·za'tion

pas'teur·ize

pas'teur·ized

pas·tiche'

pas·tille'

pas'time'

past'i·ness

pas'tor

pas'to·ral

pas'to·ral·ly

pas'tor·ate

pas'try

pas'try·man

pas'tur·age

pas'ture

pas'tured

past'y

pat

Pat'a·go'ni·an

patch

patched

patch'ou·li

patch'work'

patch'y

pa·tel'la

pa·tel'lar

pat'ent

pat'ent·a·ble

pat'ent·ed

pat'ent·ee'

pa'ter·fa·mil'i·as

pa·ter'nal

pa·ter'nal·ism

pa·ter'nal·is'tic

pa·ter'nal·ly

pa·ter'ni·ty

path

pa·thet'ic

pa·thet'i·cal·ly

path'less

pa·thol'o·gist

pa·thol'o·gy

pa'thos

path'way'

pa'tience

pa'tient

pat'i·na

pa'ti·o

pat'ness

pat'ois

pa'tri·arch

pa'tri·ar'chal

pa'tri·arch'ate

pa'tri·arch'y

pa·tri'cian

pat'ri·cide

pat'ri·mo'ni·al

pat'ri·mo'ny

pa'tri·ot

pa'tri·ot'ic

pa'tri·ot'i·cal·ly

pa'tri·ot·ism

pa·tris'tic

pa·trol'

pa·trolled'

pa·trol'man

pa'tron

pa'tron·age

pa'tron·ess

pa'tron·ize

pa'tron·ized	pay	peb'bled
pat'ro·nym'ic	pay'a·ble	peb'ble·ware'
pa·troon'	pay'day'	peb'bly
pat'ted	pay'ee'	pe·can'
pat'ten	pay'ees'	pec'ca·dil'lo
pat'ter	pay'er	pec'can·cy
pat'tered	pay'mas'ter	pec'cant
pat'tern	pay'ment	pec'ca·ry
pat'terned	pay'roll'	peck
pau'ci·ty	pea	pec'tase
Paul'ist	peace	pec'tin
paunch	peace'a·ble	pec'to·ral
paunch'i·ness	peace'a·bly	pec'u·late
pau'per	peace'ful	pec'u·lat'ed
pau'per·ism	peace'mak'er	pec'u·la'tion
pau'per·i·za'tion	peach	pec'u·la'tor
pau'per·ize	pea'cock'	pe·cul'iar
pau'per·ized	peak	pe·cu'li·ar'i·ty
pause	peaked	pe·cul'iar·ly
paused	peal	pe·cu'ni·ar'y
pave	pealed	ped'a·gog'ic
paved	pea'nut'	ped'a·gog'i·cal
pave'ment	pear	ped'a·gog'i·cal·ly
pav'er	pearl	ped'a·gogue
pa·vil'lion	pearl'ite	ped'a·go'gy
paw	pearl'y	ped'al
pawed	peas'ant	ped'aled
pawl	peas'ant·ry	ped'ant
pawn	pea'shoot'er	pe·dan'tic
pawn'bro'ker	peat	pe·dan'ti·cal
pawned	pea'vey	pe·dan'ti·cism
pawn'shop'	peb'ble	ped'ant·ry

ped'dle

ped'dled

ped'dler

ped'es·tal

pe·des'tri·an

pe·des'tri·an·ism

pe'di·a·tri'cian

pe'di·at'rics

pe·dic'u·lar

pe·dic'u·lo'sis

ped'i·cure

ped'i·gree

ped'i·greed

ped'i·ment

pe·dom'e·ter

peek

peel

peeled

peel'ings

peen

peep

peer

peer'age

peered

peer'less

pee'vish

peg

Peg'a·sus

pegged

pe'jo·ra'tive

pe'koe

pe·lag'ic

pelf

pel'i·can

pe·lisse'

pel·la'gra

pel'let

pel·lu'cid

pe·lo'ta

pelt

pelt'ed

pel'try

pel'vic

pel'vis

pem'mi·can

pen

pe'nal

pe'nal·i·za'tion

pe'nal·ize

pe'nal·ized

pen'al·ty

pen'ance

pen'chant'

pen'cil

pen'ciled

pend'ant

pend'en·cy

pend'ing

pen'du·lous

pen'du·lum

pen'e·tra·bil'i·ty

pen'e·tra·ble

pen'e·trant

pen'e·trate

pen'e·trat'ed

pen'e·trat'ing·ly

pen'e·tra'tion

pen'e·tra'tive

pen'guin

pen'hold'er

pen'i·cil'lin

pen·in'su·la

pen·in'su·lar

pen'i·tence

pen'i·tent

pen'i·ten'tial

pen'i·ten'tial·ly

pen'i·ten'tia·ry

pen'i·tent·ly

pen'knife'

pen'man

pen'man·ship

pen'nant

pen'ni·less

pen'non

pen'ny

pen'ny·roy'al

pen'ny·weight'

pe·nol'o·gist

pe·nol'o·gy

pen'sion

pen'sion·ar'y

pen'sioned

pen'sion·er

pen'sive

pen'stock'

pent

pen·ta·gon

pen·tag'o·nal

pen·tam'e·ter

Pen'ta·teuch

pen·tath'lon

pen'ta·ton'ic

Pen'te·cost

pent'house'

pent·ox'ide

pe'nult

pe·nul'ti·mate

pe·num'bra

pe·nu'ri·ous

pen'u·ry

pe'on

pe'on·age

pe'o·ny

peo'ple

peo'pled

pep'lum

pep'per

pep'pered

pep'per·i·ness

pep'per·mint

pep'per·y

pep'sin

pep'tic

pep'tone

per'ad·ven'ture

per·am'bu·late

per·am'bu·la'tor

per·bo'rate

per·cale'

per·ceiv'a·ble

per·ceive'

per·ceived'

per·cent'

per·cent'age

per·cen'tile

per'cept

per·cep'ti·bil'i·ty

per·cep'ti·ble

per·cep'tion

per·cep'tive

per·cep'tu·al

per·cep'tu·al·ly

perch

per·chance'

per·cip'i·en·cy

per·cip'i·ent

per'co·late

per'co·la'tion

per'co·la'tor

per·cus'sion

per·cus'sive

per·di'tion

per·du'

per·dur'a·ble

per'e·gri·na'tion

per·emp'to·ri·ly

per·emp'to·ri·ness

per·emp'to·ry

per·en'ni·al

per·en'ni·al·ly

per'fect

per·fect'ed

per·fect'i·bil'i·ty

per·fect'i·ble

per·fec'tion

per·fec'tion·ism

per·fec'tion·ist

per'fect·ly

per·fec'to

per·fid'i·ous

per'fi·dy

per'fo·rate

per'fo·rat'ed

per'fo·ra'tion

per'fo·ra'tive

per'fo·ra'tor

per·force'

per·form'

per·form'a·ble

per·form'ance

per·formed'

per·form'er

per·fume'

per·fumed'

per·fum'er

per·fum'er·y

per·func'to·ri·ly

per·func'to·ri·ness

per·func'to·ry

per·fuse'

per·fused'

per'go·la

per·haps'

per'i·car'di·al

per'i·car·di'tis

per'i·car'di·um

per'i·gee

per'il·ous

per'il·ous·ly

per·im'e·ter

pe'ri·od

per·i'o·date

pe'ri·od'ic

pe'ri·od'i·cal

pe'ri·od'i·cal·ly

pe'ri·o·dic'i·ty

per'i·os'te·um

per'i·pa·tet'ic

pe·riph'er·al

pe·riph'er·al·ly

pe·riph'er·y

per'i·phras'tic

per'i·scope

per'i·scop'ic

per'ish

per'ish·a·ble

per'ished

per'i·stal'sis

per'i·stal'tic

per'i·stal'ti·cal·ly

per'i·style

per'i·to·ne'um

per'i·to·ni'tis

per'i·win'kle

per'jure

per'jured

per'jur·er

per·ju'ri·ous·ly

per'ju·ry

perk'y

perm'al·loy'

per'ma·nence

per'ma·nent

per'ma·nent·ly

per·man'ga·nate

per'me·a·bil'i·ty

per'me·a·ble

per'me·ate

per'me·at'ed

per'me·a'tion

per·mis'si·bil'i·ty

per·mis'si·ble

per·mis'sion

per·mis'sive·ness

per·mit'

per·mit'ted

per'mu·ta'tion

per·mute'

per·mut'ed

per·ni'cious

per'o·ra'tion

per·ox'ide

per'pen·dic'u·lar

per'pen·dic'u·lar'i·ty

per'pe·trate

per'pe·trat'ed

per'pe·tra'tion

per'pe·tra'tor

per·pet'u·al

per·pet'u·al·ly

per·pet'u·ate

per·pet'u·at'ed

per·pet'u·a'tion

per·pet'u·a'tor

per'pe·tu'i·ty

per·plex'

per·plexed'

per·plex'ed·ly

per·plex'ing·ly

per·plex'i·ty

per'qui·site

per'qui·si'tion

per'se·cute

per'se·cut'ed

per'se·cu'tion

per'se·cu'tor

per'se·ver'ance

per·sev'er·a'tion

per'se·vere'

per'se·vered'

per'si·flage

per·sim'mon

per·sist'

per·sist'ence

per·sist'en·cy

per·sist'ent

per·sist'ing·ly

per'son

per'son·a·ble

per'son·age

per'son·al

per'son·al'i·ty

per'son·al·ize

per'son·al·ly

per'son·al·ty

per·son'i·fi·ca'tion

per·son'i·fied

per·son'i·fy

per'son·nel'

per·spec'tive

per'spi·ca'cious

per'spi·cac'i·ty

per·spic'u·ous

per'spi·ra'tion

per·spir'a·to'ry

per·spire'

per·spired'

per·suade'

per·suad'ed

per·suad'er

per·sua'sion

per·sua'sive

per·sua'sive·ness

per·sul'phate

pert

per·tain'

per·tained'

per'ti·na'cious

per'ti·nac'i·ty

per'ti·nence

per'ti·nent

per·turb'

per·turb'a·ble

per'tur·ba'tion

per·turbed'

pe·rus'al

pe·ruse'

pe·rused'

Pe·ru'vi·an

per·vade'

per·vad'ed

per·vad'ing·ly

per·va'sion

per·va'sive

per·verse'

per·ver'sion

per·ver'si·ty

per·ver'sive

per·vert'

per·vert'ed

per'vi·ous

pes'si·mism

pes'si·mist

pes'si·mis'tic

pes'si·mis'ti·cal·ly

pest

pes'ter

pes'tered

pest'hole'

pest'house'

pes·tif'er·ous

pes'ti·lence

pes'ti·lent

pes'ti·len'tial

pes'ti·len'tial·ly

pes'tle

pet

pet'al

pe·tard'

pe·tite'

pe·ti'tion

pe·ti'tioned

pe·ti'tion·er

pet'rel

pet'ri·fac'tion

pet'ri·fac'tive

pet'ri·fy

pet'rol

pet'ro·la'tum

pe·tro'le·um

pe·trol'o·gy

pet'ted

pet'ti·coat

pet'ti·er

pet'ti·est

pet'ti·fog'ger

pet'ti·ly

pet'ti·ness

pet'tish

pet'ty

pet'u·lance

pet'u·lant

pe·tu'ni·a

pew	phil'an·throp'i·cal	phon'ic
pew'ter	phi·lan'thro·pist	pho'no·graph
pha'e·ton	phi·lan'thro·py	phos'phate
phag'o·cyte	phil'a·tel'ic	phos'phide
phal'ange	phi·lat'e·list	phos'phite
phal'an·ster'y	phi·lat'e·ly	phos'pho·resce'
pha'lanx	phil'har·mon'ic	phos'pho·res'cence
phan'tasm	phi·lip'pic	phos·phor'ic
phan·tas'ma·go'ri·a	Phil'ip·pine	phos'pho·rous
phan'tom	Phil·is'tine	phos'pho·rus
Phar'aoh	phi·lol'o·gist	pho'to·cop'i·er
phar'ma·ceu'tic	phi·lol'o·gy	pho'to·e·lec'tric
phar'ma·ceu'ti·cal	phi·los'o·pher	pho'to·en·grav'ing
phar'ma·ceu'tics	phil'o·soph'ic	pho'to·gen'ic
phar'ma·cist	phil'o·soph'i·cal	pho'to·graph
phar'ma·col'o·gy	phi·los'o·phize	pho'to·graphed
phar'ma·co·poe'ia	phi·los'o·phy	pho·tog'ra·pher
phar'ma·cy	phil'ter	pho'to·graph'ic
phar'yn·gi'tis	phle·bi'tis	pho·tog'ra·phy
phar'ynx	phle·bot'o·my	pho'to·gra·vure'
phase	phlegm	pho'to·lith'o·graph
phased	phleg·mat'ic	pho'to·mi'cro·graph
pheas'ant	phleg·mat'i·cal·ly	pho'ton
phe'nol	phlo'em	pho'to·play'
phe·nom'e·na	phlox	pho'to·sen'si·tize
phe·nom'e·nal	pho'bi·a	Pho'to·stat
phe·nom'e·nol'o·gy	phoe'nix	pho'to·syn'the·sis
phe·nom'e·non	phone	phrase
phi'al	pho·net'ic	phrased
phi·lan'der	pho·net'i·cal·ly	phra'se·ol'o·gy
phi·lan'der·er	pho'ne·ti'cian	phre·net'ic
phil'an·throp'ic	pho·net'ics	phren'ic

phre·nol'o·gist

phre·nol'o·gy

phthi'sis

phy·lac'ter·y

phys'ic

phys'i·cal

phys'i·cal·ly

phy·si'cian

phys'i·cist

phys'ics

phys'i·og'no·my

phys'i·o·log'i·cal

phys'i·o·log'i·cal·ly

phys'i·ol'o·gy

phy·sique'

pi·a·nis'si·mo

pi·an'ist

pi·a'no

pi·an'o·for'te

pi·az'za

pi'ca

pic'a·resque'

pic'co·lo

pick

pick'ax

picked

pick'er

pick'er·el

pick'et

pick'et·ed

pick'ings

pick'le

pick'led

pick'lock'

pick'pock'et

pick'up'

pic'nic

pic'nick·er

pic'ric

pic'to·graph

pic·to'ri·al

pic·to'ri·al·ly

pic'ture

Pic'ture·phone

pic'tur·esque'

pie

pie'bald'

piece

piece'meal'

piece'work'

pie'crust'

pied

pie'plant'

pier

pierce

pierced

pi'e·ty

pig

pi'geon

pi'geon·hole'

pig'fish'

pig'ger·y

pig'gish

pig'head'ed

pig'let

pig'ment

pig'men·tar'y

pig'men·ta'tion

pig'ment·ed

pig'nut'

pig'pen'

pig'skin'

pig'stick'er

pig'sty'

pig'tail'

pig'weed'

pike

pik'er

pike'staff'

pi·las'ter

pil'chard

pile

piled

pile'work'

pile'worm'

pil'fer

pil'fer·age

pil'fered

pil'fer·ings

pil'grim

pil'grim·age

pill

pil'lage

pil'laged

pil'lar

pil'lion

pil'lo·ry

pil'low

pil'low·case'

pil'lowed

pi'lot

pi'lot·ed

pi·men'to

pim'per·nel

pim'ple

pin

pin'a·fore'

pin'cers

pinch

pinched

pin'cush'ion

pine

pine'ap'ple

pined

pin'feath'er

pin'fish'

ping'-pong'

pin'guid

pin'hole'

pin'ion

pink

pink'ish

pink'weed'

pink'wood'

pin'nace

pin'na·cle

pinned

pi'noch'le

pin'prick'

pint

pin'to

pin'weed'

pin'worm'

pi'o·neer'

pi'o·neered'

pi'ous

pi'ous·ly

pip

pip'age

pipe

piped

pipe'line'

pip'er

pipe'stem'

pipe'stone'

pi·pette'

pipe'wood'

pip'ing·ly

pip'ings

pip'it

pip'kin

pip·sis'se·wa

pi'quan·cy

pi'quant

pique

pi·qué'

piqued

pi'ra·cy

pi'rate

pi'rat·ed

pi·rat'ic

pi·rat'i·cal

pi·rogue'

pir'ou·ette'

pir·ou·et'ted

pis'ca·tol'o·gy

pis'ca·to'ri·al

pis'ca·to'ri·al·ly

pis·tach'i·o

pis'tol

pis·tole'

pis'ton

pit

pitch

pitched

pitch'er

pitch'fork'

pit'e·ous

pit'e·ous·ness

pit'fall'

pith

pith'i·ly

pith'i·ness

pith'y

pit'i·a·ble

pit'i·ful

pit'i·less

pit'i·less·ly

pit'i·less·ness

pit'tance

pit'ted

pi·tu'i·tar'y

pit'y	plain'ly	plas'ma
pit'y·ing·ly	plain'ness	plas'ter
piv'ot	plaint	plas'tered
piv'ot·al	plain'tiff	plas'ter·er
piv'ot·ed	plain'tive	plas'ter·work'
pla'ca·bil'i·ty	plait	plas'tic
pla'ca·ble	plait'ed	plas·tic'i·ty
plac'ard	plait'ings	plas'tron
pla'cate	plan	plate
pla'cat·ed	plan·chette'	pla·teau'
pla'ca·tive·ly	plane	plat'ed
pla'ca·to'ry	plan'et	plate'hold'er
place	plan'e·tar'i·an	plate'let
pla·ce'bo	plan'e·tar'i·um	plat'en
place'man	plan'e·tar'y	plat'er
place'ment	plan'et·oid	plat'form'
pla·cen'ta	plan'gent	plat'i·na
plac'er	plan'i·sphere	plat'i·nate
plac'id	plank	plat'ings
pla·cid'i·ty	planked	pla·tin'ic
plac'id·ly	plank'ton	plat'i·nize
plack'et	plan'less	plat'i·noid
pla'gi·a·rism	planned	plat'i·num
pla'gi·a·rist	pla'no·graph'ic	plat'i·tude
pla'gi·a·rize	plant	plat'i·tu'di·nize
pla'gi·a·ry	plan'tain	plat'i·tu'di- nous
plague	plan'tar	pla·toon'
plagued	plan·ta'tion	plat'ter
plaid	plant'ed	plat'y·pus
plain	plant'er	plau'dit
plain'er	plant'ings	plau'si·bil'i·ty
plain'est	plaque	plau'si·ble

play	pleat	plinth
play'back'	ple·be'ian	plod
play'bill'	pleb'i·scite	plod'ded
play'boy'	pledge	plod'der
played	pledged	plod'ding·ly
play'er	pledg'ee'	plot
play'ful	pledge'or'	plot'ted
play'ful·ness	pledg'er	plot'ter
play'ground'	pledg'et	plough
play'ings	ple'na·ri·ly	plov'er
play'mate'	ple'na·ry	plow
play'read'er	plen'i·po·ten'ti·ar'y	plow'boy
play'room'	plen'i·tude	plow'ings
play'script'	plen'te·ous	plow'man
play'thing'	plen'ti·ful	plow'share'
play'time'	plen'ty	pluck
play'wright'	ple'num	plucked
pla'za	ple'o·nasm	pluck'i·er
plea	ple'o·nas'tic	pluck'i·est
plead	pleth'o·ra	pluck'i·ly
plead'ed	ple·thor'ic	pluck'i·ness
plead'er	pleu'ra	pluck'y
plead'ing·ly	pleu'ral	plug
plead'ings	pleu'ri·sy	plugged
pleas'ant	plex'us	plum
pleas'ant·ly	pli'a·bil'i·ty	plum'age
pleas'ant·ness	pli'a·ble	plumb
pleas'ant·ry	pli'an·cy	plum·ba'go
please	pli'ant	plum'bate
pleased	pli'ers	plumbed
pleas'ur·a·ble	plight	plumb'er
pleas'ure	plight'ed	plum'bic

plum'bous	plu·to'ni·um	point'less
plume	ply	point'less·ly
plumed	pneu·mat'ic	poise
plum'met	pneu·mat'i·cal·ly	poised
plum'met·ed	pneu·mat'ics	poi'son
plump	pneu·mo'ni·a	poi'soned
plump'er	poach	poi'son·er
plump'est	poach'er	poi'son·ous
plump'ly	pock'et	poke
plump'ness	pock'et·book'	poked
plun'der	pock'et·knife'	pok'er
plun'dered	pock'mark'	poke'weed'
plun'der·er	pod	po'lar
plunge	po·dag'ra	po·lar'i·ty
plunged	po·di'a·try	po'lar·i·za'tion
plung'er	po'di·um	po'lar·ize
plunk	po'em	po'lar·ized
plunked	po'e·sy	po'lar·iz'er
plu'ral	po'et	pole
plu'ral·ism	po'et·as'ter	pole'cat'
plu'ral·ist	po·et'ic	po·lem'ic
plu·ral·is'tic	po·et'i·cal	po·lem'i·cal
plu·ral'i·ty	po'et·ry	po·lem'i·cist
plu'ral·ize	po'i	po·lem'ics
plu'ral·ized	poign'an·cy	pole'star'
plus	poign'ant	po·lice'
plush	poin'ci·an'a	po·liced'
plu·toc'ra·cy	poin·set'ti·a	po·lice'man
plu'to·crat	point	pol'i·cy
plu'to·crat'ic	point'ed	pol'ish
plu'to·crat'i·cal·ly	point'ed·ly	pol'ished
plu·ton'ic	point'er	pol'ish·er

po·lite′	pol′y·gon	pon′der·os′i·ty
po·lite′ly	po·lyg′o·nal	pon′der·ous
po·lite′ness	pol′y·mer′ic	pond′fish′
pol′i·tic	po·lym′er·ism	pond′weed′
po·lit′i·cal	pol′y·mer·i·za′tion	pon·gee′
po·lit′i·cal·ly	pol′y·mer·ize	pon′iard
pol′i·ti′cian	pol′y·no′mi·al	pon′tiff
pol′i·tics	pol′yp	pon·tif′i·cal
pol′ka	po·lyph′o·ny	pon·tif′i·cal·ly
poll	pol′y·syl·lab′ic	pon·tif′i·cate
pol′lard	pol′y·tech′nic	pon·toon′
pol′lard·ed	po·made′	po′ny
polled	po·man·der	poo′dle
pol′len	po·ma′tum	pool
pol′li·nate	pome′gran′ate	pooled
pol′li·na′tion	Pom·er·a′ni·an	pool′room′
poll′ster	pom′mel	poor
pol·lute′	pom′meled	poor′er
pol·lut′ed	po·mol′o·gy	poor′est
pol·lu′tion	pomp	poor′house′
po′lo	pom′pa·dour	poor′ly
pol′o·naise′	pom′pa·no	poor′ness
po·lo′ni·um	Pom·pe′ian	pop
pol·troon′	pom′pon	pop′corn′
pol′y·an′drous	pom·pos′i·ty	pop′gun′
pol′y·an′dry	pomp′ous	pop′in·jay
pol′y·chrome	pon′cho	pop′lar
pol′y·clin′ic	pond	pop′lin
po·lyg′a·mist	pon′der	pop′o′ver
po·lyg′a·mous	pon′der·a·ble	popped
po·lyg′a·my	pon′dered	pop′pet
pol′y·glot	pon′der·o′sa	pop′py

pop'u·lace

pop'u·lar

pop'u·lar'i·ty

pop'u·lar·i·za'tion

pop'u·lar·ize

pop'u·lar·ized

pop'u·late

pop'u·lat'ed

pop'u·la'tion

pop'u·lous

por'ce·lain

porch

por'cu·pine

pore

pored

por'gy

pork

por·nog'ra·phy

po·ros'i·ty

po'rous

por'phy·ry

por'poise

por'ridge

por'rin·ger

port

port'a·ble

por'tage

por'tal

port·cul'lis

por·tend'

por·tend'ed

por'tent

por·ten'tous

por'ter

por'ter·house'

port·fo'li·o

port'hole'

por'ti·co

por·tiere'

por'tion

por'tioned

port·man'teau

por'trait

por'trait·ist

por'trai·ture

por·tray'

por·tray'al

por·trayed'

Por'tu·guese

por'tu·la'ca

pose

posed

po·si'tion

pos'i·tive

pos'i·tiv·ism

pos'i·tiv·is'tic

pos'i·tron

pos'se

pos·sess'

pos·sessed'

pos·ses'sion

pos·ses'sive

pos·ses'sor

pos·ses'sor·ship

pos'si·bil'i·ty

pos'si·ble

pos'si·bly

pos'sum

post

post'age

post'al

post'box'

post'date'

post'dat'ed

post'ed

post'er

pos·te'ri·or

pos·ter'i·ty

pos'tern

post·grad'u·ate

post'haste'

post'hole'

post'hu·mous

pos·til'ion

post'im·pres'sion·ism

post'ings

post'lude

post'man

post·mar'i·tal

post'mark'

post'mas'ter

post'me·rid'i·an

post'mis'tress

post'-mor'tem

post·nup'tial

post'op'er·a·tive

post'paid'	pot'house'	pow'ered
post·pone'	po'tion	pow'er·ful
post·poned'	pot'latch'	pow'er·ful·ly
post·pone'ment	pot'luck'	pow'er·less
post·pran'di·al	pot'pie'	pow'er·less·ly
post'script	pot'pour'ri'	pow'er·less·ness
pos'tu·lant	pot'sherd'	pow'wow'
pos'tu·late	pot'tage	prac'ti·ca·bil'i·ty
pos'tu·lat'ed	pot'ter	prac'ti·ca·ble
pos'tu·la'tion	pot'ter·y	prac'ti·ca·bly
pos'ture	pouch	prac'ti·cal
pos'tured	poult	prac'ti·cal'i·ty
pos'tur·ings	poul'ter·er	prac'ti·cal·ly
po'sy	poul'tice	prac'tice
pot	poul'ticed	prac'ticed
po'ta·bil'i·ty	poul'try	prac'ti·cum
po'ta·ble	pounce	prac·ti'tion·er
pot'ash'	pounced	prag·mat'ic
po·tas'si·um	pound	prag·mat'i·cal
po·ta'tion	pound'age	prag·mat'i·cal·ly
po·ta'to	pound'cake'	prag'ma·tism
pot'boil'er	pound'ed	prag'ma·tist
po'ten·cy	pound'ings	prai'rie
po'tent	pour	praise
po'ten·tate	poured	praised
po·ten'tial	pout	praise'wor·thy
po·ten'ti·al'i·ty	pout'ed	pra'line
po·ten'tial·ly	pov'er·ty	prance
po·ten'ti·om'e·ter	pow'der	pranced
pot'herb'	pow'dered	pranc'ing·ly
pot'hole'	pow'der·y	prank
pot'hook'	pow'er	prank'ster

prate	pre·cep′tress	pre·cool′
prat′ed	pre·ces′sion	pre·cur′sor
prat′ings	pre·chill′	pre·cur′so·ry
pra·tique′	pre′cinct	pre·da′ceous
prat′tle	pre·ci·os′i·ty	pre·dac′i·ty
prat′tling·ly	pre′cious	pre·date′
prawn	pre′cious·ly	pre·da′tion
pray	prec′i·pice	pred′a·tive
prayed	pre·cip′i·tan·cy	pred′a·tor
prayer	pre·cip′i·tant	pred′a·to′ry
prayer′ful	pre·cip′i·tate	pre′de·cease′
prayer′ful·ly	pre·cip′i·tat′ed	pred′e·ces′sor
preach	pre·cip′i·tate·ly	pre′de·cide′
preached	pre·cip′i·ta′tion	pre·des′ig·nat′ed
preach′er	pre·cip′i·tous	pre·des·ig·na′tion
preach′ment	pré·cis′	pre·des′ti·nar′i·an
preach′y	pre·cise′	pre·des′ti·nar-i·an·ism
pre′ad·o·les′cent	pré·cised′	pre·des′ti·na′tion
pre′am′ble	pre·cise′ly	pre·des′tine
pre′ar·range′	pre·cise′ness	pre·des′tined
pre′ar·range′ment	pre·ci′sion	pre′de·ter′mi·nant
preb′en·dar′y	pre·ci′sion·ist	pre′de·ter′mi·nate
pre·can′celed	pre·clin′i·cal	pre′de·ter′mi·na-tion
pre·car′i·ous	pre·clude′	pre′de·ter′mine
pre·cau′tion	pre·clud′ed	pre′de·ter′mined
pre·cau′tion·ar′y	pre·clu′sion	pre′di·as·tol′ic
pre·cede′	pre·co′cious	pre·dic′a·ment
pre·ced′ed	pre·co′cious·ly	pred′i·cate
pre·ced′ence	pre·coc′i·ty	pred′i·cat′ed
prec′e·dent	pre·con·ceived′	pred′i·ca′tion
pre′cept	pre′con·cep′tion	pred′i·ca′tive
pre·cep′tor	pre·cook′	pre·dict′

pre·dict'a·ble

pre·dict'ed

pre·dic'tion

pre·dic'tion·al

pre·dic'tive

pre'di·gest'

pre'di·gest'ed

pre'di·ges'tion

pre'di·lec'tion

pre'dis·clo'sure

pre'dis·pose'

pre'dis·posed'

pre'dis·po·si'tion

pre·dom'i·nance

pre·dom'i·nant

pre·dom'i·nate

pre·dom'i·nat'ed

pre·dom'i·nate·ly

pre·dom'i·nat'ing·ly

pre·draft'

pre·dry'

pre-em'i·nence

pre-em'i·nent

pre-empt'

pre-empt'ed

pre-emp'tion

pre-emp'tive

preen

preened

pre-es'ti·mate

pre'-ex·ist'

pre'-ex·ist'ent

pref'ace

pref'aced

pre·fash'ion

pref'a·to'ry

pre'fect

pre'fec·ture

pre·fer'

pref'er·a·ble

pref'er·a·bly

pref'er·ence

pref'er·en'tial

pref'er·en'tial·ly

pre·fer'ment

pre·ferred'

pre·fig'ure

pre·fig'ured

pre'fix

pre'fix·al

pre'fixed'

pre·form'

pre·formed'

pre·gath'er

preg'nan·cy

preg'nant

pre·har'vest

pre·hen'sile

pre'hen·sil'i·ty

pre'his·tor'ic

pre'im·ag'ine

pre'in·au'gu·ral

pre'in·cline'

pre'in·clined'

pre·in'ven·to'ry

pre·judge'

pre·judged'

prej'u·diced

prej'u·di'cial

prej'u·di'cial·ly

prel'a·cy

prel'ate

pre·lim'i·nar'y

pre·lit'er·ate

prel'ude

pre'ma·ter'ni·ty

pre'ma·ture'

pre·med'i·cal

pre·med'i·tate

pre·med'i-
  tat'ed

pre'med·i·ta'tion

pre'mi·er

prem'ise

prem'is·es

pre'mi·um

pre'mo·ni'tion

pre·mon'i·to'ry

pre·na'tal

pre·na'tal·ly

pre·oc'cu·pa'tion

pre·oc'cu·pied

pre·oc'cu·py

pre·op'er·a'tive

pre'or·dain'

pre'or·dained'

pre·paid'

prep′a·ra′tion

pre·par′a·tive

pre·par′a·to′ry

pre·pare′

pre·pared′

pre·par′ed·ness

pre·pay′

pre·pay′ment

pre·pense′

pre·pon′der·ance

pre·pon′der·ant

pre·pon′der·ate

pre·pon′der·at′ing·ly

prep′o·si′tion

prep′o·si′tion·al

pre′pos·sess′

pre′pos·ses′sion

pre·pos′ter·ous

pre·print′

pre′re·lease′

pre·req′ui·site

pre·rog′a·tive

pre·sage′

pre·saged′

pres′by·ter

Pres′by·te′ri·an

pres′by·ter′y

pre′sci·ence

pre′sci·ent

pre·scribe′

pre·scribed′

pre·scrip′tion

pre·scrip′tive

pres′ence

pres′ent

pre·sent′a·bil′i·ty

pre·sent′a·ble

pres′en·ta′tion

pre·sent′ed

pre·sen′ti·ment

pres′ent·ly

pre·sent′ment

pres′er·va′tion

pre·serv′a·tive

pre·serve′

pre·serv′er

pre·side′

pre·sid′ed

pres′i·den·cy

pres′i·dent

pres′i·den′tial

press

press′board′

pressed

pres′sings

press′man

press′room′

pres′sure

press′work′

pres′ti·dig′i·ta′tor

pres·tige′

pres·tig′i·ous

pres′to

pre·sum′a·ble

pre·sume′

pre·sumed′

pre·sum′ed·ly

pre·sump′tion

pre·sump′tive

pre·sump′tu·ous

pre′sup·pose′

pre′sys·tol′ic

pre·tend′

pre·tend′ed

pre·tend′er

pre·tense′

pre·ten′sion

pre·ten′tious

pre·ten′tious·ly

pre·ten′tious·ness

pret′er·it

pre′ter·mit′

pre′ter·mit′ted

pre′ter·nat′u·ral

pre′text

pret′ti·er

pret′ti·est

pret′ti·ly

pret′ti·ness

pret′ty

pret′zel

pre·vail′

pre·vailed′

pre·vail′ing·ly

prev′a·lence

prev′a·lent

prev'a·lent·ly

pre·var'i·cate

pre·var'i·cat'ed

pre·var'i·ca'tion

pre·var'i·ca'tor

pre·vent'

pre·vent'a·bil'i·ty

pre·vent'a·ble

pre·vent'ed

pre·ven'tion

pre·ven'tive

pre'view'

pre'vi·ous

pre·vi'sion

pre'vo·ca'tion·al

prey

price

priced

price'less

prick

pricked

prick'le

prick'led

prick'li·ness

prick'ly

pride

pride'ful

priest

priest'ess

priest'hood

priest'ly

prig'gish

prim

pri'ma·cy

pri'mal

pri'ma·ri·ly

pri'ma·ry

pri'mate

pri'mate·ship

prime

primed

prim'er

pri·me'val

prim'i·tive

prim'i·tiv·ism

prim'ly

prim'ness

pri'mo·gen'i·ture

pri·mor'di·al

prim'rose'

prince

prince'li·ness

prince'ling

prince'ly

prin'ces

prin'cess

prin'ci·pal

prin'ci·pal'i·ty

prin'ci·pal·ly

prin'ci·ple

prin'ci·pled

print

print'a·ble

print'ed

print'er

print'ings

print'out

pri'or

pri·or'i·ty

pri'o·ry

prism

pris·mat'ic

pris'on

pris'on·er

pris'tine

pri'va·cy

pri'vate

pri'va·teer'

pri'vate·ly

pri'vate·ness

pri·va'tion

priv'et

priv'i·lege

priv'i·ly

priv'i·ty

priv'y

prize

prized

prob'a·bil'i·ty

prob'a·ble

prob'a·bly

pro'bate

pro·ba'tion

pro·ba'tion·ar'y

probe

prob'i·ty

prob′lem

prob′lem·at′ic

pro·bos′cis

pro·ce′dur·al

pro·ce′dure

pro·ceed′

pro·ceed′ed

pro·ceed′ings

proc′ess

proc′essed

proc′ess·es

pro·ces′sion

proc′ess·or

pro·claim′

pro·claimed′

proc′la·ma′tion

pro·cliv′i·ty

pro·con′sul

pro·cras′ti·nate

pro·cras′ti·nat′ed

pro·cras′ti·na′tion

pro·cras′ti·na′tor

pro′cre·a′tion

pro′cre·a′tive

proc′tor

pro·cur′a·ble

proc′u·ra′tion

proc′u·ra′tor

pro·cure′

pro·cured′

pro·cure′ment

prod

prod′ded

prod′i·gal

prod′i·gal′i·ty

prod′i·gal·ly

pro·di′gious

pro·di′gious·ly

prod′i·gy

pro·duce′

pro·duced′

pro·duc′er

prod′uct

pro·duc′tion

pro·duc′tive

pro′duc·tiv′i·ty

pro′em

prof′a·na′tion

pro·fan′a·to′ry

pro·fane′

pro·faned′

pro·fan′i·ty

pro·fess′

pro·fessed′

pro·fess′ed·ly

pro·fes′sion

pro·fes′sion·al

pro·fes′sion·al·ism

pro·fes′sion·al·ize

pro·fes′sion·al·ly

pro·fes′sor

pro·fes·so′ri·al

pro·fes′sor·ship

prof′fer

prof′fered

pro·fi′cien·cy

pro·fi′cient

pro·fi′cient·ly

pro′file

prof′it

prof′it·a·ble

prof′it·a·bly

prof′it·ed

prof′it·eer′

prof′it·less

prof′li·ga·cy

prof′li·gate

pro·found′

pro·found′ness

pro·fun′di·ty

pro·fuse′

pro·fuse′ly

pro·fuse′ness

pro·fu′sion

pro·gen′i·tor

prog′e·ny

prog·no′sis

prog·nos′tic

prog·nos′ti·cate

prog·nos′ti-
cat′ed

pro′gram

pro′gramed

pro′gram·er

pro·gress′

pro·gressed′

pro·gres′sion

pro·gres'sive

pro·hib'it

pro·hib'it·ed

pro'hi·bi'tion

pro'hi·bi'tion·ist

pro·hib'i·tive

pro·hib'i·to'ry

pro·ject'

pro·ject'ed

pro·jec'tile

pro·jec'tion

pro·jec'tive

pro·jec'tor

pro'le·tar'i·an

pro'le·tar'i·at

pro·lif'er·ate

pro·lif'er·a'tion

pro·lif'ic

pro·lif'i·ca'tion

pro·lix'

pro·lix'i·ty

pro'logue

pro·long'

pro·lon'gate

pro'lon·ga'tion

pro·longed'

prom'e·nade'

prom'e·nad'ed

prom'i·nence

prom'i·nent

prom'is·cu'i·ty

pro·mis'cu·ous

pro·mis'cu·ous·ly

pro·mis'cu·ous·ness

prom'ise

prom'ised

prom'is·ing·ly

prom'is·so'ry

prom'on·to'ry

pro·mote'

pro·mot'ed

pro·mot'er

pro·mo'tion

pro·mo'tion·al

prompt

prompt'ed

prompt'er

prompt'est

promp'ti·tude

prompt'ly

prompt'ness

pro·mul'gate

pro·mul'gat·ed

pro'mul·ga'tion

pro'nate

pro·na'tion

prone

prong

prong'horn'

pro·nom'i·nal

pro'noun

pro·nounce'

pro·nounce'a·ble

pro·nounced'

pro·nounce'ment

pro·nun'ci·a'tion

proof

proofed

prop

prop'a·gan'da

prop'a·gan'dist

prop'a·gate

prop'a·gat'ed

prop'a·ga'tion

pro·pel'

pro·pel'lant

pro·pelled'

pro·pel'ler

pro·pen'si·ty

prop'er

prop'er·ly

prop'er·ty

proph'e·cy

proph'e·sied

proph'e·sy

proph'et

pro·phet'ic

pro·phet'i·cal·ly

pro'phy·lac'tic

pro'phy·lax'is

pro·pin'qui·ty

pro·pi'ti·ate

pro·pi'ti·at'ed

pro·pi'ti·a'tion

pro·pi'ti·a·to'ry

pro·pi'tious

pro·po'nent

pro·por'tion

pro·por'tion·a·ble

pro·por'tion·al

pro·por'tion·al·ly

pro·por'tion·ate

pro·por'tion·ate·ly

pro·por'tioned

pro·pos'al

pro·pose'

pro·posed'

prop'o·si'tion

pro·pound'

pro·pound'ed

pro·pri'e·tar'y

pro·pri'e·tor

pro·pri'e·to'ri·al

pro·pri'e·to'ri·al·ly

pro·pri'e·tor·ship'

pro·pri'e·to'ry

pro·pri'e·ty

pro·pul'sion

pro·pul'sive

pro'rate'

pro'rat'ed

pro·ra'tion

pro'ro·ga'tion

pro·rogue'

pro·rogued'

pro·sa'ic

pro·sa'i·cal·ly

pro·sce'ni·um

pro·scribe'

pro·scribed'

pro·scrip'tion

prose

pros'e·cute

pros'e·cut·ed

pros'e·cu'tion

pros'e·cu'tor

pros'e·lyte

pros'e·lyt'ed

pros'e·lyt·ize

pros'e·lyt·iz'er

pros'i·er

pros'i·est

pros'i·fy

pros'i·ly

pros'i·ness

pros'o·dy

pros'pect

pros'pect·ed

pro·spec'tive

pros'pec·tor

pro·spec'tus

pros'per

pros'pered

pros·per'i·ty

pros'per·ous

pros'per·ous·ly

pros'the·sis

pros·thet'ic

pros'trate

pros'trat·ed

pros·tra'tion

pros'y

pro·tag'o·nist

pro'te·an

pro·tect'

pro·tect'ed

pro·tect'ing·ly

pro·tec'tion

pro·tec'tion·ism

pro·tec'tion·ist

pro·tec'tive

pro·tec'tive·ly

pro·tec'tive·ness

pro·tec'tor

pro·tec'tor·ate

pro'té·gé

pro'te·in

pro·test'

prot'es·tant

prot'es·ta'tion

pro·test'ed

pro·test'ers

pro·thon'o·tar'y

pro'to·col

pro'ton

pro'to·plasm

pro'to·type

pro·tox'ide

Pro'to·zo'a

pro·tract'

pro·tract'ed

pro·trac'tile

pro·trac′tion	pro·vin′cial·ism	prud′ish
pro·trac′tive	pro·vin′ci·al′i·ty	prune
pro·trac′tor	pro·vin′cial·ly	pruned
pro·trude′	pro·vi′sion	pru′ri·ence
pro·trud′ed	pro·vi′sion·al	pru′ri·ent
pro·tru′sion	pro·vi′sion·al·ly	pru·ri′tus
pro·tru′sive	pro·vi′so	Prus′sian
pro·tu′ber·ance	pro·vi′so·ry	pry
pro·tu′ber·ant	prov′o·ca′tion	pry′ing·ly
proud	pro·voc′a·tive	psalm
proud′er	pro·voke′	psalm′book′
proud′est	pro·voked′	psalm′ist
proud′ly	pro·vok′ing·ly	psal′mo·dist
prov′a·ble	prov′ost	psal′mo·dy
prove	prow	psal′ter
proved	prow′ess	pseu′do·nym
prov′en	prowl	pso·ri′a·sis
prov′e·nance	prowled	psy′chi·at′ric
Prov′en·çal′	prowl′er	psy′chi·at′ri·cal·ly
prov′en·der	prox′i·mal	psy·chi′a·trist
prov′erb	prox′i·mal·ly	psy·chi′a·try
pro·ver′bi·al	prox′i·mate	psy′chic
pro·ver′bi·al·ly	prox·im′i·ty	psy′chi·cal
pro·vide′	prox′i·mo	psy′chi·cal·ly
pro·vid′ed	prox′y	psy′cho·a·nal′y·sis
prov′i·dence	prude	psy′cho·bi·ol′o·gy
prov′i·dent	pru′dence	psy′cho·dy·nam′ics
prov′i·den′tial	pru′dent	psy′cho·gen′e·sis
prov′i·den′tial·ly	pru·den′tial	psy′cho·ge·net′ic
pro·vid′er	pru·den′tial·ly	psy′cho·log′i·cal
prov′ince	pru′dent·ly	psy·chol′o·gist
pro·vin′cial	prud′er·y	psy·chol′o·gy

psy'cho·path'ic	puff'y	pul'sa·to'ry
psy'cho·pa·thol'o·gy	pug	pulse
psy·chop'a·thy	pu'gil·ism	pul'ver·i·za'tion
psy·cho'sis	pu'gil·ist	pul'ver·ize
psy·chot'ic	pu'gil·is'tic	pul'ver·iz'er
Ptol'e·ma'ic	pug·na'cious·ly	pum'ice
pto'maine	pug·nac'i·ty	pump
pub'lic	pu'is·sance	pum'per·nick'el
pub'li·ca'tion	pu'is·sant	pump'kin
pub'li·cist	pul'chri·tude	pun
pub·lic'i·ty	pul'chri·tu'di·nous	punch
pub'lic·ly	pul'ing	punched
pub'lish	pul'ing·ly	pun'cheon
pub'lished	pull	punch'ings
pub'lish·er	pulled	punc·til'i·o
puce	pul'let	punc·til'i·ous
puck	pul'ley	punc·til'i·ous·ly
puck'er	Pull'man	punc·til'i·ous·ness
puck'ered	pul'lu·late	punc'tu·al
pud'dings	pul'mo·nar'y	punc'tu·al'i·ty
pud'dle	Pul'mo'tor	punc'tu·al·ly
pud'dled	pulp	punc'tu·ate
pud'dler	pulp'i·er	punc'tu·at'ed
pu'den·cy	pulp'i·est	punc'tu·a'tion
pudg'i·ness	pulp'i·ness	punc'ture
pudg'y	pul'pit	punc'tured
pueb'lo	pul'pit·eer'	pun'dit
pu'er·ile	pulp'y	pung
pu'er·il'i·ty	pul'sate	pun'gen·cy
puff	pul'sat·ed	pun'gent
puf'fin	pul·sa'tion	pu'ni·ness
puff'i·ness	pul·sa'tor	pun'ish

pun'ish·a·ble	pur'ist	pur'sy
pun'ished	Pu'ri·tan	pu'ru·lence
pun'ish·ment	pu'ri·tan'ic	pu'ru·len·cy
pu'ni·tive	pu'ri·tan'i·cal	pu'ru·lent
punk	Pu'ri·tan·ism	pur·vey'
punt	pu'ri·ty	pur·vey'ance
pu'ny	purl	pur·vey'or
pup	pur'lieu	pur'view
pu'pa	pur·loin'	pus
pu'pae	pur'ple	push
pu'pil	pur'plish	push'cart'
pup'pet	pur·port'	push'er
pup'pet·eer'	pur·port'ed	pu'sil·la·nim'i·ty
pup'pet·ry	pur'pose	pu'sil·lan'i·mous
pup'py	pur'pose·ful	puss'y·foot'
pur'blind'	pur'pose·ful·ly	pus'tu·lant
pur'chase	pur'pose·ful·ness	pus'tu·lar
pur'chased	pur'pose·less	pus'tu·late
pur'chas·er	pur'pose·ly	pus'tu·la'tion
pure	pur'pos·ive	pus'tule
pure'ly	purr	put
pur'er	purred	pu'ta·tive
pur'est	purse	pu'tre·fac'tion
pur'ga·tive	pursed	pu'tre·fac'tive
pur'ga·to'ry	purs'er	pu'tre·fied
purge	purs'lane	pu'tre·fy
purged	pur·su'ance	pu·tres'cence
pu'ri·fi·ca'tion	pur·su'ant	pu·tres'cent
pu'ri·fied	pur·sue'	pu'trid
pu'ri·fi'er	pur·sued'	putt
pu'ri·fy	pur·suit'	putt'tee
pur'ism	pur'sui·vant	putt'er

put′ty

puz′zle

puz′zled

puz′zler

puz′zles

py·e′mi·a

pyg′my

py·ja′ma

py′lon

py·lo′rus

py′or·rhe′a

pyr′a·mid

py·ram′i·dal

pyre

py′rex

py·rex′i·a

py·ri′tes

py·rog′ra·phy

py′ro·ma′ni·a

py·rom′e·ter

py′ro·tech′nics

py·rox′y·lin

Pyr′rhic

py′thon

Q

quack	quag′mire′	quan′ti·ty
quack′er·y	qua′hog	quan′tum
quad	quail	quar′an·tine
quad′ran′gle	quailed	quar′an·tined
quad·ran′gu·lar	quaint	quar′rel
quad′rant	quaint′ly	quar′reled
quad′rat	quaint′ness	quar′rel·some
quad·rat′ic	quake	quar′ri·er
quad·rat′ics	quaked	quar′ry
quad′ra·ture	quak′er	quar′ry·man
quad·ren′ni·al	quak′ing·ly	quart
quad·ren′ni·al·ly	qual′i·fi·ca′tion	quar′tan
quad·ren′ni·um	qual′i·fied	quar′ter
quad′ri·lat′er·al	qual′i·fi′er	quar′ter·back′
qua·drille′	qual′i·fy	quar′tered
quad′ri·par′tite	qual′i·ta′tive	quar′ter·ings
quad′ru·ped	qual′i·ties	quar′ter·ly
quad·ru′ple	qual′i·ty	quar′ter·mas′ter
quad′ru·plet	qualm	quar′ter·saw′
quad′ru·plex	quan′da·ry	quar·tet′
quad·ru′pli·cate	quan′ti·ta′tive	quar′tile
quaff	quan′ti·ties	quar′to

235

quartz	queue	quin·tet'
quash	quib'ble	quin'tu·plet
qua'si	quick	quip
qua·ter'na·ry	quick'en	qui'pu
quat'rain	quick'ened	quire
quat're·foil'	quick'er	quirk
qua'ver	quick'est	quirt
qua'vered	quick'lime'	quit
qua'ver·ing·ly	quick'ly	quit'claim'
quay	quick'ness	quite
quay'age	quick'sand'	quit'rent'
quea'sy	quick'sil'ver	quit'tance
queen	quick'step'	quit'ter
queen'ly	quid'di·ty	quiv'er
queer	qui·es'cence	quiv'ered
queer'er	qui'et	quiv'er·ing·ly
queer'est	qui'et·ed	quix·ot'ic
quell	qui'et·ly	quiz
quelled	qui'et·ness	quiz'zi·cal
quench	qui'e·tude	quoin
quenched	qui·e'tus	quoit
quench'less	quill	quon'dam
que'ried	quilled	quo'rum
quer'u·lous	quill'work'	quo'ta
que'ry	quilt	quot'a·ble
quest	quilt'ed	quo·ta'tion
quest'ing·ly	quince	quote
ques'tion	qui'nine	quot'ed
ques'tion·a·ble	quin·quen'ni·al	quoth
ques'tion·er	quin'tal	quo·tid'i·an
ques'tion·ing·ly	quint·es'sence	quo'tient
ques'tion·naire'	quin'tes·sen'tial	quot'ing

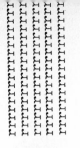

R

rab'bet

rab·bin'i·cal

rab'bit

rab'bit·ry

rab'ble

rab'id

rab'id·ly

ra'bi·es

rac·coon'

race

raced

rac'er

race'way'

ra·chit'ic

ra·chi'tis

ra'cial

ra'cial·ly

rac'i·ly

rac'i·ness

rac'ism

rac'ist

rack'et

rac'y

ra'di·al

ra'di·al·ly

ra'di·ance

ra'di·ant

ra'di·ant·ly

ra'di·ate

ra'di·at'ed

ra'di·a'tion

ra'di·a'tor

rad'i·cal

rad'i·cal·ism

rad'i·cal·ly

ra·dic'u·lar

ra'di·i

ra'di·o

ra'di·o·ac'tive

ra'di·o·ac·tiv'i·ty

ra'di·o·gram'

ra'di·o·graph'

ra'di·om'e·ter

ra'di·o·phone'

ra'di·o·pho'to·graph

ra'di·o·scope'

ra'di·o·sen'si·tive

ra'di·o·tel'e·gram

rad'ish

ra'di·um

ra'di·us

ra'di·us·es

ra'dix

ra'don

raf'fi·a

raf'fle

raf'fled

raft

raft'er

rafts'man

rag

rag'a·muf'fin

rage

raged

rag'ged

rag'lan

ra·gout'	ram	ranked
rag'pick'er	ram'ble	ran'kle
rag'time'	ram'bled	ran'kled
rag'weed'	ram'bler	rank'ling·ly
raid	ram·bunc'tious	ran'sack
rail	ram'e·kin	ran'som
rail'bird'	ram'i·fi·ca'tion	ran'somed
railed	ram'i·fied	rant
rail'head'	ram'i·fy	rant'ed
rail'ing·ly	rammed	rant'ing·ly
rail'ings	ram'mer	ra·pa'cious
rail'ler·y	ramp	ra·pac'i·ty
rail'road'	ram'page	rap'id
rail'road'er	ramp'ant	ra·pid'i·ty
rail'way'	ram'part	rap'id·ly
rai'ment	ram'rod'	ra'pi·er
rain	ram'shack'le	rap'ine
rain'bow'	ranch	rap·port'
rain'coat'	ranch'er	rap·scal'lion
rained	ran·che'ro	rapt
rain'fall'	ranch'man	rap·to'ri·al
rain'spout'	ran'cho	rap'ture
rain'storm'	ran'cid	rap'tur·ous
rain'y	ran·cid'i·ty	rap'tur·ous·ly
raise	ran'cid·ly	rap'tur·ous·ness
raised	ran'cor	rare
rai'sin	ran'cor·ous	rar'e·fac'tion
ra'ja	ran'dom	rar'e·fy
rake	range	rare'ly
rak'ish	ranged	rare'ness
ral'lied	rang'er	rar'er
ral'ly	rank	rar'est

rar'i·ty

ras'cal

ras·cal'i·ty

ras'cal·ly

rash

rash'er

rash'est

rash'ly

rash'ness

rasp

rasp'ber'ry

rasped

rasp'ing·ly

rat

rat'a·ble

ratch'et

rate

rat'ed

rath'er

raths'kel'ler

rat'i·fi·ca'tion

rat'i·fied

rat'i·fy

rat'ings

ra'tio

ra'ti·oc'i·na'tion

ra'ti·oc'i·na'tive

ra'tion

ra'tion·al

ra'tion·al·ism

ra'tion·al·ist

ra'tion·al·is'tic

ra'tion·al·i·za'tion

ra'tion·al·ize

ra'tion·al·ized

ra'tion·al·ly

ra'tioned

rat'line

rat·tan'

rat'ter

rat'tle

rat'tle·brain'

rat'tle·brained'

rat'tled

rat'tle·head'ed

rat'tler

rat'tle·snake'

rat'tlings

rat'tly

rau'cous

rav'age

rav'aged

rave

raved

rav'el

rav'eled

ra'ven

rav'en·ous

rav'en·ous·ly

rav'en·ous·ness

ra'vi'gote'

ra·vine'

rav'ings

ra·vi·o'li

rav'ish

rav'ished

rav'ish·er

rav'ish·ing·ly

rav'ish·ment

raw

raw'boned'

raw'er

raw'est

raw'hide'

raw'ness

ray

ray'less

ray'on

raze

razed

ra'zor

ra'zor·back'

ra'zor·edge'

reach

reached

reach'ings

re·act'

re·act'ance

re·ac'tion

re·ac'tion·ar'y

re·ac'ti·vate

re'ac·ti·va'tion

read

read'a·bil'i·ty

read'a·ble

read'er

read'i·ly	reap'er	re·bel'lion
read'i·ness	re'ap·pear'	re·bel'lious
read'ings	re'ap·pear'ance	re·bind'
re'ad·just'	re'ap·point'	re·birth'
re'ad·just'a·ble	re'ap·point'ment	re·born'
re'ad·just'ment	rear	re·bound'
re'ad·mis'sion	reared	re·buff'
re'ad·mit'	re·ar'gue	re·buffed'
read'y	re·arm'	re·build'
re'af·firm'	re·ar'ma·ment	re·built'
re'af·fir·ma'tion	re·armed'	re·buke'
re·a'gent	rear'most	re·buked'
re'al	re'ar·range'	re·buk'ing·ly
re·a·lign'	re'ar·range'ment	re'bus
re'al·ism	rear'ward	re·but'
re'al·ist	rea'son	re·but'tal
re'al·is'tic	rea'son·a·ble	re·but'ted
re'al·is'ti·cal·ly	rea'son·a·ble·ness	re·but'ter
re·al'i·ty	rea'son·a·bly	re·cal'ci·trance
re'al·iz'a·ble	rea'soned	re·cal'ci·trant
re'al·i·za'tion	re'as·sem'ble	re·call'
re'al·ize	re·as·sert'	re·called'
re'al·ized	re·as·sert'ed	re·cant'
re'al·ly	re·as·sign'	re'can·ta'tion
realm	re·as·sume'	re·cant'ed
re'al·tor	re'as·sur'ance	re·cap'i·tal·ize
re'al·ty	re'as·sure'	re'ca·pit'u·late
ream	re'as·sured'	re'ca·pit'u·lat'ed
reamed	re'bate	re'ca·pit'u·la'tion
ream'er	re'bat·ed	re'ca·pit'u·la·to'ry
re·an'i·mate	re·bel'	re·cap'ture
reap	re·belled'	re·cast'

re·cede'

re·ced'ed

re·ceipt'

re·ceipt'ed

re·ceiv'a·ble

re·ceiv'a·bles

re·ceive'

re·ceived'

re·ceiv'er

re·ceiv'er·ship

re'cent

re'cent·ly

re·cep'ta·cle

re·cep'tion

re·cep'tion·ist

re·cep'tive

re·cep'tive·ly

re·cep'tive·ness

re'cep·tiv'i·ty

re·cep'tor

re·cess'

re·cessed'

re·cess'es

re·ces'sion

re·ces'sion·al

re·ces'sive

re·charge'

re·charged'

re·cher'ché'

re·cid'i·vism

re·cid'i·vist

rec'i·pe

re·cip'i·ent

re·cip'ro·cal

re·cip'ro·cal·ly

re·cip'ro·cate

re·cip'ro·cat'ed

re·cip'ro·ca'tion

re·cip'ro·ca'tive

re·cip'ro·ca'tor

rec'i·proc'i·ty

re·cit'al

re·cit'al·ist

rec'i·ta'tion

rec'i·ta·tive'

re·cite'

re·cit'ed

reck

reck'less

reck'less·ly

reck'less·ness

reck'on

reck'oned

reck'on·er

reck'on·ings

re·claim'

re·claim'a·ble

re·claimed'

rec'la·ma'tion

re·cline'

re·clined'

re·cluse'

rec'og·ni'tion

rec'og·niz'a·ble

re·cog'ni·zance

rec'og·nize

rec'og·nized

re·coil'

re·coiled'

rec'ol·lect'

rec'ol·lect'ed

rec'ol·lec'tion

re'com·mence'

rec'om·mend'

rec'om·men·da'tion

rec'om·mend'a·to'ry

rec'om·mend'ed

re'com·mit'

rec'om·pen'sa·ble

rec'om·pense

rec'om·pensed

rec'on·cil'a·ble

rec'on·cile

rec'on·ciled

rec'on·cile'ment

rec'on·cil'i·a'tion

rec'on·cil'i·a·to'ry

rec'on·dite

re·con'nais·sance

rec'on·noi'ter

rec'on·noi'tered

re·con'quer

re'con·sid'er

re'con·sti·tute

re'con·struct'

re'con·struct'ed

re·con·struc'tion

re·con·struc'tive

re·con'vert

re·con·vey'

re·cord'

re·cord'ed

re·cord'er

re·cord'ings

re·count'

re·count'ed

re·coup'

re·couped'

re·coup'ment

re·course'

re·cov'er

re·cov'er·a·ble

re·cov'er·y

rec're·ant

re'-cre·ate'

rec're·a'tion

rec're·a'tion·al

re·crim'i·nate

re·crim'i·na'tion

re·crim'i·na'tive

re·crim'i·na·to'ry

re'cru·des'cence

re'cru·des'cent

re·cruit'

re·cruit'ed

re·cruit'ment

re'crys·tal·li·za'tion

re·crys'tal·lize

rec'tan'gle

rec·tan'gu·lar

rec·tan'gu·lar'i·ty

rec'ti·fi'a·ble

rec'ti·fi·ca'tion

rec'ti·fied

rec'ti·fi'er

rec'ti·fy

rec'ti·lin'e·ar

rec'ti·tude

rec'tor

rec'tor·ate

rec·to'ri·al

rec'to·ry

re·cum'ben·cy

re·cum'bent

re·cu'per·ate

re·cu'per·at'ed

re·cu'per·a'tion

re·cu'per·a'tive

re·cu'per·a·to'ry

re·cur'

re·curred'

re·cur'rence

re·cur'rent

re·cur'rent·ly

re·cy'cle

red

red'bird'

red'breast'

red'bud'

red'den

red'dened

red'der

red'dest

red'dish

re·deal'

re·deem'

re·deem'a·bil'i·ty

re·deem'a·ble

re·deemed'

re·deem'er

re·demp'tion

Re·demp'tor·ist

re·demp'to·ry

re'de·ter'mine

re'de·vel'op

re'di·rect'

re'di·rect'ed

re·dis'count

re'dis·cov'er

re'dis·trib'ute

re'dis·tri·bu'tion

re·dis'trict

red'ness

red'o·lence

red'o·lent

re·dou'ble

re·doubt'

re·doubt'a·ble

re·dound'

re·draft'

re·dress'

re·dressed'

re·duce'

re·duced'

re·duc'er

re·duc'i·ble

re·duc'tion

re·dun'dance

re·dun'dan·cy

re·dun'dant

re·dun'dant·ly

re·du'pli·cate

re·du'pli·cat'ed

re·du·pli·ca'tion

red'wood'

re·ech'o

re·ech'oed

reed

reed'bird'

reed'i·ness

re-ed'it

re-ed'u·cate

re'-ed·u·ca'tion

reed'y

reef

reef'er

reek

reek'ing·ly

reel

re'-e·lect'

re'-em·bark'

re'-em·bar·ka'tion

re'-em·ploy'

re'-en·act'

re'-en·force'

re'-en·force'ment

re'-en·gage'

re'-en·grave'

re'-en·list'

re-en'ter

re-en'trance

re-en'try

re'-es·tab'lish

re'-ex·am'i·na'tion

re'-ex·am'ine

re'-ex·port'

re'-ex·por·ta'tion

re·fec'to·ry

re·fer'

ref'er·a·ble

ref'er·ee'

ref'er·ence

ref'er·en'dum

re·ferred'

re·fig'ure

re'fill

re'fi·nance'

re·fine'

re·fined'

re·fine'ment

re·fin'er

re·fin'er·y

re·fit'

re·flect'

re·flect'ed

re·flect'ing·ly

re·flec'tion

re·flec'tive

re·flec'tor

re'flex

re·flex'ive

re'flux

re'for·est·a'tion

re·form'

ref'or·ma'tion

re·form'a·tive

re·form'a·to'ry

re·formed'

re·form'er

re·fract'

re·fract'ed

re·frac'tion

re·frac'tion·ist

re·frac'tive

re'frac·tiv'i·ty

re·frac'tor

re·frac'to·ry

re·frain'

re·frained'

re·fresh'

re·freshed'

re·fresh'er

re·fresh'ing·ly

re·fresh'ment

re·frig'er·ant

re·frig'er·ate

re·frig'er·at'ed

re·frig'er·a'tion

re·frig'er·a'tive

re·frig'er·a'tor

ref'uge

ref'u·gee'

re·ful'gence

re·ful'gent

re·fund'

re·fund'ed

re·fur'nish

re·fus'al

re·fuse'

re·fused'

ref'u·ta'tion

re·fute'

re·fut'ed

re·gain'

re·gained'

re'gal

re·gale'

re·galed'

re·gale'ment

re·ga'li·a

re·gal'i·ty

re'gal·ly

re·gard'

re·gard'ed

re·gard'ful

re·gard'less

re·gat'ta

re'ge·la'tion

re'gen·cy

re·gen'er·a·cy

re·gen'er·ate

re·gen'er·at'ed

re·gen'er·a'tion

re·gen'er·a'tive

re·gen'er·a'tor

re'gent

reg'i·cid'al

reg'i·cide

re·gime'

reg'i·men

reg'i·ment

reg'i·men'tal

reg'i·men'tals

reg'i·men·ta'tion

reg'i·ment'ed

re'gion

re'gion·al

re'gion·al·ism

re'gion·al·ize

re'gion·al·ly

reg'is·ter

reg'is·tered

reg'is·trar

reg'is·tra'tion

reg'is·try

re'gress

re·gres'sion

re·gres'sive

re·gret'

re·gret'ful

re·gret'ful·ly

re·gret'ful·ness

re·gret'ta·ble

re·gret'ted

reg'u·lar

reg'u·lar'i·ty

reg'u·lar·i·za'tion

reg'u·lar·ize

reg'u·late

reg'u·lat'ed

reg'u·lates

reg'u·la'tion

reg'u·la'tor

re·gur'gi·tate

re·gur'gi·tat'ed

re·gur'gi·ta'tion

re'ha·bil'i·tate

re'ha·bil'i·tat'ed

re'ha·bil'i·ta'tion

re·hash'

re·hears'al

re·hearse'

re·hearsed'

re·heat'

reign

reigned

re'im·burse'

re'im·bursed'

re'im·port'

re'im·por·ta'tion

rein

re'in·car'nate

re'in·car·na'tion

rein'deer'

reined

re·in·force'

re·in·forced'

re·in·sert'

re·in·stall'

re·in·state'

re·in·stat·ed

re·in·state'ment

re·in·sur'ance

re·in·sure'

re·in'te·grate

re·in·tro·duce'

re·in·vest'

re·in·vig'o·rate

re·is'sue

re·it'er·ate

re·it'er·at'ed

re·it'er·a'tion

re·it'er·a'tive

re·ject'

re·ject'ed

re·jec'tion

re·joice'

re·joiced'

re·joic'es

re·joic'ing·ly

re·join'

re·join'der

re·ju've·nate

re·ju've·nat'ed

re·ju've·na'tion

re·ju've·na'tive

re·ju've·nes'cence

re·ju've·nes'cent

re·kin'dle

re·lapse'

re·lapsed'

re·late'

re·lat'ed

re·la'tion

re·la'tion·al

re·la'tion·ship

rel'a·tive

rel'a·tive·ly

rel'a·tiv·ism

rel'a·tiv'i·ty

re·la'tor

re·lax'

re'lax·a'tion

re·laxed'

re·lax'es

re·lay'

re·layed'

re·lease'

re·leased'

rel'e·gate

rel'e·gat'ed

rel'e·ga'tion

re·lent'

re·lent'ed

re·lent'ing·ly

re·lent'less

rel'e·vance

rel'e·van·cy

rel'e·vant

re·li'a·bil'i·ty

re·li'a·ble

re·li'ant

rel'ic

re·lief'

re·lieve'

re·lieved'

re·li'gion

re·li'gious

re·li'gious·ly

re·lin'quish

re·lin'quished

re·lin'quish·ment

rel'i·quar'y

rel'ish

rel'ished

re·live'

re·load'

re·lo'cate

re·lo'cat·ed

re'lo·ca'tion

re·lo'ca·tor

re·lu'cent

re·luc'tance

re·luc'tant

re·luc'tant·ly

re·ly'

re·main'

re·main'der

re·mained'

re·make'

re·mand'

re·mand'ed

re·mark'

re·mark'a·ble

re·mar'ried

re·mar'ry

re·me'di·a·ble

re·me'di·al

rem'e·died

rem'e·dy

re·mem'ber

re·mem'bered

re·mem'brance

re·mind'

re·mind'ed

re·mind'er

re·mind'ful

re·mind'ing·ly

rem'i·nis'cence

rem'i·nis'cent

re·miss'

re·mis'sion

re·mit'

re·mit'tal

re·mit'tance

re·mit'ted

re·mit'tent

re·mit'ter

rem'nant

re·mod'el

re·mon'e·ti·za'tion

re·mon'e·tize

re·mon'strance

re·mon'strant

re·mon'strate

re·mon'strat·ed

re·mon'strat·ing·ly

re'mon·stra'tion

re'mon'stra·tive

re·morse'

re·morse'ful

re·morse'ful·ly

re·morse'less

re·mote'

re·mote'ness

re·mot'er

re·mot'est

re·mount'

re·mov'a·bil'i·ty

re·mov'a·ble

re·mov'al

re·move'

re·moved'

re·moves'

re·mu'ner·ate

re·mu'ner·at'ed

re·mu'ner·a'tion

re·mu'ner·a'tive

ren'ais·sance'

re'nal

re·nas'cent

rend

ren'der

ren'dered

ren'der·ings

ren'dez·vous

ren·di'tion

ren'e·gade

re·nege'

re·ne·go'ti·ate

re·new'

re·new'a·ble

re·new'al

re·newed'

ren'net

re·nom'i·nate

re·nom'i·na'tion

re·nounce'

re·nounced'

ren'o·vate

ren'o·vat'ed

ren'o·va'tion

re·nown'

re·nowned'

rent

rent'al

rent'ed

re·num'ber

re·nun'ci·a'tion

re·nun'ci·a'tive

re·nun'ci·a·to'ry

re·o'pen

re·or'der

re'or·gan·i·za'tion

re·or'gan·ize

re·o'ri·ent

re·paid'

re·paint'

re·pair'

re·paired'

re·pair'er

rep'a·ra·ble

rep'a·ra'tion

re·par'a·tive

rep'ar·tee'

re·past'

re·pa'tri·ate

re·pay'

re·pay'ment

re·peal'

re·pealed'

re·peal'er

re·peat'

re·peat'ed·ly

re·peat'er

re·pel'

re·pelled'

re·pel'lence

re·pel'len·cy

re·pel'lent

re·pel'ling·ly

re·pent'

re·pent'ance

re·pent'ed

re'per·cus'sion

re'per·cus'sive

rep'er·toire

rep'er·to'ry

rep'e·tend

rep'e·ti'tion

rep'e·ti'tious

re·pet'i·tive

re·phrase'

re·pine'

re·pined'

re·place'

re·placed'

re·place'ment

re·plant'

re·plen'ish

re·plen'ished

re·plen'ish·ment

re·plete'

re·ple'tion

re·plev'in

rep'li·ca

rep'li·ca'tion

re·plied'

re·ply'

re·port'

re·port'ed

re·port'er

re·pose'

re·posed'

re·pose'ful

re·pos'i·to'ry

re'pos·sess'

re'pos·sessed'

rep're·hend'

rep're·hen'si·ble

rep're·hen'sion

rep're·hen'sive

rep're·sent'

rep're·sen·ta'tion

rep're·sent'a·tive

rep're·sent'ed

re·press'

re·pres'sion

re·pres'sive

re·prieve'

re·prieved'

rep'ri·mand

rep'ri·mand'ed

rep'ri·mand'ing·ly

re'print'

re·print'ed

re·pris'al

re·prise'

re·proach'

re·proached'

re·proach'ful

re·proach'ful·ly

re·proach'ful·ness

rep'ro·bate

rep'ro·ba'tion

re'pro·duce'

re'pro·duc'er

re'pro·duc'tion

re'pro·duc'tive

re·proof'

re·prove'

re·proved'

re·prov'ing·ly

rep'tile

rep·til'i·an

re·pub'lic

re·pub'li·can

re·pub'li·can·ism

re·pub'li·can·ize

re·pub'lish

re·pu'di·ate

re·pu'di·a'tion

re·pug'nance

re·pug'nant

re·pulse'

re·pulsed'

re·pul'sion

re·pul'sive

re·pul'sive·ness

re·pur'chase

rep'u·ta·ble

rep'u·ta'tion

re·pute'

re·put'ed

re·put'ed·ly

re·quest'

re'qui·em

re·quire'

re·quired'

re·quire'ment

req'ui·site

req'ui·si'tion

re·quit'al

re·quite'

re·quit'ed

rere'dos

re·run'

re·sale'

re·scind'

re·scind'ed

re·scis'sion

re·score'

res'cue

res'cued

re·search'

re·search'er

re·sec'tion

re·sem'blance

re·sem'ble

re·sem'bled

re·sent'

re·sent'ed

re·sent'ful

re·sent'ful·ness

re·sent'ment

res'er·va'tion

res'er·va'tion·ist

re·serve'

re·served'

re·serv'ist

res'er·voir

re·set'

re·set'tle

re·set'tle·ment

re·ship'

re·ship'ment

re·side'

re·sid'ed

res'i·dence

res'i·den·cy

res'i·dent

res'i·den'tial

re·sid'u·al

re·sid'u·ar'y

res'i·due

re·sid'u·um

re·sign'

res'ig·na'tion

re·signed'

re·sign'ed·ly

re·sil'i·en·cy

re·sil'i·ent

res'in

res'in·ous

re·sist'

re·sist'ance

re·sist'ant

re·sist'i·ble

re·sis'tive

re'sis·tiv'i·ty

re·sist'less

re·sol'u·ble

res'o·lute

res'o·lute·ness

res'o·lu'tion

re·solv'a·ble

re·solve'

re·solved'

re·sol'vent

res'o·nance

res'o·nant

res'o·nate

res'o·na'tor

re·sort'

re·sort'ed

re·sound'

re·sound'ed

re·sound'ing·ly

re·source'

re·source'ful

re·source'ful·ness

re·spect'

re·spect'a·bil'i·ty

re·spect'a·ble

re·spect'ed

re·spect'er

re·spect'ful

re·spec'tive

re·spec'tive·ly

re·spell'

re·spir'a·ble

res'pi·ra'tion

res'pi·ra'tor

re·spir'a·to'ry

re·spire'

re·spired'

res'pite

re·splend'ence

re·splend'en·cy

re·splend'ent

re·spond'

re·spond'ed

re·spond'ent

re·sponse'

re·spon'si·bil'i·ties

re·spon'si·bil'i·ty

re·spon'si·ble

re·spon'sive

re·spon'sive·ness

rest

re·state'

re·state'ment

res'tau·rant

res'tau·ra·teur'

rest'ed

rest'ful

rest'ful·ly

rest'ful·ness

res'ti·tu'tion

res'tive

res'tive·ly

res'tive·ness

rest'less

rest'less·ness

re·stock'

res'to·ra'tion

re·stor'a·tive

re·store'

re·stored'

re·strain'

re·strained'

re·strain'ed·ly

re·strain'ing·ly

re·straint'

re·strict'

re·strict'ed

re·stric'tion

re·stric'tive

re·sult'

re·sult'ant

re·sum'a·ble

re·sume'

re·sumed'

re·sump'tion

re·sur'gence

re·sur'gent

res'ur·rect'

res'ur·rect'ed

res'ur·rec'tion

re·sus'ci·tate

re·sus'ci·tat'ed

re·sus'ci·ta'tion

re·sus'ci·ta'tive

re·sus'ci·ta'tor

re'tail

re'tailed

re'tail·er

re·tain'

re·tained'

re·tain'er

re·take'

re·tal'i·ate

re·tal'i·at'ed

re·tal'i·a'tion

re·tal'i·a'tion·ist

re·tal'i·a'tive

re·tal'i·a·to'ry

re·tard'

re'tar·da'tion

re·tard'ed

re·tard'er

retch

retched

re·tell'

re·tell'ings

re·ten'tion

re·ten'tive

re'ten·tiv'i·ty

ret'i·cence

ret'i·cent

ret'i·cent·ly

ret'i·cle

re·tic'u·lar

re·tic'u·late

re·tic'u·lat'ed

re·tic'u·la'tion

ret'i·cule

ret'i·na

ret'i·nal

ret'i·ni'tis

ret'i·nue

re·tire'

re·tired'

re·tire'ment

re·tir'ing·ly

re·told'

re·tort'

re·tort'ed

re·touch'

re·touch'er

re·trace'

re·trace'a·ble

re·tract'

re·tract'ed

re·trac'tile

re·trac'tion

re·trac'tive

re·trac'tor

re-tread'

re·treat'

re·treat'ed

re·trench'

re·trenched'

re·trench'ment

re·tri'al

ret'ri·bu'tion

re·trib'u·tive

re·triev'al

re·trieve'

re·trieved'

re·triev'er

ret'ro·ac'tive

ret'ro·ac·tiv'i·ty

ret'ro·cede'

ret'ro·ces'sion

ret·ro·ces'sive

ret'ro·flex

ret'ro·flex'ion

ret'ro·grade

ret'ro·grad'ed

ret'ro·gress

ret'ro·gres'sion

ret'ro·gres'sive

ret'ro·spect

ret'ro·spec'tion

ret'ro·spec'tive

ret'ro·ver'sion

re·turn'

re·turn'a·ble

re·turned'

re·un'ion

re'u·nite'

re-use'

re-used'

re·vac'ci·nate

re·val'i·date

re·val'or·ize

re·val'u·a'tion

re·val'ue

re·vamp'

re·veal'

re·vealed'

re·veal'ing·ly

re·veal'ment

rev'eil·le

rev'el

rev'e·la'tion

rev'e·la·to'ry

rev'eled

rev'el·er

rev'el·ry
re·venge'
re·venged'
re·venge'ful
rev'e·nue
re·ver'ber·ant
re·ver'ber·ate
re·ver'ber·at'ed
re·ver'ber·a'tion
re·ver'ber·a'tive
re·ver'ber·a'tor
re·ver'ber·a·to'ry
re·vere'
re·vered'
rev'er·ence
rev'er·end
rev'er·ent
rev'er·en'tial
rev'er·ie
re·ver'sal
re·verse'
re·versed'
re·vers'i·bil'i·ty
re·vers'i·ble
re·ver'sion
re·ver'sion·ar'y
re·vert'
re·vert'ed
re·vert'i·ble
re·vest'
re·vet'
re·vet'ment

re·vict'ual
re·view'
re·viewed'
re·view'er
re·vile'
re·viled'
re·vile'ment
re·vil'ing·ly
re·vin'di·cate
re·vise'
re·vised'
re·vis'er
re·vi'sion
re·vi'sion·ism
re·vi'sion·ist
re·vis'it
re·viv'al
re·viv'al·ism
re·viv'al·ist
re·vive'
re·vived'
re·viv'i·fi·ca'tion
re·viv'i·fi'er
re·viv'i·fy
rev'o·ca'tion
re·vok'a·ble
re·voke'
re·voked'
re·volt'
re·volt'ed
re·volt'ing·ly
rev'o·lu'tion

rev'o·lu'tion·ar'y
rev'o·lu'tion·ist
rev'o·lu'tion·ize
rev'o·lu'tion·ized
re·volve'
re·volved'
re·volv'er
re·vue'
re·vul'sion
re·vul'sive
re·ward'
re·ward'ed
re·ward'ing·ly
re·wind'
re·wire'
re·word'
re·worked'
re·write'
re·writ'ten
rhap·sod'ic
rhap'so·dist
rhap'so·dize
rhap'so·dized
rhap'so·dy
rhe'ni·um
rhe'o·stat
rhe'sus
rhet'o·ric
rhe·tor'i·cal
rhet'o·ri'cian
rheum
rheu·mat'ic

rheu'ma·tism	rich'ness	right'eous
rheu'ma·toid	rich'weed'	right'eous·ly
rheum'y	rick'ets	right'eous·ness
rhine'stone'	ric'o·chet'	right'ful
rhi·ni'tis	rid'dance	right'ful·ly
rhi·noc'er·os	rid'den	right'ly
rhi·nol'o·gy	rid'dle	right'ness
rhi'no·scope	ride	rig'id
rhi·nos'co·py	rid'er	ri·gid'i·ty
rhi'zome	rid'er·less	rig'id·ly
rho'di·um	ridge	rig'id·ness
rhom'boid	ridged	rig'or
rhom'bus	rid'i·cule	rig'or·ous
rhu'barb	rid'i·culed	rig'or·ous·ly
rhyme	ri·dic'u·lous	rile
rhymed	ri·dic'u·lous·ly	riled
rhythm	ri·dot'to	rill
rhyth'mic	rife	rim
rhyth'mi·cal	rif'fle	rime
Ri·al'to	rif'fled	rind
ri'ant	riff'raff'	ring
rib	ri'fle	ring'bolt'
rib'ald	ri'fled	ring'bone'
rib'ald·ry	ri'fle·man	ringed
ribbed	ri'flings	ring'er
rib'bon	rift	ring'ing·ly
rice	rig	ring'lead'er
rich	rig'a·doon'	ring'let
rich'er	rigged	ring'let·ed
rich'es	rig'ger	ring'mas'ter
rich'est	right	ring'side'
rich'ly	right'ed	ring'worm'

rink		rite		roared	
rinse		rit′u·al		roar′ings	
rinsed		rit′u·al·ism		roast	
ri′ot		rit′u·al·ist		roast′ed	
ri′ot·ed		rit′u·al·is′tic		roast′er	
ri′ot·er		rit′u·al·ly		rob	
ri′ot·ous		ri′val		robbed	
ri′ot·ous·ly		ri′valed		rob′ber	
ri′ot·ous·ness		ri′val·ry		rob′ber·y	
rip		rive		robe	
ri·par′i·an		riv′er		robed	
ripe		riv′er·side′		rob′in	
ripe′ly		riv′et		ro′bot	
rip′en		riv′et·ed		ro·bust′	
rip′ened		riv′et·er		ro·bust′ly	
rip′er		riv′u·let		ro·bust′ness	
rip′est		roach		rock	
ri·poste′		road		rock′er	
rip′ple		road′a·bil′i·ty		rock′et	
rip′pled		road′bed′		rock′fish′	
rip′pling·ly		road′house′		rock′weed′	
rip′ply		road′man		rock′work′	
rip′rap′		road′side′		rock′y	
rise		road′stead		ro·co′co	
ris′en		road′ster		rod	
ris′er		road′way′		ro′dent	
ris′i·bil′i·ty		road′weed′		ro′de·o	
ris′i·ble		roam		rod′man	
ris′ings		roamed		roe	
risk		roam′er		roent′gen	
risked		roam′ings		rogue	
risk′y		roar		ro′guer·y	

ro'guish	room'i·ness	ro'tat·ed
ro'guish·ly	room'mate'	ro·ta'tion
ro'guish·ness	room'y	ro·ta'tion·al
roil	roost	ro'ta·tive
roiled	roost'er	ro'ta·tor
roist'er	root	ro'ta·to'ry
roll	root'ed	rote
rolled	root'er	ro'te·none
roll'er	root'let	ro'to·gra·vure'
roll'mop'	root'worm'	ro'tor
ro·maine'	rope	rot'ten
Ro'man	rope'danc'er	rot'ten·ness
ro·mance'	rope'mak'er	rot'ter
Ro'man·esque'	rope'work'	ro·tund'
ro·man'tic	ro·quet'	ro·tun'da
ro·man'ti·cal·ly	ro·sa'ceous	ro·tun'di·ty
ro·man'ti·cism	ro'sa·ry	rouge
ro·man'ti·cist	rose	rouged
ro·man'ti·cize	ro'se·ate	rough
romp	rose'mar'y	rough'age
romp'ers	ro·sette'	rough'cast'
ron'deau	rose'wood'	rough'dry'
ron'do	ros'i·ly	rough'en
roof	ros'in	rough'ened
roof'er	ros'i·ness	rough'er
roof'less	ros'ter	rough'est
roof'tree'	ros'trum	rough'hew'
rook'er·y	ros'y	rough'hewn'
room	rot	rough'house'
roomed	Ro·tar'i·an	rough'ish
room'er	ro'ta·ry	rough'ly
room'ful	ro'tate	rough'neck'

rough'ness	row	ru'bri·ca'tor
rough'rid'er	row	ru'by
rou·lade'	row'boat	ruch'ing
rou·leau'	row'dy	ruck'sack'
rou·lette'	rowed	ruck'us
round	row'el	rud'der
round'a·bout'	row'eled	rud'der·post'
round'ed	row'en	rud'di·er
roun'de·lay	row'er	rud'di·est
round'er	row'lock	rud'di·ly
round'est	roy'al	rud'di·ness
round'fish'	roy'al·ism	rud'dy
round'house'	roy'al·ist	rude
round'ish	roy'al·ly	rude'ly
round'ly	roy'al·ty	rude'ness
round'ness	rub	rud'er
rounds'man	rubbed	rud'est
round'worm'	rub'ber	ru'di·ment
rouse	rub'ber·ize	ru'di·men'tal
roused	rub'ber·ized	ru'di·men'ta·ry
rous'ing·ly	rub'ber·y	rue
roust'a·bout'	rub'bings	rued
rout	rub'bish	rue'ful
route	rub'ble	ruff
rout'ed	rub'down'	ruf'fi·an
rout'ed	ru'be·fa'cient	ruf'fi·an·ism
rou·tine'	ru'be·fac'tion	ruf'fle
rou·tin'i·za'tion	ru·be'o·la	ruf'fled
rou·tin'ize	ru'bi·cund	Rug'by
rov'er	ru·bid'i·um	rug'ged
rov'ing·ly	ru'ble	rug'ged·ness
rov'ings	ru'bric	ru'gose

ru·gos'i·ty

ru'in

ru'in·a'tion

ru'ined

ru'in·ous

rule

ruled

rul'er

rul'ings

rum

rum'ble

rum'bled

rum'bling·ly

rum'blings

ru'mi·nant

ru'mi·nate

ru'mi·nat'ed

ru'mi·nat'ing·ly

ru'mi·na'tion

ru'mi·na'tive

rum'mage

rum'maged

rum'my

ru'mor

ru'mored

rump

rum'ple

rum'pled

rum'pus

run

run'a·bout'

run'a·gate

rune

rung

ru'nic

run'ner

run'off'

runt

run'way'

ru·pee'

rup'ture

rup'tured

ru'ral

ru'ral·ism

ru'ral·i·za'tion

ru'ral·ize

ru'ral·ly

ruse

rush

rush'ing·ly

rush'light'

rusk

rus'set

Rus'sian

rust

rust'ed

rus'tic

rus'ti·cate

rus'ti·cat'ed

rus'ti·ca'tion

rus'ti·cism

rus·tic'i·ty

rus'tic·ly

rust'i·er

rust'i·est

rus'tle

rus'tled

rus'tler

rus'tling·ly

rus'tlings

rust'proof'

rust'y

rut

ru'ta·ba'ga

ruth

ru·the'ni·um

ruth'less

rye

S

Sab'ba·tar'i·an	sa'cred	sad'ly
Sab'bath	sa'cred·ly	sad'ness
sab·bat'i·cal	sa'cred·ness	sa·fa'ri
sab'ba·tine	sac'ri·fice	safe
sa'ber	sac'ri·ficed	safe'guard'
sa'ble	sac'ri·fi'cial	safe'keep'ing
sab'o·tage'	sac'ri·lege	safe'ly
sac'cha·rine	sac'ri·le'gious	safe'ness
sac'er·do'tal	sac'ris·tan	saf'er
sa'chem	sac'ris·ty	saf'est
sa·chet'	sac'ro·sanct	safe'ty
sack'but	sa'crum	saf'fron
sack'cloth'	sad	sag
sacked	sad'der	sa'ga
sack'ful	sad'dest	sa·ga'cious
sa'cral	sad'dle	sa·ga'cious·ly
sac'ra·ment	sad'dle·back'	sa·gac'i·ty
sac'ra·men'tal	sad'dle·bag'	sag'a·more
sac'ra·men'tal·ism	sad'dled	sage
sac'ra·men'tal·ist	sad'dler	sagged
sac'ra·men'tal·ly	sad'dler·y	sag'it·tal
sac'ra·men·tar'i·an	sad'i'ron	sa'go

sa'hib

said

sail

sail'boat'

sailed

sail'fish'

sail'ings

sail'or

saint

saint'ed

saint'hood

saint'li·ness

saint'ly

sake

sa'ker

sa·laam'

sal'a·bil'i·ty

sal'a·ble

sa·la'cious

sa·la'cious·ly

sa·la'cious·ness

sal'ad

sal'a·man'der

sal'a·ried

sal'a·ry

sale

sal'e·ra'tus

sales'man

sales'man·ship

sales'peo'ple

sales'per'son

sales'room'

sales'wom'an

sal'i·cyl'ic

sa'li·ence

sa'li·ent

sa·lif'er·ous

sa'line

sa·li'va

sal'i·vant

sal'i·vate

sal'i·va'tion

sal'low

sal'low·er

sal'low·est

sal'ly

salm'on

sa·loon'

sal'si·fy

salt

sal'ta·to'ry

salt'cel'lar

salt'ed

salt'i·er

salt'i·est

salt'pe'ter

salt'y

sa·lu'bri·ous

sa·lu'bri·ty

sal'u·tar'y

sal'u·ta'tion

sa·lu'ta·to'ri·an

sa·lu'ta·to'ry

sa·lute'

sa·lut'ed

sal'vage

sal'vaged

sal·va'tion

salve

salved

sal'ver

sal'vo

Sa·mar'i·tan

sa·ma'ri·um

same

same'ness

sam'ite

Sa·mo'an

sam'o·var

sam'pan

sam'ple

sam'pled

sam'pler

sam'plings

sam'u·rai

san'a·tive

san'a·to'ri·um

san'a·to'ry

sanc'ti·fi·ca'tion

sanc'ti·fied

sanc'ti·fy

sanc'ti·mo'ni·ous

sanc'ti·mo'ni·ous·ly

sanc'ti·mo'ni·ous·ness

sanc'tion

sanc'tioned

sanc'ti·tude	san'guine	sar'do·nyx
sanc'ti·ty	san'i·tar'i·um	sar·gas'so
sanc'tu·ar'y	san'i·tar'y	sa'ri
sanc'tum	san'i·ta'tion	sa·rong'
sand	san'i·ty	sar'sa·pa·ril'la
san'dal	sank	sar·to'ri·al
san'dal·wood'	San'skrit	sash
sand'bag'	sap	sas'sa·fras
sand'bank'	sa'pi·ence	sat
sand'blast'	sa'pi·ent	Sa'tan
sand'box'	sap'lings	sa·tan'ic
sand'bur'	sa·pon'i·fi·ca'tion	satch'el
sand'ed	sa·pon'i·fy	sate
sand'er	sap'per	sat'ed
sand'fish'	sap'phire	sa·teen'
sand'flow'er	sap'pi·er	sat'el·lite
sand'i·ness	sap'pi·est	sa'ti·ate
sand'man'	sap'py	sa'ti·at'ed
sand'pa'per	sap'wood'	sa'ti·a'tion
sand'pip'er	sar'a·band	sa·ti'e·ty
sand'stone'	Sar'a·cen	sat'in
sand'storm'	sar'casm	sat'i·nette'
sand'wich	sar·cas'tic	sat'ire
sand'wiched	sar·cas'ti·cal·ly	sa·tir'ic
sand'worm'	sar·co'ma	sa·tir'i·cal
sand'y	sar·co'ma·ta	sa·tir'i·cal·ly
sane	sar'co·phag'ic	sat'i·rist
sane'ly	sar·coph'a·gus	sat'i·rize
san'er	sar·dine'	sat'i·rized
san'est	Sar·din'i·an	sat'is·fac'tion
sang	sar·don'ic	sat'is·fac'to·ri·ly
san'gui·nar'y	sar·don'i·cal·ly	sat'is·fac'to·ry

sat'is·fied	sav'a·ble	sca'lar
sat'is·fy	sav'age	scald
sat'is·fy'ing·ly	sav'age·ly	scald'ed
sa'trap	sav'age·ry	scale
sat'u·rate	sa·van'na	scaled
sat'u·rat'ed	sa·vant'	sca·lene'
sat'u·ra'tion	save	scal'er
Sat'ur·day	saved	scal'lion
Sat'urn	sav'ings	scal'lop
sat'ur·nine	sav'ior	scalp
sat'yr	sa'vor	scalped
sat'yr·esque'	sa'vor·less	scal'pel
sauce	sa'vor·y	scalp'er
sauce'boat'	saw	scal'y
sauce'dish'	saw'dust'	scamp
sauce'pan'	sawed	scamped
sau'cer	saw'fish'	scam'per
sau'cer·like'	saw'fly'	scam'pered
sau'ci·er	saw'horse'	scan
sau'ci·est	saw'mill'	scan'dal
sau'ci·ly	saw'yer	scan'dal·i·za'tion
sau'cy	Sax'on	scan'dal·ize
saun'ter	say	scan'dal·ized
saun'tered	say'ings	scan'dal·ous
saun'ter·er	says	scan'dal·ous·ly
saun'ter·ing·ly	scab	Scan'di·na'vi·a
saun'ter·ings	scab'bard	scan'di·um
sau'ri·an	scab'by	scanned
sau'sage	sca'bi·es	scan'ner
sau·té'	sca'bi·ous	scan'sion
sau·téed'	sca'brous	scan·so'ri·al
sau·terne'	scaf'fold	scant

scant'ed

scant'i·ly

scant'i·ness

scant'lings

scant'y

scape'goat'

scape'grace'

scap'u·la

scap'u·lar

scar

scar'ab

scarce

scarce'ly

scarc'er

scarc'est

scar'ci·ty

scare

scared

scarf

scar'i·fi·ca'tion

scar'i·fied

scar'i·fi'er

scar'i·fy

scar'la·ti'na

scar'let

scarred

scathed

scathe'less

scath'ing

scath'ing·ly

scat'ter

scat'ter·brain'

scat'tered

scat'ter·ing·ly

scat'ter·ings

scav'en·ger

sce·na'ri·o

scen'er·y

scene'shift'er

sce'nic

sce'ni·cal

scent

scent'ed

scent'less

scent'wood'

scep'ter

scep'tered

sched'ule

sched'uled

sche·mat'ic

sche·mat'i·cal·ly

sche'ma·tize

sche'ma·tized

scheme

schemed

schem'er

schem'ing·ly

scher·zan'do

scher'zo

schism

schis·mat'ic

schis·mat'i·cal

schist

schiz'oid

schiz'o·phre'ni·a

schiz'o·phren'ic

schnapps

schnau'zer

schnit'zel

schol'ar

schol'ar·ly

schol'ar·ship

scho·las'tic

scho·las'ti·cal

scho·las'ti·cal·ly

scho·las'ti·cism

scho'li·ast

scho'li·um

school

school'book'

schooled

school'house'

school'man

school'mas'ter

schoon'er

schot'tische

sci·at'ic

sci·at'i·ca

sci'ence

sci'en·tif'ic

sci'en·tif'i·cal·ly

sci'en·tist

scim'i·tar

scin·til'la

scin'til·lant

scin'til·late

scin'til·lat'ed

scin'til·lat'ing·ly

scin'til·la'tion

sci'on

scis'sors

scle·ri'tis

scle·ro'sis

scle·rot'ic

scle'ro·ti'tis

scle·rot'o·my

scoff

scoffed

scoff'er

scoff'ing·ly

scoff'law'

scold

scold'ed

scold'ing·ly

scold'ings

sco'li·o'sis

sconce

scone

scoop

scooped

scoop'ing·ly

scoot

scoot'er

scope

scorch

scorched

scorch'er

scorch'ing·ly

score

scored

scor'er

scor'ings

scorn

scorned

scorn'er

scorn'ful

scorn'ful·ly

scor'pi·on

Scot

Scotch

Scotch'man

Scots'man

Scot'tish

scoun'drel

scoun'drel·ly

scour

scoured

scour'er

scourge

scourged

scourg'ing·ly

scour'ings

scout

scout'ed

scow

scowl

scowled

scowl'ing·ly

scrab'ble

scrab'bled

scrab'blings

scrag'gy

scram'ble

scram'bled

scram'blings

scrap

scrap'book'

scrape

scraped

scrap'er

scrap'ing·ly

scrap'ings

scrap'man

scrap'pi·er

scrap'pi·est

scrap'ple

scrap'py

scratch

scratched

scratch'i·ness

scratch'ings

scratch'y

scrawl

scrawled

scrawl'ings

scraw'ni·ly

scraw'ni·ness

scraw'ny

scream

screamed

scream'ing·ly

screech

screeched

screech'i·er

screech'i·est

screech'y

screed

screen

screened

screen'ings

screen'play'

screw

screw'driv'er

screwed

scrib'ble

scrib'bled

scrib'bler

scrib'bling·ly

scrib'blings

scribe

scrib'er

scrim

scrim'mage

scrimp

scrimped

scrimp'i·ly

scrimp'i·ness

scrimp'ing·ly

scrim'shaw'

scrip

script

scrip'tur·al

scrip'tur·al·ism

scrip'tur·al·ist

scrip'ture

scrive'ner

scrod

scrof'u·la

scrof'u·lous

scroll

scrolled

scroll'work'

scroug'er

scrounge

scrub

scrub'bed

scrub'bi·er

scrub'bi·est

scrub'bings

scrub'by

scrub'land'

scruff

scrum'mage

scrump'tious

scrunch

scrunched

scru'ple

scru'pled

scru'pu·los'i·ty

scru'pu·lous

scru'pu·lous·ly

scru'pu·lous·ness

scru'ti·ni·za'tion

scru'ti·nize

scru'ti·nized

scru'ti·niz'ing·ly

scru'ti·ny

scud

scud'ded

scuff

scuffed

scuf'fle

scuf'fled

scuf'fling·ly

scuf'flings

scull

sculled

scull'er

scul'ler·y

scul'lion

scul'pin

sculp'tor

sculp'tur·al

sculp'ture

sculp'tur·esque'

scum

scum'my

scup'per

scup'per·nong

scurf

scur·ril'i·ty

scur'ril·ous

scur'ril·ous·ly

scur'ril·ous·ness

scur'ry

scur'vy

scut'tle

scut'tled

scut'tle·ful	sea'sick'ness	sec're·tar'i·al
scu'tum	sea'side'	sec're·tar'i·at
scythe	sea'son	sec're·tar'y
sea	sea'son·a·ble	se·crete'
sea'board'	sea'son·al	se·cret'ed
sea'coast'	sea'son·al·ly	se·cre'tion
sea'far'er	sea'soned	se·cre'tive
sea'fowl'	sea'son·ings	se·cre'tive·ly
sea'go'ing	seat	se·cre'tive·ness
seal	seat'ed	se'cret·ly
sealed	sea'ward	se·cre'to·ry
seal'er	sea'wor'thi·ness	sect
seal'skin'	sea'wor'thy	sec·tar'i·an
seam	se·ba'ceous	sec·tar'i·an·ism
sea'man	se'cant	sec'ta·ry
sea'man·like'	se·cede'	sec'tion
sea'man·ship	se·ced'ed	sec'tion·al
seamed	se·ces'sion	sec'tion·al·ism
seam'stress	se·ces'sion·ism	sec'tion·al·ize
seam'y	se·ces'sion·ist	sec'tion·al·ized
sea'plane'	se·clude'	sec'tion·al·ly
sea'port'	se·clud'ed	sec'tor
sear	se·clu'sion	sec'u·lar
search	sec'ond	sec'u·lar·ism
searched	sec'ond·ar'i·ly	sec'u·lar·ist
search'er	sec'ond·ar'y	sec'u·lar'i·ty
search'ing·ly	sec'ond·ed	sec'u·lar·i·za'tion
search'light'	sec'ond·er	sec'u·lar·ize
seared	sec'ond·hand'	sec'u·lar·ized
sea'scape	sec'ond·ly	sec'u·lar·iz'er
sea'shore'	se'cre·cy	se·cure'
sea'sick'	se'cret	se·cured'

se·cure'ly	seed'ed	se'gui·dil'la
se·cu'ri·ty	seed'i·er	seine
se·dan'	seed'i·est	seis'mic
se·date'	seed'i·ness	seis'mo·graph
se·date'ly	seed'less	seis·mol'o·gy
se·date'ness	seed'less·ness	seiz'a·ble
se·da'tion	seed'lings	seize
sed'a·tive	seed'y	seized
sed'en·tar'y	seek	sei'zure
sedge	seek'er	sel'dom
sed'i·ment	seem	se·lect'
sed'i·men'tal	seemed	se·lect'ed
sed'i·men'ta·ry	seem'ing·ly	se·lec'tion
sed'i·men·ta'tion	seem'ly	se·lec'tive
se·di'tion	seen	se·lec'tiv'i·ty
se·di'tious	seep	se·lect'man
se·di'tious·ly	seep'age	se·lect'men
se·di'tious·ness	seep'weed'	se·lec'tor
se·duce'	se'er	sel'e·nate
se·duced'	seer'ess	se·le'nic
se·duc'er	seer'suck'er	sel'e·nide
se·duc'i·ble	see'saw'	sel'e·nite
se·duc'tion	seethe	se·le'ni·um
se·duc'tive	seethed	self
se·duc'tive·ly	seg'ment	self'-as·ser'tion
se·duc'tive·ness	seg·men'tal	self'-as·ser'tive
sed'u·lous	seg'men·tar'y	self'-as·sured'
sed'u·lous·ly	seg'men·ta'tion	self'-cen'tered
sed'u·lous·ness	seg're·gate	self'-col'ored
se'dum	seg're·gat'ed	self'-com·mand'
see	seg're·ga'tion	self'-com·pla'cent
seed	seg're·ga'tion·ist	self'-com·posed'

self'-con·ceit'

self'-con·cern'

self'-con'fi·dence

self'-con'scious

self'-con'scious·ness

self'-con·tained'

self'-con'tra·dic'tion

self'-con·trol'

self'-cov'ered

self'-de·ceit'

self'-de·fense'

self'-de·ni'al

self'-de·struc'tion

self'-de·ter'mi·na'tion

self'-de·ter'mined

self'-dis'ci·pline

self'-dis·trust'

self'-ed'u·cat'ed

self'-ef·face'ment

self'-ef·fac'ing·ly

self'-es·teem'

self'-ev'i·dent

self'-ex·am'i·na'tion

self'-ex'e·cut'ing

self'-ex·plain'ing

self'-ex·plan'a·to'ry

self'-ex·pres'sion

self'-for·get'ful

self'-gov'erned

self'-gov'ern·ment

self'-help'

self'-im·por'tance

self'-im·prove'ment

self'-in·duced'

self'-in·duc'tance

self'-in·dul'gent

self'-in'ter·est

self'ish

self'ish·ly

self'ish·ness

self'-knowl'edge

self'less

self'-lim'it·ed

self'-liq'ui·dat'ing

self'-love'

self'-made'

self'-mas'ter·y

self'-o·pin'ion·at·ed

self'-pos·sessed'

self'-pos·ses'sion

self'-pres'er·va'tion

self'-pro·pel'ling

self'-rat'ing

self'-read'ing

self'-re'al·i·za'tion

self'-re·gard'

self'-reg'is·ter·ing

self'-re·li'ance

self'-re·li'ant

self'-re·nun'ci·a'tion

self'-re·proach'

self'-re·proach'ful

self'-re·proach'ing·ly

self'-re·spect'

self'-re·straint'

self'-right'eous

self'-right'eous·ness

self'-sac'ri·fice

self'-sac'ri·fic'ing·ly

self'same'

self'-sat'is·fied

self'-seek'er

self'-serv'ice

self'-start'er

self'-stud'y

self'-styled'

self'-suf·fi'cien·cy

self'-suf·fi'cient

self'-sup·port'

self'-sur·ren'der

self'-sus·tain'ing

self'-un'der·stand'ing

self'-will'

self'-willed'

self'-wind'ing

sell

sell'er

sell'out'

Selt'zer

sel'vage

se·man'tic

sem'a·phore

sem'blance

se·mes'ter

sem'i·an'nu·al

sem'i·cir'cle

sem'i·civ'i·lized

sem'i·co'lon

sem'i·con'scious

sem'i·de·tached'

sem'i·fi'nal

sem'i·fi'nal·ist

sem'i·fin'ished

sem'i·month'ly

sem'i·nar'

sem'i·nar'i·an

sem'i·nar'y

Sem'i·nole

sem'i·per'me·a·ble

sem'i·pre'cious

sem'i·se'ri·ous

sem'i·skilled'

Sem'ite

Se·mit'ic

Sem'i·tism

sem'i·tone'

sem'i·week'ly

sem'o·li'na

sem'pi·ter'nal

sen'ate

sen'a·tor

sen'a·to'ri·al

sen'a·to'ri·al·ly

sen'a·tor·ship'

send

send'er

Sen'e·ca

se·nes'cence

se·nes'cent

sen'es·chal

se'nile

se·nil'i·ty

sen'ior

sen·ior'i·ty

sen'na

sen'nit

sen'sate

sen·sa'tion

sen·sa'tion·al

sen·sa'tion·al·ism

sen·sa'tion·al·ly

sense

sense'less

sense'less·ly

sense'less·ness

sen'si·bil'i·ty

sen'si·ble

sen'si·tive

sen'si·tive·ly

sen'si·tive·ness

sen'si·tiv'i·ty

sen'si·ti·za'tion

sen'si·tize

sen'si·tized

sen'si·tiz'er

sen'si·tom'e·ter

sen·so'ri·um

sen'so·ry

sen'su·al

sen'su·al·ism

sen'su·al·ist

sen'su·al·is'tic

sen'su·al'i·ty

sen'su·al·i·za'tion

sen'su·al·ize

sen'su·al·ized

sen'su·al·ly

sen'su·ous

sen'su·ous·ly

sen'su·ous·ness

sen'tence

sen'tenced

sen·ten'tious

sen·ten'tious·ly

sen·ten'tious·ness

sen'ti·ence

sen'ti·en·cy

sen'ti·ment

sen'ti·men'tal

sen'ti·men'tal·ism

sen'ti·men'tal·ist

sen'ti·men·tal'i·ty

sen'ti·men'tal·ize

sen'ti·men'tal·ized

sen'ti·nel

sen'try

sep'a·ra·bil'i·ty

sep'a·ra·ble

sep'a·rate

sep'a·rat'ed

sep'a·rate·ly

sep'a·ra'tion

sep′a·ra′tion·ist	Se·quoi′a	se′ri·ous·ness
sep′a·ra·tism	se·ragl′io	ser′mon
sep′a·ra′tist	se·ra′pe	ser′mon·ize
sep′a·ra′tive	ser′aph	ser′mon·ized
sep′a·ra′tor	se·raph′ic	se′rous
sep′a·ra·to′ry	se·raph′i·cal	ser′pent
se′pi·a	ser′a·phim	ser′pen·tine
se′poy	Ser′bi·an	ser·pig′i·nous
sep′sis	sere	ser′rate
Sep·tem′ber	ser′e·nade′	ser·ra′tion
sep·ten′ni·al	ser′e·nad′ed	ser′ried
sep·tet′	ser′e·nad′er	se′rum
sep′tic	ser′e·na′ta	serv′ant
sep′ti·ce′mi·a	ser′en·dip′i·ty	serve
Sep′tu·a·gint	se·rene′	served
sep′tum	se·rene′ly	serv′er
sep′ul·cher	se·rene′ness	serv′ice
se·pul′chral	se·ren′i·ty	serv′ice·a·bil′i·ty
se·pul′tur·al	serf	serv′ice·a·ble
sep′ul·ture	serf′dom	serv′ice·a·bly
se′quel	serge	serv′iced
se·que′la	ser′geant	Serv′i·dor
se′quence	se′ri·al	ser′vile
se′quenc·er	se′ri·al·i·za′tion	ser·vil′i·ty
se·quen′tial	se′ri·al·ize	serv′ings
se·quen′tial·ly	se′ri·al·ly	ser′vi·tor
se·ques′ter	se′ri·a′tim	ser′vi·tude
se·ques′tered	ser′i·cul′ture	ser′vo·mech′a·nism
se·ques′trate	se′ries	ser′vo·mo′tor
se·ques′trat·ed	ser′if	ses′a·me
se·ques·tra′tion	se′ri·ous	ses′qui·sul′phide
se′quin	se′ri·ous·ly	ses′sion

ses'terce	sex·tet'	shak'en
ses·tet'	sex'ton	shak'er
set	sex'tu·ple	Shake·spear'e·an
set'back'	sex·tu'pli·cate	shake'-up'
set'off'	shab'bi·ly	shak'i·er
set·tee'	shab'bi·ness	shak'i·est
set'ter	shab'by	shak'i·ly
set'tings	shack	shak'i·ness
set'tle	shack'le	shak'o
set'tled	shack'led	shak'y
set'tle·ment	shade	shale
set'tler	shad'ed	shall
sev'er	shad'i·er	shal'lop
sev'er·a·ble	shad'i·est	shal·lot'
sev'er·al	shad'i·ly	shal'low
sev'er·al·ly	shad'i·ness	shal'lowed
sev'er·al·ty	shad'ings	shal'low·er
sev'er·ance	shad'ow	shal'low·est
sev'er·a'tion	shad'owed	shal'low·ly
se·vere'	shad'ow·less	shal'low·ness
sev'ered	shad'ow·y	sham
se·vere'ly	shad'y	sha'man
se·ver'er	shaft	sham'ble
se·ver'est	shag	sham'bled
se·ver'i·ty	shag'bark'	sham'bling·ly
sew	shag'gi·er	shame
sew'age	shag'gi·est	shamed
sewed	shag'gi·ly	shame'faced'
sew'er	shag'gy	shame·fac'ed·ly
sew'er·age	sha·green'	shame'ful
sewn	shake	shame'ful·ly
sex'tant	shake'down'	shame'ful·ness

shame′less·ly	sharp′ness	sheep′skin′
shame′less·ness	sharp′shoot′er	sheer
shammed	sharp′-wit′ted	sheer′er
sham′mer	shas′tra	sheer′est
sham·poo′	shat′ter	sheer′ly
sham·pooed′	shat′tered	sheet
sham′rock	shat′ter·ing·ly	sheet′ed
shan′dy·gaff	shat′ter·proof′	sheet′ings
shang·hai′	shave	sheet′ways′
shang·haied′	shaved	sheet′wise′
shank	shav′er	sheet′work′
shan′t	shave′tail′	shek′el
shan′ty	shav′ings	shel′drake′
shape	shaw	shelf
shaped	shawl	shell
shape′less	she	shel·lac′
shape′less·ly	sheaf	shell′back′
shape′less·ness	shear	shell′burst′
shape′li·ness	sheared	shelled
shape′ly	shear′ings	shell′fish′
shard	shears	shell′proof′
share	sheathe	shell′work′
shared	sheathed	shel′ter
share′hold′er	sheaves	shel′tered
shark	shed	shel′ter·ing·ly
sharp	sheen	shel′ter·less
sharp′en	sheep	shelve
sharp′ened	sheep′herd′er	shelved
sharp′en·er	sheep′ish	shelves
sharp′er	sheep′ish·ly	shep′herd
sharp′est	sheep′ish·ness	shep′herd·ed
sharp′ly	sheep′man	shep′herd·ess

Sher'a·ton	shin'gled	shirt'ings
sher'bet	shin'i·ly	shirt'less
sher'iff	shin'i·ness	shiv'er
Sher'pa	shin'ing·ly	shiv'ered
sher'ry	shin'ny	shiv'er·ing·ly
Shet'land	shin'plas'ter	shiv'er·ings
shew'bread'	Shin'to'	shoal
shib'bo·leth	Shin'to·ism	shoal'ness
shied	Shin'to·ist	shock
shield	Shin'to·is'tic	shocked
shield'ed	shin'y	shock'ing·ly
shift	ship	shod
shift'ed	ship'board'	shod'di·er
shift'i·er	ship'build'er	shod'di·est
shift'i·est	ship'load'	shod'dy
shift'i·ly	ship'mas'ter	shoe
shift'i·ness	ship'mate'	shoe'horn'
shift'less	ship'ment	shoe'lace'
shift'y	ship'own'er	shoe'less
shil·le'lagh	ship'per	shoe'mak'er
shil'lings	ship'shape'	shoe'man
shim	ship'worm'	shoes
shimmed	ship'wreck'	shoe'string'
shim'mer	ship'wright'	sho'gun'
shim'mered	ship'yard'	shook
shim'mer·ing·ly	shire	shoot
shim'mer·y	shirk	shoot'er
shin	shirked	shoot'ings
shin'bone'	shirk'er	shop
shine	shirr	shop'keep'er
shin'er	shirred	shop'lift'er
shin'gle	shirt	shop'man

shop'per

shop'work'

shop'worn'

shore

shored

shorn

short

short'age

short'bread'

short'cake'

short'change'

short'com'ings

short'en

short'ened

short'en·ing

short'er

short'est

short'fall'

short'hand'

short'hand'ed

short'horn'

short'ish

short'leaf'

short'-lived'

short'ly

short'ness

short'-range'

short'sight'ed

short'-time'

shot

shot'gun'

shot'ted

should

shoul'der

shoul'dered

shout

shout'ed

shove

shoved

shov'el

shov'eled

shov'el·head'

show

show'boat'

show'down'

showed

show'er

show'ered

show'i·er

show'i·est

show'i·ly

show'i·ness

show'ings

show'man

show'man·ship

shown

show'room'

show'y

shrank

shrap'nel

shred

shred'ded

shred'der

shrew

shrewd

shrewd'er

shrewd'est

shrewd'ly

shrewd'ness

shriek

shrieked

shrift

shrike

shrill

shrilled

shrill'er

shrill'est

shrill'ness

shrill'y

shrimp

shrimp'er

shrine

Shrin'er

shrink

shrink'age

shrink'er

shrink'ing·ly

shrive

shriv'el

shriv'eled

shriv'en

shroud

shroud'ed

shrub

shrub'ber·y

shrub'wood'

shrug	sib'yl	siege
shrugged	sib'yl·line	si·en'na
shrunk	Si·cil'i·an	si·er'ra
shrunk'en	sick	si·es'ta
shuck	sick'bed'	sieve
shucked	sick'en	sift
shud'der	sick'ened	sift'age
shud'dered	sick'en·ing·ly	sift'ed
shud'der·ing·ly	sick'er	sift'ings
shud'der·ings	sick'est	sigh
shuf'fle	sick'le	sighed
shuf'fled	sick'li·er	sigh'ing·ly
shuf'fling·ly	sick'li·est	sigh'ings
shuf'flings	sick'li·ness	sight
shun	sick'ly	sight'ed
shunt	sick'ness	sight'ings
shunt'ed	sick'room'	sight'less
shut	side	sight'li·ness
shut'off'	side'board'	sight'ly
shut'ter	side'car'	sig'ma
shut'tered	sid'ed	sign
shut'tle	side'long'	sig'nal
shut'tled	side'piece'	sig'naled
shy	si·de're·al	sig'nal·ize
shy'ly	sid'er·ite	sig'nal·ized
shy'ness	side'split'ting	sig'nal·ly
shy'ster	side'walk'	sig'na·to'ry
Si'a·mese'	side'ways'	sig'na·ture
sib'i·lance	side'wise'	sign'board'
sib'i·lant	sid'ings	signed
sib'i·late	si'dle	sign'er
sib'ling	si'dled	sig'net

sig·nif′i·cance

sig·nif′i·cant

sig·nif′i·cant·ly

sig′ni·fi·ca′tion

sig′ni·fied

sig′ni·fy

sign′post′

sign′writ′er

si′lage

si′lence

si′lenced

si′lenc·er

si′lent

si′lent·ly

si′lent·ness

si′lex

sil′hou·ette′

sil′i·ca

sil′i·cate

sil′i·con

sil′i·co′sis

silk

silk′en

silk′i·er

silk′i·est

silk′i·ly

silk′i·ness

silk′weed′

silk′worm′

silk′y

sil′la·bub

sil′li·er

sil′li·est

sil′li·ness

sil′ly

si′lo

silt

sil·ta′tion

silt′ed

sil′van

sil′ver

sil′vered

sil′ver·smith′

sil′ver·ware′

sil′ver·y

sim′i·an

sim′i·lar

sim′i·lar′i·ty

sim′i·lar·ly

sim′i·le

si·mil′i·tude

sim′mer

sim′mered

sim′mer·ing·ly

sim′o·ny

si·moon′

sim′per

sim′pered

sim′per·ing·ly

sim′ple

sim′pler

sim′plest

sim′ple·ton

sim′plex

sim·plic′i·ty

sim′pli·fi·ca′tion

sim′pli·fied

sim′pli·fy

sim′ply

sim′u·la′crum

sim′u·late

sim′u·la′tion

sim′u·la′tor

si′mul·ta′ne·ous

sin

since

sin·cere′

sin·cere′ly

sin·cere′ness

sin·cer′er

sin·cer′est

sin·cer′i·ty

sine

si′ne·cure

sin′ew

sin′ew·y

sin′ful

sin′ful·ly

sin′ful·ness

sing

sing′a·ble

singe

singed

sing′er

sin′gle

sin′gled

sin'gle·ness	sip'per	siz'es
sin'gle·ton	sir	siz'ings
sin'gly	sir·dar'	siz'zle
sin'gu·lar	sire	siz'zled
sin'gu·lar'i·ty	sired	siz'zling·ly
sin'gu·lar·ly	si'ren	skate
sin'is·ter	sir'loin'	skat'ed
sin'is·tral	si·roc'co	skat'er
sink	sir'up	skein
sink'age	sir'up·y	skel'e·tal
sink'er	si'sal	skel'e·ton
sink'hole'	sis'kin	skel'e·ton·ize
sink'ings	sis'si·fied	skel'e·ton·ized
sink'less	sis'sy	skep'tic
sin'less	sis'ter	skep'ti·cal
sin'less·ly	sis'ter·hood	skep'ti·cal·ly
sin'less·ness	sis'ter-in-law'	skep'ti·cism
sinned	sis'ter·ly	sketch
sin'ner	Sis'tine	sketched
Sin'o·log'i·cal	sis'trum	sketch'i·ly
Si·nol'o·gist	sit	sketch'i·ness
Sin'o·logue	site	sketch'y
Sin'o·phile	sit'ter	skew
sin'ter	sit'tings	skewed
sin'u·os'i·ty	sit'u·ate	skew'er
sin'u·ous	sit'u·at'ed	skew'ered
si'nus·i'tis	sit'u·a'tion	skew'ings
Sioux	sixth	ski
sip	siz'a·ble	ski'a·gram
si'phon	size	ski'a·graph
si'phoned	sized	ski·am'e·try
sipped	siz'er	skid

skid'ded	skir'mished	sky'writ'ing
skied	skir'mish·er	slab
skiff	skir'mish·ing·ly	slack
ski·jor'ing	skirt	slacked
skill	skirt'ed	slack'en
skilled	skirt'ings	slack'ened
skil'let	skit	slack'er
skill'ful	skit'ter	slack'est
skill'ful·ly	skit'tish	slack'ness
skill'ful·ness	skit'tish·ly	slag
skim	skit'tish·ness	slain
skimmed	skit'tles	slake
skim'mer	skive	slaked
skim'ming·ly	skived	slam
skimp	skiv'er	slammed
skimped	skiv'ings	slan'der
skimp'i·ness	skoal	slan'dered
skimp'y	skulk	slan'der·er
skin	skulked	slan'der·ing·ly
skin'flint'	skull	slan'der·ous
skink'er	skunk	slan'der·ous·ly
skinned	skunk'weed'	slan'der·ous·ness
skin'ner	sky	slang
skin'ni·er	sky'jack'er	slang'y
skin'ni·est	sky'larked'	slank
skin'ny	sky'light'	slant
skin'worm'	sky'rock'et	slant'ed
skip	sky'scape	slant'ing·ly
skipped	sky'scrap'er	slant'ways'
skip'per	sky'shine'	slant'wise'
skip'ping·ly	sky'ward	slap
skir'mish	sky'writ'er	slap'dash'

slap'stick'	sleek'er	slick'est
slash	sleek'est	slid
slashed	sleek'ly	slide
slash'er	sleek'ness	sli'er
slash'ing·ly	sleep	sli'est
slash'ings	sleep'er	slight
slate	sleep'i·er	slight'ed
slat'er	sleep'i·est	slight'er
slat'ted	sleep'i·ly	slight'est
slat'tern	sleep'i·ness	slight'ing·ly
slat'tern·ly	sleep'less	slight'ly
slaugh'ter	sleep'less·ness	slight'ness
slaugh'tered	sleep'y	slim
slaugh'ter·er	sleet	slime
slaugh'ter·house'	sleeve	slim'i·er
slave	sleigh	slim'i·est
slaved	sleight	slim'i·ly
slav'er	slen'der	slim'i·ness
slav'er·y	slen'der·er	slim'mer
slav'ish	slen'der·est	slim'mest
slav'ish·ly	slen'der·ness	slim'ness
slav'ish·ness	slept	slim'y
slaw	sleuth	sling
slay	sleuthed	slink
slay'er	sleuth'hound'	slink'i·er
slay'ings	slew	slink'i·est
sleave	slewed	slink'y
slea'zi·ness	slice	slip
slea'zy	sliced	slip'case'
sled	slic'er	slip'knot'
sledge	slick	slip'page
sleek	slick'er	slipped

slip'per	sloth'ful·ness	sluice
slip'per·i·ness	slot'ted	sluiced
slip'per·y	slouch	sluice'way'
slip'shod'	slouched	sluic'ings
slit	slouch'i·ly	slum
slith'er	slouch'i·ness	slum'ber
slith'ered	slouch'ing·ly	slum'bered
slit'ter	slough	slum'ber·er
sliv'er	slough	slum'ber·ing·ly
sliv'ered	sloughed	slum'ber·land'
sliv'er·y	slov'en	slum'ber·ous
slob	slov'en·li·ness	slump
slob'ber	slov'en·ly	slumped
sloe	slow	slung
sloe'ber'ry	slowed	slur
slog	slow'er	slurred
slo'gan	slow'est	slur'ring·ly
slo'gan·eer'	slow'go'ing	slur'ry
slogged	slow'ly	slush
sloop	slow'poke'	slush'i·ly
slop	sloyd	slush'i·ness
slope	slub	slush'y
sloped	slubbed	slut'tish
slop'ing·ly	sludge	sly
slopped	slug	sly'boots'
slop'py	slug'gard	sly'ly
slosh	slug'gard·ly	sly'ness
sloshed	slugged	smack
slot	slug'ger	smacked
sloth	slug'gish	smack'ing·ly
sloth'ful	slug'gish·ly	small
sloth'ful·ly	slug'gish·ness	small'er

small'est	smil'ing·ly	smooth'ing·ly
small'ness	smirch	smooth'ly
small'pox'	smirched	smooth'ness
smart	smirk	smote
smart'ed	smirked	smoth'er
smart'en	smirk'ing·ly	smoth'ered
smart'ened	smirk'ish	smoth'er·ing·ly
smart'er	smite	smudge
smart'est	smith	smudged
smart'ing·ly	Smith·so'ni·an	smudg'i·ly
smart'ly	smith'y	smudg'i·ness
smart'ness	smit'ten	smudg'y
smash	smock	smug
smash'up'	smoke	smug'gle
smat'ter	smoked	smug'gled
smat'ter·ings	smoke'house'	smug'gler
smear	smoke'less	smug'ly
smeared	smoke'proof'	smug'ness
smear'i·er	smok'er	smut
smear'i·est	smoke'stack'	smut'ted
smear'i·ness	smoke'wood'	smut'ti·er
smear'y	smok'i·er	smut'ti·est
smell	smok'i·est	smut'ti·ly
smelled	smok'i·ness	smut'ti·ness
smelt	smok'y	smut'ty
smelt'ed	smol'der	snack
smelt'er	smol'dered	snaf'fle
smelt'er·y	smooth	sna·fu'
smidg'en	smooth'bore'	snag
smi'lax	smoothed	snag'ged
smile	smooth'er	snag'gled
smiled	smooth'est	snail

snake	snatch'y	snip'pet
snake'bird'	snath	snip'pi·er
snaked	sneak	snip'pi·est
snake'like'	sneaked	snip'pi·ness
snake'stone'	sneak'er	snip'py
snake'weed'	sneak'i·er	sniv'el
snake'wood'	sneak'i·est	sniv'eled
snak'i·er	sneak'ing·ly	sniv'el·er
snak'i·est	sneak'y	sniv'el·ings
snak'i·ly	sneer	snob
snak'i·ness	sneered	snob'ber·y
snak'y	sneer'ing·ly	snob'bish
snap	sneeze	snob'bish·ly
snap'drag'on	sneezed	snob'bish·ness
snapped	sneeze'weed'	snood
snap'per	snick'er	snook'er
snap'pi·er	snick'ered	snoop
snap'pi·est	snick'er·ing·ly	snoop'er
snap'ping·ly	snick'er·ings	snoot
snap'pish	sniff	snooze
snap'py	sniffed	snore
snap'shot'	sniff'i·ly	snored
snap'weed'	sniff'i·ness	snor'ing·ly
snare	sniff'ing·ly	snor'ings
snared	sniff'ings	snor'kel
snarl	snif'fle	snort
snarled	snif'fled	snort'ing·ly
snarl'ing·ly	sniff'y	snort'ings
snarl'y	snig'ger·ing·ly	snout
snatch	snip	snow
snatched	snipe	snow'ball'
snatch'ing·ly	snipped	snow'bell'

snow'ber'ry

snow'bird'

snow'bound'

snow'bush'

snow'cap'

snow'drift'

snow'drop'

snowed

snow'fall'

snow'flake'

snow'flow'er

snow'i·er

snow'i·est

snow'plow'

snow'shed'

snow'shoe'

snow'slide

snow'slip

snow'storm

snow'worm'

snow'y

snub

snubbed

snub'ber

snub'bing·ly

snub'bings

snuff

snuffed

snuff'er

snuf'fle

snuf'fled

snuf'fling·ly

snuf'flings

snug

snug'ger

snug'ger·y

snug'gest

snug'gle

snug'gled

snug'ly

snug'ness

so

soak

soaked

soap

soap'box'

soaped

soap'i·ness

soap'root'

soap'stone'

soap'suds'

soap'y

soar

soared

soar'ing·ly

sob

sobbed

sob'bing·ly

so·be'it

so'ber

so'bered

so'ber·er

so'ber·est

so'ber·ing·ly

so'ber·ly

so'ber·sides'

so·bri'e·ty

so'bri·quet

soc'age

soc'cer

so'cia·bil'i·ty

so'cia·ble

so'cia·bly

so'cial

so'cial·ism

so'cial·ist

so'cial·is'tic

so'cial·i·za'tion

so'cial·ize

so'cial·ized

so'cial·iz'er

so·ci'e·tal

so·ci'e·tar'i·an

so·ci'e·tar'i·an·ism

so·ci'e·ty

so'ci·o·log'i·cal

so'ci·o·log'i·cal·ly

so'ci·ol'o·gist

so'ci·ol'o·gy

sock

sock'et

sock'et·ed

So·crat'ic

sod

so'da

so·dal'i·ty

sod'den	sol'e·cism	sol'i·tude
so'di·um	soled	so'lo
so'fa	sole'ly	so'loed
soft	sol'emn	so'lo·ist
sof'ten	so·lem'ni·ty	sol'stice
sof'tened	sol'em·ni·za'tion	sol'u·bil'i·ty
sof'ten·er	sol'em·nize	sol'u·ble
soft'er	sol'em·nized	sol'ute
soft'est	sol'emn·ly	so·lu'tion
soft'ly	so'le·noid	solv'a·ble
soft'ware	so'le·noi'dal	sol'vate
soft'wood'	sole'print'	sol·va'tion
sog'gi·ly	sol'fe·ri'no	solve
sog'gi·ness	so·lic'it	solved
sog'gy	so·lic'i·ta'tion	sol'ven·cy
soil	so·lic'it·ed	sol'vent
soiled	so·lic'i·tor	so·mat'ic
so·journ'	so·lic'it·ous	so'ma·tol'o·gy
so·journed'	so·lic'i·tude	som'ber
so·journ'er	sol'id	som·bre'ro
sol'ace	sol'i·dar'i·ty	some
sol'aced	so·lid'i·fi'a·ble·ness	some'bod'y
so'lar	so·lid'i·fi·ca'tion	some'how
so·lar'i·um	so·lid'i·fy	some'one'
sold	so·lid'i·ty	som'er·sault
sol'der	sol'id·ly	some'thing
sol'dered	so·lil'o·quize	some'time'
sol'dier	so·lil'o·quized	some'what'
sol'diered	so·lil'o·quy	some'where'
sol'dier·ly	sol'i·taire'	som·nam'bu·lism
sol'dier·y	sol'i·tar'i·ly	som·nam'bu·list
sole	sol'i·tar'y	som'no·lent

son	so·phis'tic	sort
so'nant	so·phis'ti·cal	sort'ed
so·na'ta	so·phis'ti·cate	sort'er
so'na·ti'na	so·phis'ti·cat'ed	sor'tie
song	so·phis'ti·ca'tion	sor'ti·lege
song'bird'	soph'ist·ry	sos'te·nu'to
song'book'	soph'o·more	sot
song'ful	soph'o·mor'ic	sot'tish
song'ful·ness	soph'o·mor'i·cal	sot'tish·ness
song'ster	so'po·rif'ic	sou·brette'
son'ic	so'pra·ni'no	souf'flé'
son'-in-law'	so·pra'no	sought
son'net	sor'cer·er	soul
son'net·eer'	sor'cer·ess	soul'ful
so·nor'i·ty	sor'cer·y	soul'ful·ly
so·no'rous	sor'did	soul'ful·ness
soon	sor'did·ness	soul'less
soon'er	sore	soul'less·ly
soon'est	sore'head'	soul'less·ness
soot	sore'ly	sound
soot'ed	sore'ness	sound'ed
soothe	sor'ghum	sound'er
soothed	so·ror'i·ty	sound'est
sooth'ing·ly	so·ro'sis	sound'ing·ly
sooth'say'er	sor'rel	sound'ings
soot'i·er	sor'ri·er	sound'less
soot'i·est	sor'ri·est	sound'less·ly
soot'i·ly	sor'row	sound'less·ness
soot'y	sor'rowed	sound'ly
sop	sor'row·ful	sound'ness
soph'ism	sor'row·ful·ly	sound'proof'
soph'ist	sor'ry	soup

soup'bone'	sowed	spare'rib'
sour	sow'er	spar'ing·ly
source	sow'ings	spark
soured	soy	spark'ed
sour'er	soy'bean'	spar'kle
sour'est	spa	spar'kled
souse	space	spar'kler
soused	space'craft	spar'kling·ly
sou·tane'	space'man	sparred
south	spa'cious	spar'ring·ly
south'east'	spa'cious·ly	spar'row
south'east'er	spa'cious·ness	sparse
south'east'er·ly	spade	sparse'ly
south'east'ern	spad'ed	sparse'ness
south'er·ly	spade'fish'	spars'er
south'ern	spade'work'	spars'est
south'ern·er	spa·ghet'ti	spar'si·ty
south'ern·most	spal·peen'	Spar'tan
south'ward	span	spasm
south'west'	span'drel	spas·mod'ic
south'west'er	span'gle	spas·mod'i·cal
south'west'er·ly	span'gled	spas·mod'i·cal·ly
sou've·nir'	Span'iard	spas'tic
sov'er·eign	span'iel	spas'ti·cal·ly
sov'er·eign·ty	Span'ish	spas·tic'i·ty
so'vi·et'	spank	spat
so'vi·et'ism	spanked	spat'ter
so'vi·et'i·za'tion	spank'ing·ly	spat'tered
so'vi·et·ize	spank'ings	spat'ter·ing·ly
so'vi·et·ol'o·gist	span'ner	spat'ter·ings
sow	spare	spat'ter·proof'
sow	spared	spat'ter·work'

spat'u·la

spat'u·late

spav'ined

spawn

spawned

speak

speak'er

spear

speared

spear'fish'

spear'head'

spear'mint'

spear'wood'

spe'cial

spe'cial·ist

spe'cial·i·za'tion

spe'cial·ize

spe'cial·ized

spe'cial·ly

spe'cial·ty

spe'cie

spe'cies

spe·cif'ic

spe·cif'i·cal·ly

spec'i·fi·ca'tion

spec'i·fied

spec'i·fy

spec'i·men

spe'cious

spe'cious·ly

spe'cious·ness

speck

specked

speck'le

speck'led

spec'ta·cle

spec'ta·cles

spec·tac'u·lar

spec·tac'u·lar·ly

spec·ta'tor

spec'ter

spec'tral

spec·trom'e·ter

spec'tro·scope

spec'trum

spec'u·late

spec'u·lat'ed

spec'u·la'tion

spec'u·la'tive

spec'u·la'tive·ly

spec'u·la'tive·ness

spec'u·la'tor

spec'u·la·to'ry

spec'u·lum

speech

speech'less

speech'less·ly

speech'less·ness

speed

speed'boat'

speed'ed

speed'er

speed'i·er

speed'i·est

speed'i·ly

speed'i·ness

speed'ing·ly

speed·om'e·ter

speed'way'

speed'y

spe'le·ol'o·gist

spe'le·ol'o·gy

spell

spell'bind'er

spell'bound'

spelled

spell'er

spell'ings

spel'ter

Spen·ce'ri·an

spend

spend'er

spend'ings

spend'thrift'

spent

sper'ma·ce'ti

spew

spewed

sphag'num

sphere

spher'i·cal

spher'i·cal·ly

sphe·ric'i·ty

sphe'roid

sphinx

spice

spiced	spin'y	splash'ings
spic'i·ly	spi'ral	splash'y
spic'i·ness	spi'raled	splat'ter
spic'y	spi'ral·ly	splat'ter·work'
spi'der	spire	splayed
spi'der·y	spired	splay'foot'
spied	spir'it	spleen
spig'ot	spir'it·ed	splen'did
spike	spir'it·ed·ly	splen'did·ly
spiked	spir'it·u·al	splen'dor
spik'y	spir'it·u·al·ism	splen'dor·ous
spile	spir'it·u·al·ist	sple·net'ic
spiled	spir'it·u·al·is'tic	splen'i·tive
spill	spir'it·u·al'i·ty	splice
spilled	spir'it·u·al·ize	spliced
spill'way'	spir'it·u·al·ized	splic'er
spin	spir'it·u·al·ly	splic'ings
spin'ach	spir'it·u·ous	splint
spi'nal	spi'ro·chete	splint'ed
spin'dle	spit	splin'ter
spine	spit'ball'	splin'tered
spine'less	spite	splin'ter·proof'
spin'et	spite'ful	split
spin'i·er	spite'ful·ly	split'tings
spin'i·est	spite'ful·ness	split'worm'
spin'na·ker	spit'fire'	splotch
spin'ner	spit·toon'	splotched
spin'ner·et	splash	splotch'y
spin'ney	splash'down	splurge
spin'ning·ly	splash'i·er	splurged
spin'ster	splash'i·est	splut'ter
spin'ster·hood	splash'ing·ly	splut'tered

spoil	spooled	spout'ings
spoil'age	spoon	sprain
spoiled	spoon'bill'	sprained
spoils'man	spooned	sprang
spoil'sport'	spoon'er·ism	sprat
spoke	spoon'ful	sprawl
spo'ken	spoon'fuls	sprawled
spoke'shave'	spoor	sprawl'ing·ly
spokes'man	spo·rad'ic	spray
spo'li·a'tion	spore	sprayed
spo'li·a'tive	sport	spray'er
spo'li·a·to'ry	sport'ed	spread
spon'dee	spor'tive	spread'er
sponge	spor'tive·ly	spread'ing·ly
sponge'cake'	sports'cast'er	spree
sponged	sports'man	sprig
spong'er	sports'man·ship	spright'li·er
spon'gi·er	sports'wear'	spright'li·est
spon'gi·est	sport'y	spright'li·ness
spong'ings	spot	spright'ly
spon'gy	spot'less	spring
spon'sor	spot'less·ly	spring'board'
spon'sor·ship	spot'less·ness	spring'bok'
spon'ta·ne'i·ty	spot'light'	spring'fish'
spon·ta'ne·ous	spot'ted	spring'i·ly
spon·ta'ne·ous·ly	spot'ter	spring'i·ness
spon·ta'ne·ous·ness	spot'ti·er	spring'ing·ly
spoof	spot'ti·est	spring'time'
spook	spot'ty	spring'wood'
spook'i·ness	spouse	spring'y
spook'y	spout	sprin'kle
spool	spout'ed	sprin'kled

sprin'kler	spurt'ed	squashed
sprin'kling·ly	sput'nik	squat
sprin'klings	sput'ter	squat'ted
sprint	sput'tered	squat'ter
sprint'er	sput'ter·ing·ly	squaw
sprite	sput'ter·ings	squaw'fish'
sprit'sail'	spu'tum	squawk
sprock'et	spy	squeak
sprout	spy'glass'	squeal
sprout'ed	squab	squealed
sprout'ling	squab'ble	squeam'ish
spruce	squab'bled	squee'gee
spruc'er	squab'bling·ly	squeeze
spruc'est	squab'blings	squeezed
sprung	squad	squelch
spry	squad'ron	squelched
spud	squal'id	squelch'ing·ly
spume	squa·lid'i·ty	squib
spumed	squal'id·ly	squid
spu·mo'ne	squall	squig'gle
spun	squalled	squig'gly
spunk	squall'ings	squint
spunk'i·er	squall'y	squint'ed
spunk'i·est	squal'or	squint'ing·ly
spunk'y	squan'der	squire
spur	squan'dered	squirm
spu'ri·ous	square	squirmed
spu'ri·ous·ly	squared	squirm'ing·ly
spurn	square'head'	squirm'ings
spurned	square'ly	squir'rel
spurred	square'ness	squir'rel·fish'
spurt	squash	squir'rel·proof'

squirt	stag'nat·ed	stamped
stab	stag·na'tion	stam·pede'
stabbed	staid	stam·ped'ed
stab'bing·ly	stain	stamp'er
stab'bings	stained	stamp'ings
sta·bil'i·ty	stain'less	stance
sta'bi·li·za'tion	stair	stanch
sta'bi·lize	stair'case'	stan'chion
sta'bi·lized	stair'way'	stand
sta'bi·liz'er	stake	stand'ard
sta'ble	staked	stand'ard·i·za'-
stac·ca'to	sta·lac'tite	tion
stack	sta·lag'mite	stand'ard·ize
sta'di·a	stale	stand'ings
sta'di·um	stale'mate'	stand'off'
staff	stal'er	stand'pipe'
stag	stal'est	stand'point'
stage	stalk	stand'still'
stage'coach'	stalked	stank
stage'craft'	stalk'er	stan'nate
staged	stalk'ing·ly	stan'nic
stage'hand'	stall	stan'nous
stag'er	stalled	stan'za
stage'wor'thy	stal'lion	sta'ple
stag'ger	stal'wart	sta'pled
stag'gered	sta'men	sta'pler
stag'ger·ing·ly	stam'i·na	star
stag'horn'	stam'mer	star'board
stag'hound'	stam'mered	starch
stag'hunt'	stam'mer·er	starched
stag'nant	stam'mer·ing·ly	starch'y
stag'nate	stamp	stare
		stared

star'fish'	states'man·like'	steak
star'gaz'er	stat'ic	steal
star'ing·ly	sta'tion	stealth
stark	sta'tion·ar'y	stealth'i·er
star'less	sta'tioned	stealth'i·est
star'let	sta'tion·er	stealth'i·ly
star'light'	sta'tion·er'y	steam
star'like'	stat'ism	steam'boat'
star'lings	stat'ist	steamed
starred	sta·tis'ti·cal	steam'er
star'ri·er	sta·tis'ti·cal·ly	steam'i·er
star'ri·est	stat'is·ti'cian	steam'i·est
star'ry	sta·tis'tics	steam'i·ness
start	stat'u·ar'y	steam'ship'
start'ed	stat'ue	steam'y
start'er	stat'u·esque'	ste'a·tite
star'tle	stat'u·ette'	steel
star'tled	stat'ure	steel'head'
star'tling·ly	sta'tus	steel'work'
star·va'tion	stat'ute	steel'yard
starve	stat'u·to'ry	steep
starved	stave	steep'er
starve'ling	stay	steep'est
state	stayed	stee'ple
stat'ed	stead	stee'ple·chase'
state'hood	stead'fast	steer
State'house'	stead'fast·ly	steer'age
state'li·ness	stead'fast·ness	steered
state'ly	stead'i·er	steer'ing
state'ment	stead'i·est	steers'man
state'room'	stead'i·ly	stein
states'man	stead'y	stel'lar

stem	stern'er	stiff'est
stemmed	stern'est	stiff'ness
stench	stern'ly	sti'fle
sten'cil	stern'ness	sti'fled
sten'ciled	stern'post'	sti'fling·ly
ste·nog'ra·pher	ster'num	stig'ma
sten'o·graph'ic	ster'nu·ta'tion	stig·mat'a
ste·nog'ra·phy	ster'to·rous	stig·mat'ic
ste·no'sis	stet	stig'ma·tism
sten·to'ri·an	steth'o·scope	stig'ma·ti·za'tion
step	ste've·dore'	stig'ma·tize
step'child'	stew	stig'ma·tized
step'daugh'ter	stew'ard	stile
step'lad'der	stew'ard·ess	sti·let'to
step'moth'er	stewed	still
steppe	stick	still'born'
stepped	stick'er	stilled
step'sis'ter	stick'ful	still'er
step'son'	stick'i·er	still'est
ster'e·o	stick'i·est	still'ness
ster'e·o·phon'ic	stick'i·ly	still'room'
ster'e·op'ti·con	stick'i·ness	still'y
ster'e·o·scope'	stick'le·back'	stilt
ster'e·o·scop'ic	stick'ler	stilt'ed
ster'ile	stick'pin'	stim'u·lant
ste·ril'i·ty	stick'weed'	stim'u·late
ster'i·li·za'tion	stick'y	stim'u·lat'ed
ster'i·lize	stiff	stim'u·lat'ing
ster'i·lized	stiff'en	stim'u·la'tion
ster'i·liz'er	stiff'ened	stim'u·lus
ster'ling	stiff'en·er	sting
stern	stiff'er	sting'er

sting'fish'	stir'rings	stodg'i·er
stin'gi·er	stir'rup	stodg'i·est
stin'gi·est	stitch	stodg'y
sting'ing·ly	stitched	sto'gy
stin'gy	stitch'er	sto'ic
stink	stitch'ings	sto'i·cal
stink'bug'	stitch'work'	sto'i·cal·ly
stink'er	sti'ver	sto'i·cism
stink'ing·ly	sto'a	stoke
stink'pot'	stoat	stoked
stink'weed'	stock	stoke'hold'
stink'wood'	stock·ade'	stok'er
stint	stock·ad'ed	stole
stint'ed	stock'breed'er	sto'len
stint'ing·ly	stock'bro'ker	stol'id
stipe	stocked	sto·lid'i·ty
sti'pend	stock'fish'	stol'id·ly
sti·pen'di·ar'y	stock'hold'er	stom'ach
sti·pen'di·um	stock'house'	stom'ach·ful
stip'ple	stock'i·ness	sto·mach'ic
stip'pled	stock'i·net'	stone
stip'plings	stock'ings	stone'boat'
stip'u·late	stock'job'ber	stoned
stip'u·lat'ed	stock'keep'er	stone'fish'
stip'u·lates	stock'mak'er	stone'ma'son
stip'u·la'tion	stock'man	stone'ware'
stip'u·la·to'ry	stock'own'er	stone'weed'
stir	stock'pile'	stone'wood'
stir'pes	stock'pot'	stone'work'
stirps	stock'tak'er	stone'yard'
stirred	stock'y	ston'i·er
stir'ring·ly	stock'yard'	ston'i·est

ston'i·ly	sto'ry	strain
ston'y	sto'ry·tell'er	strained
stood	stoup	strain'er
stool	stout	strain'ing·ly
stoop	stout'er	strain'ings
stooped	stout'est	strait
stoop'ing·ly	stout'heart'ed	strait'en
stop	stout'ly	strait'ened
stop'cock'	stout'ness	strait'er
stope	stove	strait'est
stop'gap'	stow	strake
stop'o'ver	stow'age	strand
stop'page	stra·bis'mus	strand'ed
stopped	strad'dle	strange
stop'per	strad'dled	strange'lings
stop'pered	strad'dling·ly	strange'ly
stop'ple	strafe	strange'ness
stor'age	strag'gle	stran'ger
store	strag'gled	strang'est
stored	strag'gler	stran'gle
store'house'	strag'gling·ly	stran'gled
store'keep'er	straight	stran'gler
store'room'	straight'edge'	stran'gles
sto'ried	straight'en	stran'gling·ly
stork	straight'ened	stran'glings
storm	straight'er	stran'gu·late
storm'bound'	straight'est	stran'gu·lat'ed
stormed	straight'for'ward	stran'gu·la'tion
storm'i·er	straight'for'ward·ly	strap
storm'i·est	straight'for'ward·ness	strap'less
storm'ing·ly	straight'way'	strap·pa'do
storm'y	straight'ways'	strapped

strap'pings

stra'ta

strat'a·gem

stra·te'gic

stra·te'gi·cal

strat'e·gist

strat'e·gy

strat'i·fi·ca'tion

strat'i·fied

strat'i·fy

strat'o·sphere

stra'tum

straw

straw'ber'ry

straw'flow'er

stray

strayed

streak

streaked

streak'i·er

streak'i·est

streak'y

stream

streamed

stream'er

stream'ing·ly

stream'line'

stream'way'

street

strength

strength'en

strength'ened

strength'en·er

stren'u·ous

stren'u·ous·ly

stren'u·ous·ness

stress

stressed

stress'ful

stretch

stretched

stretch'er

stretch'er·man

stretch'-out'

strew

strewed

strewn

stri'ate

stri'at·ed

stri·a'tion

strick'en

strict

strict'ly

strict'ness

stric'ture

stride

stri'dent

stri'dent·ly

strid'ing·ly

strid'u·lous

strife

strig'il

strike

strike'break'er

strik'er

strik'ing·ly

string

stringed

strin'gen·cy

strin'gent

strin'gent·ly

string'er

string'i·er

string'i·est

string'piece'

string'y

strip

stripe

striped

strip'lings

strip'per

strip'pings

strive

striv'en

strob'o·scope

strode

stroke

stroked

strok'ings

stroll

strolled

stroll'er

strong

strong'box'

strong'er

strong'est

strong'hold'	stub'born	stump
strong'ly	stub'by	stump'age
stron'ti·um	stuc'co	stumped
strop	stuck	stump'i·er
stro'phe	stud	stump'i·est
stroph'ic	stud'book'	stump'y
strove	stud'ded	stun
struck	stu'dent	stung
struc'tur·al	stud'fish'	stunk
struc'tur·al·ly	stud'horse'	stunned
struc'ture	stud'ied	stun'ner
struc'tured	stu'di·o	stun'ning·ly
stru'del	stu'di·ous	stunt
strug'gle	stu'di·ous·ly	stunt'ed
strug'gled	stu'di·ous·ness	stu'pe·fa'cient
strug'gler	stud'work'	stu'pe·fac'tion
strug'gling·ly	stud'y	stu'pe·fied
strug'glings	stuff	stu'pe·fy
strum	stuffed	stu·pen'dous
strummed	stuff'er	stu'pid
strung	stuff'ings	stu·pid'i·ty
strut	stuff'i·er	stu'pid·ly
strut'ted	stuff'i·est	stu'por
strut'ter	stuff'i·ly	stu'por·ous
strut'ting·ly	stuff'i·ness	stur'di·ly
strut'tings	stuff'y	stur'di·ness
strych'nine	stul'ti·fi·ca'tion	stur'dy
stub	stul'ti·fied	stur'geon
stubbed	stul'ti·fy	stut'ter
stub'bi·ness	stum'ble	stut'tered
stub'ble	stum'bled	stut'ter·er
stub'bly	stum'bling·ly	stut'ter·ing·ly

sty

Styg'i·an

style

style'book'

styled

styl'ings

styl'ish

styl'ish·ness

styl'ist

sty·lis'tic

sty·lis'ti·cal·ly

styl'ize

styl'ized

sty'lo·graph

sty'lo·graph'ic

sty'lus

sty'mie

styp'tic

Styx

su'a·bil'i·ty

su'a·ble

sua'sion

suave

suave'ly

suave'ness

suav'i·ty

sub'a·cute'

sub'a·dult'

sub·a'gent

sub·al'tern

sub'a·quat'ic

sub·a'que·ous

sub·arc'tic

sub'a·tom'ic

sub·cal'i·ber

sub'cap'tion

sub'cel'lar

sub'class'

sub'com·mit'tee

sub·con'scious

sub·con'scious·ly

sub·con'scious·ness

sub'con·stel·la'tion

sub·con'ti·nent

sub'con'tract

sub'con·tract'ed

sub'con·trac'tor

sub'cu·ta'ne·ous

sub·dea'con

sub'di·vide'

sub'di·vid'ed

sub'di·vi'sion

sub·due'

sub·dued'

sub·du'ing·ly

sub·ed'i·tor

sub·fam'i·ly

sub'foun·da'tion

sub'grade'

sub'group'

sub'head'

sub'head'ings

sub·hu'man

sub'ject

sub·ject'ed

sub·jec'tion

sub·jec'tive

sub·jec'tive·ly

sub·jec'tive·ness

sub·jec'tiv·ism

sub'jec·tiv'i·ty

sub·join'

sub·join'der

sub·joined'

sub'ju·gate

sub'ju·gat'ed

sub'ju·ga'tion

sub·junc'tive

sub·king'dom

sub'lap·sar'i·an

sub'lease'

sub·les·see'

sub·les'sor

sub'let'

sub'li·mate

sub'li·mat'ed

sub'li·ma'tion

sub·lime'

sub·limed'

sub·lim'er

sub·lim'est

sub·lim'i·nal

sub·lim'i·ty

sub'lu·nar'y

sub'lux·a'tion

sub·mar'gin·al

sub′ma·rine′

sub′ma·rin′er

sub·merge′

sub·merged′

sub·mer′gence

sub·mers′i·ble

sub·mer′sion

sub·me′ter·ing

sub·mis′sion

sub·mis′sive

sub·mis′sive·ly

sub·mis′sive·ness

sub·mit′

sub·mit′tal

sub·mit′ted

sub·mit′ting·ly

sub·nor′mal

sub′nor·mal′i·ty

sub′o·ce·an′ic

sub·or′der

sub·or′di·nate

sub·or′di·nat′ed

sub·or′di·nat′ing·ly

sub·or′di·na′tion

sub·or′di·na′tive

sub·orn′

sub′or·na′tion

sub·orned′

sub·orn′er

sub·phy′lum

sub′plinth′

sub′plot′

sub·poe′na

sub·poe′naed

sub·ro·ga′tion

sub·scribe′

sub·scribed′

sub·scrib′er

sub′script

sub·scrip′tion

sub′se·quent

sub′se·quent·ly

sub·serve′

sub·served′

sub·ser′vi·ence

sub·ser′vi·en·cy

sub·ser′vi·ent

sub·side′

sub·sid′ed

sub·sid′ence

sub·sid′i·ar′y

sub′si·dize

sub′si·dized

sub′si·dy

sub·sist′

sub·sist′ed

sub·sist′ence

sub′soil′

sub′spe′cies

sub′stance

sub·stand′ard

sub·stan′tial

sub·stan′tial·ly

sub·stan′ti·ate

sub·stan′ti·at′ed

sub·stan′ti·a′tion

sub′stan·tive

sub′sta′tion

sub′sti·tute

sub′sti·tut′ed

sub′sti·tu′tion

sub·stra′tum

sub·struc′ture

sub·sur′face

sub·tan′gent

sub·ten′ant

sub·tend′

sub·tend′ed

sub′ter·fuge

sub′ter·ra′ne·an

sub′ter·ra′ne·ous

sub′ti′tle

sub′tle

sub′tler

sub′tlest

sub′tle·ty

sub′tly

sub·tract′

sub·tract′ed

sub·trac′tion

sub′tra·hend′

sub·treas′ur·y

sub·trop′i·cal

sub′urb

sub·ur′ban

sub·ur′ban·ite

sub·ven'tion		suc'tion		suf·fused'	
sub·ver'sion		sud'den		suf·fu'sion	
sub·ver'sive		sud'den·ly		sug'ar	
sub·vert'		sud'den·ness		sug'ared	
sub·vert'ed		su'dor·if'er·ous		sug'ar·plum'	
sub'way'		su'dor·if'ic		sug'ar·y	
suc·ceed'		suds		sug·gest'	
suc·ceed'ed		sue		sug·gest'ed	
suc·ceed'ing·ly		sued		sug·gest'i·bil'i·ty	
suc·cess'		suède		sug·gest'i·ble	
suc·cess'ful		su'et		sug·ges'tion	
suc·cess'ful·ly		suf'fer		sug·ges'tive	
suc·ces'sion		suf'fer·a·ble		sug·ges'tive·ness	
suc·ces'sive		suf'fer·ance		su'i·cid'al	
suc·ces'sor		suf'fered		su'i·cid'al·ly	
suc·cinct'		suf'fer·er		su'i·cide	
suc·cinct'ly		suf'fer·ing·ly		suit	
suc'cor		suf'fer·ings		suit'a·bil'i·ty	
suc'cored		suf·fice'		suit'a·ble	
suc'co·tash		suf·ficed'		suit'case'	
suc'cu·lence		suf·fi'cien·cy		suite	
suc'cu·lent		suf·fi'cient		suit'ed	
suc'cu·lent·ly		suf'fix		suit'ing·ly	
suc·cumb'		suf'fo·cate		suit'ings	
suc·cumbed'		suf'fo·cat'ed		suit'or	
such		suf'fo·cat'ing·ly		sulk	
suck		suf'fo·ca'tion		sulked	
sucked		suf'fo·ca'tive		sulk'i·er	
suck'er		suf'fra·gan		sulk'i·est	
suck'le		suf'frage		sulk'i·ly	
suck'led		suf'fra·gist		sulk'i·ness	
suck'lings		suf·fuse'		sulk'y	

sul'len

sul'len·ly

sul'len·ness

sul'lied

sul'ly

sul'phate

sul'phide

sul'phite

sul'phur

sul·phu'ric

sul'phu·rous

sul'tan

sul·tan'a

sul·tan·ate

sul'tri·er

sul'tri·est

sul'try

sum

su'mac

sum'ma·ri·ly

sum'ma·ri·ness

sum'ma·rize

sum'ma·rized

sum'ma·ry

sum·ma'tion

summed

sum'mer

sum'mered

sum'mer·y

sum'mit

sum'mon

sum'moned

sump

sump'ter

sump'tu·ar'y

sump'tu·ous

sump'tu·ous·ly

sump'tu·ous·ness

sun

sun'beam'

sun'bon'net

sun'burn'

sun'burned

sun'burst'

sun'dae

Sun'day

sun'der

sun'der·ance

sun'dered

sun'di'al

sun'dry

sun'fish'

sun'flow'er

sun'glass'

sun'glow'

sunk

sunk'en

sun'less

sun'light'

sun'lit'

sunned

sun'ni·ness

sun'ny

sun'proof'

sun'rise'

sun'room'

sun'set'

sun'shade'

sun'shine'

sun'shin'y

sun'spot'

sun'stone'

sun'stroke'

sun'ward

sup

su'per·a·ble

su'per·a·bun'dance

su'per·a·bun'dant

su'per·an'nu·ate

su'per·an'nu·at'ed

su'per·an'nu·a'tion

su·perb'

su'per·bowl

su'per·cal'en-
dered

su'per·car'go

su'per·charg'er

su'per·cil'i·ous

su'per·cil'i·ous·ly

su'per·cil'i·ous·ness

su'per·con·duc'-
tance

su'per·con·duc-
tiv'i·ty

su'per·con·duc'-
tor

su'per·cool'

su'per·dread'-
nought'

su'per·em'i·nence

su'per·em'i·nent

su'per·er'o·ga'tion

su'per·fam'i·ly

su'per·fi'cial

su'per·fi·ci·al'i·ty

su'per·fi'cial·ly

su'per·fine'

su'per·flu'i·ty

su·per'flu·ous

su·per'flu·ous·ly

su·per'flu·ous·ness

su'per·heat'

su'per·heat'ed

su'per·het'er·o·dyne'

su'per·hu'man

su'per·hu'man·ly

su'per·im·pose'

su'per·im·posed'

su'per·im'po·si'tion

su'per·im·po'sure

su'per·in·duce'

su'per·in·duced'

su'per·in·tend'

su'per·in·tend'ed

su'per·in·tend'ence

su'per·in·tend'en·cy

su'per·in·tend'ent

su·pe'ri·or

su·pe'ri·or'i·ty

su'per·jet

su·per'la·tive

su'per·man'

su·per'nal

su·per'nal·ly

su'per·nat'u·ral

su'per·nat'u·ral·ly

su'per·nat'u·ral·ism

su'per·nat'u·ral·ist

su'per·nor'mal

su'per·nu'mer·ar'y

su'per·po·si'tion

su'per·sat'u·rate

su'per·sat'u·rat'ed

su'per·sat'u·ra'tion

su'per·scribe'

su'per·scribed'

su'per·scrip'tion

su'per·sede'

su'per·sed'ed

su'per·ses'sion

su'per·son'ic

su'per·sti'tion

su'per·sti'tious

su'per·sti'tious·ly

su'per·stra'tum

su'per·struc'ture

su'per·tax'

su'per·vene'

su'per·vened'

su'per·vise'

su'per·vised'

su'per·vi'sion

su'per·vi'sor

su'per·vi'so·ry

su·pine'

su·pine'ness

sup'per

sup·plant'

sup·plant'ed

sup'ple

sup'ple·ment

sup'ple·men'tal

sup'ple·men'ta·ry

sup'ple·men·ta'tion

sup'ple·ment'ed

sup'pli·ant

sup'pli·cant

sup'pli·cate

sup'pli·cat'ed

sup'pli·cat'ing·ly

sup'pli·ca'tion

sup'pli·ca·to'ry

sup·plied'

sup·pli'er

sup·ply'

sup·port'

sup·port'ed

sup·port'er

sup·pose'

sup·posed'

sup·pos'ed·ly

sup'po·si'tion

sup·pos'i·ti'tious

sup·pos'i·ti'tious·ly

sup·press'

sup·pressed'

sup·pres'sion

sup·pres'sive

sup'pu·rate

sup'pu·rat'ed

sup'pu·ra'tion

sup'pu·ra'tive

su·prem'a·cy

su·preme'

su·preme'ly

sur·base'

sur·cease'

sur·charge'

sur·charged'

sur'cin'gle

surd

sure

sure'ly

sure'ness

sure'ty

sure'ty·ship

surf

sur'face

sur'faced

sur'fac·ings

sur'feit

sur'feit·ed

surge

surged

sur'geon

sur'ger·y

sur'gi·cal

sur'li·er

sur'li·est

sur'li·ness

sur'ly

sur·mise'

sur·mised'

sur·mount'

sur·mount'ed

sur'name'

sur'named'

sur·pass'

sur·passed'

sur·pass'ing·ly

sur'plice

sur'pliced

sur'plus

sur'plus·age

sur·prise'

sur·prised'

sur·pris'ed·ly

sur·pris'ing·ly

sur're·but'tal

sur're·but'ter

sur're·join'der

sur·ren'der

sur·ren'dered

sur'rep·ti'tious

sur'rep·ti'tious·ly

sur'rep·ti'tious·ness

sur'rey

sur'ro·gate

sur'ro·ga'tion

sur·round'

sur·round'ed

sur·round'ings

sur'tax'

sur·tout'

sur·veil'lance

sur·vey'

sur·veyed'

sur·vey'or

sur·viv'al

sur·viv'al·ism

sur·vive'

sur·vived'

sur·vi'vor

sur·vi'vor·ship

sus·cep'ti·bil'i·ty

sus·cep'ti·ble

sus·cep'ti·bly

sus·pect'

sus·pect'ed

sus·pend'

sus·pend'ed

sus·pend'ers

sus·pense'

sus·pense'ful

sus·pen'sion

sus·pen'sive

sus·pen'sive·ly

sus·pen'sive·ness

sus·pi'cion

sus·pi'cious

sus·pi'cious·ly

sus·pi'cious·ness

sus·pire'

sus·tain′	swal′low-tailed′	sweat′box′
sus·tained′	swa′mi	sweat′er
sus·tain′ed·ly	swamp	sweat′i·er
sus·tain′ing·ly	swamped	sweat′i·est
sus′te·nance	swan	sweat′i·ly
sus′ten·tac′u·lar	swan′herd′	sweat′i·ness
sus′ten·ta′tion	swank	sweat′shop
su′sur·ra′tion	swank′i·er	sweat′y
sut′ler	swank′i·est	Swed′ish
sut·tee′	swank′y	sweep
su′ture	swans′down′	sweep′er
su′tured	swap	sweep′ing·ly
su′ze·rain	swapped	sweep′ings
su′ze·rain·ty	sward	sweep′stake′
svelte	swarm	sweet
swab	swarmed	sweet′bread′
swabbed	swart	sweet′bri′er
swad′dle	swarth′y	sweet′en
swad′dled	swash	sweet′ened
swad′dling	swas′ti·ka	sweet′en·er
swad′dlings	swat	sweet′en·ings
swag	swatch	sweet′heart′
swage	swath	sweet′ish
swaged	swathe	sweet′ish·ly
swag′ger	swat′ter	sweet′ly
swag′gered	sway	sweet′meat′
swag′ger·ing·ly	swayed	sweet′ness
Swa·hi′li	sway′ing·ly	sweet′root′
swain	swear	sweet′shop′
swal′low	swear′ing·ly	sweet′wa′ter
swal′lowed	sweat	sweet′weed′
swal′low·er	sweat′band′	sweet′wood′

swell	swipe	sworn
swelled	swiped'	swung
swell'er	swirl	swum
swell'fish'	swirled	syb'a·rite
swell'ings	swirl'ing·ly	syc'a·more
swel'ter	swish	syc'o·phan·cy
swel'tered	swished	syc'o·phant
swel'ter·ing·ly	Swiss	syc'o·phan'tic
swept	switch	syl'la·bi
swerve	switch'blade'	syl·lab'ic
swerved	switch'board'	syl·lab'i·cate
swift	switch'gear'	syl·lab'i·cat'ed
swift'er	switch'keep'er	syl·lab'i·ca'tion
swift'est	switch'man	syl·lab'i·fi·ca'tion
swift'ly	switch'tail'	syl·lab'i·fy
swift'ness	switch'yard'	syl'la·ble
swig	swiv'el	syl'la·bus
swigged	swiv'eled	syl'la·bus·es
swill	swol'len	syl'lo·gism
swilled	swoon	syl'lo·gis'tic
swim	swooned	syl'lo·gize
swim'mer	swoon'ing·ly	sylph
swim'ming·ly	swoop	syl'van
swin'dle	swooped	sym'bi·o'sis
swin'dled	sword	sym'bi·ot'ic
swin'dler	sword'bill'	sym'bol
swine	sword'fish'	sym·bol'ic
swine'herd'	sword'play'	sym·bol'i·cal
swing	swords'man	sym·bol'i·cal·ly
swing'ing·ly	sword'stick'	sym'bol·ism
swin'ish	sword'tail'	sym'bol·ist
swink	swore	sym'bol·i·za'tion

sym'bol·ize

sym'bol·ized

sym·met'ri·cal

sym'me·try

sym'pa·thec'to·my

sym'pa·thet'ic

sym'pa·thet'i·cal·ly

sym'pa·thize

sym'pa·thized

sym'pa·thiz'er

sym'pa·thiz'ing·ly

sym'pa·thy

sym·phon'ic

sym'pho·ny

sym'phy·sis

sym·po'si·um

symp'tom

symp'to·mat'ic

symp'tom·a·tol'o·gy

syn'a·gogue

syn·apse'

syn·ap'sis

syn'chro·nism

syn'chro·ni·za'tion

syn'chro·nize

syn'chro·nized

syn'chro·nous

syn'co·pate

syn'co·pat'ed

syn'co·pa'tion

syn'co·pe

syn'cre·tism

syn'dic

syn'di·cal

syn'di·cal·ism

syn'di·cal·ize

syn'di·cate

syn'di·cat'ed

syn'di·ca'tion

syn'dro·me

syn'er·gis'tic

syn'od

syn'od·ist

syn'o·nym

syn·on'y·mous

syn·op'ses

syn·op'sis

syn·op'tic

syn·o'vi·al

syn'o·vi'tis

syn·tac'ti·cal

syn'tax

syn'the·ses

syn'the·sis

syn'the·size

syn'the·sized

syn·thet'ic

syn·thet'i·cal·ly

syr'inge

syr'up

sys'tem

sys'tem·at'ic

sys'tem·a·ti·za'tion

sys'tem·a·tize

sys'tem·a·tized

sys'tem·a·tiz'er

sys'tem·a·tol'o·gy

sys·tem'ic

sys·tem'i·cal·ly

sys'to·le

sys·tol'ic

syz'y·gy

T

tab	tab'u·late	tac'ti·cal
tab'ard	tab'u·lat'ed	tac·ti'cian
ta·bas'co	tab'u·la'tion	tac'tics
tab'er·nac'le	tab'u·la'tor	tac'tile
tab'er·nac'led	ta·chis'to·scope	tact'less
ta'bes	ta·chom'e·ter	tact'less·ly
tab'la·ture	ta·chyg'ra·pher	tact'less·ness
ta'ble	ta·chyg'ra·phy	tad'pole'
ta'bleau	tac'it	taf'fe·ta
ta'ble·cloth'	tac'it·ly	taff'rail
ta'bled	tac'i·turn	taf'fy
ta'ble·maid'	tac'i·tur'ni·ty	tag
ta'ble·man	tack	tag'board'
ta'ble·spoon'	tacked	tagged
tab'let	tack'le	Ta·hi'ti·an
ta'ble·ware'	tack'led	tail
tab'loid	tack'ler	tail'board'
ta·boo'	tack'y	tailed
ta'bor	tact	tail'first'
tab'o·ret	tact'ful	tail'ings
ta·bu'	tact'ful·ly	tail'less
tab'u·lar	tact'ful·ness	tai'lor

tai'lored	tal'lowed	tan'gent
tail'piece'	tal'low·i·ness	tan·gen'tial
tail'race'	tal'low·root'	tan·gen'ti·al'i·ty
tail'stock'	tal'low·wood'	tan'ge·rine'
taint	tal'low·y	tan'gi·ble
taint'ed	tal'ly	tan'gi·bly
take	tal'ly·ho'	tan'gle
take'down'	tal'ly·man	tan'gled
tak'en	Tal'mud	tan'gle·root'
tak'er	Tal·mud'ic	tan'gling·ly
tak'ing·ly	tal'on	tan'go
tak'ing·ness	tal'oned	tang'y
tak'ings	tam'a·rack	tank
talc	tam'a·rind	tank'age
tal'cum	tam'bour	tank'ard
tale	tam'bou·rine'	tanked
tale'bear'er	tame	tank'er
tal'ent	tamed	tan'nage
tal'ent·ed	tame'ness	tanned
tal'i·pes	tam'er	tan'ner
tal'is·man	tam'est	tan'ner·y
tal'is·man'ic	Tam'il	tan'nic
talk	Tam'ma·ny	tan'nin
talk'a·tive	tamp'er	tan'nings
talked	tam'pered	tan'sy
talk'er	tam'per·proof'	tan'ta·li·za'tion
tall	tam'pon	tan'ta·lize
tall'er	tan	tan'ta·lized
tall'est	tan'a·ger	tan'ta·lum
tall'ish	tan'bark'	tan'ta·lus
tall'ness	tan'dem	tan'ta·mount'
tal'low	tang	tan'trum

tan·vat	tar′di·ness	taste
tan′wood′	tar′dy	tast′ed
tap	tare	taste′ful
tape	tar′flow′er	taste′ful·ly
taped	targe	taste′ful·ness
tape′line′	tar′get	taste′less
tape′man	tar′iff	taste′less·ly
ta′per	tar′la·tan	taste′less·ness
ta′pered	tar′nish	tast′er
ta′per·ing·ly	tar′nished	tast′i·er
tap′es·try	tar′ot	tast′i·est
tape′worm′	tar·pau′lin	tast′i·ly
tap′hole′	tar′pon	tast′ing·ly
tap′house′	tar′ra·gon	tast′ings
tap′i·o′ca	tarred	tast′y
ta′pir	tar′ried	Ta′tar
tap′per	tar′ry	tat′ter
tap′pet	tar′ry·ing·ly	tat′tered
tap′pings	tart	tat′ting
tap′room′	tar′tan	tat′tle
tap′root′	tar′tar	tat′tled
tap′ster	tart′let	tat′tler
tar	tart′ness	tat·too′
tar′an·tel′la	tar′trate	tat·tooed′
ta·ran′tu·la	tar′weed′	tat·too′er
tar′board′	task	taught
tar·boosh′	task′mas′ter	taunt
tar′brush′	task′mis′tress	taunt′ed
tar′bush′	task′work′	taunt′ing·ly
tar′di·er	Tas·ma′ni·an	taupe
tar′di·est	tas′sel	tau′rine
tar′di·ly	tas′seled	taut

taut'en

taut'ened

tau·to·log'i·cal

tau·tol'o·gy

tav'ern

taw'dri·er

taw'dri·est

taw'dri·ly

taw'dri·ness

taw'dry

taw'ny

tax

tax'a·ble

tax·a'tion

taxed

tax'es

tax'i

tax'i·cab'

tax'i·der'mist

tax'i·der'my

tax'i·me'ter

tax'ing·ly

tax·on'o·my

tax'paid'

tax'pay'er

tea

tea'ber'ry

tea'cart'

teach

teach'a·bil'i·ty

teach'a·ble

teach'er

teach'er·age

teach'ing·ly

teach'ings

tea'cup'

teak

tea'ket'tle

teal

team

teamed

team'mate'

team'ster

team'work'

tea'pot'

tear

tear

tear'ful

tear'ful·ly

tear'ful·ness

tear'less

tear'less·ly

tea'room'

tear'stain'

tear'y

tease

teased

teas'er

teas'ing·ly

tea'spoon'

tea'spoon·ful

tea'tast'er

tech'ni·cal

tech'ni·cal'i·ty

tech'ni·cal·ly

tech·ni'cian

tech·nique'

tech·noc'ra·cy

tech'no·crat

tech'no·log'i·cal

tech·nol'o·gy

te'di·ous

te'di·ous·ly

te'di·ous·ness

te'di·um

tee

teed

teem

teemed

teem'ing·ly

tee'ter

tee'ter·board'

tee'tered

teeth

tee·to'tal

tee·to'tal·er

tee·to'tal·ly

tel·au'to·graph

tel'e·cast

tel'e·com·mu'ni·ca'tion

tel'e·gram

tel'e·graph

te·leg'ra·pher

tel'e·graph'ic

te·leg'ra·phy

tel'e·ol'o·gy

tel′e·path′ic	tem′pered	ten′ant
te·lep′a·thy	tem′pest	ten′ant·a·ble
tel′e·phone	tem·pes′tu·ous	ten′ant·ed
tel′e·phon′ic	tem·pes′tu·ous·ly	ten′ant·less
tel′e·pho′to	tem·pes′tu·ous·ness	ten′ant·ry
Tel′e-Promp-Ter	tem′plate	tend
tel′e·scope	tem′ple	tend′ed
tel′e·scop′ic	tem′pled	tend′en·cy
tel′e·type	tem′po	tend′er
tel′e·type′set′ter	tem′po·ral	ten′dered
tel′e·type′writ′er	tem′po·ral·ty	ten′der·er
tel′e·vise	tem′po·rar′i·ly	ten′der·est
tel′e·vised	tem′po·rar′y	ten′der·foot′
tel′e·vi′sion	tem′po·ri·za′tion	ten′der·loin′
tel′ford	tem′po·rize	ten′der·ly
tell	tem′po·rized	ten′der·ness
tell′er	tem′po·riz′er	ten′don
tell′ing·ly	tem′po·riz′ing·ly	ten′dril
tell′ings	tempt	Ten′e·brae
tell′tale′	temp·ta′tion	ten′e·brous
tel·lu′ri·um	tempt′ed	ten′e·ment
tel′pher	tempt′er	ten′et
Tel′star	tempt′ing·ly	ten′nis
te·mer′i·ty	tempt′ing·ness	ten′on
tem′per	tempt′ress	ten′or
tem′per·a·ment	ten′a·bil′i·ty	ten′pins′
tem′per·a·men′tal	ten′a·ble	tense
tem′per·a·men′tal·ly	te·na′cious	tense′ly
tem′per·ance	te·na′cious·ly	tense′ness
tem′per·ate	te·na′cious·ness	tens′er
tem′per·ate·ly	te·nac′i·ty	tens′est
tem′per·a·ture	ten′an·cy	ten′sile

ten'sion	ter'mite	ters'est
ten'sor	term'less	ter'tian
tent	tern	ter'ti·ar'y
ten'ta·cle	ter'na·ry	tes'sel·late
ten'ta·tive	ter'race	tes'sel·lat'ed
ten'ter·er	ter'raced	tes'sel·la'tion
ten'ter·hooks'	ter·rain'	test
ten·u'i·ty	ter'ra·pin	tes'ta·ment
ten'u·ous	ter·raz'zo	tes'ta·men'ta·ry
ten'u·ous·ly	ter·res'tri·al	tes·ta'tor
ten'ure	ter'ri·ble	test'ed
te'pee	ter'ri·bly	tes'ter
tep'id	ter'ri·er	tes'ti·fied
te·pid'i·ty	ter·rif'ic	tes'ti·fy
tep'id·ly	ter·rif'i·cal·ly	tes'ti·mo'ni·al
ter'a·tol'o·gy	ter'ri·fied	tes'ti·mo'ny
ter·cen'te·nar'y	ter'ri·fy	test'ing·ly
te·re'do	ter'ri·fy'ing·ly	test'ings
ter'gi·ver·sate'	ter·rine'	tes'ty
term	ter'ri·to'ri·al	tet'a·nus
ter'ma·gant	ter'ri·to'ri·al'i·ty	teth'er
termed	ter'ri·to'ry	teth'ered
ter'mi·na·ble	ter'ror	tet'ra·gon
ter'mi·nal	ter'ror·ism	te·trag'o·nal
ter'mi·nate	ter'ror·ist	te·tral'o·gy
ter'mi·nat'ed	ter'ror·is'tic	te·tram'e·ter
ter'mi·na'tion	ter'ror·i·za'tion	te'trarch
ter'mi·na'tive	ter'ror·ize	te·trig'id
ter'mi·no·log'i·cal	ter'ror·ized	Tex'an
ter'mi·no·log'i·cal·ly	terse	tex'as
ter'mi·nol'o·gy	terse'ness	text
ter'mi·nus	ters'er	text'book'

tex'tile	the·at'ri·cal·ly	the'o·ry
tex'tu·al	the·at'ri·cals	the'o·soph'ic
tex'tu·al·ism	thee	the'o·soph'i·cal
tex'tu·al·ist	theft	the'o·soph'i·cal·ly
tex'tu·al·ly	their	the·os'o·phism
tex'tur·al	theirs	the·os'o·phist
tex'tur·al·ly	the'ism	the·os'o·phy
tex'ture	the'ist	ther'a·peu'tic
tex'tured	the·is'tic	ther'a·peu'ti·cal
tha·las'sic	them	ther'a·peu'ti·cal·ly
thal'li·um	the·mat'ic	ther'a·py
than	the·mat'i·cal	there
than'a·top'sis	theme	there'a·bouts'
thane	them·selves'	there'a·bove'
thank	then	there·aft'er
thanked	thence	there·at'
thank'ful	thence'forth'	there·by'
thank'ful·ly	thence'for'ward	there'fore
thank'ful·ness	the·oc'ra·cy	there·from'
thank'less	the·od'o·lite	there·in'
thanks	the'o·lo'gi·an	there'in·aft'er
thanks·giv'ing	the'o·log'i·cal	there·in'be·fore'
that	the'o·log'i·cal·ly	there·of'
thatch	the·ol'o·gy	there·on'
thatched	the'o·rem	there·to'
thau'ma·tur'gist	the'o·ret'ic	there·to·fore'
thau'ma·tur'gy	the'o·ret'i·cal	there·un'der
thaw	the'o·ret'i·cal·ly	there·un·to'
the'a·ter	the'o·rist	there'up·on'
the·at'ri·cal	the'o·rize	there·with'
the·at'ri·cal·ism	the'o·rized	ther'mal
the·at'ri·cal'i·ty	the'o·riz'er	therm'i·on

therm′i·on′ic	thigh	thorn
ther′mite	thill	thorn′bush′
ther′mo·e·lec′tric	thim′ble	thorned
ther·mom′e·ter	thim′ble·ful	thorn′i·er
ther′mo·met′ric	thim′ble·rig′ger	thorn′i·est
ther′mo·met′ri·cal	thin	thorn′y
ther′mo·met′ri·cal·ly	thing	thor′ough
ther′mo·stat	things	thor′ough·bred′
the·sau′rus	think	thor′ough·fare′
these	think′a·ble	thor′ough·go′ing
the′ses	think′er	thor′ough·ly
the′sis	think′ing·ly	thor′ough·ness
thew	thinks	those
they	thin′ly	thou
thick	thin′ner	though
thick′en	thin′ness	thought
thick′ened	thin′nest	thought′ful
thick′en·er	third	thought′ful·ly
thick′er	thirst	thought′ful·ness
thick′est	thirst′ed	thought′less
thick′et	thirst′i·ly	thought′less·ly
thick′et·ed	thirst′i·ness	thought′less·ness
thick′head′ed	thirst′ing·ly	thou′sand
thick′ly	thirst′y	thou′sand·fold′
thick′ness	this	thou′sandth
thick′set′	this′tle	thrall
thick′-skinned′	thith′er	thrall′dom
thick′-wit′ted	thole	thrash
thief	thong	thrashed
thiev′er·y	tho·rac′ic	thrash′er
thiev′ing·ly	tho′rax	thrash′ings
thiev′ish	Thor	thra·son′i·cal

thread	thrips	thrown
thread'bare'	thrive	throw'off'
thread'ed	thriv'ing·ly	thrum
thread'weed'	throat	thrummed
thread'worm'	throat'ed	thrush
thread'y	throat'i·er	thrust
threat	throat'i·est	thud
threat'en	throat'i·ly	thud'ded
threat'ened	throat'i·ness	thud'ding·ly
threat'en·ing·ly	throat'root'	thug
three	throat'wort'	thug'ger·y
three'some	throat'y	thu'li·um
thren'o·dy	throb	thumb
thre'nos	throbbed	thumbed
thresh	throb'bing·ly	thumb'mark'
threshed	throes	thumb'nail'
thresh'er	throm·bo'sis	thumb'piece'
thresh'old	throm'bus	thumb'print'
threw	throne	thump
thrice	throne'less	thumped
thrift	throne'like'	thump'ing·ly
thrift'i·er	throng	thump'ings
thrift'i·est	thronged	thun'der
thrift'i·ly	throng'ing·ly	thun'der·bird'
thrift'i·ness	throt'tle	thun'der·bolt'
thrift'less	throt'tled	thun'dered
thrift'less·ly	throt'tling·ly	thun'der·fish'
thrift'less·ness	through	thun'der·head'
thrift'y	through·out'	thun'der·ing
thrill	throw	thun'der·ing·ly
thrilled	throw'back'	thun'der·ings
thrill'ing·ly	throw'er	thun'der·ous

thun'der·show'er

thun'der·struck'

thun'der·y

thun'drous

thu'ri·ble

Thurs'day

thus

thwack

thwacked

thwack'ing·ly

thwart

thwart'ed

thwart'ing·ly

thy

thyme

thy'mus

thy'roid

thy·self'

ti·ar'a

tib'i·a

tick

ticked

tick'er

tick'et

tick'et·ed

tick'ings

tick'le

tick'led

tick'ler

tick'ling·ly

tick'lish

tick'lish·ly

tick'lish·ness

tid'al

tid'bit'

tide

tid'ed

tide'race'

tide'wa'ter

tide'way'

ti'died

ti'di·er

ti'di·est

ti'di·ly

ti'di·ness

ti'dings

ti'dy

tie

tie'back'

tied

tier

tiered

tiff

tif'fa·ny

tiffed

tif'fin

ti'ger

ti'ger·ish

ti'ger·like'

ti'ger·wood'

tight

tight'en

tight'ened

tight'en·er

tight'en·ing

tight'er

tight'est

tight'fist'ed

tight'ly

tight'rope'

tight'wad'

til'bu·ry

til'de

tile

tiled

tile'fish'

til'er

tile'root'

till

till'a·ble

till'age

tilled

till'er

tilt

tilt'ed

tilth

tilt'yard'

tim'bale

tim'ber

tim'bered

tim'ber·land'

tim'ber·wood'

tim'ber·work'

time

timed

time'keep'er

time′less

time′less·ly

time′less·ness

time′li·ness

time′ly

time′piece′

tim′er

time′serv′ing

time′ta′ble

tim′id

ti·mid′i·ty

tim′id·ly

tim′ings

tim′or·ous

tim′or·ous·ly

tin

tinct

tinct′ed

tinc′ture

tinc′tured

tin′der

tin′der·box′

tine

tined

tine′weed′

tinge

tinged

tin′gle

tin′gled

tin′gling·ly

tin′glings

tin′horn′

tink′er

tink′ered

tin′kle

tin′kled

tin′kling·ly

tin′klings

tinned

tin′ni·er

tin′ni·est

tin′ni·ly

tin′ni·ness

tin·ni′tus

tin′ny

tin′sel

tin′seled

tin′smith′

tint

tint′ed

tin′tin·nab′u·la′tion

tin′type′

tin′ware′

tin′work′

ti′ny

tip

tipped

tip′pet

tip′ple

tip′pled

tip′pler

tip′si·er

tip′si·est

tip′ster

tip′sy

tip′toe′

tip′toed′

tip′toe′ing·ly

tip′top′

ti′rade

tire

tired

tire′less

tire′less·ly

tire′less·ness

tire′some

tire′some·ly

tire′some·ness

tir′ing·ly

tis′sue

tis′sued

tis′sues

Ti′tan

ti·tan′ic

ti′tan·if′er·ous

ti·ta′ni·um

tit′bit′

tith′a·ble

tithe

tithed

tith′ings

ti′tian

tit′il·late

tit′il·lat′ed

tit′il·lat′ing·ly

tit′il·la′tion

tit'il·la'tive

tit'i·vate

tit'i·vat'ed

tit'i·va'tion

ti'tle

ti'tled

ti'tle·hold'er

tit'mouse'

ti'trate

ti'trat·ed

ti·tra'tion

tit'ter

tit'tered

tit'ter·ing·ly

tit'ter·ings

tit'tle

tit'tup

tit'u·lar

tit'u·lar·ly

tit'u·lar'y

to

toad

toad'fish'

toad'root'

toad'stone'

toad'stool'

toad'y

toast

toast'ed

toast'er

to·bac'co

to·bog'gan

to·bog'ganed

toc·ca'ta

toc'sin

to·day'

tod'dle

tod'dled

tod'dler

tod'dy

toe

toe'cap'

toed

toe'nail'

toe'plate'

tof'fee

to'ga

to·geth'er

to·geth'er·ness

tog'gle

tog'gled

toil

toiled

toil'er

toi'let

toi'let·ry

toi'let·ware'

toil'ing·ly

To·kay'

to'ken

to'kened

told

tol'er·a·ble

tol'er·a·bly

tol'er·ance

tol'er·ant

tol'er·ate

tol'er·at'ed

tol'er·a'tion

tol'er·a'tion·ism

tol'er·a'tive

toll

tolled

toll'gate'

toll'house'

tom'a·hawk

to·ma'to

tomb

tombed

tom'bo·la

tom'boy'

tomb'stone'

tom'cat'

tom'cod'

tome

tom'fool'

tom'fool'er·y

tom'fool'ish·ness

to·mor'row

ton

ton'al

ton'al·ist

to·nal'i·ty

tone

toned

tone'less

tongs	tooth'less·ness	top'side'
tongue	tooth'pick'	top'stone'
tongued	tooth'some	toque
ton'ic	too'tle	torch
ton'i·cal·ly	too'tled	torch'light'
to·nic'i·ty	top	torch'weed'
to·night'	to'paz	torch'wood'
ton'ka	top'coat'	tore
ton'nage	top'er	tor'e·a·dor'
ton·neau'	to'pi·a·rist	tor·ment'
ton'sil	to'pi·ar'y	tor·ment'ed
ton'sil·li'tis	top'ic	tor·ment'ing·ly
ton·so'ri·al	top'i·cal	tor·men'tor
ton'sure	top'knot'	tor·na'do
ton'tine	top'less	tor·pe'do
too	top'loft'y	tor·pe'doed
took	top'man	tor'pid
tool	top'mast'	tor·pid'i·ty
tool'box'	top'most	tor'pid·ly
tooled	to·pog'ra·pher	tor'por
tool'ings	top'o·graph'ic	torque
tool'mak'er	top'o·graph'i·cal	tor'rent
tool'room'	top'o·graph'i·cal·ly	tor·ren'tial
tool'smith'	to·pog'ra·phy	tor·ren'tial·ly
toot	topped	tor'rid
toot'ed	top'per	tor·rid'i·ty
tooth	top'piece'	tor'rid·ly
tooth'ache'	top'ping·ly	tor'sion
tooth'brush'	top'pings	tor'sion·al
toothed	top'ple	tor'so
tooth'less	top'pled	tort
tooth'less·ly	top'sail'	tor'toise

tor'tu·os'i·ty	tot'tered	tou'sle
tor'tu·ous	tot'ter·ing·ly	tou'sled
tor'tu·ous·ly	tot'ter·ings	tout
tor'tu·ous·ness	tot'ter·y	tout'ed
tor'ture	tou·can'	to·va'rish
tor'tured	touch	tow
tor'tur·er	touch'a·ble	tow'age
tor'tur·ing·ly	touch'down'	to'ward
tor'tur·ous	touched	to'wards
tor'tur·ous·ly	touch'hole'	tow'boat'
To'ry	touch'i·er	towed
toss	touch'i·est	tow'el
tossed	touch'i·ly	tow'el·ings
toss'ing·ly	touch'i·ness	tow'er
toss'ings	touch'ing·ly	tow'ered
toss'up'	touch'stone'	tow'er·ing·ly
to'tal	touch'wood'	tow'er·man
to'taled	touch'y	tow'head'
to·tal'i·tar'i·an	tough	tow'line'
to·tal'i·tar'i·an·ism	tough'en	town
to·tal'i·ty	tough'ened	town'folk'
to'tal·i·za'tion	tough'er	town'ship
to'tal·i·za'tor	tough'est	towns'man
to'tal·ize	tou·pee'	town'wear'
to'tal·ized	tour	tow'path'
to'tal·iz'er	toured	tow'rope'
to'tal·ly	tour'ism	tox·e'mi·a
tote	tour'ist	tox'ic
tot'ed	tour'ma·line	tox·ic'i·ty
to'tem	tour'na·ment	tox'i·co·log'i·cal
toth'er	tour'ney	tox'i·col'o·gist
tot'ter	tour'ni·quet	tox'i·col'o·gy

tox'i·co'sis	trac'tive	trained
tox'oid	trac'tor	train'er
toy	trac'tor·ize	train'ful
toyed	trade	train'load'
toy'ing·ly	trad'ed	train'man
toy'man	trad'er	trait
toy'shop'	trades'man	trai'tor
trace	tra·di'tion	trai'tor·ous
trace'a·ble	tra·di'tion·al	trai'tor·ous·ly
traced	tra·di'tion·al·ism	tra·jec'to·ry
trac'er	tra·di'tion·al·ly	tram
trac'er·y	tra·duce'	tram'car'
tra'che·a	tra·duced'	tram'mel
tra'che·al	tra·duc'er	tram'meled
tra·cho'ma	tra·duc'ing·ly	tram'mel·ing·ly
trac'ings	traf'fic	tra·mon'tane
track	traf'ficked	tramp
track'age	trag'a·canth	tramped
tracked	tra·ge'di·an	tram'ple
track'er	tra·ge'di·enne'	tram'pled
track'lay'er	trag'e·dy	tram'po·lin
track'less	trag'ic	tram'road'
track'man	trag'i·cal	tram'way'
track'mas'ter	trag'i·cal·ly	trance
tract	trag'i·com'e·dy	trance'like'
trac'ta·bil'i·ty	tra'gus	tran'quil
trac'ta·ble	trail	tran'quil·i·za'tion
trac'ta·bly	trailed	tran'quil·ize
trac·tar'i·an	trail'er	tran'quil·ized
trac'tate	trail'ing·ly	tran'quil·iz'er
trac'tile	train	tran'quil·iz'ing·ly
trac'tion	train'band'	tran·quil'li·ty

tran'quil·ly

trans·act'

trans·act'ed

trans·ac'tion

trans·al'pine

trans·at·lan'tic

tran·scend'

tran·scend'ed

tran·scend'ence

tran·scend'en·cy

tran·scend'ent

tran'scen·den'tal

tran'scen·den'tal·ism

tran'scen·den'tal·ist

trans'con·ti·nen'tal

tran·scribe'

tran·scribed'

tran·scrib'er

tran'script

tran·scrip'tion

trans·duc'er

trans·duc'tion

tran'sept

trans·fer'

trans·fer'a·bil'i·ty

trans·fer'a·ble

trans·fer'al

trans·fer'ence

trans'ferred'

trans·fer'rer

trans·fig'u·ra'tion

trans·fig'ure

trans·fig'ured

trans·fig'ure·ment

trans·fix'

trans·fixed'

trans·form'

trans'for·ma'tion

trans·formed'

trans·form'er

trans·form'ing·ly

trans·fuse'

trans·fused'

trans·fu'sion

trans·fu'sions

trans·gress'

trans·gressed'

trans·gress'ing·ly

trans·gres'sion

trans·gres'sor

tran'sient

tran·sis'tor

tran·sis'tor·ize

trans'it

tran·si'tion

tran·si'tion·al

tran·si'tion·al·ly

tran'si·tive

tran'si·tive·ly

tran'si·tive·ness

tran'si·to'ry

trans·lat'a·ble

trans·late'

trans·lat'ed

trans·la'tion

trans·la'tor

trans·la'to·ry

trans·lit'er·ate

trans·lu'cence

trans·lu'cen·cy

trans·lu'cent

trans·lu'cent·ly

trans'ma·rine'

trans'mi'grant

trans'mi·gra'tion

trans·mis'si·ble

trans·mis'sion

trans·mit'

trans·mit'tal

trans·mit'ted

trans·mit'ter

trans·mog'ri·fi·ca'tion

trans·mog'ri·fied

trans·mog'ri·fy

trans·mut'a·ble

trans'mu·ta'tion

trans·mute'

trans·mut'ed

tran'som

trans'pa·cif'ic

trans·par'en·cy

trans·par'ent

tran'spi·ra'tion

tran·spir'a·to'ry

tran·spire'

tran·spired'

trans·plant′	trau′ma·ta	treas′ur·y
trans′plan·ta′tion	trau·mat′ic	treat
trans·plant′ed	trau·mat′i·cal·ly	treat′ed
trans·port′	trau′ma·tism	trea′tise
trans′por·ta′tion	trau′ma·tize	treat′ment
trans·port′ed	trav′ail	trea′ty
trans·port′ing·ly	trav′el	tre′ble
trans·pos′al	trav′eled	tre′bled
trans·pose′	trav′el·er	tree
trans·posed′	trav′e·logue	treed
trans′po·si′tion	trav′ers·a·ble	tree′nail′
trans·ship′	trav′ers·al	trek
trans·ship′ment	trav′erse	trekked
tran′sub·stan′ti·a′tion	trav′ersed	trel′lis
trans·ver′sal	trav′er·tine	trel′lised
trans·verse′	trav′es·ty	trem′ble
trap	trawl	trem′bled
trap door	trawl′er	trem′bling·ly
tra·peze′	tray	trem′blings
tra·pe′zi·um	treach′er·ous	tre·men′dous
trap′e·zoid	treach′er·ous·ly	tre·men′dous·ly
trapped	treach′er·ous·ness	tre′mo·lan′do
trap′per	treach′er·y	trem′o·lo
trap′pings	trea′cle	trem′or
Trap′pist	tread	trem′u·lous
trap′rock′	trea′dle	trem′u·lous·ly
trap′shoot′ing	tread′mill′	trem′u·lous·ness
trash	trea′son	trench
trash′i·er	trea′son·a·ble	trench′an·cy
trash′i·est	treas′ure	trench′ant
trash′y	treas′ured	trench′ant·ly
trau′ma	treas′ur·er	trench′er

trench'er·man

trend

trend'ed

tre·pan'

tre·phine'

tre·phined'

trep'i·da'tion

tres'pass

tres'passed

tres'pass·er

tress

tres'tle

tres'tle·work'

tri'ad

tri·ad'ic

tri'al

tri'an'gle

tri·an'gu·lar

tri·an'gu·lar'i·ty

tri·an'gu·late

tri·an'gu·lat'ed

tri·an'gu·la'tion

trib'al

trib'al·ism

tri·bas'ic

tribe

tribes'man

trib'u·la'tion

tri·bu'nal

trib'une

trib'u·tar'y

trib'ute

trice

tri'ceps

tri·chi'na

trich'i·no'sis

tri·chot'o·my

trick

tricked

trick'er·y

trick'i·er

trick'i·est

trick'i·ly

trick'i·ness

trick'le

trick'led

trick'ling·ly

trick'lings

trick'ster

trick'sy

trick'y

tri'col'or

tri'corn

tri'cot

tri'cy·cle

tri'dent

tried

tri·en'ni·al

tri·en'ni·al·ly

tri'fle

tri'fled

tri'fler

tri'fling·ly

tri'flings

trig

trig'ger

trig'gered

trig'ger·fish'

tri'glyph

trig'o·no·met'-
ric

trig'o·no·met'-
ri·cal

trig'o·nom'-
e·try

tri·lem'ma

tri·lin'gual

trill

trilled

tril'lion

Tril'li·um

tri'lo·bite

tril'o·gy

tri·mes'ter

trimmed

trim'mer

trim'mings

trim'ness

tri·month'ly

trin'i·ty

trin'ket

tri·no'mi·al

tri'o

tri'ode

tri'o·let

trip

tri·par'tite

tripe

triph'thong

tri′ple		tri′umph·ing·ly		troth	
tri′pled		tri·um′vir		trot′line′	
tri′plet		tri·um′vi·rate		trot′ted	
tri′plex		tri′une		trot′ter	
trip′li·cate		tri·va′lent		trou′ba·dour	
trip′li·cat′ed		triv′et		trou′ble	
trip′li·ca′tion		triv′i·a		trou′bled	
tri′ply		triv′i·al		trou′ble·some	
tri′pod		triv′i·al′i·ty		trou′ble·some·ly	
tripped		triv′i·al·ly		trou′ble·some·ness	
trip′per		tro·cha′ic		trou′bling·ly	
trip′ping·ly		tro′che		trou′blous	
trip′tych		troi′ka		trough	
tri′reme		troll		trough′like′	
tri′sect′		trolled		trounce	
tri′sect′ed		trol′ley		trounced	
tri·sec′tion		trom′bone		trounc′ings	
tri·sec′tor		troop		troupe	
tris·kel′i·on		trooped		troup′er	
tris′yl·lab′ic		troop′er		trou′sers	
trite		troop′ship′		trous′seau′	
trite′ly		trope		trout	
trite′ness		tro′phy		trout′let	
Tri′ton		trop′ic		trout′ling	
tri′tone′		trop′i·cal		trow′el	
trit′u·rate		trop′i·cal·ly		trow′eled	
trit′u·rat′ed		tro′pism		troy	
trit′u·ra′tion		trop′ist		tru′an·cy	
tri′umph		tro·pol′o·gy		tru′ant	
tri·um′phal		trop′o·pause		tru′ant·ism	
tri·um′phant		trop′o·sphere		truce	
tri′umphed		trot		tru′cial	

truck	trun'cat·ed	tub
truck'age	trun·ca'tion	tu'ba
trucked	trun'cheon	tubbed
truck'er	trun'dle	tub'bi·er
truck'le	trun'dled	tub'bi·est
truck'led	trunk	tub'bings
truck'ling·ly	trun'nion	tub'by
truck'man	truss	tube
truc'u·lence	trussed	tu'ber
truc'u·lent	truss'ings	tu'ber·cle
trudge	trust	tu·ber'cu·lar
trudged	trus·tee'	tu·ber'cu·lin
trudg'en	trus·tee'ship	tu·ber'cu·lo'sis
true	trust'ful	tu·ber'cu·lous
trued	trust'ful·ly	tu'ber·os'i·ty
true'love'	trust'ful·ness	tu'ber·ous
true'ness	trust'i·er	tub'ings
truf'fle	trust'i·est	tu'bu·lar
truf'fled	trust'ing·ly	tu'bu·la'tion
tru'ism	trust'wor'thi·ness	tuck
tru'ly	trust'wor'thy	tucked
trump	trust'y	Tu'dor
trumped	truth	Tues'day
trump'er·y	truth'ful	tuft
trum'pet	truth'ful·ly	tuft'ed
trum'pet·ed	truth'ful·ness	tuft'ings
trum'pet·er	try	tug
trum'pet·ings	try'ing·ly	tug'boat'
trum'pet·like'	try'sail'	tugged
trum'pet·weed'	tryst	tug'ging·ly
trum'pet·wood'	tryst'ed	tug'gings
trun'cate	tset'se	tu·i'tion

tu'la·re'mi·a	tung'sten	turn'coat'
tu'lip	tu'nic	turn'cock'
tu'lip·wood'	tun'ings	turned
tulle	Tu·ni'sian	turn'er
tum'ble	tun'nel	turn'ings
tum'bled	tun'neled	tur'nip
tum'bler	tun'ny	turn'key'
tum'ble·weed'	tu'pe·lo	turn'off'
tum'bling·ly	tur'ban	turn'out'
tum'brel	tur'bid	turn'o'ver
tu'me·fac'tion	tur·bid'i·ty	turn'pike'
tu'me·fied	tur'bid·ly	turn'spit'
tu'me·fy	tur'bi·nate	turn'stile'
tu'mid	tur'bine	tur'pen·tine
tu·mid'i·ty	tur'bot	tur'pi·tude
tu'mor	tur'bu·lence	tur'quoise
tu'mor·ous	tur'bu·lent	tur'ret
tu'mult	tur'bu·lent·ly	tur'ret·ed
tu·mul'tu·ous	tu·reen'	tur'tle
tu·mul'tu·ous·ly	turf	Tus'can
tu·mul'tu·ous·ness	turfed	tusk
tu'mu·lus	turf'man	tusked
tun	tur'gid	tus'sle
tu'na	tur·gid'i·ty	tus'sled
tun'dra	tur'gid·ly	tus'sock
tune	Turk	tu'te·lage
tuned	tur'key	tu'te·lar'y
tune'ful	Turk'ish	tu'tor
tune'less	tur'mer·ic	tu'tored
tune'less·ly	tur'moil	tu·to'ri·al
tune'less·ness	turn	tux·e'do
tun'er	turn'buck'le	twad'dle

twad'dled	twin'klings	ty'phoid
twain	twirl	ty·phoi'dal
twang	twirled	ty·phoon'
twanged	twist	ty'phous
tweak	twist'ed	ty'phus
tweaked	twist'er	typ'i·cal
tweed	twist'ings	typ'i·cal·ly
tweez'ers	twit	typ'i·fi·ca'tion
twice	twitch	typ'i·fy
twid'dle	twitched	typ'ings
twid'dled	twit'ted	typ'ist
twig	twit'ter	ty·pog'ra·pher
twi'light'	twit'tered	ty'po·graph'ic
twill	twit'ter·ing·ly	ty·pog'ra·phy
twilled	twit'ter·ings	ty·poth'e·tae
twin	two	ty·ran'ni·cal
twin'born'	two'fold'	ty·ran'ni·cide
twine	two'some	tyr'an·nize
twined	ty·coon'	tyr'an·nized
twinge	type	ty'ran·niz'ing·ly
twinged	typed	tyr'an·nous
twin'kle	type'set'ter	tyr'an·ny
twin'kled	type'writ'er	ty'rant
twin'kling·ly	type'writ·ten	ty'ro

U

u·biq'ui·tous	ul'ti·mate	um·brel'la
u·biq'ui·tous·ly	ul'ti·mate·ly	um'laut
u·biq'ui·ty	ul'ti·ma'tum	um'pire
ud'der	ul'ti·mo	um'pired
ug'li·er	ul'tra·ism	un·a'ble
ug'li·est	ul'tra·le·gal'i·ty	un'a·bridged'
ug'li·ness	ul'tra·ma·rine'	un'ac·cent'ed
ug'ly	ul'tra·mi'cro·scope	un'ac·cept'a·ble
uh'lan	ul'tra·mod'ern	un'ac·com'mo·dat'ing
u·kase'	ul'tra·mon'tane	un'ac·com'pa·nied
u'ku·le'le	ul'tra·na'tion·al·ism	un'ac·count'a·ble
ul'cer	ul'tra·na'tion·al·ist	un'ac·cus'tomed
ul'cer·ate	ul'tra·red'	un'ac·quaint'ed
ul'cer·at·ed	ul'tra·son'ic	un'a·dorned'
ul'cer·a'tion	ul'tra·vi'o·let	un'a·dul'ter·at·ed
ul'cer·a'tive	ul'u·late	un'af·fect'ed
ul'cer·ous	ul'u·lat'ed	un'al·loyed'
ul'cer·ous·ly	ul'u·la'tion	un·al'ter·a·ble
ul'na	um'ber	un·al'tered
ul'nar	um'bra	un'-A·mer'i·can
ul'ster	um'brage	un·a'mi·a·ble
ul·te'ri·or	um·bra'geous	u·nan'i·mous

un·an'swer·a·ble

un'ap·peas'a·ble

un'ap·proach'a·ble

un'ap·pro'pri·at'ed

un'ap·prov'ing·ly

un·armed'

un'a·shamed'

un·asked'

un'as·sail'a·ble

un'as·signed'

un'as·sim'i·lat'ed

un'as·sist'ed

un'as·sum'ing·ly

un'at·tached'

un'at·tain'a·ble

un'at·tempt'ed

un'at·trac'tive·ly

un·au'thor·ized

un'a·vail'a·ble

un'a·vail'ing·ly

un'a·void'a·ble

un'a·ware'

un·bal'anced

un·bal'last·ed

un·bar'

un·barred'

un·bear'a·bly

un·beat'a·ble

un'be·com'ing·ly

un'be·fit'ting·ly

un'be·known'

un'be·knownst'

unbe·lief'

un'be·liev'a·ble

un'be·liev'er

un'be·liev'ing·ly

un'be·liev'ing·ness

un·bend'

un·bend'ing·ly

un·bi'ased

un·bid'den

un·bind'

un·blem'ished

un·blessed'

un·blocked'

un·blush'ing·ly

un·bolt'

un·bolt'ed

un·born'

un·bos'om

un·bos'omed

un·bound'

un·bound'ed

un·bowed'

un·break'a·ble

un·bri'dled

un·bro'ken

un·buck'le

un·bur'den

un·bur'dened

un·burned'

un·busi'ness·like'

un·but'ton

un·but'toned

un·cage'

un·can'ny

un·cap'ti·vat'ed

un·car'pet·ed

un·cat'a·logued

un·ceas'ing·ly

un'cer·e·mo'ni·ous

un·cer'tain

un·cer'tain·ly

un·cer'tain·ness

un·cer'tain·ty

un·chal'lenged

un·change'a·ble

un·change'a·bly

un·chang'ing·ly

un·char'i·ta·ble

un·chid'ing·ly

un·chris'tened

un·chris'tian

un'ci·al

un·civ'il

un·civ'i·lized

un·clad'

un·claimed'

un·clasp'

un'cle

un·clean'

un·clean'ly

un·closed'

un·clothe'

un·coil'

un'col·lect'ed

un·colt'	un'con·trolled'	un·dam'aged
un·com'fort·a·ble	un'con·ven'tion·al	un·damped'
un·com'fort·a·ble·ness	un'con·ven'tion·al·ly	un·dashed'
un·com'mon	un'con·vert'ed	un·dat'ed
un·com·mu'ni·ca'tive	un'con·vinced'	un·daunt'ed
un·com'pa·nied	un'con·vinc'ing·ly	un'de·ceive'
un·com'pro·mis'ing	un'co-op'er·a'tive	un'de·ceived'
un'con·cerned'	un·cork'	un'de·cid'ed
un'con·di'tion·al	un·corked'	un'de·ci'pher·a·ble
un'con·di'tion·al'i·ty	un'cor·rect'ed	un'de·ci'phered
un'con·fined'	un'cor·rupt'ed	un·dec'o·rous
un'con·firmed'	un'count'a·ble	un'de·feat'ed
un'con·form'i·ty	un·count'ed	un'de·fend'ed
un'con·gen'ial	un·cou'ple	un'de·filed'
un·con'quer·a·ble	un·cou'pled	un'de·fin'a·ble
un·con'quered	un·couth'	un'de·liv'er·a·ble
un·con'scion·a·ble	un·couth'ness	un'dem·o-crat'ic
un·con'scious	un·cov'er	un'de·mon'stra-tive
un·con'scious·ly	un·cov'ered	un'de·ni'a·ble
un·con'scious·ness	un·cowed'	un'de·pend'a·ble
un·con'se·crat'ed	un·creased'	un'de·pos'it·ed
un·con'se·quen'tial	un·crit'i·cal	un'der
un'con·se·quen'tial·ly	un·crit'i·ciz'ing·ly	un'der·a·chiev'er
un'con·sid'er·ate·ly	un·crowd'ed	un'der·arm'
un'con·sid'ered	un·crowned'	un'der·bid'
un'con·sti·tu'tion·al	unc'tion	un'der·bod'y
un'con·sti·tu'tion·al·ly	unc'tu·ous	un'der·brush'
un'con·strained'	un·cul'ti·vat'ed	un'der·buy'
un'con·strain'ed·ly	un·cul'tured	un'der·cap'i·tal·i·za'tion
un'con·tam'i·nat'ed	un·curbed'	un'der·cap'i·tal·ize
un'con·tra·dic'to·ry	un·curl'	un'der·car'riage
un'con·trol'la·ble	un·cut'	un'der·charge'

un'der·charged'	un'der·mined'	un'der·tak'er
un'der·class'man	un'der·neath'	un'der·tak'ings
un'der·clothes'	un'der·nour'ish	un'der·things'
un'der·coat'	un'der·nour'ished	un'der·tone'
un'der·con·sump'tion	un'der·nour'ish·ment	un'der·took'
un'der·cov'er	un'der·pass'	un'der·tow'
un'der·cur'rent	un'der·pin'nings	un'der·turn'
un'der·cut'	un'der·priv'i·leged	un'der·val'ue
un'der·done'	un'der·pro·duc'tion	un'der·wa'ter
un'der·dose'	un'der·quote'	un'der·wear'
un'der·es'ti·mate	un'der·rate'	un'der·weight'
un'der·ex·pose'	un'der·rat'ed	un'der·world'
un'der·feed'	un'der·score'	un'der·write'
un'der·foot'	un'der·scored'	un'der·writ'er
un'der·gar'ment	un'der·sec're·tar'y	un'de·scrib'a·ble
un'der·glaze'	un'der·sell'	un'de·served'
un'der·go'	un'der·shirt'	un'de·sir'a·ble
un'der·grad'u·ate	un'der·shot'	un'de·sired'
un'der·ground'	un'der·signed'	un'de·stroyed'
un'der·growth'	un'der·sized'	un'de·tect'ed
un'der·hand'ed	un'der·skirt'	un'de·ter'mined
un'der·hand'ed·ly	un'der·slung'	un'de·vel'oped
un'der·hand'ed·ness	un'der·sparred'	un'di·ag·nosed'
un'der·hung'	un'der·stand'	un·di'a·pered
un'der·laid'	un'der·stand'ing·ly	un'di·gest'ed
un'der·lay'	un'der·stand'ings	un·dig'ni·fied
un'der·lie'	un'der·state'	un'di·lut'ed
un'der·line'	un'der·state'ment	un'di·min'ished
un'der·lined'	un'der·stood'	un·dimmed'
un'der·lings	un'der·stud'y	un'di·rect'ed
un'der·manned'	un'der·take'	un·dis'ci·plined
un'der·mine'	un'der·tak'en	un'dis·closed'

un'dis·cov'ered

un'dis·crim'i·nat'ing·ly

un'dis·guised'

un'dis·tin'guished

un'dis·trib'ut·ed

un'di·vid'ed

un·do'

un'do·mes'ti·cat·ed

un·done'

un·doubt'ed

un·doubt'ed·ly

un'dra·mat'i·cal·ly

un·draped'

un·drawn'

un·dress'

un·dressed'

un·drink'a·ble

un·due'

un'du·lant

un'du·late

un'du·lat'ed

un'du·la'tion

un·du'ly

un·du'ti·ful

un·dy'ing·ly

un·earned'

un·earth'

un·earthed'

un·earth'ly

un·eas'i·er

un·eas'i·est

un·eas'i·ly

un·eas'i·ness

un·eas'y

un·eat'a·ble

un·ed'u·ca·ble

un·ed'u·cat'ed

un'em·bar'rassed

un'em·bit'tered

un'em·broi'dered

un'e·mo'tion·al

un'em·ploy'a·ble

un'em·ploy'a·ble·ness

un'em·ployed'

un'em·ploy'ment

un'en·cum'bered

un'en·dan'gered

un·end'ing

un'en·dorsed'

un'en·dur'a·ble

un'en·force'a·ble

un'en·gaged'

un'en·graved'

un'en·grossed'

un'en·larged'

un'en·light'ened

un'en·slaved'

un·en'tered

un'en·ter·pris'ing

un'en·ter·tain'ing

un'en·thu'si·as'tic

un'en·thu'si·as'ti·cal·ly

un·en'vi·a·ble

un·en'vi·a·bly

un·en'vied

un·e'qual

un·e'qual·a·ble

un·e'qualed

un·e'qual·ize

un·e'qual·ized

un·e'qual·ly

un'e·quipped'

un'e·quiv'o·cal

un'e·rad'i·cat'ed

un'e·ras'a·ble

un'e·rased'

un·err'ing

un·err'ing·ly

un·es·sen'tial

un·es'ti·mat'ed

un·eth'i·cal

un·eth'i·cal·ly

un·e'ven

un·e'ven·ly

un·e'vent'ful

un·e'vent'ful·ly

un·ex·am'pled

un'ex·celled'

un'ex·cep'tion·a·ble

un'ex·cep'tion·al

un'ex·cit'a·ble

un'ex·cit'ing

un'ex·cused'

un·ex'e·cut'ed

un'ex·haust'ed

un'ex·pect'ed

un'ex·pect'ed·ly

un'ex·pect'ed·ness

un'ex·plain'a·ble

un'ex·plained'

un'ex·ploit'ed

un'ex·posed'

un·ex·pressed'

un·ex·press'i·ble

un·ex'pur·gat'ed

un'ex·tin'guished

un'ex·tri·cat·ed

un·fad'ed

un·fad'ing·ly

un·fail'ing·ly

un·fair'

un·fair'ly

un·fair'ness

un·faith'ful

un·faith'ful·ly

un·faith'ful·ness

un·fal'ter·ing

un'fa·mil'iar

un·farmed'

un·fash'ion·a·ble

un·fash'ion·a·bly

un·fas'ten

un·fas'tened

un·fa'ther·ly

un·fath'om·a·ble

un·fath'omed

un'fa·tigue'a·ble

un'fa·tigued'

un·fa'vor·able

un·fa'vor·a·bly

un·fear'ing·ly

un·fea'si·ble

un·fea'si·bly

un·fed'

un·feel'ing·ly

un·feigned'

un·felt'

un·fem'i·nine

un·fenced'

un'fe·nes'trat·ed

un'fer·ment'ed

un·fer'ti·lized

un·fet'ter

un·fet'tered

un·filed'

un·fil'i·al

un·fil'i·al·ly

un·fill'a·ble

un·fil'tered

un·fin'ished

un·fit'

un·fit'ting·ly

un·flag'ging·ly

un·flat'ter·ing·ly

un·flick'er·ing·ly

un·flinch'ing·ly

un·flinch'ing·ness

un·flood'ed

un·flur'ried

un·flus'tered

un·fo'cused

un·fold'

un·fold'ed

un·forced'

un'fore·see'a·ble

un'fore·seen'

un'fore·tell'a·ble

un·for'feit·ed

un'for·get'ta·ble

un'for·get'ting·ly

un'for·giv'a·ble

un'for·giv'en

un'for·giv'ing·ly

un'for·giv'ing·ness

un'for·got'ten

un·for'mal·ized

un·formed'

un·for'ti·fied

un·for'tu·nate

un·for'tu·nate·ly

un·found'ed

un·frayed'

un'fre·quent'ed

un·friend'ed

un·friend'li·ness

un·friend'ly

un·frock'

un·frocked'

un·fru'gal

un·fruit'ful

un·fu'eled

un'ful·filled'

un·fund'ed
un·fun'ny
un·fur'bished
un·furl'
un·furled'
un·fur'nished
un·gain'li·ness
un·gain'ly
un·gal'lant
un·gar'land·ed
un·gar'nished
un·gen'er·ous
un·gen'tle
un·gen'tle·man·ly
un·ger'mi·nat'ed
un·gift'ed
un·girt'
un·glazed'
un·glo'ri·ous
un·gloved'
un·god'li·ness
un·god'ly
un·gov'ern·a·ble
un·gov'ern·a·bly
un·gra'cious
un·gra'cious·ly
un·grad'ed
un'gram·mat'i·cal
un·grate'ful
un·grate'ful·ly
un·grate'ful·ness
un·ground'ed

un·grudg'ing·ly
un·guard'ed
un·guard'ed·ly
un'guent
un·guid'ed
un·gummed'
un·hack'neyed
un·hal'lowed
un·ham'pered
un·hand'i·ness
un·hand'some
un·hand'y
un·hanged'
un·hap'pi·er
un·hap'pi·est
un·hap'pi·ly
un·hap'pi·ness
un·hap'py
un·hard'ened
un·harmed'
un·har'ness
un·har'nessed
un·har'vest·ed
un·hatched'
un·healed'
un·health'ful
un·health'ful·ness
un·health'y
un·heard'
un·heat'ed
un·heed'ed
un·heed'ful·ly

un·heed'ing·ly
un·help'ful
un·her'ald·ed
un'he·ro'ic
un·hes'i·tat'ing
un·hes'i·tat'ing·ly
un·hin'dered
un·hinge'
un·hinged'
un·hitch'
un·hitched'
un·ho'li·ness
un·ho'ly
un·home'like'
un·hon'ored
un·hook'
un·hooked'
un·hoped'
un·horse'
un·hum'bled
un·hu'mor·ous
un·hurt'
un'hy·gi·en'ic
un·hy'phen·at'ed
u'ni·corn
u'ni·cy'cle
un·i'den'ti·fi'a·ble
un·i'den'ti·fied
u'ni·fi·ca'tion
u'ni·fied
u'ni·form
u'ni·formed

u'ni·form'i·ty

u'ni·fy

u'ni·lat'er·al

u'ni·lat'er·al·ly

un·il·lu'mi·nat'ing

un'im·ag'i·na·ble

un'im·ag'i·na'tive

un'im·paired'

un'im·peach'a·ble

un'im·ped'ed

un'im·por'tant

un'im·por'tant·ly

un'im·pos'ing

un'im·pressed'

un'im·pres'sion·a·ble

un'im·pres'sive

un'im·proved'

un'in·cor'po·rat'ed

un'in·dem'ni·fied

un·in'dexed

un·in·dict'ed

un·in'flu·enced

un'in·formed'

un'in·hab'it·a·ble

un'in·hab'it·ed

un'in·hib'it·ed

un·in'jured

un·inked'

un'in·scribed'

un'in·spired'

un'in·spir'ing·ly

un'in·struct'ed

un'in·struc'tive

un·in'su·lat'ed

un'in·sur'a·ble

un'in·sured'

un·in'te·grat'ed

un'in·tel'li·gent

un'in·tel'li·gi·ble

un'in·tend'ed

un'in·ten'tion·al

un'in·ten'tion·al·ly

un·in'ter·est·ed

un·in'ter·est·ed·ly

un·in'ter·est·ing·ly

un'in·ter·mit'ting·ly

un'in·ter·rupt'ed·ly

un·in'ti·mat'ed

un'in·tim'i·dat'ed

un'in·tox'i·cat'ed

un'in·vad'ed

un'in·ven'tive

un'in·vig'o·rat'ed

un'in·vit'ing·ly

un'ion

un'ion·ism

un'ion·ist

un'ion·i·za'tion

un'ion·ize

un'ion·ized

u·nique'

u·nique'ly

u·nique'ness

un'ir·ra'di·at'ed

u'ni·son

un·is'sued

u'nit

U'ni·tar'i·an

U'ni·tar'i·an·ism

u'ni·tar'y

u·nite'

u·nit'ed

u·nit'ed·ly

u'ni·ty

u'ni·ver'sal

U'ni·ver'sal·ist

u'ni·ver·sal'i·ty

u'ni·ver'sal·ly

u'ni·verse

u'ni·ver'si·ty

un·jok'ing·ly

un·just'

un·jus'ti·fi'a·ble

un·jus'ti·fi'a·bly

un·jus'ti·fied

un·just'ly

un·kempt'

un·killed'

un·kind'

un·kind'li·ness

un·kind'ly

un·know'a·ble

un·know'ing·ly

un·known'

un·la'beled

un·lace'

un·laced'

un·la'dy·like'

un'la·ment'ed

un·lashed'

un·latch'

un·law'ful

un·law'ful·ly

un·law'ful·ness

un·lead'ed

un·learn'

un·leash'

un·leashed'

un·leav'ened

un·less'

un·let'tered

un·lib'er·at'ed

un·li'censed

un·light'ed

un·lik'a·ble

un·like'

un·like'li·hood

un·like'ly

un·lim'ber

un·lim'bered

un·lim'it·ed

un·lined'

un·list'ed

un·load'

un·load'ed

un·lo'cal·ized

un·lock'

un·locked'

un·looked'

un·loos'en

un·loved'

un·lov'ing·ly

un·luck'i·ly

un·luck'y

un·made'

un·mag'ni·fied

un·maid'en·ly

un·mail'a·ble

un·make'

un·man'

un·man'age·a·ble

un·man'li·ness

un·man'ly

un·manned'

un·man'ner·li·ness

un·man'ner·ly

un·marked'

un·mar'riage·a·ble

un·mar'ried

un·mask'

un·masked'

un·matched'

un·meas'ur·a·ble

un·meas'ured

un·men'tion·a·ble

un·men'tioned

un·mer'ci·ful

un·mer'ci·ful·ly

un·mer'it·ed

un·me'tered

un·mind'ful

un'mis·tak'a·ble

un·mit'i·gat'ed

un·mixed'

un'mo·lest'ed

un·moored'

un·mort'gaged

un·mo'ti·vat'ed

un·mount'ed

un·moved'

un·mov'ing·ly

un·named'

un·nat'u·ral

un·nat'u·ral·ly

un·nav'i·ga·ble

un·nec'es·sar'i·ly

un·nec'es·sar'y

un·need'ed

un·neigh'bor·ly

un·nerve'

un·no'tice·a·ble

un·no'ticed

un·num'bered

un'ob·serv'ant

un'ob·served'

un'ob·tain'a·ble

un·oc'cu·pied

un'of·fi'cial

un·o'pened

un'o·pin'ion·at'ed

un'op·posed'

un·or'ches·trat'ed

un·or'gan·ized
un·or'tho·dox
un'os·ten·ta'tious
un·pac'i·fied
un·pack'
un·paged'
un·paid'
un·paint'ed
un·pal'at·a·ble
un·par'al·leled
un·par'don·a·ble
un·par'doned
un'par·lia·men'ta·ry
un·pas'teur·ized
un·pat'ent·a·ble
un·pat'ent·ed
un'pa·tri·ot'ic
un'pa·tri·ot'i·cal·ly
un'pa·trolled'
un·paved'
un'per·ceived'
un'per'fo·rat'ed
un'per·formed'
un'per·turbed'
un·pit'y·ing
un·pit'y·ing·ly
un·planned'
un·plas'tered
un·play'a·ble
un·pleas'a·ble
un·pleas'ant
un·pleas'ant·ly

un·pleas'ant·ness
un·pleas'ing·ly
un·pledged'
un·plowed'
un·plugged'
un·plumbed'
un'po·et'ic
un'po·liced'
un·pol'ished
un'pol·lut'ed
un'pop'u·lar
un·pop'u·lat'ed
un·pop'u·lous
un·prac'ticed
un·prec'e·dent'ed
un·prec'e·dent'ed·ly
un'pre·dict'a·ble
un·prej'u·diced
un'pre·med'i·tat'ed
un'pre·pared'
un'pre·par'ed·ness
un'pre·pos·sess'ing
un'pre·sent'a·ble
un'pre·tend'ing·ly
un'pre·ten'tious
un'pre·ten'tious·ly
un'pre·ten'tious·ness
un·prin'ci·pled
un·print'a·ble
un·print'ed
un'pro·duced'
un'pro·duc'tive

un'pro·fes'sion·al
un·prof'it·a·ble
un'pro·gres'sive
un·prom'is·ing
un·prompt'ed
un'pro·nounce'a·ble
un'pro·pi'tious
un'pro·tect'ed
un·prov'a·ble
un·proved'
un'pro·vid'ed
un'pro·voked'
un·pub'lished
un·punc'tu·al
un'punc·tu·al'i·ty
un·punc'tu·al·ly
un·pun'ished
un·qual'i·fied
un·quelled'
un·quench'a·bly
un·ques'tion·a·ble
un·ques'tion·a·bly
un·ques'tioned
un·ques'tion·ing·ly
un·ran'somed
un·rav'el
un·rav'eled
un·reach'a·ble
un·read'
un·read'a·ble
un·re'al
un're·al·is'tic

un're·al'i·ty

un·re'al·ized

un·rea'son·a·ble

un·rea'son·a·bly

un·rea'soned

un·rea'son·ing·ly

un're·buked'

un're·ceipt'ed

un're·cep'tive

un're·claim'a·ble

un·rec'og·niz'a·ble

un·rec'og·nized

un·rec'og·niz'ing·ly

un're·con·cil'a·ble

un're·cord'ed

un're·deem'a·ble

un're·deemed'

un·re·fill'a·ble

un·re·fined'

un're·frig'er·at'ed

un're·fut'ed

un're·gen'er·ate

un·reg'u·lat'ed

un're·hearsed'

un're·lat'ed

un're·lent'ing·ly

un're·li·a·bil'i·ty

un're·li'a·ble

un're·mit'ting

un're·mu'ner·a'tive

un're·mu'ner·a'tive·ly

un·rent'a·ble

un·rent'ed

un're·pent'ed

un're·port'a·ble

un're·port'ed

un're·pre·sent'a·tive

un're·proach'ing·ly

un're·proved'

un're·quit'ed

un're·served'

un're·serv'ed·ly

un're·sist'ing·ly

un're·solved'

un're·source'ful

un're·spon'sive

un·rest'

un·rest'ed

un're·strained'

un're·strict'ed

un're·veal'ing·ly

un're·ward'ed

un·rhymed'

un·right'eous

un·right'eous·ly

un·right'ful·ly

un·ripe'

un·ri'pened

un·ri'valed

un·roll'

un·rolled'

un·ruf'fle

un·ruf'fled

un·ruled'

un·rul'y

un·sad'dened

un·sad'dle

un·sad'dled

un·safe'

un·said'

un·sal'a·ble

un·sal'a·ried

un·sanc'ti·fied

un·sa'ti·at·ed

un'sat·is·fac'to·ri·ly

un'sat·is·fac'to·ry

un·sat'is·fied

un·sat'is·fy'ing·ly

un·sat'u·rat'ed

un·sa'vor·i·ly

un·sa'vor·y

un·scathed'

un·scent'ed

un·schooled'

un'sci·en·tif'ic

un·scram'ble

un·screw'

un·screwed'

un·scru'pu·lous

un·scru'pu·lous·ly

un·seal'

un·sealed'

un·sea'son·a·ble

un·sea'soned

un·seat'ed

un·sea'wor'thy

un·sec'ond·ed

un'se·cured'

un·see'ing·ly

un·seem'ing·ly

un·seem'ly

un·seen'

un'se·lect'ed

un·self'ish

un·self'ish·ly

un·sen'si·tized

un'sen·ti·men'tal

un·sep'a·rat'ed

un·serv'ice·a·ble

un·set'tle

un·set'tled

un·shack'le

un·shack'led

un·shad'ed

un·shak'a·ble

un·shak'en

un·sharp'ened

un·shav'en

un·sheathe'

un·shed'

un·shel'tered

un·shield'ed

un·ship'

un·shipped'

un·shrink'a·ble

un·shuf'fled

un·sight'ed

un·sight'ly

un·signed'

un·sing'a·ble

un·sink'a·ble

un·sis'ter·ly

un·sized'

un·skilled'

un·skill'ful

un·skimmed'

un·smil'ing·ly

un·smirched'

un·smoked'

un·smudged'

un·snarl'

un·so'cia·ble

un·soft'ened

un·soil'

un·soiled'

un·sold'

un·sol'dier·ly

un'so·lic'it·ed

un'so·phis'ti·cat'ed

un·sought'

un·sound'

un·sound'ly

un·speak'a·ble

un·spe'cial·ized

un·spec'i·fied

un·spoiled'

un·spo'ken

un·sports'man·like'

un·spot'ted

un·sprin'kled

un·sta'ble

un·stained'

un·stamped'

un·stead'i·ly

un·stead'y

un·ster'i·lized

un·stint'ed

un·stint'ing·ly

un·strained'

un·stressed'

un·strung'

un'sub·stan'tial

un'sub·stan'ti·at'ed

un'suc·cess'ful

un·suf'fer·a·ble

un·suit'a·ble

un·sul'lied

un·sum'moned

un·sung'

un'su·per·vised'

un·sure'

un'sur·pass'a·ble

un'sur·passed'

un'sus·pect'ed

un'sus·pect'ing

un'sus·pect'ing·ly

un·swayed'

un·sweet'ened

un·swerv'ing·ly

un·sworn'

un'sym·pa·thet'ic

un·sym'pa·thiz'ing·ly

un'sys·tem·at'ic

un·sys'tem·a·tized

un·taint'ed

un·tal'ent·ed

un·tamed'

un·tan'gle

un·tanned'

un·tast'ed

un·taught'

un·tax'a·ble

un·taxed'

un·teach'a·ble

un·tech'ni·cal

un·tempt'ed

un·ten'ant·a·ble

un·ten'ant·ed

un·tend'ed

un·ter'ri·fied

un·thick'ened

un·think'a·ble

un·think'ing

un·think'ing·ly

un·ti'di·ly

un·ti'dy

un·tie'

un·tied'

un·til'

un·time'ly

un·tint'ed

un·tir'ing·ly

un·ti'tled

un'to

un·told'

un·touch'a·ble

un·touched'

un·to'ward

un·trace'a·ble

un·trad'ed

un·trained'

un·tram'meled

un'trans·lat'a·ble

un·trav'eled

un·tried'

un·trimmed'

un·trod'den

un·trou'bled

un·true'

un·trussed'

un·trust'wor'thy

un·truth'

un·truth'ful

un·tuned'

un·turned'

un·tu'tored

un·twine'

un·twist'

un'un·der·stand'a·ble

un'up·braid'ing·ly

un·us'a·ble

un·used'

un·u'su·al

un·u'su·al·ly

un·ut'ter·a·ble

un·ut'ter·a·bly

un·ut'tered

un·val'i·dat'ed

un·val'ued

un·van'quished

un·var'ied

un·var'nished

un·var'y·ing·ly

un·vaunt'ing·ly

un·veil'

un·veiled'

un·ver'bal·ized

un·ver'i·fied

un·versed'

un·vis'it·ed

un·voiced'

un·walled'

un·war'i·ly

un·warned'

un·war'rant·a·ble

un·war'rant·ed

un·war'y

un·washed'

un·wa'tered

un·wa'ver·ing·ly

un·wea'ried

un·wea'ry·ing·ly

un·wed'

un·wed'ded

un·wel'come

un·well'

un·wept'

un·whole'some

un·whole′some·ly	un·yoked′	up·raised′
un·wield′i·ness	up	up′right′
un·wield′y	u′pas	up′right′ly
un·will′ing	up′beat′	up′right′ness
un·will′ing·ly	up·braid′	up·ris′ings
un·will′ing·ness	up·braid′ed	up′roar′
un·winc′ing·ly	up·braid′ing·ly	up·roar′i·ous
un·wind′	up·bring′ing	up·roar′i·ous·ness
un·wind′ing·ly	up′coun′try	up′root′
un·wink′ing·ly	up′draft′	up·root′ed
un·wise′	up′grade′	up·set′
un·wit′nessed	up′growth′	up·set′ting·ly
un·wit′ting·ly	up·heav′al	up′shot′
un·wom′an·ly	up·held′	up′side′
un·wont′ed	up′hill′	up′stairs′
un·work′a·ble	up·hold′	up′start′
un·work′man·like′	up·hold′er	up′state′
un·world′li·ness	up·hol′ster	up′stream′
un·world′ly	up·hol′stered	up′stroke′
un·worn′	up·hol′ster·er	up′take′
un·wor′ried	up·hol′ster·y	up′-to-date′
un·wor′thi·ly	up′keep′	up′town′
un·wor′thi·ness	up′land′	up·turn′
un·wor′thy	up·lift′	up·turned′
un·wound′	up·lift′ed	up′ward
un·wound′ed	up·lift′ing·ly	up′wind′
un·wrap′	up′most	u·ra′ni·um
un·wrapped′	up·on′	ur′ban
un·wreathe′	up′per	ur·bane′
un·wrin′kled	up′per·most	ur·bane′ly
un·writ′ten	up′pers	ur′ban·ite
un·yield′ing·ly	up·raise′	ur·ban′i·ty

ur'ban·i·za'tion	use'ful·ness	u·til'i·tar'i·an·ism
ur'ban·ize	use'less	u·til'i·ties
ur'ban·ized	use'less·ly	u·til'i·ty
ur'chin	use'less·ness	u'ti·liz'a·ble
urge	us'er	u'ti·li·za'tion
urged	us'es	u'ti·lize
ur'gen·cy	ush'er	u'ti·lized
ur'gent	ush'ered	ut'most
ur'gent·ly	u'su·al	u·to'pi·a
urg'ings	u'su·al·ly	u·to'pi·an
urn	u'su·fruct	u·to'pi·an·ism
us	u'su·rer	ut'ter
us'a·bil'i·ty	u·su'ri·ous	ut'ter·ance
us'a·ble	u·surp'	ut'tered
us'age	u'sur·pa'tion	ut'ter·ly
use	u·surp'er	ut'ter·most
used	u'su·ry	u'vu·la
use'ful	u·ten'sil	u'vu·lar
use'ful·ly	u·til'i·tar'i·an	

va'can·cy	vag'a·bon'di·a	va·le'ri·an
va'cant	vag'a·bond·ism	val'et
va'cate	vag'a·bond·ize	val'e·tu'di·nar'i·an
va'cat·ed	va·gar'y	Val·hal'la
va·ca'tion	va'gran·cy	val'iant
va·ca'tioned	va'grant	val'id
va·ca'tion·ist	vague	val'i·date
vac'ci·nate	va'guer	val'i·dat'ed
vac'ci·nat'ed	va'guest	val'i·da'tion
vac'ci·na'tion	va'gus	va·lid'i·ty
vac'ci·na'tor	vain	val'id·ly
vac'cine	vain'glo'ri·ous	va·lise'
vac'il·late	vain'glo'ry	val'ley
vac'il·lat'ed	vain'ly	val'or
vac'il·la'tion	vain'ness	val'or·i·za'tion
vac'il·lat'ing·ly	val'ance	val'or·ize
vac'il·la·to'ry	vale	val'or·ous
va·cu'i·ty	val'e·dic'tion	val'u·a·ble
vac'u·ous	val'e·dic·to'ri·an	val'u·a'tion
vac'u·um	val'e·dic'to·ry	val'ue
vag'a·bond	va'lence	val'ued
vag'a·bond'age	val'en·tine	val'ue·less

valve	var'i·a'tion	vault
val'vu·lar	var'i·col'ored	vault'ed
vamp	var'i·cose	vaunt
vam'pire	var'i·cos'i·ty	vaunt'ed
va·na'di·um	var'ied	vaunt'ing·ly
van'dal	var'i·e·gate	veal
van'dal·ism	var'i·e·gat'ed	vec'tor
van'dal·ize	var'i·e·ga'tion	ve·dette'
vane	va·ri'e·tal	veer
van'guard'	va·ri'e·ty	veered
va·nil'la	va·ri'o·la	veg'e·ta·ble
van'il·lin	var'i·o'rum	veg'e·tar'i·an
van'ish	var'i·ous	veg'e·tar'i·an·ism
van'ished	var'i·ous·ly	veg'e·tate
van'ish·ing·ly	var'let	veg'e·tat'ed
van'i·ty	var'nish	veg'e·ta'tion
van'quish	var'nished	veg'e·ta'tive
van'quished	var'nish·ings	ve'he·mence
van'tage	var'y	ve'he·ment
vap'id	var'y·ing·ly	ve'he·ment·ly
vap'id·ly	vas'cu·lar	ve'hi·cle
va'por	vase	ve'hi·cles
va'por·ings	Vas'e·line	ve·hic'u·lar
va'por·i·za'tion	vas'sal	veil
va'por·ize	vas'sal·age	veiled
va'por·ized	vast	vein
va'por·iz'er	vast'er	veined
va'por·ous	vast'est	vein'ings
var'i·a·bil'i·ty	vast'ly	vein'let
var'i·a·ble	vat	vel'lum
var'i·ance	Vat'i·can	ve·loc'i·pede
var'i·ant	vaude'ville	ve·loc'i·ty

ve'lo·drome

ve·lours'

vel'vet

vel'vet·een'

vel'vet·y

ve'nal

ve·nal'i·ty

ve'nal·i·za'tion

ve'nal·ize

ve·na'tion

vend

vend'ed

vend·ee'

ven·det'ta

vend'i·ble

ven'dor

ve·neer'

ve·neered'

ven'er·a·ble

ven'er·ate

ven'er·at'ed

ven'er·a'tion

ven'er·a'tive

Ve·ne'tian

venge'ance

venge'ful

venge'ful·ness

ve'ni·al

ve·ni·al'i·ty

ve'ni·al·ly

ven'i·son

ven'om

ven'om·ous

ven'om·ous·ly

vent

vent'ed

vent'hole'

ven'ti·late

ven'ti·lat'ed

ven'ti·la'tion

ven'ti·la'tor

ven'tral

ven'tri·cle

ven·tric'u·lar

ven·tril'o·quism

ven·tril'o·quist

ven'ture

ven'tured

ven'ture·some

ven'ue

ve·ra'cious

ve·ra'cious·ly

ve·rac'i·ty

ve·ran'da

ver'bal

ver'bal·ism

ver'bal·ist

ver'bal·i·za'tion

ver'bal·ize

ver'bal·ized

ver'bal·ly

ver·ba'tim

ver·be'na

ver'bi·age

ver·bose'

ver·bos'i·ty

ver'dant

ver'dict

ver'di·gris

ver'dure

verge

verged

ver'ger

ver'i·est

ver'i·fi'a·ble

ver'i·fi·ca'tion

ver'i·fied

ver'i·fy

ver'i·ly

ver'i·si·mil'i·
   tude

ver'ism

ver'i·ta·ble

ver'i·ta·bly

ver'i·ties

ver'i·ty

ver'meil

ver'mi·cel'li

ver'mi·cide

ver·mic'u·late

ver·mic'u·la'tion

ver·mic'u·lite

ver'mi·form

ver'mi·fuge

ver·mil'ion

ver'min

ver'min·ous

ver·nac'u·lar
ver'nal
ver'ni·er
ver'sa·tile
ver'sa·til'i·ty
verse
ver'si·cle
ver'si·fi·ca'tion
ver'si·fied
ver'si·fi'er
ver'si·fy
ver'sion
ver'so
ver'sus
ver'te·bra
ver'te·brae
ver'te·brate
ver'tex
ver'ti·cal
ver'ti·cal·ly
ver·tig'i·nous
ver'ti·go
ver'vain
verve
ver'y
ves'i·cle
ves'per
ves'sel
vest
ves'tal
vest'ed
ves·tib'u·lar

ves'ti·bule
ves'tige
ves·tig'i·al
vest'ment
ves'try
ves'ture
vetch
vet'er·an
vet'er·i·nar'i·an
vet'er·i·nar'y
ve'to
ve'toed
vex
vex·a'tion
vex·a'tious
vexed
vi'a
vi·a·bil'i·ty
vi'a·ble
vi'a·duct
vi'al
vi'and
vi·at'i·cum
vi'bran·cy
vi'brant
vi'brate
vi'brat·ed
vi'brat·ing·ly
vi·bra'tion
vi·bra'tion·less
vi·bra'to
vi'bra·tor

vi'bra·to'ry
vic'ar
vic'ar·age
vi·car'i·ate
vi·car'i·ous
vi·car'i·ous·ly
vice
vice·ge'ral
vice·ge'rent
vice'reine
vice'roy
vic'i·nage
vi·cin'i·ties
vi·cin'i·ty
vi'cious
vi'cious·ly
vi'cious·ness
vi·cis'si·tude
vic'tim
vic'tim·ize
vic'tim·ized
vic'tor
Vic·to'ri·an
vic·to'ri·ous
vic·to'ri·ous·ly
vic'to·ry
Vic·tro'la
vict'ual
vi·cu'ña
vid'e·o
vid'e·o·tape
vie

view

viewed

vig'il

vig'i·lance

vig'i·lant

vig'i·lan'te

vig'i·lant·ly

vi·gnette'

vi·gnett'ed

vig'or

vig'or·ous

vig'or·ous·ly

vi'kings

vile

vil'er

vil'est

vil'i·fi·ca'tion

vil'i·fi'er

vil'i·fy

vil'la

vil'lage

vil'lag·er

vil'lain

vil'lain·ous

vil'lain·ous·ly

vil'lain·y

vil'la·nelle'

vin'ai·grette'

vin'cu·lum

vin·di·ca·ble

vin'di·cate

vin'di·cat'ed

vin'di·ca'tion

vin·dic'tive

vine

vin'e·gar

vine'yard

vin'i·fi·ca'tion

vi'nous

vin'tage

vint'ner

vi'ol

vi·o'la

vi'o·late

vi'o·lat'ed

vi'o·la'tion

vi'o·la'tive

vi'o·la'tor

vi'o·lence

vi'o·lent

vi'o·lent·ly

vi'o·let

vi'o·lin'

vi'o·lin'ist

vi'o·lon·cel'list

vi'o·lon·cel'lo

vi'per

vi'per·ous

vi·ra'go

vir'e·o

vir'gin

vir'gin·al

vir·gin'i·ty

vir'ile

vi·ril'i·ty

vir'tu·al

vir'tu·al·ly

vir'tue

vir'tu·os'i·ty

vir'tu·o'so

vir'tu·ous

vir'tu·ous·ly

vir'tu·ous·ness

vir'u·lence

vir'u·len·cy

vir'u·lent

vi'rus

vi'sa

vis'age

vis'-à-vis'

vis'cer·a

vis'cer·al

vis'cid

vis·cid'i·ty

vis'cid·ly

vis'cose

vis·cos'i·ty

vis'count'

vis'cous

vise

vis'i·bil'i·ty

vis'i·ble

vis'i·bly

vi'sion

vi'sion·ar'y

vis'it

vis'it·a'tion

vis'it·ed

vis'i·tor

vis'ta

vis'u·al

vis'u·al·i·za'tion

vis'u·al·ize

vis'u·al·ized

vis'u·al·ly

vi'tal

vi·tal'i·ty

vi'tal·ize

vi'tal·ized

vi'tal·ly

vi'ta·min

vi'ti·ate

vi'ti·at'ed

vi'ti·a'tion

vit're·ous

vit'ri·fac'tion

vit'ri·fi·ca'tion

vit'ri·fied

vit'ri·fy

vit'ri·ol

vit'ri·ol'ic

vi·tu'per·ate

vi·tu'per·at'ed

vi·tu'per·a'tion

vi·tu'per·a·tive

vi·tu'per·a·tive·ly

vi·va'cious

vi·va'cious·ly

vi·vac'i·ty

vi·var'i·um

viv'id

viv'id·ly

viv'i·fy

vi·vip'a·rous

viv'i·sect

viv'i·sec'tion

viv'i·sec'tion·ist

vix'en

vix'en·ish

viz'ard

vi·zier'

vo'ca·ble

vo·cab'u·lar'y

vo'cal

vo'cal·ism

vo'cal·ist

vo'cal·i·za'tion

vo'cal·ize

vo'cal·ized

vo'cal·ly

vo·ca'tion

vo·ca'tion·al

vo·ca'tion·al·ly

voc'a·tive

vo·cif'er·ate

vo·cif'er·at'ed

vo·cif'er·a'tion

vo·cif'er·ous

vod'ka

vogue

voice

voiced

voice'less

voice'less·ly

voice'less·ness

void

void'a·ble

void'ed

vol'a·tile

vol'a·til'i·ty

vol'a·til·i·za'tion

vol'a·til·ize

vol'a·til·ized

vol·can'ic

vol·ca'no

vol·can·ol'o·gy

vo·li'tion

vo·li'tion·al

vo·li'tion·al·ly

vol'ley

vol'ley·ball'

vol'leyed

volt

volt'age

vol·ta'ic

volt·tam'e·ter

volt'am'me·ter

volt'me·ter

vol'u·bil'i·ty

vol'u·ble

vol'u·bly

vol'ume

vol'u·met'ric

vo·lu'mi·nous

vo·lu'mi·nous·ly

vo·lu'mi·nous·ness

vol'un·tar'i·ly

vol'un·tar'y

vol'un·teer'

vol'un·teered'

vo·lup'tu·ar'y

vo·lup'tu·ous

vo·lup'tu·ous·ly

vo·lup'tu·ous·ness

vo·lute'

vol'vu·lus

vom'it

vom'it·ed

vom'i·to'ry

voo'doo

voo'doo·ism

vo·ra'cious

vo·rac'i·ty

vor'tex

vor'ti·cal

vor'ti·cal·ly

vo'ta·ry

vote

vot'ed

vot'er

vo'tive

vouch

vouched

vouch'er

vouch·safe'

vouch·safed'

vow

vowed

vow'el

vow'el·i·za'tion

vow'el·ize

voy'age

voy'aged

voy'ag·er

vul'can·i·za'tion

vul'can·ize

vul'can·ized

vul'can·iz'er

vul'gar

vul·gar'i·an

vul'gar·ism

vul·gar'i·ty

vul'gar·i·za'tion

vul'gar·ize

vul'gar·ized

vul'gar·iz'er

vul'gar·ly

vul'gate

vul'ner·a·bil'i·ty

vul'ner·a·ble

vul'ner·a·bly

vul'ture

W

wad	wag'gling·ly	wake
wad'ded	Wag·ne'ri·an	waked
wad'dings	wag'on	wake'ful
wad'dle	wag'tail'	wake'ful·ly
wad'dling·ly	waif	wake'ful·ness
wade	wail	wak'en
wad'ed	wailed	wak'ened
wad'er	wail'ing·ly	wak'ing·ly
wa'fer	wail'ings	wale
waf'fle	wain	waled
waft	wain'scot	walk
wag	waist	walked
wage	waist'band'	walk'er
waged	waist'coat'	walk'o'ver
wa'ger	waist'line'	walk'-up'
wa'gered	wait	walk'way'
wa'ger·ings	wait'ed	wall
wag'es	wait'er	wall'board'
wag'ged	wait'ress	walled
wag'gish	waive	wal'let
wag'gle	waived	wall'eyed'
wag'gled	waiv'er	walk'out

349

Wal·loon'		ward'ed		war'rant	
wal'lop		ward'en		war'rant·a·ble	
wal'low		ward'er		war'rant·ed	
wal'lowed		ward'robe'		war'ran·tor	
wall'pa'per		ward'room'		war'ran·ty	
wal'nut		ware'house'		warred	
wal'rus		ware'house'man		war'ren	
waltz		ware'room'		war'ship'	
waltzed		wares		wart	
wam'pum		war'fare'		war'time'	
wan		war'i·ly		wart'less	
wand		war'i·ness		war'y	
wan'der		war'like'		was	
wan'dered		war'lock		wash	
wan'der·er		warm		wash'a·ble	
wan'der·ing·ly		warmed		wash'board'	
wan'der·ings		warm'er		wash'bowl'	
wane		warm'est		wash'cloth'	
waned		warm'heart'ed		washed	
wan'gle		warm'ly		wash'er	
wan'gled		warm'ness		wash'house'	
want		war'mon'ger		wash'ings	
want'ed		warmth		wash'out'	
want'ing·ly		warn		wash'room'	
wan'ton		warned		wash'stand'	
war		warn'ing·ly		wash'-up'	
war'ble		warn'ings		wash'wom'an	
war'bled		warp		wasp	
war'bler		warp'age		wasp'ish	
war'bling·ly		war'path'		was'sail	
war'blings		warped		wast'age	
ward		war'plane'		waste	

waste'bas'ket	wa'ter·log'	wax'i·ness
wast'ed	wa'ter·logged'	wax'ing·ly
waste'ful	Wa'ter·loo'	wax'wing'
waste'ful·ly	wa'ter·man	wax'work'
waste'ful·ness	wa'ter·mark'	wax'y
waste'land'	wa'ter·mel'on	way
waste'pa'per	wa'ter·proof'	way'bill'
wast'er	wa'ter·proofed'	way'far'er
wast'ing·ly	wa'ter·shed'	way'fel'low
wast'rel	wa'ter·side'	way'laid'
watch	wa'ter·spout'	way'lay'
watch'case'	wa'ter·way'	way'side'
watch'dog'	wa'ter·weed'	way'ward
watched	wa'ter·works'	we
watch'er	wa'ter·y	weak
watch'ful	watt	weak'en
watch'ful·ly	watt'age	weak'ened
watch'ful·ness	wat'tle	weak'er
watch'house'	wat'tled	weak'est
watch'keep'er	watt'me'ter	weak'ling
watch'mak'er	wave	weak'ly
watch'man	waved	weak'ness
watch'tow'er	wave'me'ter	weal
watch'word'	wa'ver	wealth
wa'ter	wa'vered	wealth'i·er
wa'tered	wa'ver·ing·ly	wealth'i·est
wa'ter·fall'	wa'ver·ings	wealth'y
wa'ter·find'er	wav'i·ness	wean
wa'ter·fowl'	wav'y	weaned
wa'ter·i·ness	wax	weap'on
wa'ter·ings	waxed	weap'on·less
wa'ter·line'	wax'en	wear

wear'a·bil'i·ty	weed'ed	wel'fare'
wear'a·ble	weed'i·er	wel'kin
wear'er	weed'i·est	well
wea'ried	weed'y	well'born'
wea'ri·er	week	welled
wea'ri·est	week'day'	well'head'
wea'ri·ly	week'end'	well'hole'
wea'ri·ness	week'lies	well'spring'
wear'ings	week'ly	welt
wea'ri·some	weep	welt'ed
wea'ri·some·ness	weep'ing·ly	wel'ter
wea'ry	wee'vil	wel'tered
wea'sel	weft	wen
weath'er	weigh	wench
weath'er·board'	weighed	wend
weath'er·cock'	weigh'mas'ter	wend'ed
weath'ered	weight	went
weath'er·proof'	weight'ed	wept
weath'er·proofed'	weight'i·er	were
weave	weight'i·est	were'wolf'
weav'er	weight'ings	west
web	weight'less·ness	west'er·ly
webbed	weight'y	west'ern
web'bings	weir	west'ern·er
wed	weird	west'ward
wed'ded	weird'ly	wet
wed'dings	weird'ness	wet'ness
wedge	wel'come	wet'ta·bil'i·ty
wedged	wel'comed	wet'ta·ble
wed'lock	wel'com·ing·ly	wet'ted
Wednes'day	weld	wet'ter
weed	weld'ed	wet'test

wet'tings

we've

whack

whacked

whale

whale'back'

whale'bone'

whale'man

whal'er

wharf

wharf'age

wharf'in·ger

what

what·ev'er

what'not'

what'so·ev'er

wheat

wheat'en

wheat'worm'

whee'dle

whee'dled

whee'dling·ly

wheel

wheel'bar'row

wheeled

wheel'house'

wheel'wright'

wheeze

wheezed

wheez'i·er

wheez'i·est

wheez'i·ly

wheez'ing·ly

wheez'y

whelk

whelp

whelped

when

whence

whence'forth'

when·ev'er

when'so·ev'er

where

where'a·bouts'

where·aft'er

where·as'

where·at'

where·by'

where'fore

where·from'

where·in'

where·of'

where·on'

where'so·ev'er

where'up·on'

wher·ev'er

where·with'

where'with·al'

wher'ry

whet

wheth'er

whet'ted

whet'stone'

whey

which

which·ev'er

which'so·ev'er

whiff

whiffed

whif'fle

whif'fled

Whig

while

whiled

whi'lom

whim

whim'per

whim'pered

whim'per·ing·ly

whim'per·ings

whim'sey

whim'si·cal

whine

whined

whin'ing·ly

whin'ings

whin'nied

whin'ny

whip

whip'cord'

whipped

whip'per·snap'per

whip'pet

whip'ping·ly

whip'pings

whip'poor·will'

whip'saw'		whit'en		why	
whip'stitch'		whit'ened		wick	
whip'stock'		white'ness		wick'ed	
whip'worm'		white'wash'		wick'ed·ly	
whir		white'washed'		wick'ed·ness	
whirl		white'wing'		wick'er	
whirled		white'wood'		wick'er·work'	
whirl'i·gig'		whith'er		wick'et	
whirl'ing·ly		whit'ings		wide	
whirl'pool'		whit'ish		wide'ly	
whirl'wind'		whit'low		wid'en	
whirred		whit'tle		wid'ened	
whisk		whit'tled		wide'ness	
whisked		whit'tlings		wid'er	
whisk'er		who		wide'spread'	
whisk'ered		who·ev'er		wid'est	
whis'ky		whole		wid'ow	
whis'per		whole'heart'ed		wid'owed	
whis'pered		whole'heart'ed·ly		wid'ow·er	
whis'per·er		whole'sale'		wid'ow·hood	
whis'per·ing·ly		whole'sal'er		width	
whis'per·ings		whole'some		wield	
whist		whole'some·ly		wield'ed	
whis'tle		whol'ly		wife	
whis'tled		whom		wife'hood	
whis'tling·ly		whom·ev'er		wife'less	
whis'tlings		whom'so·ev'er		wife'ly	
whit		whoop		wig	
white		whooped		wig'gle	
white'cap'		whoop'ing·ly		wig'gled	
whit'ed		whose		wig'gler	
white'fish'		who'so·ev'er		wig'glings	

wight	wind'break'	wing'spread'
wig'mak·er	wind'ed	wink
wig'wag'	wind'er	winked
wig'wam'	wind'fall'	wink'ing·ly
wild	wind'i·ly	win'kle
wild'er	wind'i·ness	win'ner
wil'der·ness	wind'ing·ly	win'ning·ly
wild'est	wind'ings	win'nings
wild'fire'	wind'jam'mer	win'now
wild'ness	wind'lass	win'nowed
wile	wind'mill'	win'some
wil'i·er	win'dow	win'ter
wil'i·est	win'dowed	win'tered
will	win'dow·pane'	win'ter·ize
willed	wind'pipe'	wipe
will'ful	wind'row'	wiped
will'ful·ly	wind'rowed'	wip'er
will'ful·ness	wind'shield'	wire
will'ing·ly	wind'storm'	wired
will'ing·ness	wind'ward	wire'less
wil'low	wind'ward ly	wire'pull'er
wilt	wind'way'	wire'pull'ing
wilt'ed	wind'y	wire'way'
wil'y	wine	wire'work'
win	wine'ber'ry	wire'work'er
wince	wined	wire'worm'
winced	wine'glass'	wir'y
winc'ing·ly	wine'skin'	wis'dom
wind	wing	wise
wind	winged	wise'a'cre
wind'age	wing'fish'	wise'crack'
wind'bag'	wing'less	wise'crack'er

wise'ly	with'ered	woe'be·gone'
wise'ness	with'er·ing·ly	woe'ful
wis'er	with·held'	woe'ful·ly
wis'est	with·hold'	woe'ful·ness
wish	with·hold'ings	wolf
wish'bone'	with·in'	wolfed
wished	with·out'	wolf'hound'
wish'ful	with·stand'	wolf'ish
wish'ful·ly	with·stood'	wol'ver·ine'
wish'ful·ness	wit'less	wolves
wish'ing·ly	wit'less·ly	wom'an
wisp	wit'less·ness	wom'an·hood
wisp'i·er	wit'ness	wom'an·ish
wisp'i·est	wit'nessed	wom'an·kind'
wisp'y	wit'ti·cism	wom'an·like'
wis·te'ri·a	wit'ti·er	wom'an·li·ness
wist'ful	wit'ti·est	wom'an·ly
wist'ful·ly	wit'ting·ly	wom'en
wist'ful·ness	wit'ty	won
wit	wived	won'der
witch	wives	won'dered
witch'craft'	wiz'ard	won'der·ful
witch'er·y	wiz'ard·ly	won'der·ful·ly
witch'ing·ly	wiz'ard·ry	won'der·ing·ly
witch'weed'	wiz'ened	won'der·land'
with	woad	won'der·ment
with·al'	wob'ble	won'der·work'
with·draw'	wob'bled	won'drous
with·draw'al	wob'bli·ness	won'drous·ly
with·drawn'	wob'bling·ly	won't
with·drew'	wob'bly	wont
with'er	woe	woo

wood

wood'bin'

wood'bine'

wood'chuck'

wood'craft'

wood'cut'

wood'ed

wood'en

wood'en·head'

wood'fish'

wood'land

wood'man

wood'peck'er

wood'pile'

wood'shop'

woods'man

wood'work'

wood'work'er

wood'worm'

wooed

woo'er

woof

wool

wool'en

wool'li·er

wool'li·est

wool'li·ness

wool'ly

wool'work'

wool'work'er

wooz'y

word

word'age

word'build'ing

word'ed

word'i·er

word'i·est

word'i·ly

word'i·ness

word'less

word'play'

word'y

wore

work

work'a·bil'i·ty

work'a·ble

work'bag'

work'bas'ket

work'bench'

work'book'

work'box'

work'day'

worked

work'er

work'house'

work'ing·man'

work'ings

work'less

work'man

work'man·like'

work'man·ship

work'men

work'out'

work'pan'

work'peo'ple

work'place'

work'room'

work'shop'

work'ta'ble

work'wom'an

work'wom'en

world

world'li·ness

world'ly

worm

wormed

worm'hole'

worm'i·er

worm'i·est

worm'like'

worm'proof'

worm'wood'

worm'y

worn

wor'ried

wor'ried·ly

wor'ri·er

wor'ri·ment

wor'ri·some

wor'ri·some·ness

wor'ry

worse

wors'en

wors'ened

wor'ship

wor'shiped

wor'ship·er

wor'ship·ful

wor'ship·ful·ly

worst

worst'ed

wor'sted

worth

wor'thi·er

wor'thi·est

wor'thi·ly

wor'thi·ness

worth'while'

wor'thy

would

wound

wound

wound'ed

wound'ing·ly

wound'less

wove

wo'ven

wrack

wraith

wraith'like'

wran'gle

wran'gled

wrap

wrapped

wrap'per

wrap'pings

wrath

wrath'ful

wrath'ful·ly

wrath'ful·ness

wreak

wreaked

wreath

wreathed

wreck

wreck'age

wrecked

wreck'er

wren

wrench

wrenched

wrest

wrest'ed

wres'tle

wres'tled

wres'tler

wretch

wretch'ed

wretch'ed·ly

wretch'ed·ness

wrig'gle

wrig'gled

wrig'gling·ly

wrig'gly

wring

wring'er

wrin'kle

wrin'kled

wrin'kli·er

wrin'kli·est

wrin'kly

wrist

wrist'band'

wrist'bone'

wrist'let

wrist'lock'

writ

writ'a·ble

write

writ'er

writhe

writhed

writh'ing·ly

writ'ings

writ'ten

wrong

wrong'do'er

wronged

wrong'ful

wrong'ful·ly

wrong'head'ed

wrong'ly

wrong'ness

wrote

wroth

wrought

wrung

wry

wry'neck'

X Y Z

xe'non	yard'mas'ter	yell
xen'o·phile	yard'stick'	yelled
xen'o·pho'bi·a	yarn	yel'low
xe'ro·der'ma	yar'row	yel'lowed
xe·rog'ra·phy	yat'a·ghan	yel'low·er
xe·ro'sis	yaw	yel'low·est
Xer'ox	yawl	yel'low·ish
X ray	yawn	yel'low·ish·ness
xy'lo·phone	yawned	yelp
	yawn'ing·ly	yelped
yacht	ye	yeo'man
yachts'man	yea	yeo'man·ry
yak	year	yes
Yale	year'book'	yes'ter·day
yam	year'ling	yet
yam'mer	year'ly	yew
yank	yearn	Yid'dish
Yan'kee	yearned	yield
yard	yearn'ing·ly	yield'ed
yard'age	yearn'ings	yield'ing·ly
yard'arm'	yeast	yield'ing·ness
yard'man	yeast'y	yo'del

yo'deled	youth'ful	ze'ro
yo'del·er	youth'ful·ly	zest
yo'ga	youth'ful·ness	zest'ful
yo'ghurt	youths	zig'zag'
yoke	yt·ter'bi·um	zinc
yoked	yt'tri·um	Zi'on
yoke'fel'low	Yuc'ca	Zi'on·ism
yo'kel	yule	ZIP
yo'kel·ry	yule'tide'	zip'per
yolk		zir'con
yon	za'ny	zir·co'ni·um
yon'der	zeal	zith'er
yore	zeal'ot	zo'di·ac
you	zeal'ot·ry	zone
young	zeal'ous	zoned
young'er	zeal'ous·ly	zoo
young'est	zeal'ous·ness	zo'o·log'i·cal
young'ish	ze'bra	zo·ol'o·gist
young'ster	ze'broid	zo·ol'o·gy
your	ze'bu	zoom
yours	ze'nith	zoomed
your·self'	ze'o·lite	Zu'lu
your·selves'	zeph'yr	zy'mase
youth	Zep'pe·lin	zy·mol'o·gy

PART TWO

Part Two consists of 1,314 entries of personal and geographical names divided as follows:

835 Geographical Names. The largest group consists of the names of American cities and towns that are likely to be encountered in business dictation. The names of the American states are given. A relatively small group of foreign geographical names is given—the foreign countries and cities that are most likely to occur in American business dictation. The lists are not intended to be complete or exhaustive. The attempt has been made, however, to include the geographical names that occur most frequently in ordinary business dictation.

243 Surnames. This group represents the commonest American surnames that are likely to be used in business dictation.

113 First Names of Women. This list contains the most frequently used feminine first names.

123 First Names of Men. This list contains the more frequently used masculine first names.

The four groups of names listed above are combined in one alphabetical list in Part Two.

With the exception of the states and of a few of the largest cities, the geographical names are written very fully. This is done with the understanding that the writer will use these full outlines for the names that occur only occasionally in the dictation. When some name occurs more frequently in the dictation, an abbreviated form would be used.

The shorthand writer in Oregon would ordinarily have little occasion to use the outline for *Corpus Christi*. The shorthand writer in Texas might use it so frequently that he would abbreviate it to *kk*.

The names of most cities that are composed of nouns or adjectives that appear in Part One have been omitted, names such as *Grove Hill*, *Egg Harbor*, *Spring Valley*, *Key West*. The shorthand outlines for such cities and towns are not likely to cause the writer any stenographic difficulty.

The writing and transcribing of proper names can present many traps for the shorthand writer. When he writes in shorthand the name *Pittsburgh*, he will not know whether to transcribe it *Pittsburg* or *Pittsburgh* until he knows whether the dictator had in mind *Pittsburg*, Kansas, or *Pittsburgh*, Pennsylvania. He can be tricked similarly by such a pair as *Worcester*, Massachusetts, and *Wooster*, Ohio.

The writer may confidently write *b-r-o-w-n* in his shorthand notes without realizing that the dictator may not be referring to his familiar correspondent, Mr. *Brown,* but to some strange *Browne* or *Braun.*

Unless the writer is absolutely sure of the identity of the proper names used by the dictator, he should always check them with the greatest possible care. Almost everyone is annoyed when his name or the name of his city or town is spelled incorrectly.

PERSONAL AND GEOGRAPHICAL NAMES

Aaron	Algernon	Anniston
Aberdeen	Allentown	Anthony
Abilene	Allison	Antioch
Abington	Alphonsine	Antoinette
Abraham	Alphonso	Antwerp
Adams	Alton	Appleton
Adelbert	Altoona	Arabia
Adolph	Alvin	Archibald
Agatha	Amanda	Argentina
Aiken	Amarillo	Arizona
Aileen	Amelia	Arkansas
Ainsworth	Amesbury	Arlington
Akron	Amherst	Arnold
Alabama	Amityville	Arthur
Alameda	Amsterdam	Asheboro
Alaska	Anderson	Asheville
Albany	Andover	Ashley
Albert	Angela	Astoria
Albuquerque	Angelica	Atchison
Alexander	Angora	Atkinson
Alfred	Annabel	Atlanta
Algeria	Annapolis	Atlantic

Augusta	Bedford	Blairsville
Augustin	Belfast	Blakely
Aurelia	Belgium	Blanchard
Aurora	Belinda	Bloomington
Austin	Bellefontaine	Bloomsburg
Australia	Belleville	Bluffton
Austria	Bellevue	Bogota
Avery	Bellingham	Boise
Baird	Belmont	Bolivia
Bakersfield	Beloit	Bonham
Baldwin	Belvedere	Boniface
Ballard	Bemidji	Boonville
Baltimore	Benedict	Bordeaux
Bangkok	Benjamin	Boston
Bangladesh	Bennett	Bosworth
Barberton	Bennington	Boulder
Barcelona	Bentley	Bowen
Barlow	Bergenfield	Bowman
Barnard	Berkeley	Boyd
Barnesville	Bernard	Boyle
Barrington	Bernstein	Braddock
Bartholomew	Bertha	Bradenton
Bartlett	Berwick	Bradford
Bartow	Bethlehem	Bradley
Basil	Beulah	Brattleboro
Batavia	Beverly	Brazil
Batesville	Biloxi	Bremen
Baton Rouge	Binghamton	Bremerton
Bauer	Birmingham	Brenham
Bayonne	Bismarck	Brentwood
Beatrice	Blackstone	Brian
Beckley	Blackwell	Bridgeport

Bridgeton	Camden	Centralia
Brigham	Camilla	Chalmers
Brisbane	Campbell	Chambersburg
Bristow	Canada	Chandler
Brockton	Canfield	Chanute
Bronxville	Cannon	Chapman
Brookfield	Canonsburg	Charleston
Brownsville	Canton	Charlottesville
Brunswick	Caracas	Chattanooga
Bryan	Carbondale	Cheboygan
Bryant	Carlisle	Chelsea
Bucharest	Carlotta	Cherbourg
Budapest	Carlsbad	Cherokee
Buenos Aires	Carlson	Cheyenne
Buffalo	Carlstadt	Chicago
Bulgaria	Carlton	Chicopee
Burbank	Carmel	Childress
Burke	Carnegie	Chillicothe
Burlington	Carol	Chippewa Falls
Burma	Carpenter	Chisholm
Burns	Carrollton	Christabel
Burroughs	Carson	Christchurch
Burton	Carter	Christina
Butte	Cartersville	Christine
Byron	Carthage	Christopher
Cadillac	Casper	Cicely
Caesar	Catharine	Cicero
Calcutta	Catskill	Cincinnati
Calhoun	Cecelia	Claremont
California	Cedarhurst	Clarinda
Callahan	Cedartown	Clarksburg
Calumet City	Celia	Clarksville

Claudia	Connor	Curtis
Clearfield	Conrad	Cuthbert
Clearwater	Constance	Cynthia
Cleburne	Conway	Dagmar
Clement	Cooley	Dalton
Cleveland	Coolidge	Daly
Clifford	Copenhagen	Daniel
Coaldale	Corbin	Danville
Coatesville	Cork	Daphne
Coeur d'Alene	Cornelia	Darby
Coffeyville	Corning	Davenport
Cohen	Corona	Davidson
Coldwater	Corpus Christi	Dawson
Coleman	Cortland	Dearborn
Collier	Corvallis	Deborah
Collingdale	Corwin	Dedham
Collingswood	Costa Rica	Deerfield
Collinsville	Covington	Defiance
Cologne	Crafton	Delaware
Colorado	Crandall	Delhi
Colton	Cranford	Delia
Columbia	Crawford	Denise
Columbus	Creston	Denison
Comstock	Cromwell	Denmark
Concord	Crowley	Denver
Concordia	Cuba	Des Moines
Condon	Cudahy	Detroit
Conklin	Culbertson	Dewey
Conley	Cullman	Dexter
Connecticut	Cumberland	Diana
Connersville	Cummings	Dickinson
Connolly	Cummins	Dillon

District of Columbia	Edwardsville	Enrico
Dolores	Edwin	Enright
Dominic	Effingham	Ernest
Donald	Egan	Ernestine
Donora	Egbert	Erwin
Donovan	Egypt	Esther
Dormont	Eileen	Esthonia
Dorothy	Elbert	Ethel
Dougherty	Eleanor	Ethiopia
Doyle	Electra	Euclid
Dresden	Elgin	Europe
Dublin	Elizabeth	Evangeline
Dubuque	Elizabethton	Evanston
Dudley	Elkhart	Evansville
Duluth	Elkins	Evelina
Dunbar	Ellensburg	Everard
Duncan	Elliott	Everett
Dunkirk	Ellsworth	Exeter
Dunmore	Elmhurst	Fairbanks
Dunn	Elmira	Fairbury
Duquesne	El Paso	Fairfield
Durham	Elvira	Fairmont
Dwight	Elwood	Fargo
Easthampton	Ely	Farrell
Eastman	Elyria	Fayetteville
Easton	Emil	Feldman
Eau Claire	Emily	Ferdinand
Ecuador	Emmanuel	Ferguson
Edgar	Emporia	Ferndale
Edinburgh	Endicott	Findlay
Edmonton	England	Finley
Edward	Englewood	Fisher

Fitchburg	Galion	Greeley
Fitzgerald	Gallagher	Greensboro
Flagstaff	Gallup	Greensburg
Fleming	Galveston	Greenville
Florence	Gardner	Greenwood
Florida	Garfield	Gregory
Floyd	Gasper	Gretchen
Fond du Lac	Gastonia	Griffiths
Ford	Geneva	Grinnell
Fort Atkinson	Genevieve	Guam
Fort Lauderdale	Genoa	Guatemala
Fort Madison	George	Gutenberg
Fort Myers	Georgia	Guthrie
Fort Wayne	Gerald	Hackensack
Fort Worth	Germany	Haggerty
Foster	Gertrude	Halifax
Fostoria	Gettysburg	Hamburg
Framingham	Gibson	Hamilton
Frances	Gifford	Hammond
Francis	Gilbert	Hampton
Frankfort	Girard	Hancock
Franklin	Glasgow	Hanford
Frederic	Gleason	Hanoi
Fredonia	Gloria	Hanover
Freehold	Gloversville	Hanson
Freeport	Goddard	Harding
Fullerton	Godfrey	Harold
Fulton	Goodwin	Harriet
Gabriel	Gordon	Harriman
Gaffney	Gould	Harrington
Gainesville	Grafton	Harrisburg
Galesburg	Great Britain	Harrison

Hartford	Honolulu	Isolde
Hartman	Hopewell	Israel
Hattiesburg	Hopkinsville	Istanbul
Haverford	Horatio	Ithaca
Haverstraw	Hornel	Ivan
Hawaii	Hortense	Jacksonville
Hawthorne	Houston	Jacobs
Hayward	Howard	Jacqueline
Healy	Howell	Jamaica
Hedwig	Hubert	Jamestown
Heloise	Hudson	Janesville
Hempstead	Humboldt	Janet
Henderson	Humphrey	Japan
Henrietta	Hungary	Jason
Herbert	Huntington	Jasper
Herkimer	Huron	Jeannette
Herman	Hutchinson	Jeffersonville
Higgins	Hyattsville	Jeffrey
Hilda	Iceland	Jemima
Hillsboro	Idaho	Jennifer
Hinsdale	Illinois	Jeremiah
Hinton	India	Jersey City
Hobart	Indiana	Jerusalem
Hoboken	Indianapolis	Jessamine
Hoffman	Inglewood	Jessica
Holdenville	Iowa	Jocelin
Hollywood	Ironton	Johnson
Holt	Ironwood	Johnston
Holyoke	Irvington	Johnstown
Homewood	Irwin	Jonathan
Honduras	Isaac	Jonesboro
Hong Kong	Isidore	Joplin

Joseph	La Crosse	Leipsig
Judith	Lafayette	Leningrad
Julian	Lakeland	Lenoir
Juliet	Lakewood	Leominster
Julius	Lambert	Leon
Justin	Lancaster	Leonard
Kalamazoo	Lancelot	Leonia
Kalispell	Lansdale	Leopold
Kankakee	Lansford	Leroy
Kansas	Lansing	Leslie
Kansas City	La Paz	Lettice
Karl	La Porte	Lewiston
Katharine	Larchmont	Lexington
Kathleen	Laredo	Lillian
Kearny	Larksville	Lima
Keith	Larson	Lincoln
Kennedy	La Salle	Lindstrom
Kenneth	Las Vegas	Lionel
Kenosha	Latrobe	Lisbon
Kenton	Laughlin	Litchfield
Kentucky	Laura	Lithuania
Kerrville	Laurel	Liverpool
Keyser	Laurens	Livingston
Kilgore	Lavinia	Llewellyn
Kingsford	Lawrence	Lloyd
Kingston	Lawrenceville	Lockhart
Kirkwood	Lazarus	Lockport
Knoxville	Leah	Lodi
Kokomo	Leavenworth	Logansport
Korea	Lebanon	Lois
Kuwait	Lehighton	Lombard
Lackawanna	Lehman	London

Longview	Manila	McCarthy
Lorain	Manistique	McCook
Lorenzo	Manitoba	McCormack
Los Angeles	Mannheim	McDonald
Louis	Manuel	McGregor
Louise	Maplewood	McKenzie
Louisiana	Marblehead	McKinney
Louisville	Marcella	McMillan
Lowell	Marcia	Meadville
Lubbock	Marcus	Medford
Lucretia	Margaret	Melbourne
Ludington	Marian	Melissa
Luella	Marianna	Menasha
Lufkin	Marion	Mercedes
Lumberton	Marlboro	Meriden
Luther	Marquette	Merrill
Luxembourg	Marseilles	Methuen
Lydia	Marshall	Mexico
Lynbrook	Martin	Meyer
Lynchburg	Martinsburg	Miami
Lyndhurst	Martinsville	Michigan
Lynwood	Mason	Middleboro
Lyons	Massachusetts	Midland
Madisonville	Massillon	Mildred
Magdalene	Mathilda	Milford
Maguire	Matthew	Millburn
Mahanoy City	Maxwell	Millbury
Mahoney	Maynard	Milledgeville
Malden	Maysville	Milton
Malvern	Mayville	Milwaukee
Manchester	Maywood	Minersville
Manhattan	McAdoo	Minneapolis

Minnesota	Naomi	New Zealand
Mississippi	Naperville	Niagara Falls
Missouri	Napoleon	Nicaragua
Mitchell	Nashua	Norfolk
Mobile	Nashville	Norma
Monica	Natalie	Norman
Monmouth	Natchez	Northampton
Monroe	Natchitoches	North Carolina
Montana	Nathaniel	North Dakota
Montebello	Natick	Norwalk
Montevideo	Naugatuck	Norway
Montpelier	Nazareth	Norwich
Montreal	Nebraska	Norwood
Mooresville	Needham	Nova Scotia
Moorhead	Nelson	Nyack
Morocco	Neptune	Oakwood
Morris	Netherlands	O'Brien
Morse	Nevada	Ocala
Mortimer	Newark	O'Connor
Moscow	Newberry	Odessa
Moultrie	New Britain	O'Donnell
Moundsville	New Brunswick	Oelwein
Muncie	Newburgh	Ogdensburg
Munhall	New Hampshire	Ohio
Munich	New Haven	Oklahoma
Murdock	New Jersey	Olean
Muriel	New London	Olney
Murray	New Mexico	Olson
Muscatine	New Orleans	Olympia
Muskegon	New Rochelle	Omaha
Myers	Newton	Oneida
Myrtle	New York	O'Neil

Ontario	Pelham	Portsmouth
Ophelia	Pendleton	Portugal
Oregon	Pennsylvania	Potter
Orlando	Pensacola	Pottsville
Oscar	Peoria	Poughkeepsie
Oshkosh	Percival	Powell
Oslo	Perth Amboy	Presque Isle
Ossining	Petaluma	Prichard
Oswald	Petersburg	Princeton
Oswego	Petersen	Priscilla
Ottawa	Peterson	Providence
Owego	Philadelphia	Provo
Owensboro	Philander	Pueblo
Packard	Philippine Islands	Puerto Rico
Paducah	Phillipsburg	Putnam
Pakistan	Phoenixville	Quebec
Palestine	Piedmont	Quinn
Pamela	Pittsburgh	Rachel
Panama	Pittsfield	Racine
Paraguay	Pius	Radford
Parkersburg	Plainfield	Rahway
Parsons	Plattsburg	Randall
Pasadena	Pleasantville	Randolph
Passaic	Plymouth	Rankin
Patchogue	Ponca City	Raton
Paterson	Pontiac	Ravenna
Patrick	Portage	Raymond
Pawtucket	Port Arthur	Rebecca
Peabody	Port Chester	Redwood City
Pearson	Porterville	Regina
Peekskill	Port Huron	Reginald
Pekin	Portland	Reinhardt

Rensselaer

Reuben

Revere

Reynolds

Rhea

Rhinelander

Rhode Island

Richard

Richfield

Richmond

Richwood

Ridgeway

Rio de Janeiro

Roanoke

Robbinsdale

Robert

Robinson

Rochester

Rockford

Rockland

Rockville

Roderick

Romania

Roosevelt

Rosalind

Rosemary

Roseville

Rossville

Roswell

Rotterdam

Rowena

Ruby

Rudolph

Rupert

Rushville

Russia

Rutherford

Ryan

Ryerson

Sacramento

Saigon

St. Albans

St. Augustine

St. Joseph

St. Louis

St. Petersburg

Salisbury

Salt Lake City

Sampson

Samuel

San Angelo

San Antonio

San Diego

Sandusky

San Fernando

Sanford

San Francisco

San Jose

San Luis Obispo

San Mateo

San Rafael

Santa Barbara

Santiago

Sarasota

Sault Ste. Marie

Savannah

Sawyer

Sayreville

Schenectady

Schneider

Schroeder

Schultz

Schuyler

Schwartz

Scotland

Seattle

Sedalia

Seminole

Serena

Seville

Seward

Sewickley

Sexton

Seymour

Shanghai

Sharon

Sharpsburg

Sheboygan

Sheffield

Shelbyville

Sheldon

Shenandoah

Sheridan

Sherman

Sherwood

Shippensburg

Shirley	Steubenville	Teaneck
Shorewood	Stewart	Tenafly
Shreveport	Stillwater	Tennessee
Siam	Stockholm	Terre Haute
Sicily	Stoneham	Texas
Silvester	Stoughton	Thaddeus
Silvia	Stratford	The Hague
Simmons	Straus	Theodore
Simpson	Stroudsburg	Thomasville
Sinclair	Struthers	Tifton
Singapore	Stuart	Timothy
Sioux Falls	Sturgis	Tipton
Solomon	Stuttgart	Titusville
Somerset	Suffolk	Tokyo
Somerville	Sullivan	Toledo
Sorensen	Sumner	Topeka
South America	Sumter	Toronto
Southampton	Sunbury	Torrington
South Carolina	Susan	Trenton
South Dakota	Sweetwater	Trinidad
Southington	Switzerland	Truman
Sparks	Sybil	Tucson
Spartanburg	Sydney	Tulsa
Spokane	Sylvester	Turkey
Springfield	Syracuse	Tuscaloosa
Stafford	Tacoma	Tyrone
Stamford	Tallahassee	Ukraine
Stanford	Tampa	Underhill
Stanley	Tampico	Union
Statesboro	Tarrytown	United Kingdom
Staunton	Taunton	United States
Sterling	Taylorville	Upton

Uruguay	Warsaw	Willmar
Utah	Washington	Wilmette
Utica	Waterbury	Wilmington
Valentine	Waterville	Wilson
Valeria	Watsonville	Winfield
Vanderlip	Waverly	Winifred
Van Horn	Waynesboro	Winnipeg
Venezuela	Weatherford	Winona
Vera Cruz	Webster	Winslow
Vermont	Welch	Winston-Salem
Vernon	Wellesley	Winthrop
Vicksburg	Wellington	Wisconsin
Victoria	Wellsburg	Woburn
Vienna	Westbrook	Woodbury
Viet Nam	West Chester	Woodward
Vincent	Westfield	Woonsocket
Viola	Weston	Wooster
Virgil	West Virginia	Worcester
Virginia	Westwood	Worthington
Vivian	Weymouth	Wyoming
Wabash	Wheaton	Xenia
Waddington	Wheeling	Yakima
Wadsworth	Whitman	Yates
Wakefield	Whittier	Yokohama
Walker	Wichita	Yonkers
Wallace	Wilbur	York
Wallington	Wilfred	Youngstown
Walpole	Wilkes-Barre	Ypsilanti
Walsh	Wilkinsburg	Yugoslavia
Walter	Willard	Yuma
Waltham	Williamsport	Zanesville
Warrensburg	Williston	Zion

PART THREE

Part Three consists of a compilation of 1,368 useful business phrases presented in alphabetic order.

These phrases were selected from a study of the phrasing content of 1,500 business letters representing 50 types of businesses. In all, these letters contained 250,143 running words.

Phrases for common expressions are very helpful to the writer seeking to gain shorthand speed. However, they can be a handicap to him if he cannot write them without the slightest hesitation. If the writer must pause for even the smallest fraction of a second in composing or thinking of a phrase, that phrase becomes a speed handicap rather than a help.

If the writer cannot immediately think of the phrase for a combination of words, he will be well advised to write the words separately.

FREQUENTLY USED GREGG
SHORTHAND PHRASES

able to say	and are	
about it	and have	
about my	and his	
about that	and hope	
about that time	and I will	
about the	and I will be	
about the matter	and is	
about the time	and let us	
about them	and let us know	
about this	and our	
about this time	and see	
about those	and that	
about which	and the	
about your	and they	
after that	any one	
after that time	any one of our	
after the	any one of the	
after these	any one of them	
after this	any other	
along this	any time	
among the	any way	
among these	are not	

378

are sure		as those	
are you		as though	
as a result		as to	
as if		as to that	
as it has been		as to the	
as it is		as to these	
as it will		as to this	
as it will be		as we	
as many		as we are	
as much		as we are not	
as soon as		as we can	
as soon as possible		as we cannot	
as soon as the		as well	
as soon as you can		as yet	
as that		as you	
as that is not		as you are	
as the		as you can	
as there was		as you cannot	
as there will be		as you did	
as these		as you do	
as they		as you do not	
as they are		as you have	
as they can		as you know	
as they can be		as you may	
as they cannot		as you may be	
as they did		as you may have	
as they have		as you might	
as they will		as you might be	
as this		as you might have	
as this is		as you must	
as this may		as you must be	
as this may be		as you must have	

as you will

as you will be

as you will find

as you will have

as you will not

as you will not be

as you will see

as you would

as you would be

as you would be able

as you would have

as you would not

as your

ask the

ask you

at a loss

at a time

at last

at least

at length

at such a time

at that

at that time

at the

at the time

at these

at this

at this time

at which time

be able

be done

be glad

be glad to know

be glad to see

be sure

been able

before it is

before many

before that

before that time

before the

before they

before us

before you

before you are

before you can

before your

being able

being sure

between the

between them

between these

between us

business world

by it

by mail

by means

by Mr.

by myself

by that

by that time

by the

by the time

by the way

by them		Cordially yours	
by themselves		could be	
by these		could be done	
by this		could be sure	
by this time		could have	
by those		could have been	
by us		could not	
by which		could not be	
by which it is		could not say	
by which time		could not see	
by which you can		could say	
by which you may		could see	
by you		day or two	
can be		day or two ago	
can be done		days ago	
can be sure		Dear Madam	
can have		Dear Miss	
can say		Dear Mr.	
can see		Dear Mrs.	
can you		Dear Sir	
can you give		Dear Sirs	
can you give us		did not	
cannot be		do it	
cannot be done		do not	
cannot be sure		do not have	
cannot have		do not pay	
cannot pay		do not say	
cannot say		do not see	
cannot see		do so	
can't be		do that	
centuries ago		do the	
check up		do this	

do you		few minutes ago	
do you know		few moments	
do you mean		few moments ago	
do you think		few months	
do you want		few months ago	
does not		few times	
does not have		for a few days	
doing so		for a few minutes	
during the last		for a few months	
during the past		for a long time	
during the year		for his	
during which time		for it	
each case		for me	
each day		for Mr.	
each month		for Mrs.	
each morning		for my	
each one		for myself	
each other		for next month	
each time		for next year	
ever since		for one	
every minute		for one thing	
every month		for our	
every one		for so long a time	
every one of the		for some years	
every one of them		for that	
every one of these		for the	
every one of those		for the last	
every other		for the present	
face to face		for the purpose	
few days		for the time	
few days ago		for them	
few minutes		for these	

for this		glad to say	
for those		glad to see	
for us		glad to send	
for which		good deal	
for whom		good many	
for you		good many of the	
for your convenience		good many of them	
for your information		good many of these	
for yourself		good time	
from him		great many	
from his		great many of the	
from it		great many of them	
from our		had been	
from that		had not	
from that time		had not been	
from the		has been	
from them		has been able	
from these		has been done	
from this		has come	
from time		has done	
from us		has given	
from which		has made	
from you		has not	
gave me		has not been	
gave us		has not been able	
gave you		has not yet	
give me		has not yet been	
give us		has that	
give you		has the	
glad to have		has this	
glad to hear		has to	
glad to know		has written	

have been

have been able

have done

have gone

have had

have made

have not

have not been

have not been able

have not yet

have not yet been

have you

have you made

he called

he came

he can

he can be

he can be sure

he can have

he can make

he cannot

he cannot be

he cannot have

he can't

he could

he could not

he did

he did not

he did not pay

he did not say

he did not see

he didn't

he does

he does not

he felt

he found

he gave

he gives

he is

he is not

he knew

he knows

he lost

he made

he may

he may be

he may be able

he may be sure

he may have

he mentioned

he might be

he might have

he might have been

he might not

he must

he must be

he must have

he needed

he needs

he said

he saw

he says

he seemed

he should

he should be		here is the	
he should be able		hope that	
he should have		hope you will	
he should not		hours ago	
he told		how many	
he took		how many of the	
he wanted		how many of them	
he wants		how many of these	
he was		how many times	
he will		how much	
he will be		I am	
he will be able		I am glad	
he will be glad		I am of the opinion	
he will find		I am sure	
he will have		I came	
he will not		I can	
he will not be able		I can be	
he will see		I can have	
he wished		I can say	
he would		I can see	
he would be		I cannot	
he would be able		I cannot be	
he would be glad		I cannot be sure	
he would have		I cannot have	
he would not		I can't	
he would not be		I could	
hear from him		I could be	
hear from you		I could have	
help us		I could not	
help you		I desire	
here are		I did	
here is		I did not	

I did not say

I do

I do not

I do not say

I do not see

I do not think

I doubt

I enclose

I fear

I feel

I feel sure

I felt

I find

I found

I gave

I give

I have

I have been

I have been able

I have done

I have given

I have had

I have made

I have not

I have not been able

I have not had

I have not yet

I have seen

I have tried

I hope

I hope it will

I hope it will be

I hope that

I hope you will

I knew

I know

I made

I may

I may be

I may have

I might

I might be

I might have

I must

I must be

I must have

I need

I notice

I read

I realize

I regret

I said

I saw

I say

I see

I sent

I shall

I shall be

I shall be able

I shall be glad

I shall have

I shall make

I shall not

I shall not be

I shall not be able		if it is	
I should		if it was	
I should be		if it will	
I should have		if it will be	
I suggest		if my	
I talked		if not	
I thank you		if so	
I thank you for the		if that	
I think		if the	
I thought		if there are	
I told		if there is	
I took		if they	
I want		if they are	
I want to see		if they are not	
I wanted		if they can	
I was		if they cannot	
I will		if they may	
I will be		if they would	
I will be able		if this	
I will have		if this is	
I will not		if we	
I will not be		if we are	
I will not be able		if we can	
I will see		if we can be	
I wish		if we cannot	
I would		if we could	
I would be		if we do	
I would have		if we have	
I would not		if you	
I wrote		if you are	
I wrote you		if you are sure	
if it		if you can	

if you can be		in order	
if you cannot		in order that	
if you could		in order to be	
if you did not		in order to be able	
if you do		in order to obtain	
if you do not		in order to see	
if you give		in our	
if you have		in our opinion	
if you know		in part	
if you may		in particular	
if you must		in question	
if you need		in relation	
if you think		in spite	
if you want		in such	
if you will		in such a manner	
if you will be		in such a way	
if you will have		in that	
if you wish		in the	
if you would		in the future	
if you would be		in the past	
if you would have		in the world	
in a few days		in them	
in a few minutes		in these	
in a few months		in this	
in a position		in this matter	
in addition		in this way	
in addition to the		in time	
in behalf		in which	
in case		in which case	
in fact		in which it is	
in his		in which the	
in it		in which you	

in which you are		letting us	
into it		line of business	
into the		line of goods	
into this		long ago	
is it		long time	
is not		long time ago	
is not yet		make the	
is that		many of the	
is the		many of them	
is there		many of these	
is this		many of those	
is to be		many other	
it has been		many times	
it is		may be	
it is the		may be able	
it isn't		may be done	
it was		may be sure	
it will		may have	
it will be		men and women	
it will have		might be	
it will not		might be able	
it will not be		might have	
left hand		might have been	
less and less		might not	
less than		might not be	
less than the		might not be able	
let us		months ago	
let us have		must be	
let us know		must be able	
let us make		must be done	
let us say		must have	
let us see		my time	

need not be		on it	
next day		on our	
next day or two		on our part	
next month		on request	
next time		on sale	
next year		on such	
next year's		on that	
no doubt		on that day	
none of the		on the	
none of them		on the part	
not only		on the question	
now and then		on the subject	
of course		on these	
of course it is		on this	
of his		on this case	
of its		on time	
of mine		on which	
of my		on your	
of our		once a month	
of such		once or twice	
of that		one of our	
of that time		one of the	
of the		one of the best	
of their		one of the most	
of them		one of them	
of these		one of these	
of this		one or two	
of those		one thing	
of time		one time	
of which		one way	
on behalf		only one	
on his		only one of these	

other than		shall not	
ought to be		shall not be	
ought to be able		shall not have	
ought to be done		she can	
ought to have		she cannot	
out of date		she could	
out of the		she could not	
out of the question		she could not be	
out of them		she is	
question of time		she is not	
quite sure		she may be	
reach us		she must	
reach you		she would	
realize that		should be	
relation to the		should be done	
Respectfully yours		should be made	
safe deposit		should have	
seem to be		should have been	
seems to be		should not	
send him		should not be	
send them		should see	
send this		since that time	
send us		since the	
send you		since this	
several days		Sincerely yours	
several days ago		so far	
several months		so long	
several months ago		so long a time	
several other		so many	
several times		so many of the	
shall be glad		so many of them	
shall have		so many times	

so much		that is to say	
so that		that it	
so well		that it is	
some of our		that it was	
some of that		that it will	
some of the		that it will be	
some of them		that may	
some of these		that may be	
some of this		that must	
some of those		that our	
some time		that this is	
some time ago		that the	
some years		that there are	
some years ago		that there is	
suggest that		that these	
take the		that they	
than the		that they are	
thank you		that this	
thank you for		that those	
thank you for your		that time	
thank you for your order		that will	
that are		that will be	
that are not		that will not	
that can		that would	
that can be		that would be	
that do		that would have	
that do not		the only thing	
that does not		there are	
that have		there has been	
that is		there have	
that is not		there is	
that is the		there may	

there may be

there might be

there must be

there was

there will

there will be

they are

they are not

they can

they can be

they can have

they cannot

they cannot be

they cannot have

they can't

they come

they could

they could not

they did

they did not

they do

they do not

they have

they may

they may be

they may be able

they might

they might be

they might not

they must

they must be

they must be able

they must have

they think

they want

they will

they will be

they will be able

they will have

they will not

they would

they would be

they would be able

they would be glad

they would have

this can

this can be

this cannot

this cannot be

this case

this did not

this information

this is

this is not

this is the

this matter

this may

this may be

this means

this month

this morning

this must be done

this one

this time

this was		to do the	
this way		to face	
this will		to fall	
this will be		to feel	
this would		to fill	
this would be		to find	
through its		to follow	
through that		to form	
through the		to forward	
through this		to furnish	
throughout the		to get	
throughout this		to give	
to be		to give me	
to be able		to give you	
to be done		to go	
to be sure		to have	
to become		to have been	
to begin		to have you	
to believe		to his	
to buy		to it	
to call		to keep	
to change		to know	
to charge		to make	
to check		to me	
to choose		to participate	
to come		to pass	
to continue		to pay	
to convince		to persuade	
to cover		to place	
to do		to plan	
to do it		to please	
to do so		to prepare	

to present	to time
to prevent	to try
to print	to turn
to proceed	to us
to produce	to verify
to prove	to which
to provide	to which the
to publish	to whom
to purchase	to you
to put	too much
to say	twice as much
to see	two months ago
to sell	two or three
to serve	up to
to serve you	up to date
to ship	up to the
to speak	up to the minute
to spend	up to this time
to surprise	upon request
to take	upon such
to talk	upon the
to tell	upon the subject
to thank you	upon this
to thank you for	upon which
to that	Very cordially yours
to the	very glad
to their	very glad to hear
to them	very good
to these	very important
to think	very many
to this	very much
to those	Very sincerely yours

very small

very soon

Very truly yours

very well

want to see

was done

was it

was made

was that

was the

was this

we are

we are not

we are not yet

we are of the opinion

we are sending

we are sure

we can

we can be

we can have

we cannot

we cannot be

we cannot say

we can see

we can't

we could

we could be

we could have

we could not

we desire

we did

we did not

we do

we do not

we do not say

we do not see

we do not think

we enclose

we feel

we feel sure

we felt

we find

we found

we give

we have

we have been

we have been able

we have done

we have had

we have made

we have not

we have not been

we have not yet

we have your order

we hope

we hope it will

we hope that

we hope that the

we hope this will

we hope to have

we hope you will

we hope you will not

we knew

we know

we made		we tried	
we mailed		we try	
we make		we want	
we may		we will	
we may be		we will be	
we may be able		we will be able	
we may have		we will have	
we might		we will not	
we might be		we will not be	
we might be able		we will see	
we might have		we will send you	
we must		we wish	
we must be		we would	
we must have		we would be	
we need		we would be glad	
we realize that		we would have	
we shall		we would not	
we shall be		we would not be	
we shall be able		we would not be able	
we shall be glad		we wrote	
we shall have		week or two	
we shall not		week or two ago	
we shall not be able		weeks ago	
we should		were not	
we should be		were sure	
we should be glad		what are	
we should have		what has been	
we should not be able		what is	
we thank you		what our	
we thank you for		what was	
we thank you for the		what will	
we think		when that	

when the	
when they	
when this	
when those	
when you	
when you are	
which does	
which has	
which have	
which is	
which may	
which may be	
which means	
which must	
which they have	
which was	
which way	
which we are	
which you can	
which you cannot	
who are	
who are not	
who can	
who can be	
who cannot	
who could	
who could be	
who could not	
who desire	
who do not	
who have	
who have done	

who have had	
who have not	
who is	
who is not	
who know	
who made	
who may	
who may be	
who might	
who might be	
who might have	
who must	
who need	
who should	
who should be	
who should have	
who want	
who will	
who will be	
who will be able	
who will have	
who will not	
who will not be	
who would	
who would be	
who would have	
who would have been	
who would not	
why not	
will be	
will be able	
will be done	

will be glad		years ago	
will find		years of age	
will have		you are	
will not be		you are not	
will not be able		you are sure	
will you		you can	
will you please		you can be	
wish to say		you can be sure	
with him		you can get	
with his		you can give	
with our		you can have	
with such		you can make	
with that		you cannot	
with the		you cannot have	
with them		you cannot pay	
with these		you cannot see	
with this		you could	
with us		you could be	
with which		you could have	
with whom		you could have been	
with you		you could see	
within the		you could not	
would be		you could not have	
would be able		you couldn't	
would be done		you desire	
would be glad		you did	
would have		you did not	
would have been		you did not say	
would not		you did not see	
would not be		you do	
would not have been		you do not	
written you		you don't	

you gave	
you have	
you have been	
you have had	
you have not	
you have not been	
you have not been able	
you knew	
you know	
you made	
you may	
you may be	
you may be able	
you may be sure	
you may have	
you might	
you might be	
you must	
you must be	
you must be able	
you must have	
you need	
you order	
you see	
you shall have	
you should	
you should be	
you should be able	
you should have	
you should not	
you think	
you want	

you wanted	
you will	
you will be	
you will be able	
you will be glad	
you will be sure	
you will find	
you will have	
you will not	
you will not be	
you will not be able	
you will not have	
you will see	
you would	
you would be	
you would be able	
you would be glad	
you would be sure	
you would have	
you would have been	
you would not	
you would not be	
you would not be able	
you would not have	
your inquiry	
your name	
your order	
your orders	
Yours cordially	
Yours sincerely	
Yours very sincerely	
Yours very truly	

PART FOUR

Part Four contains abbreviations for 120 expressions. A suggested shorthand outline is given for each expression.

Some expressions are dictated and transcribed almost exclusively in abbreviated form, such as *FOB (free on board)*. Others may be dictated and transcribed either in full or in the form of initials, such as *AC* for *alternating current*.

There are many variations in the use of periods and capitals in abbreviations. For example, the expression *revolutions per minute* may be expressed by *rpm,* or *r.p.m.,* or *RPM.* In the following list of abbreviations, the forms used are those given in Webster's Seventh New Collegiate Dictionary.

ABBREVIATIONS

AA	Alcoholics Anonymous	
ABC	American Broadcasting Company	
AC	alternating current	
ACE	American Council on Education	
ACTH	adrenocorticotropic hormone	
AEC	Atomic Energy Commission	
AFL-CIO	American Federation of Labor and Congress of Industrial Organizations	
a.m.	ante meridiem	
AMA	American Medical Association	
APO	army post office	
ARC	American Red Cross	
ASCAP	American Society of Composers, Authors, and Publishers	
AVA	American Vocational Association	
AWOL	absent without leave	
BA	bachelor of arts	

BBC	British Broadcasting Corporation	
B.C.	Before Christ	
BS	bachelor of science	
Btu	British thermal unit	
CAB	Civil Aeronautics Board	
CBC	Canadian Broadcasting Corporation	
cc	cubic centimeter	
CIA	Central Intelligence Agency	
CIF	cost, insurance, and freight	
CNO	chief of naval operations	
COD	cash on delivery	
CPA	certified public accountant	
CPO	chief petty officer	
DA	district attorney	
DAR	Daughters of the American Revolution	
DC	District of Columbia	
DDS	doctor of dental surgery	
DFC	distinguished flying cross	
DOA	dead on arrival	
DT	delirium tremens	

EKG	electrocardiogram
ESP	extrasensory perception
EST	eastern standard time
ETA	estimated time of arrival
et al	et alii (and others)
etc.	et cetera (and so forth)
FAA	Federal Aviation Agency
FBI	Federal Bureau of Investigation
FCC	Federal Communications Commission
FDA	Food and Drug Administration
FM	frequency modulation
FOB	free on board
GB	Great Britain
GI	general issue
GM	general manager
GOP	Grand Old Party (Republican)
GP	general practitioner
HEW	Health, Education, and Welfare
HQ	headquarters
IBM	International Business Machines

ID	identification	
i.e.	id est (that is)	
ILA	International Longshoremen's Association	
IQ	intelligence quotient	
IRS	Internal Revenue Service	
JV	junior varsity	
kc	kilocycle	
KKK	Ku Klux Klan	
KP	kitchen police	
LI	Long Island	
LLB	bachelor of laws	
LLM	master of laws	
MA	master of arts	
MC	master of ceremonies	
MD	doctor of medicine	
mm	millimeter	
MP	member of parliament	
mph	miles per hour	
MS	manuscript	
MSS	manuscripts	

MST	mountain standard time	
NASA	National Aeronautics and Space Administration	
NATO	North Atlantic Treaty Organization	
NLRB	National Labor Relations Board	
OAS	Organization of American States	
PAL	Police Athletic League	
P and L	profit and loss	
PBX	private branch exchange	
PGA	Professional Golfers' Association	
PHA	Public Housing Administration	
PhD	doctor of philosophy	
PHS	Public Health Service	
p.m.	post meridiem	
PN	promissory note	
POW	prisoner of war	
PS	post scriptum (postscript)	
PST	Pacific standard time	
PTA	Parent-Teacher Association	
PX	post exchange	
q.t.	quiet	

RAF	Royal Air Force
R and D	research and development
RBI	runs batted in
REA	Rural Electrification Administration
ROTC	Reserve Officers' Training Corps
RSVP	répondez s'il vous plait (please reply)
SBA	Small Business Administration
SEATO	Southeast Asia Treaty Organization
SEC	Securities and Exchange Commission
SRO	standing room only
SSA	Social Security Administration
TV	television
TVA	Tennessee Valley Authority
UK	United Kingdom
UNESCO	United Nations Educational, Scientific, and Cultural Organization
UP	United Press
UPI	United Press International
US	United States
USA	United States of America
USO	United Service Organizations

USSR	Union of Sov
VI	Virgin Island
VIP	very importa
WI	West Indies
wpm	words per mi

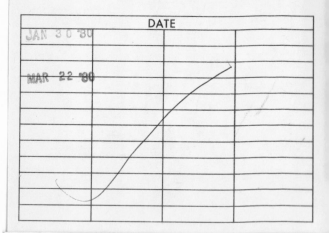

USSR	Union of Soviet Socialist Republics
VI	Virgin Islands
VIP	very important person
WI	West Indies
wpm	words per minute

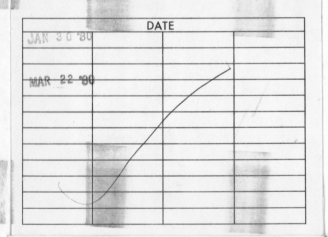

653.427 Gregg, John Robert
GRE

Gregg shorthand
dictionary

DATE		
JAN 30 '80		
MAR 22 '80		

© THE BAKER & TAYLOR CO.